Voices and Visions:
The Evolution of the Black Experience at Northwestern University

Jeffrey E. Sterling, MD
Lauren Lowery

Copyright 2018 Jeffrey E. Sterling, MD, Lauren Lowery
All rights reserved.

ISBN: 9780692124086

Contents

Introduction

Section I: Early Northwestern

    I.   The Earliest Black Attendees of Northwestern University

    II.   History of Desegregating Housing at Northwestern University

    III.   Rev. Dr. Michael Nabors: The Evanston Community and the Northwestern Black Student Experience

Section II: The Black Athlete and the Black Experience

    IV.   Norm Comer

    V.   Jim Pitts

    VI.   Dee Todd

    VII.   Joseph Webb

    VIII.   Rishal Dinkins

    IX.   Katrina Adams

    X.   Ricky Byrdsong

    XI.   Oliver Kupe

    XII.   Daryl Newell

Section III: Birth of a Community: The 1968 Takeover of the Bursar's Office

    XIII.   Stanley Hill

    XIV.   Herman Cage

    XV.   Daphne Maxwell Reid

    XVI.   Steve Colson

    XVII.   Victor Goode

    XVIII. Wayne Watson

    XIX. Kathryn Ogletree

    XX. John Bracey

    XXI. Eva Jefferson Paterson

    XXII. Participants in the Bursar's Office Takeover

Section IV: The Black House / Caring for the Community

    XXIII. Milton Wiggins

    XXIV. Alice Palmer

    XXV. Karla Spurlock-Evans

    XXVI. Duke Jenkins

    XXVII. Jerre Michelin

    XXVIII. Penny Warren

    XXIX. Debra Blade

    XXX. Kathleen Bethel

    XXXI. Ce Cole Dillon

    XXXII. Tamara Johnson

    XXXIII. Lesley-Ann Brown-Henderson

Section IV: Growth of the Black Experience

    XXXIV. Andre Bell

    XXXV. Henry Binford

    XXXVI. Robert Moore

    XXXVII. L. Stanley Davis

XXXVIII. Aldon Morris

XXXIX. Jabari Asim

XL. Harris Lennix

XLI. Asadah Kirkland

XLII. Black Greek Letter Organizations

Section V: New Challenges

XLIII. Charles Whitaker

XLIV. Tanya D. Woods

XLV. Sarah Oberholtzer

XLVI. Macs Vinson

XLVII. Kasey Brown

XLVIII. Paula Pretlow

Section VI: Modern Evolution of the Black Experience & A New Future

XLIX. Alexandria Bobbitt

L. Charla Wilson

LI. Phil Harris

LII. Sonia Waiters

LIII. Michael Wilbon

LIV. Jabbar Bennett

LV. Jonathan Holloway

LVI. Jeffrey Sterling

Introduction

In African societies, the oral tradition of storytelling has long been a prominent method by which history and legend have been passed on between generations. Although Northwestern University has embraced an initiative to establish an archive for the Black experience (i.e., The NUBAA Archives), a nod to the oral tradition continues with this volume: *Voices and Visions—The Evolution of the Black Experience at Northwestern University*. History can be described as a series of experiences and defined by the outcomes produced. This book applies a lens to the experiences and outcomes of individuals who have been formative to the Black experience or have contributed significantly to institutions that have propelled the Black experience at Northwestern.

Northwestern University is legendary for having produced incredible talent from multiple disciplines and inclusive of all ethnicities and genders. However, it is not the primary objective of this book to tell that story. This book is about the group of individuals whose actions and/or existence propelled the Black experience of Northwestern in meaningful and, sometimes, dramatic ways. These stories involve members of the student body, faculty, staff, administration, and alumni—all elements of the university's community.

Through the voices and stories of these members of the community, we believe the Black experience will reveal itself. As these stories are told, we hope you will note that personal experiences often reflected the realities and needs of Blacks on campus. Your interpretation of those experiences will likely reveal things about your interactions with the members of the Black community and your view of them; we invite and challenge you to explore the feelings that generate within you while you appreciate the variety of experiences shared by the voices of our contributors. Whatever you feel, keep in mind, as a community, we are fiercely proud to be associated with Northwestern University and proud that our university is amenable to the type of insight and introspection this book offers.

We would like to express our gratitude to everyone who has been a part of this project and to everyone who, in his or her own way, has made a difference.

The stories and opinions expressed in these first-person accounts are those of the subjects and not necessarily the authors. Every effort has been made to fact-check comments and claims. We note the existence of discrepancies between subjects on the same topic. Special thanks go to the Northwestern University Library and Archives for assistance in this regard.

Early Northwestern

- **The Earliest Black Attendees of Northwestern University**

- **History of Desegregating Housing at Northwestern University**

- **Rev. Dr. Michael Nabors:** The Evanston Community and the Northwestern Black Student Experience

The Earliest Black Attendees of Northwestern University

There is a distinction between the first African Americans who attended what is now part of Northwestern University and those who attended what was Northwestern University at the time. For example, Ferdinand L. Barnett attended Union College of Law (the "union" representing a collaboration between Northwestern University and the University of Chicago), the precursor to Northwestern's Pritzker School of Law. He graduated in 1878 and became the third Black to have passed the Illinois bar. He is noted to have married suffragist, civil right pioneer, and co-founder of the National Association for the Advancement of Colored People (NAACP), Ida B. Wells.

Another prominent example exists in Daniel Hale Williams, who is famously noted to have attended Chicago Medical College (CMC), the precursor to Northwestern's Feinberg School of Medicine. CMC was largely autonomous from Northwestern at the time, but an administrative relationship existed that eventually resulted in Northwestern annexing the institution. Daniel Hale Williams graduated in 1883 and famously performed the first successful heart surgery in 1893 in the United States. He also founded the first non-segregated US Hospital, Provident Hospital, and he was the only African American charter member of the American College of Surgeons.

John Jacob Aston Goode, originally from Xenia, Ohio, and Evanston High School, is likely the first African American to have actually attended what was named

Northwestern University at the time. John entered Northwestern in 1880 and graduated in either 1884 or 1885 as a Bachelor of Liberal Arts. John is also believed to be the father-in-law of Paul Robeson.

It is notable that that the Northwestern class of 1903 was meant to have at least three African Americans graduates, yet none of them completed their studies. Elizabeth Irma Telling of Chicago (originally from Milwaukee, WI) entered Northwestern University (NU) in 1899 but withdrew in 1900. Claude Leon Umholtz of Oklahoma City also entered NU in 1899 and withdrew in 1900. Edward Trezise of Mason City, Iowa (originally from Michigan) transferred to Northwestern in 1901 from Lawrence University but withdrew.

In contrast, Lawyer Taylor from Austin, Texas (and originally from Louisville, Kentucky) was a member of the Class of 1903, and he did go on to graduate. Lawyer had been commonly thought to be the first African American to receive an undergraduate degree from Northwestern. He entered Northwestern in 1899 and graduated with a B.S. in Liberal Arts. He was 34 years old at the time of his matriculation. After graduation, Lawyer became the Chair of Physics at Clark University in Atlanta, Ga. and a teacher of Mathematics and Astronomy. Lawyer's graduation was announced in the *Chicago Daily Tribune* on June 16, 1903. "Students of Northwestern University to the number of 1,200 made the class day memorable in Evanston yesterday by a shouting demonstration in honor of Lawyer Taylor, colored, a member of this year's graduating class and the first negro to secure a degree in the college of liberal arts."

Here is the actual lauding of Lawyer by his class at the official Northwestern Class Day program of June 15, 1903: "Laying aside all humor and cheap wit, let us give nine rahs for a fellow who has fought his way thro' college under more difficulties than any of us have encountered, who is the first of his race to receive a degree from Northwestern; let us give him a cheer as he goes forth to lead his brothers in the South. Here's to Lawyer Taylor!"

Lawyer Taylor is currently honored with a professorship in his name at Northwestern University.

History of Desegregating Housing at Northwestern University

Edwin B. Jourdain

African Americans were prohibited from living in Northwestern University housing for generations. The first vivid example of this problem is noted to have occurred in 1902, when Isabella Ellis (aka Mabel) from San Antonio, Texas was admitted to the University's Chapin Hall dormitory. Upon her arrival from Texas, her designated roommate refused to share a room with her. When the dormitory administration (Women's Educational Association, WEA) discovered that she was Black, they initially denied her entry to the dorm.

Upon her eventual admittance, thirteen White occupants of the same dormitory threatened to withdraw from the school. This prompted the WEA to allow Ellis to live in a reconfigured "special" single room at the dormitory for the school year, but without a roommate or other dorm "privileges." She withdrew from Northwestern University at the end of the year after being denied housing for the subsequent year. That same year, another Black woman applied to live in Chapin Hall in an effort to room with Ms. Ellis, but her application was denied. The WEA claimed that her dismissal was due to overcrowding of the dorm.

At the end of the 1902 school year, the WEA created an official policy of housing segregation.

Curiously, during the same time, young men students attending Northwestern were allowed to stay in the students' dormitory at Sheridan Road and Cook Street. Lawyer Taylor himself stayed there for three years. At least two Black varsity football players were also allowed to stay at the dormitory. However, shortly after the WEA's decision, struggles for Black males ensued. Lawyer Taylor, who had considered staying at Northwestern for graduate school studies, decided otherwise. He was noted to have said it was nearly impossible for Negroes to rent a room anywhere in Evanston.

These difficulties continued for decades. When the male dormitory began being used as training quarters for the football team, Black students were left without an option of campus housing. At the same time, the prejudice of Evanston landlords against Negro tenants made off-campus housing virtually non-existent. This led the faculty of Northwestern University to consider providing a separate dormitory for colored students, although this did not occur. Franklin Snyder, Northwestern University President between 1939 and 1949, is quoted in the *Daily Northwestern* as saying to NU Blacks, "Why should we concern ourselves with your housing?"

Over the succeeding years, Black students attending Northwestern often commuted to school, in most cases, from Chicago. The segregated Emerson Young Men's Christian Association (YMCA, aka "The Black Y") became a site where many Black males lived. Other Blacks were accommodated at local homes and churches, such as Second Baptist Church, Ebenezer A&M Church, and Garrett Seminary.

Lorraine Morton, Evanston's first African-American mayor and Evanston's longest serving mayor, recalls not being permitted to live in the dormitories when she attended (Lorraine graduated from NU in 1942, getting a Master's in Education). She says, "when I asked where I'd be staying, they gave me an address to a Mrs. Griffith's home on Lake Street! I just thought that was the normal way things were. I didn't know when I applied to Northwestern that you couldn't live in the dormitories."

It appears that the first desegregated housing unit at Northwestern was established in September 1947 for women at the International House (the facility designated for foreign-born students; international students were also denied campus housing at this time) on 1827 Orrington Ave. According to articles from the *Daily Northwestern*, this partially resulted from a student campaign to desegregate housing for Black students. In February of that year, the Student Governing Board (SGB) voted against a proposal to desegregate campus housing, instead recommending usage of the International House on the basis of perceived vulnerability of Black women. The SGB claimed that unrestricted housing was not feasible throughout the University, and seventy-two percent of the student population opposed the effort to desegregate. Five Black women lived at the International House in 1947.

Bill Branch, an African American sophomore and outspoken leader on campus at the time, criticized the decision to not have a stronger stand against discrimination. He recommended Black students to testify before the council about housing conditions. He mentioned that Garrett Biblical Institute (Garrett Seminary) and Hinman House had implemented successful interracial housing over the summer. *The Chicago Defender* called out Northwestern administration for ignoring the promises it had made to the Federal Housing Coordinator to combat segregation, as a result of it being an institution receiving federal aid.

As an example of acting contrarily to perceived promises and responsibilities, in 1948, Northwestern planned to build a 280-person apartment for veterans that would still deny Black veterans the right to live there, even though at least five Black veterans were attending Northwestern at the time. Alderman Edwin B. Jourdain, a Black member of the Evanston City Council, placed pressure on the National

Housing Agency to not provide curb funding to Northwestern based on its institutionalized segregated housing. At about the same time, other Big Ten universities were adopting "open dorm" policies, which was likely a response to integrated units during World War II.

Northwestern subsequently purchased property to build Ashbury Hall International House for men at 1830 Sherman Ave, formerly the property of Garrett Seminary. It opened in January 1950.

In 1953, all men dorms were desegregated.

Rev. Dr. Michael Nabors:

The Evanston Community and the Northwestern Black Student Experience

Charles "Doc" Glass

Rev. Dr. Michael Nabors is the Senior Pastor of Second Baptist Church in Evanston, Illinois. Both Rev. Nabors and the Second Baptist Church have multiple amazing points of intersection with Northwestern University. His roots in Evanston go back to 1893, when his great-grandmother arrived as a domestic and married podiatrist. His grandparents were part of the group that founded the Emerson Street YMCA, which is another key location in the history of the Black Experience at Northwestern. The Emerson Street YMCA was historically referred to as "The Black Y," as a result of being the only refuge for Blacks. As many White Evanston locals often expressed an unwillingness to have their children play with Blacks, it created a need for a separate facility at which Blacks could congregate.

Similarly, the origins of the Second Baptist Church itself are intimately tied to Northwestern. Soon after being established in 1882 in an upstairs room of the local post office, there was a concerted effort by its members to establish a permanent location. Unfortunately, their preferred location seemed unattainable because the local would-be neighborhood wasn't enthralled with the notion of a Black church within it. As luck would have it, one of the founders of the church, Nathan Branch, served as a livery worker for the current Northwestern President, and, in the course of sharing his frustration, a parcel of land that was owned by Northwestern was offered and sold for $700. This remains the location of the Second Baptist Church to this day.

For what still approximates a majority of the history of Blacks attending Northwestern University, private homes in the Evanston community instead of structures on campus housed its students, due to racist policies, and without even allowing "separate but equal" considerations in filling student housing. The Emerson YMCA was a primary location for students but, very often, members of the Second Baptist Church filled the void and offered their homes upon discovering that students who showed up for worship did not have a home to return to after the church services.

One prominent and legendary example of members of the Evanston community offering their homes for the social needs of Northwestern Blacks is the family of Charles "Doc" Glass. Doc Glass performed in some capacity as a university athletic recruiter and supporter of students beginning in either 1955 (via first person student-athlete accounts) or 1957 (according to Northwestern University records). His efforts reportedly began after observing the victory of an African American track and field athlete, noting that this athlete had no one to congratulate him and celebrate with him. From that point forward, the Glass' and several other families who were members of the Second Baptist Church spent the next decade serving as extended family members of the entire Black student body. It took the events of the 1968 takeover of the Bursar's Office at Northwestern for students to receive a dedicated safe space to socialize on the college campus at which they studied.

For the next generation, the Second Baptist Church retained and expanded its role in the life of Black Northwestern students, serving as a hub of social, community, and spiritual activities. Even after students were allowed to live on and participate in activities within campus, the search for culturally specific activities was often felt to be lacking, and the void was readily filled by a combination of barbecue from Hecky's Barbecue and attending services at the Second Baptist Church. Later, as the Northwestern Community Ensemble became a fixture within Black student life at NU, Evanston's Ebenezer A&M Church also assumed a prominent position in the social activities of students.

It wasn't a coincidence that the Second Baptist Church retained a position of primacy in the Black experience at Northwestern. The new pastor, Rev. Dr. Hycel B. Taylor, who had spent years at Garrett Seminary as a professor, was a spiritual and cultural dynamo. His brand of Black liberation theology built on 1960's civil-rights activism served as an ideal template for students looking for how to draw power and achieve success from their university degrees.

Hycel Taylor's doctrine found ready application in the lives of NU students during this time and served as a bridge between many students practicing Christianity and seemingly being opposed by those alleging to be Christian. The Second Baptist Church was a great vehicle in helping Northwestern Blacks overcome feeling overwhelmed by college life and the newness of their first experience away from home and community. As such, during the 1980's, which perhaps marked the peak of the relationship between the Second Baptist Church and NU Black student body, it was common to see dozens of students traveling together to church on Sundays, and many of Rev. Taylor's sermons served as fuel to make it through college.

Furthermore, and although it may seem odd to the uninitiated reader, it was also during this time that another cultural phenomenon occurred in Evanston that greatly affected the Black experience at Northwestern and its connection to the Evanston community. For over thirty years, Hecky Powell has brought his brand of barbecue to students across the university community. Hecky's barbecue proved to be a taste of home and a staple at Black events. However, and thankfully, the significance of Hecky Powell wasn't limited to simply bringing great food to campus. He has been omnipresent in supporting various Black organizations and individuals needing support at Northwestern. Also, his foundation, honoring his late father, impacts social causes throughout Evanston and Northwestern, and his wife, Cheryl, is an adjunct faculty member of Northwestern's School of Education and Social Policy. It is affirming to see Hecky's success grow proportionately to his service. His offerings are now distributed in dorms across campus, bringing a taste of home to students across the university.

Success has scores of unintended consequences. The incremental success of Black students, faculty, staff and administrators, combined with Northwestern eventually providing enhanced on-campus opportunities for worship, inclusion within the greater university community, and expansion of culturally-specific offerings led to steady reductions of the reliance on the Evanston community as the source providing feelings of relevance for Black students. Specifically, the emergence of Garrett Theological Seminary and, later, other campus offerings, such as House on the Rock, provided more easily accessible locales of worship, and the steady hand of the student affairs administrators at The Black House on campus combined to wean students from the need to leave campus in ways necessary in the past. Students can eat, sleep, and socialize in any number of locations consistent with their status as students at Northwestern. Even as still impressive numbers of members of the Black university community still worship at Evanston community churches, the dynamic of the relationship between the Blacks of Evanston and NU has changed.

In an ironic turn of events, the Black Evanston community has become in need of support from Northwestern's Black community. In the face of a dwindling Black population in the city of Evanston and with resources within the community becoming scarcer, the next chapter in the story of the relationship between the Black Evanston and Northwestern communities may hinge on the ability to compel the NU community to care about the circumstances in the Evanston community. As had been the case long ago, Northwestern continues to play a role in assisting the success of the city it calls home. Recent efforts by President Morton O. Schapiro, including Northwestern offering a five million-dollar grant to the city and embedding academic assistants within Evanston Township High School, have sought to reestablish and improve relations between the city of Evanston and Northwestern. Furthermore, the university has established a Neighborhood and Community Relations Department, which is meant to proactively engage city entities in mutually beneficial ways. Through its current Director, Alan Anderson, NU's Neighborhood and Community Relations Department is engaging community and civil right organizations, cultural and social clubs, churches, schools, and athletic groups to preserve the symbiotic relationship between Northwestern and Evanston.

In the meantime, the legacy of the Evanston community protecting the Black Northwestern community should not only be remembered and treasured, but it should also serve as a reminder to advance efforts to maintain a strong Black presence within the Evanston community. The message from Evanston is clear: The Black Northwestern community has been handed a baton from prior generations, and their presence and success resulted from those who acted with future students in mind and not because of any entitlement or happenstance. It is without question that members of institutions within the city that includes and surrounds Northwestern paved the way for the success of generations of Blacks at Northwestern, and that also is true for those students today who might not even think of such linkages or think to venture into the community. Based on the success during the times of need at the peak of the relationship, members of the current and future Black university communities would do well to appreciate that, perhaps, the purest expression of Black culture and community accessible to them is still waiting and wanting the fellowship there to be had. As it once proved capable of addressing feelings of isolation on campus, it may well be able to do so again.

The Black Athlete and the Black Experience

- **Norm Comer:** Football

- **Jim Pitts:** Men's Basketball

- **Dee Todd:** Women's Track Coach

- **Joseph Webb:** Football

- **Rishal Dinkins:** Women's Basketball

- **Katrina Adams:** Women's Tennis

- **Chris Martin:** Football

- **Ricky Byrdsong:** Men's Basketball Coach

- **Oliver Kupe:** Men's Soccer

- **Daryl Newell:** Football

Norm Comer

Norman Comer

Norm Comer graduated from Northwestern in 1958 from the School of Education and Social Policy.

Dr. Norman David Comer was born on December 8, 1935, in East Chicago, Indiana and, eighty-three years later, he still lives there. Although his father was born in Comer, Alabama and only obtained a sixth-grade education, educating the children was a mission for the Comer parents. Norm had five siblings with fifteen college degrees between them, including a brother who was the Associate Dean of Yale Medical School. During Norm's time at Northwestern, the Comer family had four children in college simultaneously. "My mother and my siblings worked in the steel mills, the hospitals, and one summer, I worked at Old Orchard to save money." Norm was able to save enough to buy a car in his junior year and help his siblings financially. Norm was recruited as a halfback and linebacker for Northwestern's football team in 1954.

"I always wanted to go to Northwestern from the time I was in sixth or seventh grade." Norm Comer used to listen to Northwestern games on the radio. He was a little taller and bigger than his siblings and enjoyed playing football. "My White high school football coaches were Northwestern grads. They steered me toward Northwestern, and it wasn't hard to do. Northwestern was my dream. I was recruited by Iowa and Arizona State, but my grades were quite acceptable, so I was offered an academic as well as an athletic scholarship from Northwestern. The football scholarship was the most lucrative, so I took it."

When Norman arrived at Northwestern in 1954 (the year after all men's dorms were desegregated), he was coached by George Steinbrenner and Ara Parseghian. They wanted him to stay at the YMCA. Norm told them that was unacceptable. "I was told, 'we thought *you* liked living at the Y. If you want to live in the dorms, you can live in the dorms.'"

Norman was one of the first Blacks to stay at Asbury Hall, but desegregation wasn't the only issue. "When I was a freshman, there were no Black girls on campus." There were twelve to fifteen Black men, of whom eight or nine were athletes, and Norm notes that they were all very smart. "One of the things I did learn at Northwestern is that I was not one of the smartest, as I originally thought. My mom would tell me, 'no matter how smart you are, there is always someone smarter.' Northwestern showed me that was true."

As a Black student athlete at Northwestern and the only Black player on the football team in the 1955-56 academic year, Norm had almost no social life. "You had to date women from Evanston or go into Chicago. I believe Northwestern saw that as embarrassing. By senior year, there were 25 Black girls on campus." They didn't all live on campus, but they were enrolled.

After the inclusion of Black women, Norm remembers a degree of socialization on and off campus. "Charles 'Doc' Glass and his wife opened their home to the athletes. They had some daughters, one of whom is now married to a former member of the

Chicago Bears, so his daughters and their friends would host us. Doc Glass was a custodian who lived in Evanston and a great gentleman who allowed us to socialize at his house." After so many years, Northwestern made Doc Glass the "official" welcoming agent for Black kids and their families. "Parents knew he was a kindly Black gentleman, and if they sent their child to Northwestern, they would be safe. Doc Glass had helped and recruited for NU and National College of Education for so many years that he had amassed a wall of pictures of all the athletes for whom he cared. This is where the Black students hung out. Northwestern's Black Athletes honored him in 1985 on the 30th Anniversary of Doc Glass' involvement at Northwestern."

As a young person, Norm wanted to be a dentist or work in the sciences, and his brothers wanted to be doctors and architects. "When I arrived at Northwestern, I decided to major in zoology. I quickly realized that I wasn't a healer and jettisoned the whole medical thing. My second year, I majored in math, my third year in social studies, and I graduated with a degree in English and social studies!"

Norm injured his shoulder in his junior year, so he didn't play much football after that. He then shifted his attention to tutoring other athletes in math and other subjects. He understood that athletes required help because they needed to travel and, as a result, would miss a lot of tests. Norm was prepared for this because he had faced the same. "I remember we played against Michigan. We went up on Friday, and I had missed an exam. We played on Saturday, flew into what was an old military base airfield, O'Hare, on Sunday night. We arrived at the dorms around 9 pm, and I had to study all night to take the test." Norm says that most times he had to study all night, and only sometimes would he get to party.

Norm does remember a few small incidents with White students and faculty, which he considered more reflective of real life in America at that time than a reflection of anything uniquely wrong with NU. "We didn't dislike Northwestern, we just wanted to be treated as normal people. Northwestern was my dream."

Jim Pitts

James Pitts

James (aka Jim) Pitts obtained a Bachelor of Arts in Political Science in 1966, a Master of Arts in Sociology in 1968 and became a Doctor of Philosophy in 1971—all from Northwestern's Weinberg College of Arts and Sciences.

Jim Pitts was a basketball star but quickly became an activist and scholar at Northwestern. Jim was six-feet tall; he grew up on Chicago's West Side and was a member of the John Marshall High School basketball team, the reigning national champs. Jim excelled in both academics and basketball at Marshall. In 1961, he enrolled at Northwestern with a basketball scholarship.

Jim was introduced to Northwestern through athletic recruiting. "I was on a prominent Chicago high school basketball team. They took an interest in me, and I took an interest in Northwestern." Compared to Michigan, Iowa, Illinois, and some of the other schools that were recruiting him, Northwestern was smaller and offered Jim the possibility of small-scale interactions. He saw Northwestern as preferable to the big schools.

Jim has had a long relationship with Northwestern with several types of connections. "There were two segments of attendance. One is when I entered Northwestern in 1961 as a freshman. I would have graduated in a formal sense in 1965 but chose to stay until 1966 to continue my basketball eligibility with the team. I re-enrolled in Northwestern and was given a teaching fellowship and teaching assistantship. That started my graduate career."

When Jim arrived as a freshman in 1961, he saw a different reality of the Blacks there. 'I would say Black people were scarce. Northwestern wasn't looking to include us, except as student athletes.' Nevertheless, Northwestern was not a hostile environment for him. Jim had chosen to be a student and an athlete at Northwestern, and he was focused on achieving that mix. Jim also joined a White fraternity, Phi Delta Chi. "That had been the first time that had happened at Northwestern. I had a good experience in the fraternity, and things worked well."

Jim says there were no Black women on campus—not one. "There were six Black males who I knew. Four of us were athletes: two in football and two in basketball. Then, there were two other persons who came in as normal students with their parents fitting the bill." Jim was pleased to say that all the athletes graduated.

As an undergraduate, Jim had no mentors and knew of no mentors of color on campus. He derived his emotional support from his teammate, Don Jackson, and his family in Chicago. Charles (Doc) and Helen Glass provided a social outlet for him and many other Black athletes in his era. Jim also credits the Black community in Evanston as a major help to him. He saw a few Black faces, but his academic world was mostly White.

Jim believes that the only thing that hindered him as an athlete was repeated injuries, but being a Black athlete enhanced his experience at Northwestern. "I was well-known, and students came out to cheer me, except when I missed free throws." He considers his acceptance into the White fraternity a social experiment. "Overall, the social experience for me, Don, and one or two others who came after us was positive." He enjoyed having the rare experience as a student-athlete who was also in a fraternity.

Jim is not sure if his time as a student-athlete fundamentally changed Northwestern. "It might have readied Northwestern in a subtle set of ways. Maybe they thought, 'Why not bring in talented Black students who are not athletes because the athletes are making it?'" To Jim, Northwestern didn't change until the arrival of Black people in larger numbers in the late 1960's.

Jim was a graduate student and professor at Northwestern for many years. He saw Northwestern grow over the years and include women and Black coaches and an unprecedented number of Black students and faculty in its community. His wife reminds him that he was influential in the recruitment of both. "For many years, I was involved in the recruitment of Black athletes and, then, as a faculty member, other Black faculty. In a few cases, I might have had a positive influence on some talented Black scholars who decided to become PhDs in the Social Sciences ... maybe Kathy Ogletree and maybe Clovis Semmes." Jim thinks they were so sharp that they would have gotten PhDs even if he were not at Northwestern.

Jim rarely gets back to campus. "I don't get back often for the simple reason that after I left the faculty in 1987, I've worked in institutions that are far away." Like a true Wildcat, Jim pays attention to the success, failures, and the frustrations of the athletic teams, but he hasn't been to any games. "I welcome the opportunity to be a part of the 50th Anniversary of the building take over because I really appreciate and love the people who I knew from that period of time."

Dee Todd

Dee Todd

In August 1981, while completing her PhD at Governors State University, Delores "Dee" Todd was hired as Northwestern's Women's Track Coach. She was the first Black Woman Coach at NU and, within three years of leading the team, she was awarded the Big Ten Coach of the Year in Cross Country Track. Her team also finished in the top five in the Big Ten for three years in row!

Dee moved from Washington, DC to Chicago after getting married, and she began coaching track at Rich Central and Thornridge High Schools in Chicago's South Suburbs where she led teams to State championships. While teaching a summer basketball camp with Jackie Joyner Kersey at University of Illinois, she heard about the Northwestern job. She was hired by Ted Leland, Northwestern's Associate Athletic Director (with support from Toya Wyatt, Northwestern alumnae and former athlete). In that same year, many women's teams became a part of the National Collegiate Athletic Association (NCAA).

Dee toured the campus and thought it to be beautiful, but she and her husband had just purchased a condominium in the South Suburbs, so she decided to commute to work instead. She didn't see The Black House or any Black faculty or staff, but that didn't deter her. There was also no indoor track, but Dee didn't see any negatives to taking the position. She had always wanted to coach at college level, and this was a great opportunity.

Dee hired John Capriotti (who later became Vice President of Nike) as her assistant coach. Northwestern had also just hired Dennis Green, so there was another Black coach, along with other Black assistant coaches, including Frances Peay (who later became the head football coach) and Jim Caldwell (who later became the Head Coach of the Detroit Lions.). As she didn't get to see them much or even enough to learn from them, Dee had to self-motivate!

There were several women's teams at Northwestern when Dee arrived, including tennis, field hockey, softball, and basketball, but none had Black student-athletes. The Big Ten Advisory Council was in place then, and Northwestern alumnus and popular broadcaster, Irv Cross, was one of the representatives. She remembers meeting and interacting with him, even though she didn't have many Black athletes to discuss with him in his capacity as a representative.

The Big Ten was always a very progressive conference in Dee's point of view. "The Big Ten had two teams with Black female head coaches and two teams with Black male coaches." Dee's friend, Karen Dennis, was the track coach at Michigan State (for sixteen years, Ms. Dennis has served as the Director of Track & field and Cross country at Ohio State), so Dee was surrounded by role models and sources of encouragement. Her real challenge was to build a competitive complete track team. In 1994, she heard that the new NU President, Arnold Weber, had no interest in athletics. They were not offering her scholarships to build the program. "It is hard to recruit a sprinter in Chicago when you don't have an indoor track."

When she had arrived at Northwestern, her track team was all White and not very good. She said to herself, "I could bring my high school team and run better than this!" Her team was slow and finished last in her first track meet at Michigan State. "The officials were dismantling the finish line by the time they completed the race." When she went to her first Big Ten indoor track meet at Indiana, she was so frustrated that she left her team on campus and went home all by herself. Dee was on a mission to recruit runners. She had to sell Northwestern and its great academics to recruits "because NU didn't have anything else to offer. The track team was bad, the football team was bad... everybody was bad!" The next year, she brought in four girls, including one great runner from England. In 1983, she brought in one Black student, Terry Washington. Within a few years, they became the thirteenth best cross-country team in the country.

Dee used unique tactics to motivate her team. They would run indoors at the University of Chicago, and she would threaten to drop them off at Cabrini Green to see how fast they could get back. "She recalls a meet that coincided with Northwestern's Homecoming where "they ran like crap." After the meet, they stopped at Wendy's to eat, and the girls begged, 'coach, let's hurry up so we can go to Homecoming.'" When they got back in the van, Dee put the cruise control on 50 MPH. "The next time you want to run slow, remember that I just showed you slow!" They missed homecoming but ran faster in the next meet.

Dee prided herself in championing diversity and consistently talking to her mostly White team about issues around racism. She thinks she may have oversold cultural concerns because about half of her team dated and married Black men. "I told them, 'you need to wait till you get out of school for this. You come to Northwestern and have a Black coach and, now, Black husbands. Your parents are not going to be happy!'" Dee says the girls were all good people, and she enjoyed coaching and training them on more than just sports.

In 1983, Anucha Brown joined the Women's Basketball team and became the first Black on the team. Dee immediately reached out to her. There was a group called Center Court that supported women's athletics, and they brought all Black women together. As a result, Dee was able to spend time with all the women athletes, including Anucha's teammate and Duke University current women's basketball head, coach Joanne P. McCallie, forming a sense of community.

Dee says Northwestern was always very nice, helpful, and appreciative of her work. "I have the most respect and warm feelings about my time at NU. I don't remember any negative experiences and, if there were any, I didn't want to rock the boat! I worked with what I had. I was always aware of the impact I would have on those who would follow me." She didn't focus on being the first Black woman coach at Northwestern. "I was busy trying to be the best and proving that I deserved to coach at college level. I was a competitor, and I didn't have time to deal with anything other than that."

Dee left Northwestern in 1985 to start a track team at Georgia Tech. She was saddened to learn that Northwestern discontinued the track program not long after she left. She returns to Northwestern every now and then. Dee was very happy when the women's track team was reinstated, and they invited her to speak at the Spring banquet. She enjoyed sharing her experiences with them but noticed "there were about twenty girls and no people of color. After my talk, one of the parents came to me and told me, 'now I recognize how non-diverse we are!'"

After leaving Northwestern, Dee Todd had a lot of firsts in a great career. After being the first African American coach in the Atlantic Coast Conference (ACC) in any sport, she became an assistant commissioner with the ACC. She left a significant mark in the history of North Carolina A&T State University by becoming its first female athletics director. She credits Northwestern University for being the launching pad to her career in college athletics and will always be grateful to it. She hopes her example inspires others to follow in her footsteps!

Joseph Webb

Joe Webb is a 1982 graduate of Northwestern's Weinberg College of Arts and Sciences. His Northwestern beginnings sounds a lot more like today's generation of students than someone attending in the 1970's. Attending Northwestern wasn't necessarily on Joe's radar. He was a high school football star living in a small steel town outside of Pittsburgh and was already scheduled to attend Syracuse University to study physics. Northwestern happened to be recruiting athletes in the class below Joe's and, when they noticed him on tape, NU decided he needed to be a Wildcat. Joe agreed.

Although recruitment to Northwestern was thought to be a life-changing opportunity, Joe's football career wouldn't be the defining factor of his NU experience. What proved to upend Joe's world upon attending Northwestern was the extent to which segregation would be forced upon him. In the small, integrated town in which he was raised, he had extremely close friendships with people of all races and walks of life. He was as comfortable with Whites as he was with Blacks. To know Joe is to appreciate that he's really a great guy. Who wouldn't want to be his friend?

For Joe, Northwestern couldn't have been more foreign than if he had landed in Brazil or the moon. "When I came to NU and experienced such a polarized community, I didn't know what it meant, and I didn't understand why it was. It was a culture shock of an extreme proportion to me." He became acutely aware of the polarization when the fraternity rush began; the fraternities were stopping at everyone's door except for his and those of other Blacks. When he asked why this was the case, he was told that White Greek organizations were for Whites and Black Greek-lettered organizations were for Blacks. The expectation was that Blacks would either belong to the Black fraternities or to none at all. The fact that Joe was a member of the football team didn't matter an iota. Even learning that "Black Greeks" existed was an eye-opener, to say the least.

A saving grace in this was the presence of a strong Black community that was ready, willing, and imposing, and they embraced him. Joe felt a strong pull toward the Northwestern Black community. After all, it was still just a decade removed from the 1968 takeover of the Bursar's Office, and the Blacks were still enjoying the benefits of that hard-fought victory. Joe describes the Black community as a "wondrous world, the likes of which I'd never known." Joe gained exposure to parts of his community that he had never been able to delve into prior to Northwestern. There was The Black House, the home of the Department of African American Student Affairs at that time. There were fireside chats and glorious, spiritual concerts by the Northwestern Community Ensemble. "It blew my mind that young Black students could even know all they did. I went to meetings sometimes wishing I had a Webster dictionary in my back pocket." Joe's exposure to Black engineers, multilingual students, and amazing student musicians was not only mind blowing but also empowering. He now felt supported at all times in all ways, and "this made navigating the rest of the university survivable."

This community strength proved to be necessary not just in terms of enhancing a Black experience but also in protecting the Black community from ongoing sieges. Joe notes that just ten years after the Bursar's Office Takeover, there was an effort to take away The Black House (but was successfully rebuked). The students also had to protest and repel efforts to eliminate the SAW (Summer Academic Workshop, a program providing transitioning for these mostly inner-city Blacks to the university environment), and they had to fight to maintain funding for the FMO (For Members Only, the Black student alliance of Northwestern).

In many ways, Northwestern was providing Joe a parallel education. In fact, he was getting a more rounded education as a Black person about his Blackness and using his Blackness in a world dominated by Whites. He was also learning how to organize, strategize, and debate via facts instead of simply relying on emotion. These would be skills essential later in life—and fatefully, later in college. However, Joe laments the loss of his naiveté and the absence of opportunities that barred from having an experience similar to the ways in which he had growing up. It is stark to appreciate that despite his natural inclination to do so, Joe left Northwestern without making a single lasting friendship with a White student.

At the same time that Joe was having difficulty enjoying all the benefits of the university community, he was evolving inside of the Black experience. He became an officer in FMO. He participated in marches on campus. Throughout it all, what was being impressed upon him was that the actions of the greater Black community weren't meant to improve their circumstances as much as it was meant to benefit those who would follow. This concept was a paradigm shift for Joe, but he understood he benefitted from the efforts of those who had attended NU before him, and this led to his participation in support activities on campus as well as in the Evanston community. He learned and participated in conversations about apartheid and AIDS—things that didn't affect him but allowed him to improve the lives of others. He felt himself being "expanded from the inside out."

Joe posits this same paradigm is a large part of why ongoing tensions exist between the university and the Black community, and he uses the seemingly ongoing desire of Northwestern to alter the purpose, function, and services of The Black House away from the reason it was established as Exhibit A. He allows that administrators may believe they have the "best interests" of the community in mind but continually misstep in being paternalistic and arrogant in their approach and in failing to adequately involve Black student and alumni in the planning, which is then interpreted as a lack of empathy or even a desire to understand or share feelings.

Joe notes that, based on the multiple attempts to take away or dilute the purpose or function of The Black House, "The Black community interprets the university's view of The Black House as a shack in need of repair or a building that could offer better services to the entire Northwestern community instead of an icon and an institution of refuge for the Black community. Ongoing efforts to impose solutions on the community and even to disregard the community when it tells the university what is needed (one common refrain, repeated over the years, is 'we'll take it under advisement') drives all the reminders of all the arrogant instruments of the institution that you're surrounded by that tells you that you are here by our favor, not by your merit. Anything that stimulates that notion that you are here because we've decided to allow you to be here removes the notion that we are welcomed guests and desired contributors and that we are here through some act of your grace. That is insulting, demeaning, and frustrating. And through actions like this, for fifty years, we've been fighting this same fight… How do we move to a place where we can consider Northwestern a place not where we go, battle, survive and leave, but a place where we go and feel welcome?"

Joe laments that the same logic and tactics used to "do away" with The Black House in 2015 were the same used during efforts when he attended Northwestern. He notes that the feeling he described are the same as those described to him by his wife's aunt, who had also attended Northwestern during the time of the Bursar's Office Takeover; his wife, younger brother, and daughter are all NU alumni. It is sad to him that he has had so many relatives attend the university but can't share a legacy of fond memories.

For them, the conversation always circles back to analogies of having been at war, surviving a war, and lamenting, "we're still fighting over the same things." As such, conversations about college life are surprisingly rare because "we know what we went through and don't care to relive the experiences." The fundamental question to Joe about the Black experience is "Why do we have to obtain a minor in civil disobedience? Every generation of Black students has to fight a fight of relevance. Why?"

Despite it all, the realization of separateness on campus became most acute when difficulties arose within the fraternity of football players. The nature of a football team is such that complete trust, respect, and teamwork are essential and unshakeable. In a relatively violent sport, you learn to depend on each other for success and to ensure safety. Even as the Wildcats weren't at all victorious during this time (Joe notes over 30 straight losses), those young men shared a bond that made them as close as brothers. However, that was on the field. Joe notes that as close as these teammates became in the field of play, and even with his inclination to have friends of all colors, it was difficult for his teammates and him to forge relationships outside the locker room and on the field, even if and as efforts were made. Joe asks, "Where is there a dichotomy as to why young men who already have positive feelings toward one another could be so easily evaporated after walking twenty feet away from the practice field? That wasn't my high school athletic experience ..."

The sadness of this Northwestern reality for Joe was that he realized that the other football players didn't want to feel this way. The surroundings imposed this reality on them. Joe recalls an illustrative incident that occurred after he suffered a knee injury and required surgery. Much to his surprise, the first person at his bedside after surgery was a White teammate, Tom. Joe found this shocking. Tom also belonged to and managed a fraternity house at which Joe stayed for one summer, and Joe recalls their ability to interact and enjoy each other's company, but this always occurred off-campus and when the school was on recess, seemingly removing the "normal barriers." It seemed that the surroundings on campus always prevented Tom from befriending Joe publicly. "Tom came from substantial means, and I came from none. Yet we found each other's experiences completely enthralling. Why is this the exception and not the rule? Tom was always cool and sensitive, but without that summer experience and the removal of the typical NU ebb and flow, I would have never learned what a neat guy he was. If he and I had met under different circumstances, I'm positive we would have become lifelong friends along with the many lifelong White friends who I fondly call my brothers and sisters.

The combination of Joe's on- and off-field education and experiences led him and others to participate in an action that would cause an unprecedented revolution on campus with shockwaves that would be felt across the nation. One of Joe's closest friends on campus was Ben Butler (who died in 2011). Ben was the FMO Coordinator (President) during the 1981-82 term; Joe also served on the Board. Joe recalls that Ben had humility of spirit and service and went to great lengths to explain the Black experience to the greater university community. He was always gracious and smiling and made it easy to facilitate understanding. It was in that vein that Ben and, later Joe, took it upon themselves to deal with others on campus as individuals and to insist that others dealt with them as men.

Ben, Joe, Mike Cammon (who ultimately served as spokesman for the group) and others—a total of thirty-one male and female athletes—created an organization called Black Athletes United for the Light (BAUL). BAUL was not created as an activist entity, but in hopes of contributing to an already dynamic African American community in socially conscious ways of interest to the Black athletic community, similar to the efforts of Black campus interest groups like the National Society of Black Engineers and Black Folks' Theatre. Still, it didn't take long before the group was pulled into activism because the examination of social consciousness in other aspects of campus life led to reflecting on the experience of Black athletes within the teams in which they played.

Examination of the treatment of Black athletes led to an appreciation of how unequally Black athletes were being treated and being made to feel. In contrast to how protests typically occur, there didn't appear to be a distinguishing event that served as a rallying cry; instead, there was a growing understanding that Black athletes were systematically being treated as less than men when compared to their White counterparts. Specifically, Joe reports being pressurized to return from surgery before he was ready to play and being forced to collect trash from the field as a means of "earning" his scholarship in the interim. Coach Venturi (Rick Venturi, men's Head Football Coach between 1978-1980) even allegedly stated he wished he could get rid of the entire senior class of African Americans and was accused of using a racial slur toward a student-athlete—a claim he vehemently denied. Joe says, "most of the Black players didn't believe he said those words he was accused of saying. That story came from one athlete and somehow got leaked to one of the news organizations, and it took on a life of its own, but no one representing BAUL ever accused him or anyone else of using that type of language. In fact, when Mike Cammon was asked about that specific event, Mike declaratively said he had not heard Venturi use those words, and neither had I."

Based on prior lessons learned from engaging the university for change with the Black community, BAUL took a systematic, controlled approach to presenting their grievances, using the support structure of The Black House to its full advantage. "So, when it actually got to organizing the actual grievance process, Alice Palmer and I had a lot of one-on-ones that I took back to the group to build on. The actual spearheading of the grievance was largely constructed by Tim Hill, Dana Hemphill, Mark Adams, Dean Payne, Mike Cammon, and myself. It's important to mention that we all paid a price for our involvement. We were the guys who Chris Hinton and the younger players trusted to march into those offices—not just me. Now, Mike Cammon typically was not involved in student activism, but he stepped up big time and represented us with class and grace that makes me smile to this day. It is my belief that only Mike, or Ben, could have pulled that type of mature cool, calm, and collective leadership under that type of intense pressure, and Ben wasn't available, as he had taken a quarter off because of a back injury. We took a vote, and we unanimously chose Mike to be our spokesperson."

Once they were ready, they met with the Vice President of Student Affairs, Jim Carleton, and the Athletic Director, John Pont; they presented their case on how the unequal treatment of African American athletes was impacting their lives. Strategically, BAUL didn't focus on race but quality of life considerations. The conversations involved autonomy in coursework (that prior to this point had been imposed on them) and accountability for actions, such as injury protocols and administering discipline to players. BAUL was careful to ask for considerations that would uplift the experience of all student-athletes, knowing that that standard was largely already in place for Whites.

The subsequent actions represented obtaining objectives, which would lead to the consequences of having to address the matter. Northwestern's Athletic Director, John Pont, Football Head Coach, Rick Venturi, and his staff were fired. In 1981, Coach Dennis (Denny) Green was hired, becoming the first African American football coach in the Big Ten (or any of the "power-conference" schools) and only the second to hold the position at a predominantly White institution. Northwestern had lost 31 of its last 33 games when this change was made. Denny Green was named Big Ten coach of the year in 1982, as Northwestern went 3-8 and ended their NCAA Division I Football Bowl Subdivision (FBS)-record losing streak at thirty-four games.

Coach Green remained at Northwestern until 1985, and the impact he had upon the general and Black campus community can't be overstated. For the first time in the modern era, the football program demonstrated it could again compete in the Big Ten. On campus, the presence of a strong, powerful Black man at the helm of such a high-profile aspect of the university served as a clear message that opportunities offered could turn into success at a level desired by the university, and this success could occur regardless of the color of the person leading the charge. In fact, Dennis Green's successor was Francis Peay, another African American, who became the *Sports Illustrated Coach of the Year* in 1986 and had a six-year head coaching tenure at Northwestern from 1986-91 after having been Denny Green's defensive coordinator since 1981 and interim head coach when Green left in 1985.

Ben, Joe, and other athletes learned that much of what he viewed and "understood" as a student proved not to be entirely the case. As an example, perhaps the largest consequence faced by Black athletes after the action that let to Coach Venturi being fired wasn't the withdrawal of scholarship or expulsion but the loss of trust and brotherhood between BAUL members and their teammates. Although a number of athletes spoke out in opposition to the action of BAUL, there were many others who felt as if they should have been informed, if not included, in the conversations and actions, especially given that their teammates had never given them an actual reason not to include them. Further concerns about the ability to fully comprehend situations in real time were realized when Joe returned to campus as an administrator (director of financial aid and undergraduate admissions and for minority students) and interacted with some of the same administrators as colleagues who he had viewed with skepticism as a student. It was unforeseeable that the same people who had once been thought to be foes would become necessary and able allies.

Joe looks at the recent symbols of "progress" at Northwestern and offers caution to reading too much into the presence of key individuals at the university as a measure of success and, even necessarily, a symbol of progress. Even as he admits that recent actions are meaningful, particularly the presence of Blacks in specific high-profile positions of authority, he states that the primary metric of interest and success is a proportionate representation among students, faculty, and staff, which remain well below that existing within the general population. After all, it has often been the case at Northwestern that Black staff and administrators have been used to implement measures, including changes to The Black House, which have further expanded the divide between the university and the Black community. Joe opines that it has been those instances in which the number of Black students on campus has been at its highest that has represented the most normal of times for students.

Finally, Joe offers a strong commentary on the university's trend toward multiculturalism instead of focusing on the individualized concerns of at-risk students. "I take issue with multiculturalism as an outcome to be desired as the university's goal. To me, it's just another statement of arrogance; another statement of 'here's what you need.' Don't ask me what I need or want and, then, proceed on a course of action that is divorced from any recognition of those needs but instead fully captures the administrative desire for what you think we should have. It's the very definition of arrogance. Give me the power to choose. If I don't want to be a part of a Black community or if I want to be part of a tightly knit Black community, I want that option and power, and I deserve it as a student ... Otherwise, you've just created a new way around which I have to figure out survival." In discussing his daughter's difficulties, he's remorseful that she hasn't had the benefit of the Black cultural experience that has defined his entire life. "That was my foundation."

It's especially interesting that Joe notes that upon leaving Northwestern in 1982, "normalcy returned to my life, and I felt whole again," meaning he has been able to enjoy relationships with people from all walks of life without regard to race and without detracting from his Black experience. He notes that his impression "upon leaving NU was that it was a racist institution with racist people, but I now realize that's not true at all." Still, he remains concerned that "the fact that you can leave that place feeling that way is a great injustice to the experience of all students."

Rishal Dinkins-Stanciel

Rishal Dinkins-Stanciel has two degrees from Northwestern. She received her BA in Political Science in 1987 and her MBA from Kellogg Graduate School of Management in 1993. Rishal played on the Wildcats' women's basketball team from 1985 to 1987.

Originally from Florida, Rishal studied at Stetson University from 1983 to '85. One of her coaches from Stetson (Mary Ciuk) became an assistant coach under Don Pirrelli at Northwestern. They were seeking diverse talent, and Rishal, who was a stellar student, fit the bill. "It was very unlikely that they would have accepted a transfer student-athlete at NU without a good academic history and the potential to play and who would graduate successfully within the prescribed four years. Thank you, Lord that I was." There was no other minority student on the team when she arrived. Two-time Big Ten Player of the Year, Anucha Browne Sanders, had graduated the year prior, and Rishal agreed that Northwestern had a very strong need for diversity.

Rishal describes Northwestern University as a blessing for her. Even prior to transferring, when she visited NU, the Department of Athletics took her to meet Asst. Dean of African American Student Affairs, Dr. Ulysses Duke Jenkins. "That time with Duke helped me to understand that Northwestern appreciated the connection of me as an African American athlete instead of just a general athlete. My prayer and my desire when I was in high school was to play basketball in Division 1 at a top twenty academic school. I suffered injuries in high school, and all the recruitment letters stopped coming in my senior year. I had to fight back." Luckily, Northwestern came knocking. Northwestern was very well regarded; she had an uncle (LaMar) in Chicago who had played pro ball, was familiar with NU and had taught her the game. The campus and the lake at Northwestern were absolutely beautiful. "I had a quick visit over the weekend and decided to sign."

She felt completely comfortable with her teammates. They were from Maine, Michigan, California, and New Jersey, and there was a warmth to them. "I didn't feel like I was the only one because the sense of belonging came very easily and very naturally. I think it tends to happen better for athletes because when you're in the trenches together and you've got to hit that last suicide (training drill), everybody's got to make the time." Most of her teammates continue to be her best friends.

During her junior year, Rishal would joke with her team and ask if they were traveling to places where it was safe for Blacks. "We were going into West Lafayette, Indiana, Lexington, Kentucky, and all these places that are historically racist, and I was the only Black person on the team. When Robin Garrett came in my senior year, it was phenomenally different because when you have two, it makes it easier."

Rishal met and developed relationships with a core group of Black women—Yvette Washington who worked for the basketball team and, in Sargent Hall, she met fellow athlete Katrina Adams and her friends, Lori Hayes and Wendy Willis. They formed the bridge to the African American community at Northwestern, which she considers critical. "I was coming in as a junior, I didn't know anyone other than my teammates. That bridge turned out to be the way that I really became a part of the Northwestern community. By senior year, I met Sonya Grier who became an even stronger bridge to the NU black community. I had lunch, breakfast, and dinner at Sargent, where Duke Jenkins would come by—may he rest in peace—and have great conversation. He would always pull me in because, as an African American female athlete, you're isolated because your schedule is so different." Rishal recognizes that the feeling of belonging is crucial. "I don't think we knew how significant it was. If you belong, it means that people value you for who you are, and you feel like a contributor."

Rishal came into Northwestern as a political science major. Five of her teammates were also political science majors and were in same classes as her. When they were on the road, they studied together. She remembers other Black women athletes, including Lynne Bey and sisters Ndidi and Chinazo Opia, who were softball players and are now both very successful in medicine and business. "There was something about female athletes at that time. There were not many professional opportunities for women, so that pushed us to advanced degrees."

Rishal emphasizes that there is a special level of camaraderie across athletes. She envisions a time when there is a stronger network amongst African American male and female athlete alums that could potentially serve as a baseline for the students who feel isolated "to assist the Jordans of this world who didn't feel that they quite belonged wholeheartedly." (Jordan Hankins, a Black student-athlete and Northwestern woman's basketball player who committed suicide in January of 2017.) Rishal can personally relate to this tragedy. "I know what it's like to be on a team where you're not playing a lot yet, every day, you still put in the same amount of time, you still have to go to classes, and you still have to go on the road every other weekend in the Big Ten. You can begin to question your ability at a certain point. Without that camaraderie and mentorship, it becomes difficult." Rishal continues, "If I have a concern about today, it is that without the high numbers of Black students and Black athletes and without support, a young athlete runs the risk of literally losing it altogether. Young athletes run the risk of losing themselves because they aren't able fulfill the sense of belonging to a community."

Rishal says Northwestern has a challenge ahead to really keep the numbers of Black athletes going. She references Northwestern Athletic Hall of Fame inductee, Anucha Browne Sanders' daughter, Spring Sanders. "Spring graduated in 2016 as one of the top lacrosse players in the country. Northwestern gave her an athletic scholarship to attend; she was All-American, and she was the only African American female on the Women's USA Lacrosse team. She is phenomenal as an athlete, yet where are the others? Now that Spring is gone, who else takes her place?" The priority, in Rishal's estimation, should be building a continuous pipeline of Black athletes or "Northwestern will continue to fight an uphill battle."

As a representative of the Big Ten Advisory Council that mentors Black athletes at Northwestern, Rishal discovers that "Gary Barnett, Northwestern's 1996 Rose Bowl coach, said, 'I'm going to have fifty percent of my athletes be African American.'" Rishal is not confident about whether there has ever been another coach at NU who has said that, and if there has been, it certainly was not a female.

Rishal's ongoing concern is about support, which occurs with a volume of similar individuals helping each other and with institutional support. She doesn't remember a lot of Black coaches throughout Northwestern in her day, but she does know that there were none in basketball. However, she does remember Mrs. Bertha, the administrative assistant in the Athletic Department who mentored the team like a mother figure, and that mattered.

When Rishal graduated in 1987, she stayed in the Evanston Community and coached at the City of Evanston's Fleetwood-Jourdain Community Center. She was the volunteer assistant coach at Northwestern's basketball camp, served on the Big Ten Advisory Committee, attended Kellogg Graduate School of Management, and became a graduate tutor for the NU Athletic Academic Services and a volunteer coach. She speaks to students and student-athletes as often as she can and supports the Northwestern University Black Alumni Association's "Athletes Connect" Student-Based Initiatives mentoring program.

Being a student-athlete at Northwestern was a phenomenal experience for Rishal in terms of shaping who she is today. "There are challenges, but the commitment, discipline, communication skills, camaraderie, political savviness, and managerial courage came from that Northwestern student-athlete experience." Rishal bleeds purple!

Katrina Adams

Katrina Adams

Katrina Adams is from the West Side of Chicago, and she wanted to attend college someplace warm. After winning the Illinois State Tennis Singles Championship in 1983 and 1984 while at Whitney Young High School, Katrina was heavily recruited by Northwestern and became its first Black woman tennis athlete. Katrina attended the School of Speech from 1985 to 1987 and was inducted into the Northwestern Athletic Hall of Fame in 1997.

Growing up in Chicago, Katrina knew that Northwestern had one of the top communications schools in the nation, and she was fascinated by the Wildcats and the purple and white. She remembers that cold weekend in January when she took her recruiting trip—she knew immediately she wanted to attend. Her freshman roommate was her best friend in high school, Wendy Willis. "So, when I arrived I knew the ins and outs of campus and parties. My base was set! I didn't have to feel my way through with who to hang out with and who to meet. I was very lucky!" Katrina was also already familiar with her teammates. The Northwestern tennis team was sixty in the country at the time, and she kept up with them, even while in High School.

As a student-athlete, Katrina's schedule was brutal because the tennis season was every quarter. "I didn't have a lot of free time. My classes began at 8 am, and I had to be done by 1 pm. Practice at 2:30pm, return at 5:30, then to dinner until 7 pm, back to the dorms to shower, try to relax and study." Katrina recalls a test that needed to be taken during the NCAA tennis tournament. "Most of the schools were already done for the summer during the tournament, but we get out in June!"

At times, being a student-athlete was just as challenging on the student side. Although she attended a competitive high school, she realized that there are different challenges and had to study better. "I had to take an Econ test with my coach sitting in the room next to me. The coach had to vouch I wasn't getting any extra time, and the professor required that I take it the same time as the other students." Economics was not her favorite class, but she made it through. Kat also remembers a Computer Science class where she couldn't understand the professor. "I sat in the back, moved to the middle, then to the front. I thought it would be a cool class to take." She loved public speaking, sociology, and all the classes in communications; however, she regrets not being able to take an African American studies class. "Af-Am classes were from 1 pm to 4 pm, and I was always at practice. There are limitations and sacrifices when you're an athlete."

Given her schedule, Katrina didn't consider herself very social, but she did go out on some occasions. Tuesday night and the weekends were her time to enjoy student life. There were a few other Black women athletes who lived in Sargent Hall with her, including basketball player Rishal Dinkins Stanciel, and softball players and sisters Ndidi Opia Massey and Chinazo Opia Cunningham. Lynn Bey, another resident of Sargent Hall, played both Field Hockey and Lacrosse. She remembers studying with a football player, Curtis Duncan, and thought student-athlete life enhanced her Northwestern experience. "I got to cross communicate with other athletes on other teams, and it also made me purposeful about making friends with non-athletes, which allowed me to have the lifelong friends I have today." Katrina didn't have time for extra-curricular activities, but she was fine with that. They were not Katrina's priority. "I was there to play tennis; I had my own goals and was able to achieve them."

When Katrina arrived at Northwestern, she kept doing what she was doing before— winning! "Winning was a part of who I was and what the team was already experiencing." The tennis team was already Big Ten champions before she arrived. She went on to win the 1987 NCAA tennis tournament in doubles. She and her teammate, Diane Donnelly (also a 1997 Athletic Hall of Fame Inductee), were the first NCAA champions in the sport for Northwestern as well as in Northwestern history. She didn't recognize the impact of that in real time. "Really, it was just another match—another tournament and winning. But this catapulted me to turn professional and begin my career." Now, she recognizes how huge that was for Northwestern athletics. Training for athletes today is much more professional. "Northwestern is a football school now, athletics is a business."

Kat visits Northwestern as often as she can. "I've been to Homecoming six times in the last ten years; I've participated in the Athletic Department's NU for Life events, several NUBAA events, and an ESPN*W* discussion, among many others." Katrina appreciates the success she's had in sports and professionally. Relationships with many alumni have been pivotal in her current career with the United States Tennis Association. "Judy Levering was the USTA's first woman president, Jon Vegosen was president of the United States Tennis Association (USTA) in 2011, Chris Combs was a huge tennis supporter, and Todd Martin, a former pro player and former member of the USTA board, are all Northwestern grads." They all share a love for purple and recognize it in their interactions. She knows what it means to have been a student at Northwestern and tries to give back, especially to students of color. She was the only Black player on her tennis team and is proud that many others followed suit. It was a great experience for Katrina, and she always encourages young people to become Wildcats.

Ricky Byrdsong

Ricky and Sherialyn Byrdsong

Ricky Byrdsong was gunned down on his street by a White supremacist in Evanston, Illinois on July 2, 1999 while walking with his children.

Ricky was the Northwestern University's men's basketball coach from 1993 to 1997. He was the first African American men's basketball coach at Northwestern and took NU to the National Invitational Tournament (NIT) for the 1993-94 season, becoming one of NU Athletics' more charismatic coaches along the way. Sherialyn Byrdsong, Ricky's wife of twenty years, eludes that the racist gunman knew exactly who Ricky was, targeted his house, knew his schedule, and purposefully killed him. She believes being that Black and a celebrity coach at Northwestern contributed to Ricky Byrdsong being targeted.

Sherialyn Byrdsong says that Ricky loved coaching and knew his personality would take him far. Sherialyn and Ricky were born and raised in Atlanta, Georgia and met on Christmas Day, when they were hanging out with high school friends. "We knew in high school we wanted to get married. We had so much fun together and were truly friends." Ricky was voted "most cooperative" in high school; he was the class clown, and everyone liked him, including his teachers. Ricky was kind, caring, and had a good heart.

Ricky was raised by his mom, grandmother, and aunts. They took him to church every Sunday morning and every Sunday night, and this shaped him into a genuine and authentic person. Sherialyn's family liked him early on, and Ricky became a part of their family.

"Ricky wasn't a great basketball player. He was an average to good basketball player," Sherialyn jokes. He started on his high school team by senior year and was good enough and tall enough to get a scholarship to Pratt Community College in Kansas. "God's favor was over his life. There was something about his personality where people saw leadership and that he had a way of holding things together." He was team captain in high school, junior college, and at Iowa State. "He knew how to keep everybody cool, calm, happy, and on the right track. He could talk to people and help them understand what was best."

He became a leader because he was so well liked and led by example. "We never had a conversation about it, but I don't think he came into his own as a leader until senior year at Iowa State." Sherialyn had left the University of Pennsylvania to join Ricky at Iowa State University. Ricky graduated in August of 1978, Sherialyn in 1979, and they got married that October. "After graduating from Iowa State, Ricky was asked to stay on as Graduate Assistant Coach. He was coaching Division I basketball right away! He went from there to becoming Assistant Coach at Western Michigan, Eastern Illinois, University of Arizona, Head Coach at University of Detroit and, then, Head Coach at Northwestern."

Ricky Byrdsong was on the fast track as a college basketball coach. Sherialyn knew he wouldn't be good at a desk job, so coaching fit him very well. "It was the perfect occupation for him. He had a heart for Black boys and being a basketball coach put him in a place where he could connect with them and help mold them. Ricky had a heart for everyone, but he knew that Black boys were the most in need and the most underserved."

When Ricky was coaching at Western Michigan in Kalamazoo, Sherilyn was also offered a position to coach Kalamazoo Valley College's women's basketball. Within three days, Ricky received a call to be Assistant Coach at Eastern Illinois University. "Ricky's career came first. As early as high school, we decided I would be a stay-at-home mom."

Sherialyn doesn't remember exactly how the offer to coach at Northwestern came but does vividly remember an offer while still in Detroit from the University of Arkansas at Little Rock. "We went to visit, and the money was great but, after we left, we knew it wasn't the right fit. After about a year, he got the offer from NU." Sherialyn didn't really want to come to Northwestern. She loved her church and her neighborhood. Detroit just grew on her, and she loved it. But she was happy for him. "It was the Big Ten, he was one of the first Black Big Ten coaches and Black coaches at Northwestern so, of course, we had to go—it was Northwestern!"

Sherialyn was shocked at the real estate prices. She was excited about getting a big house, but the homes were triple the price of homes the same size in Detroit. Sherialyn and her kids loved Evanston, and the kids still live there. "We lived in the Evanston, 60203 area, and my son went to St. Joan of Arc." She was a stay-at-home mom and thought Evanston was a great place to raise her children, and she got to go to basketball games at Welsh Ryan Arena. "Evanston was like Mayberry! The schools were great, PTA was great, and there was a community." She even considered the Northwestern fans and Athletic Department a community.

As Head Coach, Ricky was able to select his staff. He had one Black Assistant Coach in Detroit, Steve Mills (who later became President of the NBA's New York Knickerbockers) and one Black Graduate Assistant at Northwestern but, generally, Ricky would be comfortable in any environment. The academic requirements at NU were tough, so many of his players came from all over the country. If there were any racial issues in Evanston—with the Evanston Police, the basketball team or on campus—Sherialyn wouldn't have known. She was raising kids and "whether good or bad, I was in a bubble. My kids were young. We just all got along." Ricky didn't discuss any racial tensions, and she doesn't believe there were any. "Ricky did not see color. His best friend was his White Assistant Coach. At Iowa State, his best friend was a White guy. They were just people to Ricky. Even if he had been the target of some racial tension, he would have explained it. He didn't let too much ruffle his feathers."

Northwestern had never been a powerhouse basketball team, so Ricky had a great opportunity to take the program to the next level. "In Ricky's first year, they won the first nine games! He was on fire! Of course, they were all non-conference games. Then Ohio State and Michigan hits, and that's when reality set in, but in the last game of the season, NU beat Michigan and the Fab Five!" She believes that was the impetus to the invitation to the NIT tournament after the 1993-94 season. It was the first post-season play for the team in many years. Unfortunately, that level of success wasn't sustained and, by 1997, they knew a firing was coming, but Ricky wasn't fazed by it. "At a press conference, Ricky put a sign around his neck that read, 'will work for food.'"

Having served as a coach for nineteen years, Ricky had a good ride. Over time, Sherialyn saw Ricky beginning to change. "He had become tired of the road and tired of the expectations of college basketball. It was almost a blessing in disguise. He was a little over forty years old and had coached for almost twenty years." Ricky had a phenomenal career and was excited about what was next. Financially stable, Sherialyn was ready to head back to Atlanta, but they decided to stay in town.

When Ricky was fired from Northwestern, he became laser-focused on helping young Black youth. "He met Father Michael Phleger, and Phleger loved Ricky. He opened Ricky's eyes to what was going on with young Black boys." As the Vice President of Community Affairs at Aon Corporation, Ricky initiated many programs to benefit Black youth, most notably, his Not Just Basketball summer camp.

Ricky took life as it came. "A couple of weeks before he died, I believe he knew." Sherialyn says she also knew. She remembers that he kept singing a gospel song—*No Weapon Formed Against Me Shall Prosper*. "The people at the midweek Bible study held on Wednesdays told me that Ricky was weeping during the prayer meeting. They said there was something very different about him. I believe he knew," Sherialyn whispers. On that Friday, he was killed.

"Evanston rallied behind us after Ricky's death." Sherilyn remembers that the community was the wind beneath her wings. The Skokie Park District commissioned a plaque dedicated to Coach Ricky Byrdsong that was installed in the Skokie Sculpture Park, and the Evanston YMCA has being sponsoring the *Ricky Byrdsong Race Against Hate* for nineteen years as of 2018. The race attracts thousands of runners who are dedicated to ending racial hatred of all forms.

Ricky wrote a book entitled *Coaching Your Kids in the Game of Life* (Bethany House Publishers), in which he set down a mission for his team and his children that simply says to always be grateful and be thankful. Sherialyn laughs when she thinks of his most common saying, "It is what it is." "Ricky would say, "Wherever you are, you're in a good place … can you roll with that?" He would tell Northwestern students, "Be thankful and make the most out of your Northwestern experience and education." He'd say, "I'm Ricky Byrdsong. I am a kind, God-fearing human being. I am a competitor, and I don't have time to deal with anything other than that."

Oliver Kupe

Oliver Kupe

Oliver Kupe is a 2012 graduate of Northwestern University with a degree in economics. Oliver clearly identifies his Northwestern undergraduate experience as that of a student-athlete, with an equal emphasis on the student and athlete aspects. Although he spent his entire life preparing for a career as a soccer player, he and his family were intent on Oliver attending a university with an Ivy League-quality education and mentality.

"I thought my four years were quite wonderful. Most of my experience was primarily focused on being a soccer player, which pretty much directed what I did on a day-to-day basis. It wasn't until I left Northwestern that I realized that (soccer) pretty much limited my experience as well. When I was there, I just mostly hung out with my teammates and other athletes. So, my social circle wasn't as expansive as I realized it could have been once I'd left. However, while I was there, especially as a Black student-athlete, it really was the same kind of experience I've had my entire life."

Oliver was born overseas and describes his upbringing as being in predominantly White areas, even after his family moved to Detroit. As such, Northwestern wasn't much different, and he didn't require as much acclimation as other Black students may have required. Oliver notes that everything he touched at Northwestern offered an opportunity for interaction with people from all walks of life. "All in all—the Athletics Department, the Economics Department, my fellow teammates, the other students with whom I engaged—it was a very positive experience."

Oliver readily admits the student athlete experience at Northwestern insulated him from certain racially tinged campus realities. "It insulated me in a couple of ways. Being a student-athlete when I was there, and even more so now, was a full-time job. We practiced year-round—two to three hours a day dedicated to our sport, every single day. That made my circle very small. I was the only Black on the entire soccer team until my junior year. I was surrounded by twenty White guys all the time. I lived with them, and we all went to the same social events, which were predominantly White events, and mostly all student-athletes would be there. So there really was a student-athlete community that I was a part of, and that lacked diversity."

"I wasn't heavily involved with the African American student association (For Members Only) or the African Students Union. I think I attended The Black House maybe twice in my four years, and the first time was a welcome event during my freshman year. It wasn't that I wasn't interested; it's just that I didn't know anyone else that was going, I didn't know what the events were about, and I didn't have the time! So, those things just made me spend my time within my comfort zone, which was my team and the student-athlete world."

These were just social considerations. Oliver notes that the Department of Athletics provided the tools necessary for success at Northwestern, including class selection, mentoring, tutoring, and counseling services, as well as a group of friends with similar interests. It was easy to become immersed in this nurturing environment.

If Oliver's student-athlete experience appears to be somewhat utopian, it should also sound familiar. The experience of today's student-athlete is quite similar to the experience of African Americans in the first heyday of The Black House. For approximately the first twenty years of its existence, The Black House created a nurturing experience that kept a watchful eye over virtually every student who cared to receive the multitude of services contained within, which was delivered by individuals whose sole purpose was to ensure the success of those students. It is indicative of a formula for achievement that the success enjoyed by and the affinity expressed by students who benefitted from The Black House when it was the Department of African American Student Affairs sounds very similar to that enjoyed and expressed by today's student-athletes.

Now, Oliver was aware of concerning events occurring on campus; it's just they hadn't gotten close to him until one particular episode on campus, known as "the Blackface incident" (also known as the "Beer Olympics") A fellow student-athlete—I believe he was a wrestler—felt it would was either a good or funny idea to don a Halloween costume with stereotypical depictions of Bob Marley, complete with Black dress, dreadlocks, and his face painted Black. The Department of Athletics gathered the Black student-athletes to assure them that this was "an isolated incident" and that the person involved is "being dealt with." Yet, Oliver was not aware of any university statement or policy change, nor was any direct support offered to the Black student-athletes offended by the incident.

Oliver had another jarring moment reminding him that being a successful athlete does not insulate him from being a Black man in America. "I said that I never ran into any trouble from police or law enforcement on campus. That's not true. I've tried to block out this event, but it was very traumatizing for me. It was junior year in early November, and I was walking home early in the morning. We had an early flight to Penn State University for the Big Ten tournament so, at 4:00 am, I was walking down Ridge St. from my girlfriend's house to my apartment on Noyes, wearing shorts, flip-flops, and a hoodie with my hoodie up. This was a walk I took all the time, just looking down, walking right by the Civic Center. I always walked down the alley to the back of our home instead of staying on the main street because I never thought I would have to do otherwise.

"I remember walking and going into the alleyway and, all of a sudden, I noticed a black, unmarked car with its lights shut off slowly trailing me into the alleyway. And at this point, I'm thinking, 'okay, this is very uncomfortable.' I'm walking steadily and looking behind me, 'why aren't the lights on? And why did they purposely follow me into this alley?' So, there are two ways in this alleyway, where it breaks off into the main street and then to a smaller alley where our house was." Oliver determines that if the car turns left with him and does not continue straight, he is going to run into the back of the house. "I only had 100 yards to home, and the car turns with me, and I'm like, 'hell no, I'm going to get jumped or robbed,' so I started sprinting; I take off and, at that moment, the lights cut on, the wheels start turning on the car, and I could hear it screaming after me.

"I jump over my fence, which has sharp hedges, into our yard, into our backdoor, up the stairs where my three white teammates are showering and getting ready for us to leave. I tell them, 'somebody just chased me into the house, call the police.' So, we call 911. We hear a noise downstairs, someone opening the door—the backdoor. I call 911 and tell them, 'somebody just chased me into my house, and I think they're downstairs in our home. Please send the police!' They're like, 'oh, that is the police.'" Oliver refuses to go downstairs to confront them and sends his roommate, Peter. "Peter asks the police officers, 'what's going on?' The police answer, 'we just saw someone run into your home. Is the person here?' He's like, 'yeah, it's our roommate.'

"I walk downstairs, and it's two white cops. By this point, I'm using explicit language—'what the F are you guys doing? Why are you chasing me in the house? This is my home. Why are you guys following me?' I could tell right away one of the officers knew that they had messed up, that they had profiled me. They say they are sorry and explain they have been having a string of robberies on this block. They were just canvassing the area. I ask, 'do I fit your description?' The police officer stalled. The other guy decided to become a hard-ass and starts commenting on the alcohol in our home, 'are you guys all twenty-one?' We answer, 'yes, we're all twenty-one.' He completely tried to change the subject. Then, the cop says, 'I could have shot you.' The other cop says, 'we're sorry,' grabs his partner and gets out of there."

Oliver filed a complaint with the City of Evanston with the help of his sister, who is an attorney. She told him that realistically that incident was not going to get solved. She told Oliver that if they filed a complaint, the Evanston Police Department was simply going to toss it. They're not going to care. Oliver knew he had to go to a soccer game in Penn State. "It was a very traumatizing moment because I quickly had to forget about it and get on a plane. That was the first time that's ever happened to me, where I was profiled and chased into my own home, fearing for my life, and I had to get on a plane and play soccer."

It was a bizarre moment that Oliver never really digested until recently. "All these moments with the Bob Marley mockeries and with the hoodie ... I've never worn a hoodie on top of my head since that moment—that was 2010. I am just fearful. I still have bad memories from that." Oliver admits that he has never discussed that incident with anyone within the Athletic Department. "I really only told my sister and my significant others about it and, obviously, the guys on my team." Oliver thought to himself, "what am I supposed to do right now as a twenty-year-old? I have to finish school, and I have to play soccer. I have these obligations."

Oliver regrets not pursuing the incident further. "Now, I would have reacted differently. As a student, I was shell-shocked. I decided to swallow it and put it at the back of my head but, obviously, it's still there and will be there for the rest of my life. That was one really terrifying moment I had as a Black student at Northwestern."

It is very clear that Oliver was focused on the business of pursuing his soccer career and his economics degree, and he was succeeding in both. In 2010, Oliver was named Second Team All-Big Ten in men's soccer and, in 2011, he was named First Team All-Big Ten. Upon graduation, he was chosen by Real Salt Lake in the 2012

Major League Soccer Draft and enjoyed a brief soccer career until injured. However, in an interesting turn of events, in Oliver's senior year at Northwestern, Oliver found himself gravitating toward both the African American and general campus communities, especially after his last soccer season ended early in the academic year. It was at this point that Oliver began to realize what his Northwestern experience had been missing. He notes that his prior assertion that his experience "was fantastic" should slightly modified to "fantastic relative to what I knew."

Unfortunately, the "Blackface incident" opened Oliver's eyes to certain realities across campus. He surmises that the racial incidents might not have been as prevalent as they otherwise might have been simply because there weren't many Black students around. "My freshman class had the lowest number of Blacks in decades. There were only seventy or eighty in our entire class. It was a real trough for Black students at the university. At that point, I wasn't able to put that in context. I didn't know what the regular population levels of past student bodies at Northwestern was. It wasn't until I left that I saw the numbers increase to 150 in a class and, then, over 200 in the early '90's. That's when my stomach and heart dropped, and I realized I had been deprived of an experience. No one within the Department of Athletics, the Economics Department, or otherwise within the university reached out or had some type of town hall or other engagement to reassure us that this (low level of Blacks) wasn't just normal at Northwestern and wasn't ok for them.

"The more you get removed from your situation, the more you realize what it was. It wasn't until I got heavily involved in the Northwestern University Black Alumni Association (NUBAA) that I realized I had missed out on a lot of opportunities, and I could have been even more enriched. I didn't get involved in Black student experiences in the ways I should have. I had blinders on." Oliver became particularly interested in the happenings of NUBAA, knowing that he'd want to have access to that network at whatever point he would complete his soccer career. He attended a few NUBAA events his senior year, including one at The Black House (representing his second visit during his time at NU). This also represented his first significant exposure to other Black alumni, many of whom had also been student-athletes, and Oliver credits these interactions for helping develop his mindset about networking and planning his business career after his athletic career would end.

Oliver also came to realize how different and protective his experience had been compared to so many others and how past generations of student-athletes had also taken care to engage in and support the Black student population. This knowledge created a resolve in Oliver to provide assistance in the ways in which he could, then and in the future. "There wasn't Black student segregation back then between student-athletes and other Blacks on campus. That's much more prominent now than when I was there, primarily because of the obligations student-athletes have. Student-athletes have a much higher priority placed on the athlete part than the student part. I realized that's why I was lacking a Black experience at NU, at least until I was finished with the athlete part and, more so, as I became an alumnus."

It was after Oliver's professional athletic career ended that his experience became less defined by having been a successful student-athlete and more so as having developed a model of alumni support and giving, which is a major component of the engagement strategy of the Northwestern University Black Alumni Association (NUBAA). "It's really been a focal point of my career. My professional goals at Merrill Lynch were tied to building business and, therefore, I was out to build business relationships. NUBAA represented a natural opportunity to tap into a network of adults and professionals that could provide that business. Our connection wasn't necessarily my age or our time of graduation but we were all Black alumni."

Oliver also was compelled by the relative absence of diversity at Merrill Lynch. "I wasn't seeing a lot of Black clients walk through the doors, which was a problem. I was the only Black advisor. That was a problem." Oliver also realized that in doing this, he could simultaneously accomplish several objectives. His efforts represented an opportunity to provide a service to the alumni and his alma mater by offering professional financial advice, wealth management, and other consumer services. He could help students by providing those immediately out of college with internships and job opportunities. He could pave a path of success for financial services professionals across the country by establishing a pipeline of potential clients. Finally, the nature of the agreement being arranged meant NUBAA would receive financial support for its programming. Oliver actually sought to change the face of financial services in the Chicago area, working through NUBAA.

Via Oliver's initiative, NUBAA and Merrill Lynch were able to negotiate and develop a partnership in 2014, which has led to Merrill Lynch becoming NUBAA's largest sponsor. In fact, three graduating Northwestern students and alumni have assumed full-time positions at Merrill Lynch as a result of this effect, and four internships have been established. Significantly, the initiative, having produced a return-on-investment far beyond expectations for Merrill Lynch, has expanded to become a key strategy for them nationally with advisors from New York, Washington, D.C., and California visiting the NUBAA Summit and Salute to Excellence Gala as a prelude to involving NUBAA's local affiliates to replicate Oliver's Chicago model. The success and connections developed by Oliver have allowed him to start his own financial services entity.

This initiative coincides with a fresh push by NUBAA to expand the financial literacy and resources for members of the Black alumni community. In the ongoing effort to fully participate in university efforts, enriching and empowering the community has been deemed an essential step toward being able to advocate priorities such as endowed academic chairs, student scholarships, programming initiatives, and general university support. This partnership with Merrill Lynch was meant to demonstrate the template for alumni support of each other's entrepreneurial endeavors, while while returning the same amount of support to Northwestern. The precise means of implementing this "NUBAA Economy Project" are still being developed, but the path is clear. The ongoing evolution of the Black experience necessitates development of this component of alumni support.

Oliver has also been a prominent fixture in the NUBAA Student-Based Initiatives (SBI)—a series of alumni-student programs providing support in several different ways, including mentoring, development of internship, and job opportunities. In the Athletic SBI, called Athletes Connect, Oliver has used his experiences and path to show the way forward for successive generations of Wildcats student-athletes.

In reflecting on his time on campus and in speaking to current and future students and student-athletes, Oliver's advice is clear and relates to lessons he learned late. "Learn to look outside your lane, and see what voids exist, both in your life and in the community around you. Ask yourself are you doing enough? Find a moral and godly mission and hold true to it. I wish I had engaged more with my fellow Black students, and I wish I had engaged earlier with the Black alumni. If students would just pass up one instance of hanging out with your fellow athletes, pass that up and go to just one event at The Black House ... you never know who you're going to meet there that later in life could produce a huge business or professional opportunity for you. That's exactly what happened to me."

Daryl Newell

Daryl Newell

Daryl Newell graduated from Northwestern's Weinberg College of Arts and Science in 1986 and received executive education from the Kellogg School of Management in 2007. Daryl Newell was a football phenomenon at Northwestern. He was a Freshman All-American along with Bo Jackson and Marcus DuPree in 1982 and the ninth-ranked offensive tackle in the nation as a senior. He graduated in 1986 and has been encouraging, hiring, and guiding Northwestern's Black students and alums ever since. He is currently the treasurer of the Northwestern University Black Alumni Association—a position he has held for over twenty years.

Daryl Newell was raised in Gary, Indiana by educator parents who were proud HBCU (Historically Black Colleges and Universities) alumni. Daryl was an All-City, All-Area, All-State, and All-Academic football star from Westside High School who was heavily recruited by the University of Illinois and the University of Iowa.

"Hayden Fry (famed long-time Iowa football coach) sent me correspondence every week." Daryl was also offered a full academic scholarship to Jackson State University, his parents' alma mater. He remembers his recruiting trip to Northwestern—it was a Saturday, right before an impending blizzard. "My father and I arrived around 9 am and, by 11 am, I told Coach Denny Green I had to head home to make some money shoveling snow. Denny called me on that Tuesday and offered me the scholarship." Daryl loved football, but he was much more than an athlete. His Mississippi-born parents earned master's degrees from the University of Illinois and the University of Indiana and instilled both Black history and academic achievement into him and his brother.

Daryl started at Northwestern in June 1982 in the Minority Engineering Opportunity Program (MEOP). He started his academic pursuits as a Computer Science major in the Technological Institute. "MEOP was great. It was nice to get to campus early and spend time and interact with regular students. Me, Jimmy Wyatt, Brian Jackson, and Marlanda English hung out with the Summer Academic Workshop kids when they arrived." Then, three weeks of football camp began in August. "They've cut that down to ten days now. If you're not in shape and don't pass the tests, then you get sent home!"

The football team in the 1980's was about 40% Black, and Daryl had Black coaches, including Denny Green, Frances Peay, and Coach Webster (who later coached for the Indianapolis Colts). Daryl credits Doc Glass (an Evanston native who had been helping Northwestern athletes since the late 1950's), Don Jackson (a former Northwestern Basketball star), and Keith Cruise (a fellow student and football athlete) as mentors. Daryl remembers the older Black football players were influential for both his social and academic success. "I lived in what was called 'the football player apartment.' The apartment went from Crazy Mos (Mosby had a nervous breakdown, hence the nickname Crazy) to Keith Cruise to Dix (David Dixon) to Tex (Kelvin Scott) ... we just passed it down. The older guys told us we needed to get an internship and that, if you got cut, you still needed to get to the stadium. These invaluable informal networks were from older player to younger player." The apartment held other unique treasures. "Many of the tools I use today in my work came not just from the classroom but also from the closet of my apartment on 2127 Ridge. I found the book *How to Run Any Organization* by Theodore Caplow on the floor." Daryl still has that first-edition text. These young men were scholars and embraced every instrument available at Northwestern to build their careers.

Daryl transferred from Tech to Sociology as, by the end of freshman year, he had a 1.55 GPA. "I was playing too much football and going to too many parties." He had to be eligible to play football, so he took two summer classes, improved his GPA, and flourished in Sociology. "Northwestern was actually fairly easy. I learned from Daphne Powell that if you go to class, you should get a C. If you went to class and could write, you could earn a B. If you actually read the book and could write, you could get that A."

Daryl received great support from the African American infrastructure of Northwestern—Professor Charles R. Branham, Professor William Exum, and The Black House's Duke Jenkins always supported Daryl. "I remember taking Professor Branham's class, the History of Racial Minorities, and learning about upward mobility skills of ethnic minorities. You learn the power of talking to the deans and talking to the professors. If you're not talking, you may get kicked out! Having those conversations and those relationships can take you a long way." Daryl also remembers building relationships with professors and teaching assistants (TAs), even if he wasn't excelling in the class. "Turns out the TA is from Indiana and I'm from Indiana, and he mentions he needs tickets to the Indiana game. I ask him how many tickets he needs.." Daryl's grade received a needed boost due to the increasing attention the TA started giving him. Daryl remembers learning from the guys who formed BAUL (Black Athletes United for the Light) during his freshman and sophomore years. "I knew Joe Webb (former athlete and a founder of BAUL), who was always in The Black House. There was a *Tribute to Black Women* and *Tribute to Black Men*, where a fellow athlete, Oscar Joseph, was singing, and Duke was militant and all about Black Power ..." Daryl remembers his parents fondly when he thinks about those times in The Black House because he was trained to believe in Black people and Black unity. The environment at The Black House reminded him of his own home in Gary, Indiana.

Daryl remembers his early days as a student-athlete when President Strotz (who notoriously didn't believe in athletics) had an arsenal of professors who would not be flexible with student-athletes. He notes that in response to that inflexibility, the Athletics Department was very helpful with academic support. "Our class selections were guided. Our majors were guided. We used to commonly major in Sociology, but there was the foreign language requirement, and some players just couldn't pass Spanish. Then, they figured out it was Human Development and Social Policy. Then, it was Radio/TV/Film, then Economics!" Daryl believes this is still true today.

Northwestern's academic support was creative, and they very attentive to each student's needs. "Our tutors knew we needed notes. They knew we needed books with highlights. They knew we needed test preparation." Daryl confirms that even in the 1980's "Northwestern was all about the graduation rates for athletes." Northwestern didn't want to be known for students just playing sports. "Every year, they put you in a room, and you had to sign your scholarship. There is no four-year scholarship. Most major conference schools might determine that the student-athlete is no longer physically able to play; they take the scholarship and say goodbye."

Northwestern operated a bit differently. He remembers two students from his football class who never played football past their freshman year, and they both graduated on time. "The coaches put them to work in the equipment room or anywhere in the Athletics Department. They wouldn't let them transfer and leave because that would hurt the graduation rate." Daryl met his academic tutors every day. If classes conflicted with practice or games, they allowed night school classes at University College, now the School of Professional Studies. Daryl and his parents knew that he would be a Northwestern graduate, as it was implanted in Northwestern's athletic culture.

After graduation, Daryl served eight years as the Northwestern representative for the Big Ten Diversity Committee and, in that role, he noticed the change in concerns for Black athletes over the years. "The issues at Northwestern are not just about graduating but also about immersing culture into their experience." In Daryl's time at NU and decades before, Black athletes were able to eat dinner with other students. They cherished that hour and a half eating and interacting with regular Black students in Foster Walker Complex (The Plex) dormitory. "Now, all student athletes eat at the stadium. Both Black kids and White kids feel isolated from campus life." Daryl acknowledges that Black students in the '80's had limited social experience, but it was rich. "We only had parties in the basement of the Plex, the Shack (Shanley Hall) or at Norris Center, but it was something outside of sports." Daryl acknowledges that the erosion of events sponsored by The Black House like *Out Da Box* or *Tribute to Black Women* pigeonhole the athletes as one dimensional. "Many of my teammates play the piano, sing, and perform better than what they do on the field." Daryl says that without these normal interactions in extracurricular activities, all students suffer. Even if limited, Daryl recognizes the value of engagement. "Networking with regular students, White and Black, is critical, especially given the quality of Northwestern students and the success they will have in their lives and careers."

Daryl credits Dennis Green for him being drafted to the NFL. In his senior year, the coach moved him from defense to offense. "One day, Denny called me into the office and asked how I felt about playing left tackle—offensive left tackle! Then, I remembered T. Harrell (Terry Harrell) rejecting Dennis' request to move to offensive guard and benching him instead. I flashed back and told Coach, 'oh yeah, it's all good!'" Dennis had coached in the pros earlier and, therefore, knew the scouts. "It's not about the record all the time but about the reputation of the coach to vouch that you're ready for the next level and to open those doors for you."

Daryl thinks about Northwestern's Black Athletes United for the Light (BAUL) and their fight to bring in Denny Green as the first Black Head Coach at Northwestern (Coach Green was only the second African American Head Coach in Division I-A's history). BAUL also protested the treatment of Black athletes by the Athletics Department generally and was instrumental in overhauling the leadership from the top down. Daryl relates this 1980's fight to contemporary events like the Colin Kaepernick protests and the team-led protests at the University of Missouri. He wonders if current Black student-athletes are learning about these events and organizations. "Student-athletes are so busy now. They are only about football. The Black athletes need to know that, historically, Northwestern athletes had 'taken a knee,' long before Colin Kaepernick."

Daryl is also concerned about Northwestern's Department of Athletics addressing the ongoing concerns of Black athletes and the Evanston Police. He remembers driving with his teammates, Kenneth "Skip" McClendon, James Sutton, and Chris Johnson, when the Evanston Police pulled them over in front of Rebecca Crown Center during midday with guns drawn. He understands that it's a nationwide issue that many of his White counterparts have never encountered, and he knows more has to be done to normalize the environment when Blacks are engaged by the police.

Daryl was recruited to work with the Northwestern University Black Alumni Association by former President Kevin Sampson in the early 1990's. NUBAA and issues involving NU athletics bring him back to campus often. He stays involved in NUBAA "because it's important to have institutional knowledge, consistency, and relevancy when you're attempting to help Black students and other Black alums." He tells Black students and Black student athletes "to build a code of honor, build a legacy, and to build tradition. Build a tradition of winning by shaking hands, getting a card, getting a fifteen-minute coffee, and getting a job." Daryl has been instrumental in the careers of many athletes by finding and personally offering them internships and jobs. "I advise them on their majors and tell them 'to use the ball and not let the ball use them.'" Fellow former athlete Tracy Parsons pitched the idea of matching the student athletes with alums to Gary Barrett in the 90's with his "expect victory" campaign. Rose Bowl coach Barnett knew that to achieve that victory you must possess tradition. Daryl made sure they interacted with the kids they were assigned to. "No money, but we were just making sure they had a good experience." Now, the Athletics Department hosts a program, called "NU for Life," which prepares athletes for their future careers. Daryl suggests that "overall student-athlete's lives are programmed while at NU," but somehow, still, the Black athletes need more help. Daryl tells Black athletes how Northwestern can sell itself in their careers and with opportunities. He encourages young people to talk about Northwestern, both the good and bad aspects of their lives at NU because fellow alums will understand. "Our classmates are executives at Harris Bank and administrators at Harvard Business School, and we all have something in common." Daryl is proudly purple and continues to be an asset to NUBAA and Black athletes across the globe.

Birth of a Community: The 1968 Takeover of the Bursar's Office

- **Stanley Hill**
- **Herman Cage:** Founding Coordinator, For Members Only
- **Daphne Maxwell Reid:** Northwestern Homecoming Queen (first African American with that distinction)
- **Steve Colson**
- **Victor Goode**
- **Wayne Watson**
- **Kathryn Ogletree:** Coordinator, For Members Only
- **John Bracey**
- **Eva Jefferson Paterson:** President, Associate Student Government (first African American to hold the office)
- **Participants in the Bursar's Office Takeover**

Stanley Hill (by Stanley Hill)

Stanley L. Hill

My name is Stanley L. Hill. I was a part of the sit-in along with my black classmates who took over the Bursar's Office at Northwestern University on May 3, 1968.

In 1954, the Supreme Court of the United States in *Brown v. Board of Education* outlawed the separate-but-equal doctrine that had been the law of the land and ordered desegregation of public schools. However, the decision tore at the spiritual heart of American society, so it was rarely respected, and it went often ignored and unenforced. Those in power worked tirelessly to devise tricky and spiteful ways to get around the high court's decision. But then came the early 1960's along with newsreel footage of Blacks being beaten and bitten by dogs held by law enforcement officers—all because of the quest for freedom. After President John F. Kennedy's assassination, Lyndon Baines Johnson assumed the presidency. American presidents were vexed by race. President Johnson understood that a new era had begun when three civil rights workers—Andrew Goodman, Michael Schwerner and James Chaney—went missing and were found murdered in Mississippi in 1964.

On March 7, 1965, nine months after the Mississippi murders, civil rights activists gathered in an attempt to cross the Edmund Pettus Bridge in Selma, Alabama in a quest for voting rights. A nation saw scores of marchers viciously beaten. Northern cities were soon torched in widespread rioting. Johnson knew the time had come, as the Blacks would not retreat. He signed the landmark Civil Rights Act in 1964 that outlawed discrimination based on race, color, religion, sex, or national origin. It ended unequal application of voter registration requirements and racial segregation in schools, workplaces, and by public facilities that served the general public. Later, in 1965, Johnson signed the Voting Rights Act into law.

My classmates in 1966 were the first beneficiaries of this legislation and represented the first wave of African American youngsters admitted to impressive schools like Northwestern as a result of Johnson signing into law what was probably the most powerful piece of presidential legislation for Blacks since the Civil War and the Emancipation Proclamation. Johnson's presidency was dubbed Johnson's "Great Society." As he maneuvered this legislation through Congress, after graduating from Wendell Phillips High School (an all-black high school located in a poor neighborhood on 39th Street on Chicago's Southside), I was admitted to

Northwestern University in the summer of 1966, in a program dubbed NUCAP—Northwestern University Chicago Area Project. The objective of the project was to take Black students from allegedly disadvantaged high schools on Chicago's south and west sides into a summer program designed to acclimate us to the rigors of study and life at NU. My NUCAP classmates included Christine Price, John Higginson, Marianne Jackson, Robert "Hollywood Bob" Miller, Leslie Harris, Arnold Wright, Jacquita Harris, Dorothy Carter, Josephine Bronaugh, Mario McHarris, Herbert Melton, William "Eric" Perkins, Leaster Redmond, Charles Shepard, Andre Bell, James Digby, Andrew Greene, Michael "Stalk" Smith, Steve Broussard, Milton Gardner, and Lonnie Ratcliffe. Later in the fall, other Blacks from various parts of the country were also admitted to the university, including, but not limited to, Nelson Johnson, Delores Wilson, Sue Rhoden, Audrey Hinton, Cherilyn Wright, Millicent Brown, Victor Goode, Widmon Butler, and Daphne Maxwell.

Northwestern's efforts to diversify its historically White campus started in 1966 with Black students who were not already there on athletic scholarships. A few athletes—Dan Davis, Sterling Burke, Jim Pitts, Woody Campbell, Vernon Ford, Bob Tubbs, and Roger Ward—were already there on athletic scholarships, as were a few other non-athletes, such as Eleanor Steele, Herman Cage, and Kimya Moyo, aka Saundra Malone. Any names I've neglected to include 50 years hence, please blame my head, not my heart.

The sit-in at the Bursar's Office was a pivotal event for Northwestern's small but growing population of Black students. Our numbers had more than tripled, but our presence was still meager—there were just 160 black students on campus in 1968, compared to less than 50 in 1966. We were determined that more was needed to improve the environment for the Blacks on campus. So, on May 3, 1968, approximately 100 of us occupied the Northwestern Bursar's Office and presented a list of demands to the University that represented "a crack that cleaved along cultural fault lines into a clenched fist that did not relax" and was a starting point for when the University began meaningful growth.

We participated in a thirty-eight-hour peaceful protest after the University failed to meet a list of Black student demands, which included calls for NU to desegregate its real estate holdings, admit more Black students, and add a program in Black literature, history, and art. We originally presented these demands on April 22, 1968, but when no agreement could be reached with the administrators, we took over the Bursar's Office—now a part of the Office of Treasury Operations—on the morning of May 3, 1968. The action began shortly after 7 am on Friday, May 3, 1968 when one of us approached the Bursar's Office at 619 Clark and told the unarmed security guard that he needed to pick up a form. As the brother (I believe it was Michael "Stalk" Smith) entered the building, another group of students began yelling slogans in the Rebecca Crown Center courtyard. The guard responded to the diversion, and about 100 of us—members of FMO (For Members Only)—poured into the office and secured the windows and doors. Within ten minutes, we had assumed control of the building. Prior to the takeover, we had all planned to meet at different locations near the building.

James Turner, a 1968 doctoral candidate, was our leader. Our demands were more Black enrollment, increased financial aid, creation of dedicated student housing for Black students, creation of an African American studies curriculum, and desegregation of the university's real estate holding in Evanston. The Dean of Students, Roland Hinz, was the only White person allowed in the building housing the Bursar's Office that week and came in to negotiate. Thirty-eight-hours later, the administration agreed to a number of demands, promising to reserve student housing for Blacks, increase student participation in policy matters, and create the university's Department of African American Studies. Dean Hinz said, "We left the place better than we took it." Our approach to the situation wasn't to trash the place but to make the university a better place. The sit-in played a major role in the creation of The Black House and the establishment of an African American Studies program.[1]

Dr. Martin Luther King, Jr. was assassinated a month before we took over the Bursar's Office—he died on April 4, 1968. "Dr. King was a prophet who shed light on the enduring and urgent tensions between White and Black America over race and class. He was a prophet who led the nation out of the darkness of Jim Crow. His Promised Land was the one he conjured on the steps of the Lincoln Memorial in

---

[1] The Black Student Sit-In of 1968, Rebecca Lindell, Weinberg College-Northwestern University, 2017

1963, a place where his 'four little children ... will not be judged by the color of their skin but by the content of their character.' But he knew our country was embarking on a long twilight struggle against poverty and violence. "We've got some difficult days ahead," he preached the night before he died."[2] His impact, legacy, and mission are still alive today and will far surpass the span of any lifetime. In fact, I am certain he intended his work to live beyond him and he certainly knew that his great civil and human rights projects would require much more than one generation to be realized. In this respect, they live on within all of those willing to continue working where he left off.

It has been 50 years since this happened. How far have we come and how much farther do we need to go? Our group was called For Members Only—FMO's goal was not to educate just Black students but all students on the significance of the Bursar's Office sit-in and our demands. The demands made in 1968 must continue. We must continue to make Black students a priority by increasing Black enrollment and providing additional resources to Black students.

Today, I am an Associate Judge of the Circuit Court of Cook County. I was just sixteen years old in 1966 when I arrived at Northwestern. A fateful compilation of legislation, policy, and activism is a part of what got me there, but not all. It opened the door, but the hinges, the doorframe, the doorknob, and the door itself were

---

[2] Washingtonpost.com: Martin Luther King, Jr.: The Legacy, www.washingtonpost.com/wp-srv/national/longterm/mlk/legacy/legacy.htm, Vern E. Smith and Jon Meacham, 1998

already there. It just needed to be opened. In addition to the true qualifications I already possessed—academic excellence, civic leadership, and character fitness—it was intestinal fortitude, determination to fulfill my vision, and community and family support that helped me to stay there and continue my journey, which has led me to where I am today.

I came from a poor family. I remember my mother meticulously checking my penmanship assignments and making me start all over again if they were not perfect. Perhaps, it was this formative exercise that equipped me for the law—it developed my attention to detail, precision, and scrutiny, all of which are skills necessary for the profession. Growing up as the son of Baptist church secretary, I credit my mother for inculcating confidence and work ethic in me Even though we were a poor family, she taught me to believe that by using my talents and resources, I could overcome and win against the odds. I guess I was too young to know any better, but it turns out she was right.

My path to the law and, ultimately, to the circuit court bench began in Bronzeville, where my mother ensured I got a healthy dose of church each Sunday. She had me in there assisting with the church bulletins. I was in church from Sunday school in the morning until after the evening service. Mom's life was my greatest example of honesty, integrity, humility, stubbornness, love, and dedication to duty. The depth and value of her love and sacrificial giving was immeasurable. She was something special—brusque, tart, often short-spoken. But when I heard her call my name while praying and ask God to bless me in a special way, all the gruffness was forgotten. She taught me to believe that "God is love," that "Faith is the substance of things hoped for, and the evidence of things not seen." By God's grace and mercy, I've been blessed with a legal career that has spanned over four decades. I've been in some tough fights and situations along the way. But my Redeemer, Christ Jesus, has seen me through all my challenging experiences. He has sustained me. His love has reinforced me. His wisdom has guided me. His peace has comforted me. God will see you through, bringing the right answers through the right channels, at the right time and in the right place. God will work through the right persons and circumstances. God will see you through in the best way for the greatest good of all concerned.

If life is demanding strength you think you do not have, wisdom you think you do not possess, tact, patience, forgiveness, love, or peace that you feel are foreign to you, remember that God will see you through with His strength, His peace, and His infinite supply. Now, just tell yourself persistently and firmly that God will see you through and, then, let him.

May all your dreams come true—"The only limits are, as always, those of vision."

Herman Cage

Herman Cage

Herman Cage was born and raised in Kansas City, Missouri and was enticed by work colleagues to attend Northwestern. He attended NU from 1965 to 1969, obtaining a BS in Business Administration. He also obtained a MBA at Kellogg, graduating in 1973. In 1965, Herman states there were five African Americans in his incoming class—a football player, two basketball players, him, and one young lady. In addition to these enrollees, he recalls there being six other Blacks on campus, all of who were student-athletes. He recalls being very isolated and insignificant, "just a few spots here and there" out of approximately 6500 students on campus. His membership as a fraternity member would prove to be very important as a means of filling that void, as did being a part of the business school.

Beyond a sense of isolation as an African American, Herman's Northwestern experience was unique in other ways, which he actually didn't appreciate at the time. He "got a jump on campus life" by attending a program called the High School Institute (aka the Cherub Program), which was a transition effort for incoming business students. He first lived in Elder Hall, making him among the first non-athlete Blacks to stay on campus. Most of his early social life was had at his fraternity house, Tau Delta Phi—a Jewish fraternity. As there were no Black Greek-Letter Organizations on campus at the time, and fraternities and sororities dominated the social scene, Blacks sometimes made the effort to join fraternities and sororities (although the first Black females were not admitted to a White sorority until 1967).

Relatively speaking, Herman was enjoying his campus existence, and he really doesn't know why he migrated to campus activism. "I had been the only Black doing things for so long that hanging out with Whites at a fraternity became second nature to me. So, I was ok with that." However, he readily acknowledges that that wasn't the case with the rest of the Black community on campus, and the "esprit de corps" environment of the business school probably insulated him. Furthermore, during his first two years at Northwestern, he and the other Black students filled the voids of an absent Black experience on campus by taking refuge in the Evanston home of Charles "Doc" Glass, which had served as a home for Black students (literally and figuratively) and the place of social gathering for about ten years. "I had the best of both worlds."

Herman recalls that during the summer of 1967, there was a comparatively large enrollment of African Americans to Northwestern under NUCAPs (Northwestern University College Admissions Program), meant to provide an orientation to college life. Herman describes it as "the Cherub program applied to Black students." He recalls that with this increased number of new Blacks on campus (he approximates there were thirty-five participants in NUCAPs), you could sense the new level of racial tension. One especially significant example of this occurred after the Blacks were denied admission to a fraternity party. This incident led Herman to take action of his own.

Faced with overt and covert actions of social discrimination, Herman decided to form For Members Only (FMO, the Black Student Alliance of Northwestern University) in August of 1967. Herman was especially interested in ensuring that the Black students had an opportunity for social interaction on campus similar to that which had always needed to occur in Evanston at homes such as Doc Glass'. Herman was quite conscious of the burgeoning numbers of Black students and felt that Doc Glass' family wouldn't be able to indefinitely accommodate the ever-increasing number of students, which, at that point, had grown to "...forty, fifty or sixty students every night. We needed to develop some capacity to entertain ourselves."

The name, For Members Only, was meant to be an ironic twist on the exclusionary tactics of so many clubs that excluded Blacks at the time. In fact, it wasn't more than a day or two after the incident at the fraternity party when Herman recalls driving past Skokie Country Club and seeing a sign (still) quite common at the entrance of country clubs. The sign included the name of the club and, below it, the words "For Members Only" were prominently displayed. This verbiage had particular resonance with Herman, having seen such so often while traveling with his father, during which they were always joking about discovering where the "members" lived within the Black communities.

At approximately the same time of the formation of FMO on campus, another Black student organization, The African American Students Union (AASU), was being established with the prominent involvement of Kathy Ogletree and James Turner.

The difference between the two was fairly straightforward. Herman intended FMO to be a co-ed social outlet for the Black students that could interact with other student body entities. AASU was intended to be more politically active in nature, focusing on student involvement with NU and the university's involvement with social issues within the country at the time. During the year following the formation of FMO, the AASU members (who were participating in both groups) became very dominant in the FMO group, and things transitioned to where FMO became able to accommodate both social and activist considerations.

Herman had no issues with the change in focus of FMO. He readily admits that the individuals crossing over from AASU were generally graduate students and "a lot more worldly, and they really struck a chord with the Black students who had just come on campus."

"I can't recall having an assigned meeting place for our FMO activity and, in fact, the absence of a designated homeland was a part of the overall tension that was building during the '67-'68 school year. FMO was an orphan organization as far as NU was concerned. We had not come to either the school administration or the student governance structure to be blessed or sanctioned as acceptable, and that was part of the problem. NU was no different than any other establishment institution at the time and that simply meant that the school's administration/Board of Trustees had final say regarding what organizations could have an approved presence on campus and what activities would be sanctioned on campus. We had the audacity to start our own "Thing," and it was FMO—For Members Only! We had conceived FMO, financed FMO's existence, and began to use FMO to identify areas where the NU experience was lacking for us. Now that I think back on that time, the fact that FMO had come into existence without the university's advanced knowledge and was designed to be both a student-controlled organizational response to the way the administration ran things, as well as a vehicle for building community on our terms, had to be very disturbing."

Still, Herman recalls feeling shocked at how the others determined the Black student existence to be so intolerable that the action of taking over the Bursar's Office was necessary. "I'll be honest with you. I wasn't particularly comfortable with that decision, primarily because I didn't know if it was the right decision or the best way to make our point, but it seemed to be the "normal" way things were being done at collegiate institutions across the country at the time … So, I accepted it. I knew we needed to do something."

"I had two big concerns. If we were going to do it, we needed to do it right to maximize our chances of success and do it in a way that minimized potential danger to the participants." He believes that the organizers were successful on both fronts.

Herman notes that although he wasn't one of the organizers, he had a rather unique role in the events and a unique set of resources to assist the cause (he also admits he hasn't told this story in the fifty years since its occurrence, with a bemused consideration as to whether "statutes of limitation" for his actions have expired). Herman had just been elected treasurer of his fraternity. With the Black student group's knowledge of this, "I had the sense everyone came to the conclusion I was going to end up being the money man! I had just been elected treasurer of my fraternity and, as treasurer, I had signing authority on our checking account, and I had resources I could access!

"Once we decided to make this move, I was thinking, 'Ok, what do we need?' We needed a truck, we needed food ... I was putting together a to-do list, and somebody had to finance this! Whether or not Tau Delta Phi knew it or not, they financed the takeover!" Herman later stated that he does believe his fraternity brothers were more or less aware of his efforts and were okay with it. He chuckles even more when he recalls the exploits of Wayne Watson (then, "Baldy" and, now, Dr. Wayne Watson) and him running through a grocery store, emptying food and supplies into shopping carts, renting a truck, and parking it illegally in a student parking lot behind the Bursar's Office. It is remarkable that he speaks of these events without displaying what you might believe to be a requisite amount of nervousness about everything that was happening. "It was one of the funniest things in the world."

Herman never discussed the Bursar's Office Takeover with his family in advance, although he is sure they would have supported him. He was comfortable enough to have discussed this with a few members of his fraternity, as he felt they would be of assistance in the event the participants found themselves "in trouble." He also felt fortunate to be able to confide in Dr. Lerone Bennett, a member of the Department of History, who would subsequently become the first Chair of the new Department of African American Studies. Formation of that department was one of the prominent victories resulting from the Bursar's Office Takeover. Although Herman was aware of the risks, he states he wasn't particularly afraid of them. Even as he was at Northwestern on academic scholarship, he felt like the group did what had to be done.

After the takeover, Herman felt like the Blacks had a "march to glory." He believes that the takeover was widely supported by the students on campus, and he references the pictures of the Bursar's Office showing many majority students present outside the building with supportive signs. Herman says that his fraternity members were so pleased with the outcome that they'd joke about grabbing a plane to Berkeley or other sites of student protest. But, of course, they didn't. The Northwestern student environment was idealistic, and everyone wanted to demonstrate that they had some power and ability to make the university better. Despite expectations, the Black students didn't suffer from their participation in the Bursar's Office Takeover.

Herman was finishing his junior year at Northwestern at the time of the takeover. He states he was able to separate himself from the campus and focus on his studies during his senior year. In the instances in which he did venture away from the business school and back to the rest of campus, he noticed the university's efforts to do better in providing a suitable environment for its Black students. One especially notable example was a small building at 619 Emerson, which was set aside for Black students to congregate. This was the location of the first Black House. This presence of The Black House, the development of African American Studies, and the influx of the largest yet class of Black students all represented a concerted effort to diversify the university. It is safe to say the experience of the incoming Black experience was qualitatively different than anything ever before experienced by the Blacks at NU.

Herman also notes that after the takeover of the Bursar's Office, the students heavily involved in AASU increasingly assumed responsibility of the new direction of the Black student experience, and even after having done his part, "I didn't feel particularly necessary." Even as he stayed at Northwestern as a graduate business student at Kellogg, he lost touch with the growing Black student population and emerging student experience, as he was in the process of becoming a husband and father. Herman's experience at Kellogg was free of any controversy he had experienced during his undergraduate years.

In reviewing the decades since his time at Northwestern, Herman is actually neither aware of how massive and vital FMO has become over the years nor could he have predicted it at the time. He says, "I had no concept at that stage in my life. It never occurred to me that (FMO) could evolve in that many aspects of collegiate life at Northwestern. I am especially pleased that it evolved mostly out of student need instead of additional confrontation." He does lament that he couldn't be around much to see the growth. "In all honesty, I haven't been a very good alumnus, but I'm very encouraged and grateful." Obviously, that doesn't negate the impact he had on the generations to come.

Daphne Maxwell Reid

Daphne Maxwell Reid

Daphne Maxwell Reid is known nationally for her many achievements and acting roles, but she'll tell you that those were simply jobs. Her impact on the Black experience at Northwestern represents a legacy unto itself. She attended Northwestern between 1966 and 1970, receiving a degree in interior design and architecture.

Daphne states that she arrived as a part of a class of thirty-six Black students—the largest such class to date. She estimates that there were just a few other Blacks on campus in total. In talking with Daphne, she makes it clear that her New York City upbringing equipped her with many tools that she would need and use to not only overcome challenges at NU but also to succeed. "I came from New York City (Manhattan)—from a fully integrated society—and I was used to being the only Black involved in anything. I was the only Black in my class from fourth grade all the way through high school."

Daphne thought her orientation into Northwestern was quite smooth. She arrived early, having participated in a program called Upward Bound. In addition to giving her a leg up on the university environment, she met her future husband, who was a program counselor. However, any dreams of continuing the welcoming pre-college experience were dashed during the very first day she moved on campus. When heading to her dorm room, she got a taste of what was to come. "I got to my room with my bags, and there was a girl standing in the door. I said, "Excuse me, this is my room," and she said, "Oh no! I'm not staying here with no niggers!" I turned around and said, "Where are they?" I then went to the housemother and said, "I'd like my own room, please." And I got one ... Welcome to Northwestern.

However, Daphne recalled being completely unfazed by the experience and remained determined to have as normal of a university experience as possible. She almost pledged a White sorority (those being the only options on campus at the time), until she was told by the sorority poised to accept her, "If any of the alums ask, tell them you're Hawaiian." Her relationship with her new boyfriend, Bob Tubbs, kept her busy enough, as he was a member of the football team, and that allowed Daphne to have access to a large swathe of university life. Additionally, Daphne and the other African Americans on campus spent their weekends at the home of "Doc" Glass in Evanston, continuing the tradition of the Evanston community providing an outlet and a refuge for the Black students.

Yet, Daphne wasn't destined to literally just sit on the sidelines; she was insistent on feeling the full Northwestern experience. Having been used to working and taking leadership roles wherever she was, including having been President of the senior class at Bronx High School of Science, she felt oblivious to any notion that she might not be well received anywhere on campus because of her gender or race. During her freshman year, she was involved in student government, becoming a delegate. She even became involved in the Waa-Mu show.

Daphne was doing all of this while working in Chicago, so she was hearing about negative racial episodes more than experiencing them. Also, there was a core group of Blacks in the freshman class who was mostly from Chicago and had attended the Cherubs program (another orientation program for entering freshman), so Daphne missed out on being a part of that "core group" daily. The outcome of this was Daphne being simultaneously involved in and isolated from various aspects of university life.

It was during Daphne's sophomore year that her Northwestern experience became more acculturated. While living in the dorms, she had three Black roommates, which was a completely new experience for her, given she didn't have any sisters. It was during this year that the Blacks on campus organized and took over the Bursar's Office in an effort to improve conditions for the Blacks at NU. "I didn't know what we were doing. I didn't much care! I was a willing protestor and had a history of protesting with my mother, who'd taken me to the March on Washington and had always led civic groups and participated in community things. So, if there was going to be a demonstration, I was going to be there!"

Although there wasn't a singular event to which the students were responding by engaging in the Bursar's Office Takeover, they were quite aware of what needed to change on campus; it was a chronically bad environment. She credits the upperclassmen and graduate student leadership of the group for guiding and focusing the needs of the community, including a need for enhancement of the curriculum to include considerations of what became African American studies. "We were 'the other.' Each of us had to fight battles alone in classes. When we did get together, there was a camaraderie that served to elevate all of our situations."

Daphne expresses bemusement at certain parts of the takeover, especially how in the dark she and others were kept prior to the actual takeover. "They told us to line up in the hall at 'such and such time.' I had no idea where we were going because they didn't tell us. We marched into the Bursar's Office building, and we sat down, and the leadership did what they did."

As was the case with many members of the takeover group, she felt confident in knowing her parents would support the effort. "I remember calling my mother and saying at one point, 'We've taken over the Bursar's building, and we're having a sit-in'," to which her mother's response was simply, "Ok. Let me know if you need some bail money, and I'll get it to you." "She was fully supportive of whatever we were doing!"

She also notes that things were a lot more fluid than one might have thought. "When I was in the building, I had to leave at one point because I had a doctor's appointment. So, I went out the window, I went to the doctor's appointment, and I came back in through the window!"

It appears that the side window of the Bursar's Office was their equivalent of today's more advanced communication tools. The organizers and participants in the takeover used the window to keep those inside the office informed of the goings-on, and this fact is captured in many pictures of the event. Fortunately, Provost Eisenfeld was cooperating with the takeover organizer James Turner, and negotiations were moving forward.

Meanwhile, those in the building were talking, listening to music, eating, waiting, and making sure nothing inside the building was disturbed. "That was our upbringing. We all came from families that taught us to respect ourselves. There was no need to trash the place. We didn't know how long we were going to be in there, anyway. Disrupting the building never crossed our minds."

Another counterintuitive occurrence of the takeover was the plethora of support that accumulated outside the building from majority students. Daphne wasn't especially surprised by this occurrence. "Many of us had friends in the majority. They were supportive of what we were doing. They saw nothing wrong with asking for something we thought we needed."

After the takeover, Daphne scoffs at the notion of any campus pushback toward African-African students. "It seemed there was no change in the demeanor of the people around us, but things were starting to be different class-wise. (The administration) was setting up the (African American Studies) courses, and they were looking for people—and they hired amazing talent. They were looking for people to guide us through what we were asking for, and I wasn't (on campus) much longer after that. I got married that December, and I moved off campus."

It is an especially poignant irony that, during the time of the 1968 Bursar's Office Takeover, Daphne Maxwell was Northwestern's reigning Homecoming Queen. That occurrence simply seemed to be a part of Daphne's ongoing evolution. "When I first got to Northwestern, a junior high school teacher of mine who had been a mentor sent my picture into *Seventeen* magazine for an article on Black power on college campuses. After the article came out, the magazine asked me to be a part of the January 1967 edition, called 'The Real Girls' issue." It was a full-page picture that led to a modeling career with the Eileen Ford Agency (while still a student). That association subsequently led to her becoming the first African American woman to be on the cover of *Glamour* magazine. When her friends at NU saw the magazines, they submitted Daphne's name and picture to the Homecoming Committee. Daphne jokingly consented, thinking it would never go anywhere.

As luck would have it, Daphne's college love had now graduated and was playing professional football so, just about every weekend, Daphne was flying out of town to either visit him or go to work. She had no expectation of needing to be in town during Homecoming weekend and, in fact, she was anxious to leave town to be with her boyfriend, who was playing with the Pittsburgh Steelers that weekend. When she learned the day before during the homecoming parade that she would be joining four "sorority girls" on the court, it reminded her of the absurdity of her past episode during sorority rush. Oddly, neither she nor any of her friends (at least as much as she was aware) bothered to vote. In fact, Daphne wasn't even paying attention when her name was announced as Homecoming Queen. Her first thought was "Aww, man! Now I can't get out of town this weekend!"

As surreal as things were at that point, they only got worse. "The (Northwestern) President (J. Roscoe Miller) came over, and I could tell he was not pleased. He held a little yellow rose crown on my head and said to me, 'I have to hold this on your head until they take pictures,' then he turned and walked away." Daphne was subsequently presented to the John Evans Society with the rest of the Homecoming Court, one of whom was in tears as the others consoled her, ignoring Daphne. When each member of the court was announced, they were greeted with rapturous applause. When Daphne was announced as Queen, "You could hear a pin drop." Daphne was later told that graduate students had encouraged their classes to vote to make a point, and with the vote otherwise being divided among the other four contestants, the tally was sufficient for Daphne to have won the contest.

The next day at the Homecoming football game, the Black students were in a celebratory mood, and word had gotten around to various press outlets as well. In additional to Daphne's victory becoming a focal point for Black campus pride, it was covered far and wide, including by the *Amsterdam News*, *St. Louis News*, and other outlets including *Jet Magazine*, whose cover she graced under the title "Black Beauty Queens at White Schools."

Daphne's victory was a big deal to Black media outlets but apparently not to the Northwestern media outlets. Daphne reports seeing the one photo of her and President Miller in the *Daily Northwestern* school newspaper. However, when the yearbook came out, instead of the traditional three-page spread, she discovered just that one picture of her, and her name wasn't mentioned anywhere in the book. There was no record that Daphne Maxwell was Northwestern's Homecoming Queen in 1967, much less the first Homecoming Queen who happened to be African American.

This disrespect caused Daphne to hold such a level of disgruntlement that she vowed to "never give a dime" to the university, and she and her husband pointedly forbade their son from applying to Northwestern, even as he had expressed an interest in doing so. In fact, four decades passed before Daphne returned to Northwestern. At the request of the Northwestern University Black Alumni Association (NUBAA), she was extended an invitation to receive a "Hall of Fame Award" based on her television career. Most of them did not know that she had been a homecoming queen, which, of course, wasn't documented anywhere. Daphne recalls NUBAA's President, Ce Cole Dillon, getting on the phone with Northwestern University's President, Morton O. Schapiro, and soliciting an apology, which was received in writing along with an invitation to crown the subsequent year's Homecoming Queen.

Daphne really credits the combination of New York City grit and her upbringing for refusing to accept a victim's mentality or allowing one to be imposed upon her. "I had grown up having been in special situations. I was plucked out of grade school and was placed into a special school in the fourth grade. I was then placed into a special program in junior high school. Then I attended the Bronx High School. I was so busy living a fulfilling life that I was not exposed to the oppression of segregation and getting sprayed with water hoses and having to navigate segregated communities. My family and the force of my presence did not accept anybody disregarding me. I knew who I was, and I knew what I could do. And if you don't think I can, then get out of my way, because I can! I was naïve to what was happening in the rest of America, but things seemed to work for me at the time! Then I received the rest of my 'education' at Northwestern."

Daphne reports that she spent five years on the Board of Weinberg College of Arts and Sciences, and she was struck by how every year "the college would repeat how difficult it was to find qualified Blacks to attend the university." She grew so tired and frustrated by what she perceived to be a lack of effort in identifying able Blacks that she declined to continue after five years of service.

Looking back, Daphne appreciates the value that she and her classmates' pain has produced for the university and the subsequent generations of Blacks who have attended Northwestern. She waxes philosophically about her memories of how beautiful the university's campus was and how both the external and internal parts of the university have appeared to evolve. "All of that is in a very good place in my memory, and I appreciate the whole picture. To see it grow and to see buildings where we used to sit on rocks by the lake is enlivening to me. I am proud of having them recognize the contributions we all made as well as my place in history. I am honored that the new archivist asked for my archives, especially considering the emphasis on the interactivity and accessibility of them and the discussions that will accompany them. I'm very pleased to have been part of the arc that changed the university toward something we can be proud of at this point."

Daphne Maxwell Reid offers many lessons to those concerned with the Black experience at Northwestern. Much like every member of the Black student body, faculty, and staff, she intermittently had to be a queen and a warrior while on campus, and she had to smile through a lot of pain. Thankfully, her example exists both as motivation and as instructions for those who need it.

Steve Colson

Steve Colson

Steve Colson is a 1967 enrollee and a 1973 graduate of Northwestern's Bienan School of Music. Upon his arrival at campus, he immediately felt like a fish out of water in several ways. "I was probably one of the only students from the east coast. When I got there, I didn't know anybody. There were maybe twenty to twenty-five (African American) upperclassmen and, in my class, there were about eighty Blacks." Though that seems like a huge increase, Steve notes that the increase only elevated the Black population to about one percent of the university student enrollment. "I don't know how the upperclassmen did it because I know it was like going through hell when I got there." Steve's acclimation to campus was additionally stifled because he hadn't participated in the preparatory program many of the African American students had enjoyed in the previous month. Still, Steve created his own path toward belonging and forging an identity on campus. He was a musician and had been playing piano since the age of ten. Steve and Chico Freeman formed a jazz band named "The Life and Death Situation" that played on and off campus, and that created many opportunities to interact with others.

While still in high school in East Orange, New Jersey, Steve recalls having been favorably impressed by reports of the success of Dan Davis on Northwestern's basketball team; he was also a three-time letterman and an Academic All-American. However, once enrolled at NU, Steve found himself frustrated at how Davis and other Blacks on the team seemed to be purposely held back from really helping the team; they never seemed to play at the same time, as if it was more important to maintain the status quo by keeping a mostly White face to the team. The concept of needing to push back against those out to maintain the status quo seemed to be in Steve's mind throughout his college years and would define his university experience.

Unfortunately, it was in Steve's core reason for attending Northwestern—the decision to obtain an education—in which he was most acutely isolated and subjected to not just the status quo but also what he identified as overt racism. "I'm seventeen. I go into my English class. There are twenty-five or so students in the class, and I'm the only African American in the class. The teacher starts off the class and makes a point of emphasizing his name: Forrest Scarborough. Who do you think he was named after? Nathan Bedford Forrest (a Confederate Army general and an early leader of the Ku Klux Klan)—that's who he was named after; that was his great-grandfather. So, the first forty minutes of my first English class, he's explaining to me how the Ku Klux Klan was a good organization and how I don't belong on the campus because it's a private school. I'm thinking I just got here; I'm seventeen, and I've got to deal with this every time I go to English class, and I had absolutely no help." Steve felt as if he was constantly and explicitly reminded that he and other the Blacks should feel "privileged" to have been allowed to come to America from Africa, pick cotton, and partake in the superior European culture.

Steve's experiences in the School of Music were just as bothersome. "I was the only Black male freshman student in the music school. There were two other Black freshman women. I had so many problems because they seemed to feel as if they were keeping the White culture alive, and it was all based on a European notion that the piano started there. Now I'm a piano major, so that means (to them) it all starts with Bach ... and Mozart and Beethoven were the greatest—without them apparently realizing that Beethoven was Black, as was Franz Josef Hayden, the father of symphony." Steve notes how odd this mentality was for a prominent faculty member to express, given the prominent university legacy of Melville J. Herskovits at Northwestern, who had launched the first major interdisciplinary program in African and African American studies in 1948 (The Program of African Studies).

On a different occasion, Steve recalls participating in a large university chorus with approximately one hundred students. The play was to celebrate the Missouri compromise and highlight the challenge of whether Missouri would be admitted to the Union as a slave state or a free state. Steve was again the lone African American. "The dialogue involved whether people could bring their so-called property (slaves) into the state. So, the instructor (William Ellard) turns to me—the only African American—and says, 'Ok, you're going to say this line'. The line was 'I'm not going to give up my slaves! I'm going to keep my slaves! I paid money for these slaves!' I refused, even knowing how much trouble this would bring."

In fact, after the takeover of the Bursar's Office in 1968, even though complete amnesty had been promised to the participants, Steve believes he was punished for his involvement. "After the takeover, as soon as I came back to class, and after amnesty had been declared by the university, (Prof. Ellard) met me at the door and said, 'I don't want to see you here again. Get out. Don't come back.' It didn't matter what the university had said. He stood up like George Wallace."

Even as Steve acknowledges his experiences may have been more overtly racist than the norm (to which he largely ascribes to the subjective nature of being involved in performing arts), he also asserts that most others on campus were involved in similar struggles. It was the sum of these aggressions and substandard conditions that compelled the students to take action. By this time, and especially as a result of his activities within his jazz band, Steve had become fully integrated into the occurrences within the Black student community in general, and within For Members Only (FMO, the Black Student Alliance) and the African American Students Union (AASU). "There were about seven or eight of us who were discussing what was going on, and once Martin Luther King was assassinated, that pretty much set the table. I'll never forget the day I was walking down the street with Steve Broussard and Jeff Donaldson, and Martin Luther King had just been assassinated the day before. Here was some guy hanging around on the steps on the way to the speech building (being interviewed) on TV, saying Martin Luther King should have been killed, he deserved to get shot, and all he did was cause trouble everywhere he went. That was the first time in my life I saw red. Luckily, Jeff and Steve got to me before I got to him. After that, we knew something had to be done."

There was a small planning group comprising of James Turner, John Bracey, Eric Perkins, Michael Smith, Kathy Ogletree, Andre Bell, Wayne Watson, John Higginson, Jim Pitts, and Steve. Given the way other protest efforts, such as the Black Panthers, had been infiltrated, a decision was made to keep logistical information restricted to this core group. Additionally, as was depicted in the movie *The Battle of Algiers*, the members of the group were given specific assignments and weren't aware of the details of the assignments of other organizers.

Regarding the decision to target the Bursar's Office, the group had observed prior efforts at other universities and noted that other potential targets, such as the president's office, weren't as vital to university operations as the place where financial transactions, including paychecks, were being conducted. Additionally, the Bursar's Office held vital records and university transcripts. It was felt that putting those documents at risk would bring swift action from the university.

Steve and Andre Bell had the assignment of surveillance and establishing entry routes into the Bursar's Office. There had long been rumors of underground tunnels and connections between Rebecca Crown and the Bursar's Office. The group wanted to know if they could be ambushed from these paths or, alternatively, if the group could use these paths to their advantage. The group's plans were complex enough to have produced sketches and maps, and they also included security schedules and the time when the key doors would open. The crew took the precautions of "liberating a few chains and padlocks" and applying them to potential access locations to ensure these doors wouldn't be used to sneak up on them. Steve notes that this proved to come in handy, as the State Troopers and National Guard did, in fact, attempt to enter the building at one point.

The students felt the demands were obvious, based on the deficits in their experiences. "One thing was financial aid. We just didn't think there was enough financial aid for students coming in. Another was there was no Black Studies Program, and we had a demand that we wanted some Black professors. We put the word out that we wanted Lerone Bennett, and they kind of turned that down, saying he didn't have enough paper (publications), but we did eventually get Vernon

Jarrett. Then we demanded to have The Black House, a place where we could meet, as well as a Black Dean—someone who could address our problems. Finally, there was an emphasis on increasing the Black population. Those were the main demands, although addressing our living quarters was also a big deal. This resulted in them placing us in the North Shore Hotel, on one side of the sixth floor."

Steve is careful to acknowledge the support of the general university community during the Bursar's Office Takeover. "We had some White supporters. There were White students out there (on the steps of the Bursar's office during the takeover) protesting as well. They knew there was some racism going on, and things weren't right. I think it was the SDS (Students for a Democratic Society); they were a radical faction associated with the Weatherman (a group thought to have been aiming at overthrowing the US government)."

Steve notes that the university was "pretty good" at following through on the agreements. Milton Wiggins was brought in as Dean of the Department of African American Student Affairs. Lerone Bennett was, in fact, appointed as the first Chairman of African American Studies for a brief period of time, which was formed in 1972. The Black House was established at 619 Emerson and, later, it was relocated to a larger location at 1914 Sheridan Road. Financial aid packages improved, and the student population multiplied.

Meanwhile, Steve's education and his career path continued, even if never totally in sync at Northwestern. Steve had been playing jazz and performing prior to college and while attending NU. "I had started collecting my own records when I was about ten years old. I was familiar with Art Blakely, Miles Davis, Dizzy Gillespie, etc., but the problem was when I got to Northwestern; they didn't have any jazz courses. I didn't know that before I got there, as my high school counselor told me it would be a really great place to go to school. Now, when I got there, and they did start a jazz band, I couldn't get in the band!"

Steve suffered the indignity of being subject to professors who didn't really know jazz. "During my audition (for the jazz band), the professor told me I could play anything I wanted except blues, which, of course, is the basis for most jazz—from Duke Ellington to Charlie Parker." Steve chose to play *Dat Dere* by Bobby Timmons, a very popular jazz standard at the time. "I knew it was good because I'd been playing it for three, four, five years at that point. The first thing he said after I finished was, 'I thought I told you, no blues!'"

In an amazing irony, Steve had such difficulty maintaining his grade point average majoring in piano that he ended up majoring in saxophone in order to graduate. The final irony was found in the success Steve has had over his career as a pianist, which has included a Grammy nomination. "On some levels, I was dealing with the European aspect of it, where I was trying to learn, and the things I was really good at, I wouldn't get credit for. For example, I took a piano course, and they lost the records of it and told me I had to take it again. However, I was able to learn about theory and orchestration—those things I hadn't ever encountered before."

Steve acknowledges the presence of Northwestern's current Dean of the Bienan School of Music, Toni-Marie Montgomery, and Victor Goins to teach jazz to move Northwestern further in allowing a representation of the Black experience in music, but he still notes that Northwestern is reputed as "still a classical school ... they still have to deal with the angles of musical structure as a feeder for the Chicago Symphony Orchestra." Steve asserts that "there is nuance of expressing what is Black culture and what are the things that are part of Black culture that aren't part of the other musical culture," such as the tradition of playing from ear vs. reading music (i.e. repetition and oral vs. notation). He laments the forced application of classical traditions to the teaching of jazz and distinguishes the emphasis of repetition in the former vs. improvisation in the latter, and he strongly opposes the notion that necessarily being credible in playing classical music is a requirement for greatness or legitimacy as a jazz musician.

Even as he speaks of his experiences within the School of Music, in many ways, Steve reveals that the ongoing effort of Blacks at Northwestern to preserve and express a unique Black experience within the global university structure. Since his earliest days as a student to his memories and reflections of modern-day Northwestern, he emphasizes the need to express the Black reality beyond and in ways not defined by the status quo.

Victor Goode

Victor Goode

Victor Goode is a 1970 Northwestern graduate of the Weinberg College of Arts and Sciences.

Victor's Northwestern experience was largely defined by the campus activism that began with the building takeover in 1968. "One of the first demonstrations I took part in as a college student at Northwestern was an open housing march in Evanston, sponsored by a civil rights group because Evanston didn't have any open housing laws at the time. Black students who were trying to live off campus at the time faced discrimination in trying to find housing. I remember one of my classmates, John Higginson, and I were thinking about getting an apartment together during our sophomore year. We started making phone calls from ads in the local paper, but every time we would show up to an apartment, it had 'just been rented!' So, we knew something was up. In response, I participated in an open housing march in downtown Evanston, but this was before the 1968 federal fair housing laws were passed and before state or local laws prohibited housing discrimination.

"Evanston was a pretty segregated little suburb. But it had its own small Black community in West Evanston. I think Dodge Street was the center of the Black community. That's where we would go to a barbershop; that's where a Black man could get his hair cut, and there was a local soul food restaurant.

"Back on campus, I certainly felt isolated. There were about a half-dozen or so Blacks on campus when my class arrived. There was nothing in the literature about this part of Northwestern when I was a high school senior looking at admission materials. There was nothing to suggest there were so few Black students on Northwestern's campus. Yet, when I think about it, I recall all the pictures of African Americans in those materials were athletes. So, I just assumed that while they were on the sports teams, Blacks were also in the stands, in the dormitories and, otherwise, on campus. I remember unpacking my bags and walking down Sheridan Road that first day of moving into Northwestern. I'm looking around, and I'm not seeing any students of color at all. So, I think to myself, 'alright. I'll keep walking.' I walk all the way down Sheridan Road, and it's not until I get to the complete South end of campus past the Miller Chapel that I see a couple of African American students on the opposite side of the street. I quickly cross the street and ask, 'Where is everybody?' They responded, 'Where did you come from!' They thought they'd seen all the Black students on campus at the time! Little by little, we put our notes together and figured out that there were about fifty or sixty NUCAPS (Northwestern University Chicago Action Program Students) who were freshman and who had been on campus since the summer. Then, there were about eight or nine of us who weren't a part of NUCAP who arrived during new student orientation.

"It really was a pretty isolating environment. In my dormitory, there wasn't one Black student on my floor. There were a couple of us sprinkled on different floors. We were spread out, and we were very few. In some respects, it wasn't that we faced a great deal of hostility in the dorms, although some of the women who moved in on campus discovered that their White roommates immediately moved out when they saw who they were living with. Most of the men didn't experience that, but we had this strange situation of not having anything in common with the young men we were living with. None of them seemed to make an effort to know us. So, it was very isolating and a somewhat alienating experience during those first few months.

"When vacations came, the White students were literally going on vacation. We were just going home and, sometimes, going home to a part-time job. Even for simple social activities like going to get a pizza on a Saturday night, we literally had to see if we could afford a fifty-cent pizza, whereas many of our White classmates were heading down to Chicago to partake in social activities there."

Victor reports not only feelings of isolation but also of occasional endangerment. "About halfway through our freshman year, there were a few racial incidents. I recall some guys walking through the Fraternity Row area, and they had beer cans thrown at them. There was a verbal confrontation. There were these kinds of things that happened from time to time. Some of us were given jobs in the cafeteria as part of our work-study assignment. Although we were fellow students, we were really treated like 'the help' in those situations. It was very demeaning to be busing the table of someone you were attending classes with just the previous day. Sometimes, the other students would act as if they didn't even know you. I remember when I went and got my work-study job; I made a specific point of turning down the cafeteria job because I couldn't take a job that seemed like being the maid or house servant. Fortunately, I got assigned to the library, stuck up in the dusty shacks of Deering, shelving books, and not having to be bothered with that.

"I was involved in both FMO (For Members Only, The Black Student Alliance) and AASU (Afro-American Student Alliance). We needed a social life. Ironically, half of Northwestern's campus needed a social life in the 1960's. The Greek system controlled the entire social scene on campus, and if you weren't part of the Greek system—whether you were Black or White—you literally had nothing to do on the weekends. For Black students, it was doubly alienating. So, FMO really was an opportunity for us to gather, throw parties from time to time, spend time, and get to know one another because here we were, sixty students spread out on campus among a student body of over 6000. We dealt with our alienation and loneliness by coming together with one another, socializing, and forming bonds and good friendships.

"These FMO social events were occurring both on and off campus. Sometimes we'd go off campus, if it was convenient. The Black athletes had a home away from home at Doc Glass'. He was a local Black Evanstonian who had helped Black athletes for years to get adjusted to Northwestern's all-White environment. But FMO became our social outlet. For some of the activities, there was a procedure you could go through if you were a recognized campus organization. FMO could reserve the basement area of a dormitory for a party, so we occasionally did that. To our surprise, the White students who weren't part of the Greek system would stand in the halls and peer through the doors, wondering what was going on inside and how we managed to have a party. To them, it appeared that we were having a great time! There was music playing, folks were dancing, and it was a wonderful time on those few Saturday nights when we were able to do that.

"During those first two years, the AASU was beginning to bring in the political currents of the day and make them a part of our campus experience and campus conversations. I remember being very active in those conversations. By the mid-seventies, the civil rights movement was waning, and the Black Power movement was beginning to take its place.

"We would occasionally go into various administrative offices to complain about what was going on, and there seemed to be a split within the administration. There were some younger administrators who were in the admissions and financial aid offices that seemed to be committed to what would later be called affirmative action. Other administrators within the University were part of the old guard that was happy with Northwestern continuing its old ways. It didn't seem that they were blocking the younger group of administrators or blocking increases in Black student enrollment, it's just they weren't whole-heartedly behind it. It wasn't a full-fledged university initiative. So, we didn't get very far with the things we wanted and needed, and little by little our frustration was building.

"We were particularly dissatisfied with the lack of university response to the racial incidents that would come up. As we got to know one another, there was a lot of 'Oh this happened to you, too conversations.' There were things that people didn't ordinarily talk about, but when we finally began to get together and share stories, we began to realize these weren't just isolated incidents but a part of the Northwestern culture.

"Realize that at that time, we were undergoing our own transformation of consciousness in the sense that in 1965 and 1966, we arrived on campus as

Negroes. Then the Black Power Movement began to take off full-fledged across the country. It caused us to examine ourselves and our sense of identity. We now understood that Black students now have a different place and different role in society and on campus than did the 'Negroes' who were recruited to integrate Northwestern. So, it became clear that something had to be done to push the administration to be responsive to our needs and, in that spirit, the plans for the building takeover began to be formulated.

"An interesting thing happened along that route. Some of the sympathetic administrators from admissions and financial aid recognized that there were problems at Northwestern but asked whether we thought other schools were doing a better job. The university ended up giving us travel funds to go to various schools, meet with Black students, and write a report for the university on what these other schools were doing. Now that I look back, I can see what they were doing. They needed some ammunition to go into their meetings with their supervisors and say, 'Look. This is what's going on at Harvard, Columbia, and other universities and, if Northwestern wants to compete with those schools, they're going to have to keep up with what those schools are doing for their Black students.'"

"Eric Perkins and I were given travel funds to visit Cornell, Harvard, and Columbia in the early spring of 1968. We weren't very impressed with what was going on at Harvard. In fact, we were kind of put off by them. Harvard had hired a Black administrator named Dean Epps who seemed more interested in trying to acclimate the Blacks at Harvard to the kind of elite Ivy League society that he saw them integrating into. In other words, he was trying to take a little of the ghetto out of the Black students and make them more "respectable." I'll never forget that we walked into his office, shook his hand and he said, 'Would you chaps like some tea?' We were thinking, 'Where did this guy come from?'

"When we went to Columbia, we witnessed the emergence of a totally different experience because the Black Student Union at Columbia was beginning to hold their meetings, which very shortly led to the takeover of Hamilton Hall on campus. In fact, we began to share notes with them about the things that were going on at Columbia and how close they were to what we were experiencing at Northwestern. Although we had been sent by the University, we had our own agenda, which was to find out what the Black students unions were doing elsewhere, what we could learn from them and what we could bring back to Northwestern to advance our agenda. What we learned from our Brothers at Columbia was that they were planning for serious action, and they had made some very close connections with the local Harlem community to support their demands.

"So, we came back, and literally before we could complete our report to the administration about our trip, AASU had already started planning for the building takeover. So, we forgot about the report because we realized that a serious demonstration that pushed hard was the only way to get the administration's attention. Kathy Ogletree was the President of FMO, and Milton Gardner and Michael

Smith were also officers. Jim Turner and John Bracey were the leaders of AASU, and this combined leadership laid the plans for the takeover. We were very clear that FMO and AASU had to be seen as a single group and work together. For security purposes, the planners of the takeover gave out information on a need-to-know-basis. What everybody knew was that we were planning an action and they knew who was going to participate. We worried about what might become of our college careers, but the majority of students were saying that no matter what went down, they were going to be a part of it. Then within, that group, different roles were broken down, and different pieces of information were given out."

Victor recalls his unique role the morning of the takeover. "We were in the alley behind the Orrington Hotel. That's where we gathered that morning. Dorothy Carter and I were given the role of creating a diversion. We were running around, yelling at the guard at the front door of the Bursar's Office. We got his attention, and he began moving toward the side of the building to see what we were up to. That's when the rest of the group hit the front door and went in. By the time Dorothy and I had circled the building, we wondered what had happened because there was no one there! Everyone had gotten in so fast. The folks inside had chained the door, so Dorothy and I are wondering, 'How are we going to get inside? We did our job, now what?' Then some folks opened up the side window and yelled at us to jump in through the window. So, as more campus police were beginning to arrive, we literally had to jump through the window! We landed into welcoming arms and, suddenly, we looked up, and we were part of the demonstration on the inside.

"Inside the Bursar's Office, we were very careful not to break anything or even to disrupt the items on the various desks. One thing we were aware of was that this thing could move in stages, and the initial stages were the takeover demands and negotiations. But we were also aware that if things went bad, the police could come in— either campus police or Evanston Police. We knew there were differences between being arrested for a non-violent civil act of civil disobedience and getting into a battle with the police and being accused of property damage, assault, and those types of things. It's not that we had worked everything out, but there was a general understanding that we would follow our leadership, and our leadership would let us know when, if, and how things might need to escalate.

"Each of the demands we had for the university was to be accompanied by a presentation made by various members of the takeover group. This way, while the leaders spoke, we also let the university know that the entire group was a part of this effort and we all supported the demands. The leadership had pretty much crafted the demands before the takeover occurred. Once we were in the building, we put together a negotiating committee, and I was one of the members asked to be on the committee. So, we called the university, and they set up a meeting at Scott Hall, I believe, and we marched over. They were on one side of the table, and we were on the other. We just went through the demands, one by one, and it went back and forth. The spokespersons—it was mostly Jim and Kathy at that point—were pretty much in constant contact, back and forth, with the university officials. When the university signed off on our demands and delivered them to the Bursar's Office, I think Jim and Kathy held a press conference on the steps and announced the settlement. They announced that because of the settlement—we would return the office back to the control of the university. And we did, with hardly a paperclip out of order.

"One of the things I remember distinctly from that process was when I was sitting across the table from the university's Vice President. A part of my responsibility—we had divided up our roles—was to make the presentation on one specific topic. So, I make my pitch, and the university's VP looks at me and says, 'Young man, your presentation is perfectly reasonable and perfectly logical, but we just can't do it.' I'm taken aback. I'm thinking that we're here in this university, being taught that reason, logic, and the life of the mind are what we're supposed to be developing. Suddenly, I was faced with the reality that power politics trumped all of that! As it turned out, that demand had to do with Northwestern admitting its complicity over time to racism, both on campus and in society as a whole. Later, we did discover from the only African American administrator who was a part of that group (Lucius Gregg) that this issue was the sticking point that almost broke down the negotiations. It seems that all the way up to President (Roscoe) Miller, there was a gradual agreement that they would meet our demands, except they would not admit to institutional racism.

"Another one of the demands was related to Black student housing. There were two things under consideration at that time. One was a demand for the recognition of Black fraternities and sororities. Bill Ihlendfelt, who I think was the Director of Financial Aid at the time, was also a part of the young group of administrators who was trying to push Northwestern forward. I remember that he said, 'We don't think the Greek system is good for Northwestern—for any student. I'll tell you what we're prepared to do. If you guys agree not to push for Black fraternities and sororities, we will turn part of one of the south campus dormitories into coed housing, and it will be an all-Black dorm with men and women, which we hope will be a model for what we can do to integrate the north campus (which was all men, whereas south campus housed all women). There are a lot of things that need to be changed at Northwestern, and you guys can be a catalyst for some of those bigger changes.' This would have been a revolutionary change for Northwestern in 1968.

"I remember taking that idea back to our group and our leadership, and the sense was the demand for fraternities and sororities was what our group really wanted. We were eighteen and nineteen years old. These guys at the university were older and had more experience and had their own vision of what they were trying to accomplish and saw this moment of change that we had initiated as an opportunity to advance their agenda as well. We were simply trying to be a part of campus life, to earn our degrees, and to have some fun. So, fraternities and sororities seemed to be the way to go.

"The compromise measure was a Black student wing on the fifth or sixth floor of the North Shore Hotel. So, we did get Black student housing—not gender-integrated but Black male housing on one floor and maybe female housing on the other. I'm not sure. On that point, my memory of events is not clear. The North Shore Hotel was used because the hotel had seen better days. Northwestern had an overflow of freshman in 1966, and they had run out of student housing. So, it leased a couple of floors, turning them into student housing.

"It's really during the building takeover when the 10% demand for Black student enrollment was put on the table. Prior to that, Northwestern had its own plans to increase Negro enrollment and to recruit more. I never saw any documents to know exactly what they had in mind but, after the building takeover, one of our demands was that since Black people made up ten percent of the nation's population, we should make up ten percent of the enrollment of Northwestern.

"There were some administrators who pushed back, and others, representing the young guard of the administration who supported the idea. They agreed with the concept that this is what Black students needed to actually form a community within the overall Northwestern community. You can't expect students to be a part of the learning environment and not be a part of the social environment. For us, we didn't see a ten percent goal as a terribly radical demand at the time but, compared to what was happening at many other schools, it was significant. From our vantage point, we looked around our own high schools and communities and saw talent everywhere. If we could see the talent, why couldn't NU?

"I didn't tell my parents exactly what was going on as things led up to the takeover. As things were heating up, I wrote them a letter vaguely letting them know that I wasn't really happy, and I was thinking about possibly transferring. I didn't want to tell them that I might get arrested and thrown out of school, even though that's really what was on my mind. I think we were all aware of the risks we were taking but, at the same time, we were drawing our inspiration from what we were seeing going on around us in Chicago and in the rest of the country. We were urban kids from the north. We were not a part of the civil rights movement, but we were a part of the spirit of that movement and of the changing political awareness and debates about Black self-determination occurring around the country. I think that's what compelled us to feel that pushing for our demands was worth the risk. I never had any remorse about the Bursar's Office Takeover, but I did consider us very lucky. It could have very easily turned into a situation similar to what had occurred on other campuses, where the police were brought in, making arrests and cracking heads.

"Even after the takeover, I can't say campus life was ever really normal. In the odyssey of our campus experience, we arrive as eighteen and nineteen-year-old kids, and circumstances forced us to grow up very fast and assume levels of responsibility well beyond what our White peers had to handle within their own matriculation. In many ways, the burdens we shouldered never stopped. While the building takeover was successful, it's not as if the racial tensions magically went away. There were other confrontations, endless adjustments, and a growing Black community. We were suddenly aware that we really didn't know everyone, and there was growing campus activism in opposition to the war. There was always something going on.

"The next year, there was an incident with Triangle fraternity. There was a fight, and the university charged several Black students with violating the university's code of conduct. The incident involved a White fraternity member who had either grabbed the arm of or brushed up against an African American woman and never said 'excuse me' or 'pardon me.' There were some Black students who got really pissed off when they heard the story. Of course, as the story got retold, the rumor had morphed into an assault. So, a group of Black men stormed the fraternity and beat up some of the fraternity guys. Several of them were identified and put on trial by the university. Many of them were suspended for a quarter.

"We put on a demonstration against the university's action, which eventually turned into a hunger strike in front of Rebecca Crown Center. After the incident, we gathered in the North Shore Hotel but, when we discovered the university police had gone looking for specific individuals, we realized we couldn't stay there. People tried to maintain some level of solidarity. Eventually, some people got charged, and we staged the hunger strike, thinking in the wake of the success of the building takeover, we could put pressure on the university to get them to back down from prosecuting these students. That didn't work. So, from the elation and success of the building takeover in '68, we experienced a sense of loss and despair in '69. The Black students were charged with being the aggressors, and they were the only ones who were charged. I don't recall any Whites being charged. That incident left an air of tension throughout that year on campus."

Victor was instrumental in organizing a 40th anniversary commemoration of the Bursar's Office Takeover. "I got the idea from attending a conference at Columbia University. A friend of mine had been in SDS (Students for a Democratic Society) at Columbia, and they were having a conference on student activism. Since I had met with those guys way back in 1968, I decided I'd see what they had to say. I soon realized that Columbia had been having this conference every four to five years, with panelists and discussions. It wasn't just a reunion of friends coming together. It was a serious meeting to reflect on student activism and make connections to the current political climate. At the Columbia conference, I noticed the near-complete absence of Black alums. I also noticed that the role of the Black students in 1968 and the support of the Harlem community was almost completely omitted and, instead, the story was being told through the lens of the White students, who were really only there in a supportive role. I recognized then that a social history was being written through these conferences, and the Black role in those events was almost nonexistent.

"I decided that couldn't happen at Northwestern. I wrote to Northwestern to propose a conference to commemorate our student activism from that period. At first, it was suggested that I contact FMO and make the building takeover an afternoon conversation as a part of the Black homecoming activities. But that wasn't my vision. I emphasized this event was a critical piece of the university's social history that needed to be preserved and placed in the broader context of the history of student movements of that period. Finally, it was the African American Studies Department's chair who picked up on the idea and pursued grant money to make the 40th anniversary a well-organized event. Once they got behind it, we had the official support of the university, and I have to give them credit; they did an excellent job of helping to plan, organize, and structure the event. All of the videos from the event are now a part of the University Archives and available to future students and future researchers who might study that period.

"I have to reemphasize the importance of this being seen as a critical piece of social history. Each of us has a story to tell, each of has a part of that story that molded us and made us who we became as adults, professionals, activists, and parents. It's also a part of the history of the university. It's a part of what was occurring on campuses across the country at that time. It was a part of a changing climate within the university and across the nation, and it showed how we as students responded to those political movements. One of the things that I think was significant about 1968 was that we were trying to understand the political trends and events occurring in the nation as a whole and make them a part of our own experience. I can't emphasize enough how dramatic it was in our lives to come onto campus as eighteen-year-old Negroes and leave as African American men or women. We arrived on campus having no real political experience at all, and this defining political moment in 1968 shaped the ways we saw the world based through our efforts to challenge racism and discrimination. We had the experience of struggling to change the structure and systems of a university. We redefined what initially was an effort toward integration and transformed it into an expression of self-determination. I know for myself it was the experience of 1968 that turned me into an activist and was a defining moment for my life and career. I think the same was true for many other students."

Victor is clear regarding his goals for the upcoming and subsequent commemorations. "One of the things I think is very important about the 50th anniversary commemoration is to recognize that, once again, albeit in a very different context, African American students all over the country have to ask themselves 'What are the political and social conditions of the day? How are they affecting us and our communities?' Black students today have a responsibility to examine them and make sense of their own sense of self-determination, just as students did before us and just as we did. In the '60's, we saw ourselves as an extension of our communities. We were a resource being developed that many hoped would return and further develop our communities."

"The world has changed a lot in the last fifty years. Several interesting questions can be posed: Is there still a vision for Black empowerment? Is there still a radical political consciousness stirring on our campuses? What is the political consciousness of African American students today? What's going on outside the campus that affects those inside the campus? How do they view and respond to external events? This 50th anniversary is an excellent time to explore those issues with current students and examine those questions, both collectively and individually.

"One of the things we that we lost in 1968 was our youth. We lost the sense of being carefree, being silly college students, and being able to make the mistakes of eighteen and nineteen-year-olds as we were growing up. Instead we had to constantly—constantly—shoulder the burden of breaking open doors and creating space for those who would come along after us. Going through the struggles that led to progress was not easy by any means. I hope today's students don't have to go through the same struggles we went through. Being a student is a remarkable time to step back, learn about yourself and the world. But as I look over the social landscape, the struggles that today's students face are, in their own way, just as challenging and daunting as what we had faced. I suppose all we can really offer them from our experience 50 years ago is the importance of embracing those challenges and giving them their best. That is what we did, and as the saying from the movement of the '60's goes, 'the struggle continues.'"

Wayne Watson

Wayne Watson

Wayne Watson obtained a bachelor's degree from Northwestern University in the School of Education and Social Policy (SESP) in 1969. He also received an MA/MS degree in teaching in 1970 from SESP and a Doctor of Philosophy from Northwestern's Graduate School in 1972.

"I'm a triple Wildcat, and I have to give Northwestern University and the Athletic Department credit because they made it possible. When I completed my baccalaureate degree, the Athletic Department contacted the College of Education and informed them I had performed well for them, and I wanted to go to graduate school. I was actually at tryouts for the World Games for wrestling when the College of Education contacted me to pursue my master's and doctorate degrees. At the time, I thought it was rare for a university to take that type of interest in an athlete."

Wayne reiterates that his status on campus as an athlete provided him a different Northwestern experience than the typical Black student. "Without a doubt, athletes had privileges that the average African American student didn't. For example, my coach made sure that I, as the only Black on the wrestling team, had a better-than-average and comfortable place to live. I could walk into the fraternity houses on campus, and they would greet me, as most fraternities had athletes. I ate regularly at the frat houses, such as Lambda Xi. Obviously, the average Black student wasn't doing that. That disparity of treatment is largely why, at a number of campuses throughout the United States, Black athletes tend not to understand the issues often expressed by other Blacks.

"However, we were fortunate enough as Black athletes at Northwestern to interact daily with the general Black student body. Even though we were not confronted blatantly with some of the challenges our fellow Black classmates had or certainly not to the same extent, we were able to hear about them. Still, the athletes stepped up and didn't isolate themselves and say, 'that's your problem. They treat us well.'"

Ironically, many of the relative privileges enjoyed by athletes were a result of the intervention of Charles 'Doc' Glass, who had been advocating for support and better conditions for Black athletes since the late 1950's. Over the decade preceding

Wayne's enrollment at Northwestern, Doc Glass' effort turned from exclusive supporting the Black athletes to the entire Black student community at NU. This support was most notable in his Evanston home being the source of student interaction and support. "Doc Glass was needed four times more than what he was able to accomplish for us. He was phenomenal, and the need was great. What his story shows is how dire it was for those who were not athletes. Even among athletes, it was better, but we were still faced with racism, but just not to the same degree as the average Black student. No one on campus was going to approach Jim Pitts at 7 feet, 1 inch and say to him what they'd say to the average Black student. People were smart enough to temper their racism but, even tempered, it was sufficient to justify a Doc Glass and two or three more on top of him. He really did ensure that the few of us who were at Northwestern were able to survive."

Wayne came to Northwestern during the dawn of a significant Black presence on campus. "When I came to Northwestern in 1966 as a transfer, there were maybe twenty or thirty of Blacks on campus. They brought in maybe forty to sixty Blacks in the freshman class, and that was revolutionary. The education that took place at Northwestern took place partly in the classroom and partly in the basement of Scott Hall where Blacks would congregate on campus. We were reading about our own institution, conducting research, and discussing our history. We discovered things like the people who gave money to build the Tech building (Northwestern's Technological Institute) in the early 1940's had allegedly attached a stipulation. Part of the codicil was that Blacks would not be allowed to be in this building. Now I never saw the document, and that could have been an urban myth, but I believe it was true. We also learned that until relatively recently, Blacks had not been allowed to live on campus. It was really this—the information part of our education—that allowed us to develop and grow."

Even though the African American community wasn't large, they were extremely cohesive. "I always have to give credit to the community. This is really a situation in which it's not just verbiage. The community continually acted as one. Sometimes, we might have someone's ego get out of line, and they'd want to stand up and be seen, but the community would literally and figuratively grab that Brother and pull him back in and say, 'Guess what? This is not about you.' Nine out of ten times that Brother or Sister would quickly make the adjustment in favor of the community.

"If you put our actions during our years on campus in the context of the times, they weren't that drastic. What was drastic was how we were being made to live every day. Fifty years ago, if your girlfriend was being approached and told her female genitalia was going to be grabbed, and people on campus were making other lewd comments toward her, and you were subject to some of the other things that were happening, you'd understand that our responses were quite rational. We never went from A to Z. We always went to B and said, 'Let's talk about it.' Then, when they didn't want to talk to us, we went to C. We only went to Z, meaning taking over the Bursar's Office, after we'd gone through the entire alphabet. We tried to talk to people. We tried to meet. Remember, these young men and ladies were some of the brightest African Americans that the urban centers of the US had to offer. Northwestern really brought in some especially bright talent. If you look at them 50 years later, you'll see doctors, judges, lawyers, and engineers. There was just incredible talent in that group. They were always logical."

Wayne states that these sentiments, which were expressed with increasing frequency in the spring of 1968, were the genesis of the takeover of the Bursar's Office. "History is contextual based on what's happening throughout the world. The Bursar's takeover was a combination of what was happening with the fraternities on campus and what had been happening across the United States. We were seeing what was happening with Martin Luther King, Jr. and Malcolm X. We were seeing what was happening in our urban centers. Remember, we had students from some of the roughest communities in the United States, such as New York City, Ohio, the West Side of Chicago, and Englewood in Chicago. Yet, these were some of the brightest students, even though most of us came from very poor families. I can't ever remember my father not working three jobs. While we were at Northwestern, within all of this luxury, we were still talking to our parents about bills, to cousins getting shot, and brothers being mistreated by the police. Those realities were still a part of our lives. Meanwhile, our White counterparts were calling home and hearing the stock market had gone up, and their families had made another half-million dollars. We were calling home and hearing, 'Daddy got laid off work' or 'your brother got put in jail' or 'your sister got accosted.' That filtered through the bell jar that we were living in at Northwestern. We were at a tipping point."

The senses of community among the Blacks on campus really came through in the planning and execution of the Bursar's Office Takeover. "There was a core group, but they did a fantastic job in communicating with the larger group. Individuals were given assignments, and the planning that took place was aided by excellent leadership from the graduate students. We had Jim Turner, John Bracey, Jim Pitts, Sterling Stuckey, and Jeff Donaldson as graduate students leading and advising. They were outstanding individuals in terms of their minds. Then, we had a group of undergraduate students who were extremely sharp, including Kathy Ogletree, Stalk, Eric Perkins, John Higginson, Milton Gardner, Marion Jackson, and Victor Goode. For as many names as I've mentioned, I've left that many out.

"One strategy emphasized by the graduate students was as follows, 'this will have a better face to it if the leadership comes from the undergraduates. We will guide you and give you counsel, but the leadership to the media and administration has to be that of undergraduates.' The graduate students and undergraduate students were in lockstep. It was an opportunity to counsel, train, and educate. I hope that part is not missed. I remember Kathy Ogletree, who was President of FMO (For Members Only, the Black Student Alliance), constantly saying, 'I'm the spokesperson.' Someone else would say. 'You're the leader.' She'd continue to rebut. 'No, no, no. I'm just the spokesperson.' Regardless, and no matter how much she wanted to deny it, her leadership talents and attributes came through. Now, did we have disagreements?

Sure. However, it was worked out in a room, and it never left the room. There were so many checks and balances in place."

Wayne extends his view of the community to discuss the participation of those in and out of the building during the takeover. "The question has often come up as to who was involved in the takeover, maybe as a means of giving credit to them. I have a slightly different take on that. Let's acknowledge those who were in the building with no questions asked. However, the takeover would have never occurred if there were just the seventy students in the building because there were thirty or forty who weren't in the building who also knew about it. Those students made the decision not to go in, but they also made the decision not to tell. If they had walked out of the series of meetings and told the administration, 'Guess what. At seven o'clock tomorrow, the students are going to take over the building,' then the takeover would have never occurred. The silence of those Brothers and Sisters deserves high respect. Nat Turner wishes he had some Brothers who chose to remain silent. Denmark Veasey wishes the same. Silence can also mean support. We had support, but we also had silence that made our action possible. I don't want us to lose or minimize that. Those individuals need to be acknowledged as much as anyone else."

Wayne was uniquely positioned during the takeover. "A large part of my responsibility was logistics. We knew that we were going to have sixty to one hundred people in that building, and the fundamental question was 'What are we going to do while we're in there?' We had to survive and deal with the basic needs necessary to survive a week. I was assigned to make sure that everything got in that building that was needed to sustain us during the takeover. Later, I was responsible for escorting some people inside the building who showed up late. You may have seen a picture of me literally throwing someone through the window into the building! They had to get in!

"We gathered money because we didn't have enough. Herman Cage is one of the unsung heroes because he 'got' some money from his fraternity on our behalf. I then rented a truck, but we couldn't get food and supplies in Evanston because we knew folks would be alarmed by a bunch of Black kids filling up a truck. So, we went to Chicago and purchased food, water, and other goods. We took what Northwestern taught us about the hierarchy of needs and applied it. We went down the list, purchased what we needed, and filled up a six or eight-wheeler truck.

"The strategy to get people and supplies was simple: once security was distracted, they'd get in the building and knock on the door to the offices, then push past the staff. When that occurred, it was my cue to get the truck lined up next to the Bursar's office. The driveway had been blocked, so we made our way around the blockade. I had identified four individuals from the Evanston community to be in the back of the truck. As soon as I stopped, they threw the back of the truck open and started unloading food into the office through the side window, where Brothers on the inside were grabbing the items just as fast as it was being thrown in. The police came, but we had a plan that as soon as they got within a certain distance of us, I'd say something, and the kids would take off running. These four individuals had 'experience' of being rather fast within the community. So, these guys took off like bullets, and not one of them got caught by the police, who were, in fact, chasing them. So, they are unsung heroes of the takeover. Very few people know who they are, but they played a key role. We couldn't have survived more than a few days without them putting themselves and their future on the line for some students at a university that traditionally wouldn't have had anything to do with them.

"We got all of the food inside, and I'm standing outside, but it appears as if the police are going to arrest me because I'm with the truck, and I'm surrounded. At this point, James Turner and one or two others met with the university and told them that I had to be let go. I, or at least my freedom, basically became one of the first demands. I continued to work logistics through the sit-in, making sure there was a constant supply of things that were needed to keep people safe and healthy.

"After the takeover, I felt tired. We hadn't slept the night before. Those working with me didn't sleep much during that first day or night because we were still responsible for getting certain things done. We were preparing food and simultaneously keeping the planning and organizing going. I remember just going home that night and just crashing. There wasn't any celebrating because we only had an agreement. That didn't mean they were going to do it."

Even though the university had agreed to do what it could to improve conditions for African American students, the sentiments of students weren't subject to negotiation. It was less than one year after the takeover when ongoing interactions with fraternities presented another major challenge for African American students. "The Triangle event was one in which a female African American student was completely disrespected. She was on her way to the library to study. A number of young men from one of the Fraternities approached her and used rather vulgar language, making reference to her female genitals and their genitals. It was very inappropriate, and she was very scared. She went back to her fiancée, who was a student on campus. She felt threatened. The African American males on campus had a discussion with the women on campus and discovered this was not the only such occurrence with this fraternity. Apparently, a number of ladies had been similarly accosted previously. A number of us decided we needed to discuss and address this. A result of the action taken was that young ladies were able to walk on campus without fear and without being inappropriately approached. It changed the culture of how Black women were treated on campus."

In fact, the Triangle event was much more dramatic, and it involved violent confrontation, followed by twenty-one Black students being either suspended or being placed on academic probation. However, that is not the focus of or lesson learned by Wayne. "What you're going to find with the Bursar's Office Takeover, the Triangle event, and some other events that is we pretty much acted as a community more than anyone can imagine. If we had about 100 students on campus, then about

100 students were involved in discussions before these things happened. To show you how we worked as a community, regardless the disciplinary actions that occurred with the Triangle event, it was identified that because of their status certain individuals who had participated could not afford to be placed on probation or suspended. They were at a point in their academic careers where they were right on line to be admitted to law school or medical school, for example. On the other hand, there were other individuals who could afford to go through a disciplinary process. These decisions were made by the community that student John Doe would be allowed to step back, even though he may have participated, and student Tim Doe would step up, even though he may not have actually participated. So, Tim Doe was the name that was given up for suspension or probation." Although charges were originally brought against Wayne, they were dropped.

The negotiation regarding the fate of the participants in the Triangle event were quite dramatic. "There was the backdrop to the negotiations, and there were the actual negotiations. The Black students were conducting a starvation strike and sit-in in support of those of us at risk. Twenty young men and ladies volunteered in the cold to have a sit-in and starve themselves at Rebecca Crown Center—and it was cold! That put a lot of pressure on the university. That gave the external world a view and knowledge of what was happening at this campus where young women and men were willing to starve themselves. Then, we had another group on the inside doing the negotiating. This group was very calm, very rationale, and very respectful. Those two groups acting together was what positioned the university and the Black students to come to an agreement."

Regarding the implementation of the components of the Bursar's agreement, it never was as easy as signing a document. "There were a series of events that took place after the Bursar's takeover that made it necessary to compel the university to continue to agree to support the signed agreement. In one sense, we were treated with more respect. Within a few years, we did see that more African American students were being admitted. We saw more faculty and administrators being hired. We had Paul Black become Dean of The Black House. He had a yeoman's task. It was like herding cats. We had one of our own, Andre Bell, become the head of financial aid and admission, and he became Vice President of the SAT! So, there were those types of achievements, but there was still so much to be done and, even then, the university was trying to renege on some of the commitments."

Wayne felt that his transition from undergraduate to graduate student was eerie as he found himself stepping into the advisor role others had offered before him. "Because I had been an undergraduate student, when I became a graduate student, the undergraduates did not acknowledge me as being separate and apart from them. I was always 'Baldy.' I was always a part of them and, from my perspective, I never wanted to be apart from them.

"My graduate studies were enhanced because I was able to interact with the undergraduates. My doctoral dissertation was on oral histories and traditions in Evanston. I was able to interview individuals from the early 1900's and some individuals from the late 1800's. They would tell stories about Black students at Northwestern not being able to stay on campus and having to stay at the 'Black Y.' I used undergraduate students to help me with the research. Being connected with the community helped me complete my dissertation."

With that orientation, Wayne is especially enamored with current initiatives by the Northwestern University Black Alumni Association (NUBAA) to establish and direct a university archive and oral history of the Black experience. "Oral histories are a valuable tradition, especially in that our oral histories are something we control. Of course, the tradition goes back to our African forefathers, where the Griots carried the stories of our family, community, and nation between generations. That is pretty much what we're doing here and now. The only difference is back then, the nation controlled it entirely. We have to be careful about who is telling our story because oral histories can also be salacious. Our history is very colorful. Some of us have reason to be measured in our telling of these stories, Some of our colleagues regrettably have transitioned, and we want to protect their names and families as well as tell the proper stories. I'm very pleased at what the alumni are doing for Northwestern to keep the fight forward. It goes without saying that this 50th Anniversary of the Bursar's takeover presents an opportunity to solidity our positions on The Black House and increase Black student's enrollment closer to ten or twelve percent."

Wayne is easily able to see the lineage of actions taken in 1968 and the current progress at Northwestern. "I was a member of the Board of Trustees, partially as a result of the takeover. So many things can be traced back to that, including the number of Blacks on the board today and the number of African American administrators and faculty. I realize that there are still challenges with current administrators but let me say this: the current President that you have, you would not have that quality of a man if it had not been for the takeover. Fifty years ago, Northwestern changed its standard. It changed the values and skillsets it was looking for to head the University as a result of what happened. Fifty years ago, they would not have considered some of the deans and vice-presidents that are there now, even if they were White. I am ecstatic that Northwestern has a Provost who is African American. I have to again give credit to the students from fifty years ago, but I also have to give credit to the current President. For him to step up and do that, as well as for the university to have selected him as President, he has to have values and skills that weren't present back then.

"Toni Marie Montgomery, the Dean of the Bienan School of Music, was hired when I was on the Board. Toni is highly qualified. There were a few Blacks on the Board at that time, and we were all excited and pushing for her hire. As with the Provost, I'm glad she's African American but, as we look back 100 years, they are where they are only in part because they are Black but more so because they are qualified way beyond race. They had to be equal to or better than their colleagues to make it to Northwestern.

"We also need to acknowledge the one African American upper-level administrator we had, Lucius Gregg. Talk about someone who put his career on the line! He strategically guided us and helped us understand certain situations within the University—to the peril of his career. He could have been fired. He played a very key role in things."

Wayne became the President of Chicago State University in 2009; he was previously the Chancellor of the City Colleges of Chicago, but he has remained in touch with the events at Northwestern. "I've been locked behind a desk for the last fifteen to twenty years, taking care of my own colleges, so I haven't been on Northwestern's campus in some time. However, I guess I would say we should always put things in context. I took a lot away from Northwestern, and I definitely acknowledge the support I received. However, the university is nothing more than a reflection of the larger society. The challenges we faced, we were able to turn into positive energy, and Northwestern taught me that. I wouldn't be the man I am today without facing some of the challenges I faced at NU. Without a doubt, those challenges taught and prepared me, and they trained me to deal with challenges in the greater society. More importantly, I learned it's not an 'I,' it's a team. It's a 'we.' That part is what NUBAA is doing today, just as we did fifty years ago. I believe the outcome of these efforts today will be equal to what we did fifty years ago because you're continuing that legacy."

Kathryn Ogletree

Kathryn Ogletree

Kathryn Ogletree (aka "Twig") matriculated to NU in 1967 and graduated with a BA in Psychology in 1971 from the Weinberg College of Arts and Science, also receiving her PhD in Counseling Psychology from the Graduate School in 1976.

"Even though I'm from Chicago, Northwestern really wasn't on my radar. I was first-generation college and was looking at state schools and Black colleges. The bottom line was whoever gave me the best financial aid package was where I was going to go! It came as a surprise when schools like Northwestern started recruiting me."

When Kathy came to Northwestern, she participated in the NUCAPS (Northwestern University Chicago Action Program Students) summer enrichment program, as had many other Black enrollees from Chicago. "It was a very good experience for me. I think it helped acclimate me to the university environment, such that it was easier, and I felt more confident in the fall than I think otherwise would have been. I did notice that Northwestern seemed to be more traumatic for other students coming in who hadn't participated." Even with a positive NUCAPS' experience, Kathy didn't come to NU with expectations. She relied on the core group of students she'd already met for friendship, and that group relied on upperclassmen to provide alternatives to the social offerings on campus. "So, for homecoming, we were already motivated to have our own activities. We'd already figured out how to have our own dances and parties."

Kathy and the other Blacks were dealing with on-campus tensions. They couldn't help but notice the frequent occurrences of roommates' friends almost immediately leaving the room if they were present or even refusing to live with a Black roommate. "These were things we really weren't prepared for. I wish the University would have alerted us that this was at least a possibility. It created trauma when someone would tell you they didn't want to room with you just because you were Black."

Even with as many challenges occurring in the social life, the case remained that the primary challenge was within the classroom. "Academics were a little tough, but I was up to the challenge. When I got to Northwestern, I learned why my high school counselors were always telling me that I could compete with anyone. That was preparation for what I'd have to deal with at Northwestern. However, I did have problems with French. I got a D, and I have never received anything lower than a B in my life on anything! I was a straight-A student so, if I got a B on a test, I knew I had to do better! I didn't want to admit that Northwestern could get the best of me academically. Still, there were a lot of Black students suffering and even on academic probation. We all felt that stress, even if it wasn't happening to us individually."

Kathryn recalls the formation of FMO (For Members Only, the Black Student Alliance) in the fall of 1967 as a social outlet. "I remember going to the meetings, agreeing that we needed the group to plan activities and address our concerns and voting on the name. Herman Cage was elected as President, and the group of people I had come up with over the summer nominated me and voted me as Vice President. That's how I became Vice President, and then I became President after Herman resigned at the end of the fall quarter.

"Some students were more politically aware than many of us. I had some political motivations; I was aware of things. However, some students, like Eric Perkins and John Higginson, had actually participated in marches in the south. They were instrumental in becoming a part of an organization that became the African American Student Union (AASU). I was invited to join and was proud that they thought enough of me to bring me in it, but it mainly consisted of the upperclassmen and graduate students like James Turner, John Bracey, Jeff Donaldson and James Pitts. To the best of my knowledge, FMO was formed first and represented all students, even those who didn't identify with us. After the takeover of the Bursar's Office, somehow, they just stopped existing. Everyone was so busy with the committees and everything ... Yet, FMO continued on because there was always a need to be attuned to the social and emotional needs of the students."

During that first year, Kathy noted a lot of focus around academics and the ongoing threats of academic probation, suspensions, and dismissals. "That's why we often rallied around financial aid. People's need to work was causing problems with grades. It was evident we needed a little extra time and mental energy to study." Also, there were social challenges to address. "Although the guys lived on the north end of campus and the girls lived on the South end, often the only place we could get space to socialize was on the north end. When we'd be walking down campus, there would be cans of beer thrown out of windows or from near us. We had to navigate through things like that. Women were also afraid to walk alone because women could be accosted. People would either say something inappropriate or touch you inappropriately, and we had various situations in which both those things occurred.

"One of the biggest episodes of this demeaning of women occurred in December of that year (1967) and involved a fraternity. Two people got to fighting, and there were Whites beating up a Black student. Other Blacks jumped in, and one of the Blacks involved was from Evanston and wasn't even a student. It resulted in the police being called. It was called mob action on the part of the Black students, and many students ended up going to court. There was punishment for both sides."

Kathy is unsure if the Bursar's Office Takeover would have occurred if Dr. Martin Luther King, Jr. hadn't been assassinated and if similar episodes weren't occurring across the country. "Probably not or maybe not at that time. However, those two things in connection with the kinds of negative experiences we were having and the frustration of being on Northwestern's campus after Dr. King was assassinated led to that. Most of us weren't rioters. Still, most people on campus were looking at us like they expected us to break out at any point and start tearing up things. There were looking at us and moving away. They were definitely anticipating. Of course, there had been demonstrations at Columbia and other places that showed us what could be done."

Kathy explains how the structure of FMO was created in a way different than what one may expect. "The way we were set up was that there was a committee structure that had responsibilities so, even though I may have known what was going on, I wasn't involved in it. So, when it came to the Bursar's Office Takeover, we had demands on the table. There was a committee. We had been submitting correspondence with the university for several months. They were being ignored. They would say, 'someone is looking into it.' So, it didn't just happen when Dr. King was assassinated that we gave them some papers that said, 'you'd better do this, or else ...' It was the accumulation of all kinds of things but, without the death of Dr.

King, I don't know if there would have been the emotional fervor to follow through. Bill Hines, who was the main recruiter of most of us, was frustrated too. Sometimes, I don't think they knew what to do. They were procrastinating or didn't feel the same sense of urgency that we felt."

Even though Kathy was the President of FMO, she wasn't fully aware of or involved in the early planning of the takeover. "So, it was set up like *the Battle of Algiers*, which was a book some of us had read—probably most of the guys in the African American Student Union! After all these years, I still don't know the entire story. What I remember is we had several meetings to create the documents that were submitted to the university. People voted. Then, when the university gave its response, and we didn't feel it adequate, we had an FMO meeting to discuss what to do to take it to the next level." Interestingly, Kathy wasn't aware of what the "or else" entailed. "I thought maybe we'd do a march!" Once the conversation came around to something involving a building, Kathy recalls the efforts with wordplay. "We talked about 'occupy' vs. 'takeover.' Takeover sounded too aggressive. They meant the same thing, but one sounded less threatening."

As was the case with many participants, Kathy had a specific role, which was to get people to participate. "So, my role as the President of FMO was to bring the people along. That notion was scary to me! Herman Cage was a senior, getting ready to graduate. I'd just gotten there! I'm a freshman—and a female! The guys respected me adequately, but I didn't make too many demands of them. At that time, it was thought that a woman was supposed to be behind the men. That's how James Turner kind of ended up in the front. However, the demands were being written and approved by those working with me. Those did not come from the African-American Student Union.

"At the last meeting, we told people that we were going to meet at a certain place at a certain time, but that's all I knew too! I didn't know where we were going. I knew why it was organized that way. We knew if we said we were going to something like Rebecca Crown (the administrative building), someone was going to tell! There was no doubt in our mind that someone wouldn't agree. In retrospect, it's crazy that I had that kind of blind faith ... That's still amazing to me. More people turned out than we expected. Numbers were important. We knew if there were 120 of us on campus and only twenty of us were in the building, we'd be in trouble! One hundred of us ended up going in, and that was a strong statement. It meant the concerns we were raising were legitimate and represented the whole of our community.

"We showed up at six o'clock in the morning; someone said, 'follow me,' and we went into the Bursar's Office. I can't believe we had chains and chained the doors shut, but I'm most amazed that we had that many people because that was my job. We had a lot of people who weren't politically astute but, at that point, the university was not taking us seriously, so people decided to come along."

Kathy was one of the few participants who were both inside the Bursar's Office and came out for meetings and negotiations with the administration, but again, she wasn't aware of how the negotiation team had been established, although as FMO President, she ended up at the head of the table. Kathy recalls Bracey, Turner, Amassa Fountleroy, Leslie Harris, Vernon Forde, Victor Goode and, maybe, Dan Davis participating in negotiations. "I remember at least two meetings with the university. The first one didn't go well at all. During the second meeting, they seemed willing to work with us. Then, when we got it in writing, it was agreeable enough to be accepted by the rest of the body, and we took a vote."

Kathy's role was even more prominent in the aftermath of the takeover, when the logistics of implementing the agreement took precedence. "I remember there were committees to address every point of the demands except the first one, which involved the university admitting wrongdoing. It was actually overwhelming to me how many committees I was on and advising. Most of the Black student body was busy. We knew we had to be at every meeting to make sure our concerns were addressed. We even had to go to Washington, D.C. over the issue of the housing unit. Someone had filed charges against the university for even considering giving Blacks housing!"

One of the points of negotiation that proved to be a stumbling block involved the creation of African American Students. The students' choice for Department Chair didn't work out. "Lerone Bennett never even made it on campus as Director of Black

Studies. He did teach a course (as a visiting professor). The students wanted him, but the faculty and, even some of the Black faculty, didn't want him."

The participants of the Bursar's Office Takeover were a unit, and they were all deferent regarding accepting praise for leadership provided during the event. Kathy, the President of FMO, was no different. "I'm amazed that people are giving me as much credit for the takeover as they are. I saw my role as important, but not to the degree that people are saying. There were other underclassmen, such as Perkins or Higginson or Marianne Jackson, who could have played that role, but it just so happened that I was the elected official because Herman Cage had stepped down. I don't know how so much attention came to me other than I had the title of President. It's true that they followed me into the building, which was very stressful. If things had gone all wrong, I would have blamed myself."

Many Northwestern students and alumni wouldn't know the answer to a common FMO trivia question regarding the name "FMO Coordinator," which actually dates back to the takeover and the way it was implemented. "One of the main things that came out of the Bursar's Office Takeover is that we changed the structure of FMO, so there wouldn't be a President anymore. I remember them having a 'K.O. Day' that retired me officially. They went to having multiple coordinators and an assistant, which wasn't that different. Even when I was President, we still operated on a committee structure. I wasn't involved in everything. I might have known a little bit about things, but that's why we had to get rid of the title. We really didn't function that way, so the name changed to reflect that fact."

Kathy quickly fell back in to student life after the negotiations around the implementation of the agreement from the Bursar's Office Takeover. "I had a lot of studying to catch up on! I didn't want to be a statistic and flunk out." She really "enjoyed seeing the changes come to fruition, including financial aid, houses, and The Black House. I remember being happy when Paul Black became the Dean of African American Student Affairs."

Kathy spent much of the rest of her college days on the sidelines, even as turbulence continued to consume Northwestern through the Triangle episode of 1969 and the Vietnam war protests in 1971. "FMO didn't offer verbal support for the Vietnam protests. We didn't have that kind of relationship with Eva (Jefferson Paterson, Associate Student Government President at the time and a participant in the Bursar's Office Takeover) for some reason. She was more versatile than most of us. Because of her background, she was more able to navigate the university. She was politically astute enough to become the ASG President."

Kathryn has visited Northwestern on two occasions in the last twenty years and, in each instance, it wasn't what she expected. "I took my daughter up to Northwestern when I was doing my college search. We did not vibe very well with Northwestern for her. She ended up going to Oberlin College and did very well. This was at the time when Clovis Semmes' son was FMO Coordinator (Clovis was also a participant in the takeover)." The second occasion was during the 40th Anniversary of the takeover in 2008. "I was happy to see so many Black students, but I noticed that Asians were the dominant minority group on campus. I was taken aback by that and saw the struggle with the university transforming The Black House. So, the same struggles are ongoing.

"I'm in awe that FMO still exists fifty years later and operates much in the same way that it did then. I'm ambivalent about what some of that means. I understand they're still addressing some of the same concerns. I don't know if we made much progress if we have to deal with the same things over and over again. I am amazed it still exists. I always thought it was a funny name because it sounds exclusionary, but it's not. It's easy to see how people could misinterpret the intent."

Over time, Kathy has come to better appreciate a sense of legacy for the action of the takeover. "With all that's been happening with the 50th Anniversary Commemoration, it does impress upon me that a legacy has been viable. It also appears to me that those of us involved at the beginning should have stayed more connected with the university to support the ongoing efforts of students. I feel as if I may have abandoned the initial issues we fought for at Northwestern. There are still needs and commitments that should be fulfilled, particularly around faculty and student enrollment. We should have a greater student enrollment than what we have. Even though they've increased the minority population, we're still at the bottom of that. I know there are more numbers of qualified students than are being brought in, and Northwestern can do better. I'm sure NUBAA (Northwestern University Black Alumni Association) is more efficient than even we were, but we alumni should have more involvement in what the university decides to do."

John Bracey

John Bracey

John Bracey came to Northwestern's History Department in the fall of 1966. On one level, he was at Northwestern avoiding being drafted into the Vietnam War and taking a respite from political activism in Chicago that dated back to 1962. On another level, he was contributing to a legacy that would last even longer.

"At the graduate school level, it really wasn't very bad at all. We all had support. There weren't that many Black graduate students. There was James Pitts and James Turner in Sociology and, in History, there was Ibrahim Sundiata (Ralph Wright). Sterling Stuckey had an MA and had come back to get a doctorate. There were some

African students in the African Studies program (Program of African Studies, aka PAS), but they were told to stay away from us African Americans because we'd get them in trouble."

Northwestern is known for having the earliest African Studies programs in the nation, which was initiated by anthropologist Melville Herskovits in 1948. PAS includes the renowned Africana Library, founded at Northwestern in 1954 by Hans Panofsky; it was later renamed the Melville J. Herskovits Library of African Studies. This library serves PAS and Northwestern faculty, students, and more than a thousand U.S. and international scholars each year. It is acclaimed to be the largest separate collection of Africana in existence.

"I found out pretty early that African Studies was a State Department program, and people in African Studies were, for the most part, training for jobs in the Foreign Service. One of the students at the time was in the Congolese embassy during the assassination of Patrice Lumumba that led to Joseph-Désiré Mobutu taking power. They didn't tell us about that until after he'd graduated because they thought we might bother him, and we probably would have! So, African Studies was training straightforward liberal, corporatist, and benign imperialist types with a political science, public policy focus. Now, my outlook was Pan-African—you now call it diasporic—focusing on all Black people who had suffered in the modern world. It doesn't make any distinction about where people came from. When I came, I took almost every African history class Northwestern offered.

"To concentrate on Black people, you had to look at three areas. One was the British Empire, in which I could focus on the West Indies and Africa. Then, you had the U.S. and the American South. Then, I had, as my third field, African Americans. This allowed me to build up work on African Americans based on content from the other subject areas, and it allowed me to work on matters of the history of the world through the prism of an African American worldview. They let me do that."

A recurring theme of John's graduate school studies was the relative "ignorance" of his White counterparts, inclusive of students and faculty. Whereas, John was required to be abreast of White global historical considerations, such as colonization and American history, he would find that his teachers knew (and acknowledged that they knew) very little about African and African American history other than through the prism of a White vantage point. John vividly recalls a professor asking him and Sterling Stuckey to offer reading material to provide balance to a syllabus of a course on the American South. "It was at that point that George Fredrickson realized that what he had learned at Harvard wasn't the history of the South at all but was the history of White people. He was smart so, after that, his writings moved toward those considerations." John's evaluations became littered with comments to the effect of questioning why he was at NU because he was teaching them instead of the other way around. Still, John found Northwestern to be a very comfortable place intellectually.

It was during his studies that the undergraduates sought out John. They knew he had experience with the Black Power movement. "They found me. They came to the library and asked me if I would come to a meeting." As it turned out, some of the students had actually participated in boycotts John had organized back in Chicago. "It had never occurred to me that if I pulled out 500,000 kids from high schools in Chicago, these kids at Northwestern would be some of them!" John wasn't looking for any reason to be involved in campus activism. "I'm getting paid; I have money in the bank, so I could go to any conference I wanted, and my wife had a job in the library, so everything's cool. But, they were having problems." So, John agreed to go, and there were over one hundred students in attendance. It was at this time when John became a resource for undergraduates.

"One of the topics of discussion was the relatively new integration of the dorms." The case was that the White students who had a Black roommate could make alternate living arrangements, but Blacks who had a White roommate didn't have that option. "That was so stupid that I thought it was a joke. If we complained about having a White roommate, they told us that that was a part of the Northwestern experience and we should learn to get along with White people. The paternalistic thing at Northwestern was really, really strong." Another early consideration was a dignity campaign for the food workers in the cafeterias, where it was common for them to be dealt with in an overly casual manner by students, i.e., to call them by their first names as if they were servants more so than employees. This was also a common concern related to the maids and butlers who worked in the student dormitories. John and others sought to ensure that the methods adopted by all students to interact with these employees were respectful and appropriate.

"Still, Jim Turner and I didn't go to a lot of undergraduate meetings because what they were discussing didn't affect us. We spent a lot of time talking among ourselves. The more radical kids, Eric Perkins, John Higginson, Michael Knowles, Clovis Semmes, and Roger Ward, kept coming to me and asking me for advice about stuff, but I never ran a meeting for them. Jim and I would just spend hours standing in front of the library, talking with them. I was still doing movement stuff in Chicago, so Evanston was not my focus."

Much to everyone's surprise, during John's second year at Northwestern, he was involved in integrating a block on Foster Ave. "We got the apartment because two young White women in African Studies agreed to sublet an apartment to us. We didn't think anything about it until we had to go meet the landlord. We got there, and he looked at us like I was Jesse James! He thought we were from the Urban League, trying to set him up on housing discrimination because he didn't have any Black tenants in any of the 500 pages of listings he had.

"There were a series of incidents back on campus that we were aware of but weren't involved in. There was the episode when the fraternities were trying to get the Black women to participate in a 'plantation dance,' and the Black men were humbugging all over campus. The students would come to us when someone got locked up, and you'd have to talk them out of jail; there was that kind of stuff going on. We knew most of the Evanston Police officers by name, from Captain Scott on down. The graduate students kind of served as the peacemakers. The undergrads would listen to us because they really didn't have any other authority figures on campus.

"So, there was a steady drumbeat reflecting that this place wasn't comfortable for them. My advice to them was always 'You have to decide what you need to make yourself comfortable because the world you're talking about is not a world I'm living in.' I wasn't in crisis mode, but once they came up with what they wanted, I was willing to assist and advise. So, they came up with a list of demands. Then, I realize just how messed up this thing (their daily lives) is! The challenges of daily life were starting to eat away at them. You could tell how great the tension was. There were students like Steve Colson. I loved Steve; he was a brilliant jazz composer, but he was always into something. He was either writing the next great jazz tune or swinging on a White kid. You never knew which was coming!

"So, when the initial list of demands was ignored, I suggested to them that they should all go to the transfer office and say they wanted to transfer to a Black school. So, I think about 100 kids went over to the transfer office and said they wanted to transfer to Howard University and other places, and that got the administration's attention. At that point, Eisenfeld, who was the Dean of Students, was sent in to talk to the students. The students presented their demands, and he just blew them off."

Now, one of the demands was about the curriculum and Black Studies and, about this same time, the graduate students were having a similar dialogue with their faculty. "The head of the Faculty Governance Curriculum Committee asked us, 'Do you think there's sufficient African American literature to justify opening up the established curriculum?'" After learning what the professor's specialty was (Scandinavian literature), John pointed out that "There are more Black people in Mississippi than there are Whites in Scandinavia, and I guarantee you Richard Wright and Alice Walker have as much to say as do whatever authors you're teaching now."

"So, the kids were really frustrated, and you could sense the anger just welling up. They came to me and said, 'We've got to take over something.' My first response was 'Whoa. You might not want to do that.' The students were insistent, tired of being blown off and weren't going to take it anymore. I told them 'you figure what you want. Don't ask me and Jim (Turner) because what you want is not what we want. I don't know what you want. You put together demands that meet your needs, and I will help you as best I can to get what you want.'" Though it was ironic that John, being the activist that he was, was initially dissuading students, it was simply due to the basic concern he had about the students putting themselves in harm's way." "You see, these were a bunch of little babies. They were all first-generation college kids, and this might have been the only time they'd get to go to college. You don't know what their family life is, and their parents are worried about them. You don't do that to people. I wasn't going to just send them out there like that, falling off a cliff. I actually can say that being in a movement is a very dangerous thing. You don't want the police following you around. I was actually shot at by the Chicago Police. I didn't want these kids getting shot at. I didn't know what the White people in Evanston thought about them. I don't want them getting beat up walking downtown. So, I told them to think very carefully about the risks they were going to take. So, they had to tell me what they were going to do, and I'd tell them what the risks were, just like any movement I'd been in. Now, if they still wanted to do something at that point, then ok.

"This was the same thing I'd said to Fred Hampton when he and the Black Panthers were alive: 'If you say this, they will kill you.' So, the students had to know the range of possibilities based on various actions and not just act. These were a bunch of undergraduates, mostly freshmen and sophomores, and I told them that if they tried this, and if the university was actually as racist as portrayed, they could possibly all be expelled because if they are racist, they might not care. Now, I didn't think they would because it would be embarrassing to have all of you leave. That's why they panicked when everyone went to transfer. That made me think they didn't want the kids to go. They just didn't know what to do with them. Thus, the students had PR (public relations) leverage.

"At this point, I'm in. I'm starting to talk to people I know in Chicago—community voices—to keep their eye on Northwestern because the kids really are at the boiling point. So, community people are watching because some of the students are talking about doing some really crazy stuff that could cause an eruption, and we'd need help. So, we go to the meeting, and I say, 'Ok you can do that, but you don't just grab a building.' The students decided on the building and got the blueprint for the building. You don't just jump in a building and find out that there are no backdoors and the toilets don't work.

"I emphasized at the meeting not to tell anyone what building was being targeted. When asked why, I told them: 'There are 100 people in this room. Someone's going to tell the administration.' When disbelief was expressed because 'everyone was down,' I told them that was exactly why someone would tell. Think about this. If there were a dear friend of yours who thinks you're going to get in trouble, to save you, they would go and tell the White people. They'll go to the Dean and say, 'Perkins and Higginson are going to take over a building, and I don't want them to get in trouble, so I'm telling you.' They don't think they're selling you out. They think they're helping you! There are all kinds of ways to look at that. So, I told them not to tell anyone which building until the morning. In fact, 'call them up and just tell them where to meet.'

"Now, there were 100 people in that room, and we had to figure out who wasn't down for the event. We asked them if they'd at least be willing to just leave Evanston. We knew reporters were going to look for Blacks who weren't participating, as a means of saying there wasn't universal support, and that would dilute what we wanted to do. So, we gave everyone who didn't want to participate

$5 and sent them to the Chicago Loop to watch movies all day. People took the money, as $5 took you a long way in those days! So, we took the opposition or, at least, people who didn't want to participate out of play. The media scoured Evanston looking for a Black student who was in opposition, and they couldn't find one. We gave the athletes a free ride. We knew they were on scholarship and might have careers to consider. Especially Don Adams on the basketball team because we knew he was going to get drafted by the pros. We told them it was ok, and they didn't have to do this if they didn't want to, but they would decide if they wanted to do this. There were others who were very cautious, but eventually almost everyone was accounted for.

"That morning, we agreed to meet at an alley across from the Bursar's building. Out of the over 100 people from the meeting, there were about thirty in that alley, and the majority were females. We looked up toward the administration building (Rebecca Crown), and we saw wall to wall police. Indeed, someone told them. So, they thought we were going to take the administration building. I mean it was packed with police; we couldn't have gotten anywhere near that building. Now, at the Bursar's Office, there was a Brother who was the security guard, and there was a rotating door entrance. He's standing at the door. So, if he just pushes the slot down and stands there, the door won't turn, and we can't get in. Still, we have to get him out of the door. Some of the guys wanted to rush and fight him, but that was a 'no, you can't do that' proposition. That would take too long and, by the time you would have subdued him, others would have joined the fight. We had to get him out of the door some other way. So, we decided on the decoy thing. We got about four people and had them run full speed, screaming at the top of their lungs toward this Brother and, then, they broke toward the administration building, hoping he would follow. I didn't know if this was going to work, but it was the only thing we had.

"So, it works. Three Sisters volunteer, and the guard comes out of the doorway, looking at them, then he looks at me. I'm screaming 'go, go, go' to the students, who stream out of the alley, running past him into the building. I get between him and them, thinking maybe I can slow him down if he tries to stop them, but he never turns around. He's now standing with his back to the entrance, looking toward the administration building. As the kids are rushing past him, he's talking into his walkie-talkie: 'The building is being occupied. Please advise. The building is being occupied. Please advise.' So, I'm the last one to go in and, as I back up into the building, he looks over his shoulder at me, ensuring that everyone is in the building, and he again speaks into his walkie-talkie: 'The building has been occupied. Please advise.' Then he gives me this big grin.

"Once we get in, we secure the door. That's what the chains are for. Eric Perkins, Steve Colson, and John Higginson had them, and we chain the doors. We have everyone call their parents to let them know where they are, so they wouldn't have to worry. We made sure no one touched anything other than to put things in the desks, and we asked the secretaries to leave. We said, 'Excuse us, but we are taking over the building, and we want you to leave. If you have any personal effects, please put them in your desks, and we'll do the same for everything else. If we break anything, leave us a phone number, and we'll replace it. We're sorry for the inconvenience, but we have these problems with Northwestern.' Those White secretaries were fully in support of us. As they were leaving, they turned around and said, 'It's about time somebody shook this place up! They treat us like crap. It's about time someone stood up.' They were just smiling and giving us thumbs up. When they left the building, they were no good for interviews. They were being asked if they felt unsafe, and we heard them responding, 'Oh no. There are some nice young students who just took over the building because they had some grievances. We're just going home!' So, if you noticed, there's no footage of the White secretaries. Not a shred. Because what they said was that they supported us.

"So, we're inside the building at this point, and there are maybe forty-eight people, and there are mostly all women in there. So, the Sisters started getting on the phone and calling the Brothers. I'm just cracking up, hearing 'Where's so and so? Where's so and so?' Then, 'Hey! If you don't get your rusty ass over here in five minutes, it's over!' Then the next thing you know, here come the Brothers. They're climbing in the window and coming in through the basement!

"So inside, we're emphasizing 'Don't talk to the press until we get the building secure!' The PR piece was being handled with Jeff Kamen of WCFL radio (who later gained fame by being beaten by the Chicago Police at the 1968 Democratic convention in Chicago). I knew Jeff from the March on Washington. WCFL was the labor station in Chicago; the CFL stood for Chicago Federation of Labor. I called Jeff the night before and said, 'Jeff, they're going to try to distort what we're doing, so can I get a straight shot over the airwaves during rush hour to tell our story straight before they distort it? I can't tell you what we're going to do yet, but just be in Evanston in the morning about 7 o'clock.' He said, 'I'm there.' So, he's driving around Evanston in this radio truck until we take the building. So, then I give him a call, and he comes. He pulls up, gets out of the truck, and comes up to the building, and we open the window—we let no one in the building other than Black reporters. He puts the mike into my hand and reports, 'This is Jeff Kamen, live at the Bursar's takeover at Northwestern University, and here are the spokespeople for the students,' and we read our demands during the rush hour—complete and unfiltered. So, when some reporters started that crap about us asking for soul food and other stuff, it was clear that wasn't true.

"Meyer Weinberg, who ran the journal *Integrated Education*, called in. He said, 'Do you have a copy of the demands? I'd like to print them.' The Nation of Islam also gave us a lot of good PR, and they sent out a reporter from *Muhammad Speaks*. They were our contact with the Fruit of Islam (the Nation of Islam's security force). I knew all of those guys, including Raymond Sharif and John Ali. They said, 'Look. You're up there by yourself. If you need some help, we've got your back.' I said, 'No, no, no. I don't want the Fruit of Islam running around downtown Evanston! That's not a good vibe. However, their reporter is right there, and he has the phone numbers. He says, 'If you need any help, we can get fifty people here in half an hour.'

So, I wasn't worried about that part. Then you had the gangbanging Brothers from the South Side saying, 'Aw, man. You all have something going down up there! Can we...' John shut that down quickly, but he knew he had multiple components of an emergency backup plan.

"There was a fear that the police would launch an assault on the building in a manner in which the students could be hurt. We knew we couldn't defend the building. We weren't armed, so we would've have gotten messed up. So, there were two lines of defense. One was SDS (Students for a Democratic Society, the student organization). These White graduate and undergraduate students were kids with whom we'd interacted. They wanted to know what they could do. We asked them to surround the building, so they could form a defensive perimeter. They thought that was great. They thought they'd put their bodies on the line on the outside while we were doing so on the inside. So, to get to us, the police would have had to tromp over some rich White kids, and we figured they weren't going to do that!"

The second line of defense involved a discovery inside the Bursar's Office itself. "Roger Ward was a computer expert and was ahead of his time. Located inside the Bursar's Office, within a big bank vault, was a mainframe computer. As we were securing things, Roger sat at the computer station. When folks started asking him what he was doing, Roger said, 'this is really cool! You know what this is? These are the records for the entire university! This is the payroll and, if you hit this button here, it'll all go away!' He was just salivating over that computer. So, when the police called and said we had to get out of the building in a half an hour, or they were going to lock us up, I told them I wanted them to speak to Roger Ward about the computers. Roger proceeded to explain to them that they had a wonderful computer system, and he knew all of the stuff that was on it, and if he kept hitting the delete button, they wouldn't have any more records. The police got off the line after saying they'd get back to us. That's one of the reasons they never attacked us.

"At this point, we're getting calls from George Fredrickson and Lucious Gregg (Associate Dean of Science). Although Lucious Gregg was supposed to be 'Northwestern's favorite Negro' (by virtue of having come from the Naval Academy), and they'd hold him up as an example for us, he was suffering just like us! He'd always talk about how he had to get a new living room window every year because the White fraternity across from him kept shooting out his window with BBs. Eventually, the administration didn't want to talk to him anymore either. When Fredrickson was calling the students inside the Bursar's Office, Gregg was also providing information, including the assessment that the police couldn't mobilize enough people to remove them within twelve hours (at this point over 100 people occupied the building). So, it was clear they weren't ready at all, and the administration wasn't going to make Northwestern into Columbia (where bloodshed occurred as a result of student protests)."

Meantime, Jim Turner was late in arriving at the proceedings. "When I called Jim that morning to meet us in the alley, Jim couldn't come right away because he didn't have a babysitter yet, so he wasn't there when we took over the building. As I mentioned before, the plan was not to address the press until the building was secure, everyone had called his or her parents, and we'd gotten our word out. Then we planned to make a cohesive statement. Yet, we look out the door, and Jim is out there with a microphone in his hand, giving a talk! Everyone inside was asking what Jim was talking about, but no one knew because we couldn't hear him because the doors are closed! So, what you have on the TV makes it appear that he was leading, but he was on the outside, when the leaders were actually on the inside. He's on the outside because he was late! I love Jim, but his role in the actual takeover has been exaggerated.

"By this time, we have enough food to last a week. We have the support of the community, and White students are surrounding the building. We have an administration that's been convinced that they don't want a big mess—that's Gregg and Fredrickson convincing them that 'they don't want Columbia.' Also, they let us keep that basement window open; they knew people were coming in and out.

"We had personal stuff occurring with individual kids, which is what I was most concerned with. For example, Saundra Malone's father flew in from Cincinnati, and he was really adamant that she come out of there. That scene (of them talking through the window) was beautifully captured in the *Chicago Defender*. Eva Paterson left over parental pressure and returned. Rick Haynes showed up from the National Urban League (UL), asking what he could do. Well, there was nothing at the time, but that evolved into getting Eva on the National UL Board of Directors as a student.

"We only let Black reporters in. So, the *Chicago Defender* got in. *The Chicago Tribune* didn't have any Black reporters, so they sent a dude who was sweeping up offices (Actually, Joseph Boyce states he was the first and only Black reporter on general assignment for *The Chicago Tribune* in 1968.). The Brother shows up. He has a camera around his neck and a notepad. He crawls in the window and says, 'I work for *The Chicago Tribune*.' We say, 'BS. The Trib doesn't have any Black reporters.' He replies, 'I'm not a reporter. I was sweeping up, and they told me to go to Evanston and write a story about how bad this takeover is.' We sat him down in a corner, and our journalism majors took the camera and wrote him a story that they let him call it in to the *Tribune*. Well, he called it in, but the *Tribune* said it wasn't an accurate picture of what was going on because it was too organized and didn't include the crazy part about the soul food and fighting. He said, 'That's not what I'm seeing.' So, they ended up not running his story; the newspaper made it into that stupid editorial that was shown. See, the head of the *Tribune* was on Northwestern's Board of Trustees. One of our demands to NU was to have them back away from that editorial because they were misrepresenting us in the *Tribune*.

"Franklin Kreml was the guy we negotiated with, the Vice President for Planning and Development. He was the real deal. He had worked for the FBI. So, we had the meeting around a big table, and at the table was Kathy Ogletree, Michael Smith, me,

Jim Turner, and Victor Goode. For Northwestern, there was Dean Roland Hinz, Walter Wallace, Fredrickson, Lucious Gregg, and Kreml, who was a hard-line guy—a policeman. He had an accountant with him who had an adding machine ready.

"These were serious negotiations. Kreml said, 'I represent the President.' We wanted the President, but he said, 'No, I'm empowered to represent the institution and engage in these negotiations. What are your concerns, and why am I here? This is a matter for Student Affairs. Why am I here? Who is the Dean of Students?' When we responded 'Dean Eisenfeld,' he asked, 'why aren't you talking to him?' When the students told him that Dean Eisenfeld wouldn't talk to us, he identified him and said, 'Dean Eisenfeld, please ask anybody if they would like refreshments.' So, Dean Eisenfeld had to go around the room and take coffee and doughnut orders from everyone. He busted the Dean in front of everybody. He came back with a tray, serving everybody. Everything we responded to by saying that Dean Eisenfeld had said something, Mr. Kreml would respond with 'Dean Eisenfeld doesn't speak for this institution.' In fact, Mr. Kreml moved Dean Eisenfeld back from the table.

"Mr. Kreml advised us that some of the things we sought weren't legal, but they'd work with us on them. So, we went item by item down the demands. For example, when we said we wanted a newspaper, they responded 'How often do you want to publish it, and how many pages will it be?' He'd then point to the accountant, who was figuring out the cost. When we said we wanted housing and a Black House, they said the housing laws prohibited having a building that was confined to one race but asked if we knew a cooperative White organization that could be put on the mailbox so The Black House building could be officially integrated. So, we got SDS. They had a cubbyhole upstairs in the corner; someone came and got their mail once a week, and that was the extent of it.

"We wanted to hire faculty. Mr. Kreml responded 'I can't promise that because faculty hires faculty but, if you give me three names, we'll always pick the top one. That way the faculty will be happy.

"Everything we asked for, we got, but then he said—and he was very cold-blooded about it—' we're being tremendously pressurized by the White alumni.. They want you to be punished. They want you to be expelled. They want the school to take a hard stance against you. So, you have to allow me to be able to walk out and say I didn't yield on everything. after the pressure subsides, of course, I will stand by my word, but the *Tribune* is very upset, and the publisher is on the Board of Trustees. He's upset he had to back down (regarding the editorial). Kreml then gave a lovely speech about moving Northwestern forward into the future. We said, 'Sure, if that's what you have to say to make the deal, fine.' As long as we got what we got, that was cool. We got everything we asked for."

One item on the demand list that was particularly difficult for NU to agree to was the notion that it had been a racist institution. "What Northwestern thought they wanted to get away from was a sustained attack on them as an institution. They thought this protest would die down and, then, the institution would be able to retreat back into its normal mode of doing things. If you conduct a structural analysis of the institution itself, you'd find they very carefully set up an apparatus that allowed them to maintain control on the environment. Agreeing to things that would represent a thorn in its side forever were things they were very reluctant to do."

One consideration that the protesters were made to understand is that going from demands to implementation isn't as easy as flipping a switch. "This was all brand new. There was no blueprint. At that time, there were no Black studies programs. The course I had taken at Roosevelt was their first attempt at a Negro history course. Lerone Bennett (who was being brought in to be the first Chairman of the African American Studies Department) had never taught this kind of course. He was the editor of a magazine. C.L.R. James wasn't a teacher. He was a revolutionary. So, all of this was unchartered territory. This is why James and Bennett were designated as visiting professors.

"See, the students got their stuff. I'm thinking about what I, as a graduate student, am getting out of this deal. That involved the faculty. I thought they needed a good historical person. I wanted to dissolve the notion that these stuffy professors were the only ones who knew anything. That's why I wanted Lerone Bennett to come; he was one of the smartest Black historians in the world. He just didn't come up through their system. Lerone was still running Ebony Magazine while he was teaching. C.L.R. James came and didn't want to have anything to do with Northwestern for the long run and left to join the faculty at Federal City College in D.C.

"Actually, a big problem we had with Lerone was that he was 'jacking people up' in the classroom. He had been giving everyone C grades on the midterms, and we had to have a meeting about it. I remember explaining to him how touchy a topic it was because, even though he did have autonomy in the classroom, he was hurting the Blacks he wanted to help with the grades. Lerone kept insisting that the topic was serious, and one would have to do 'A work to get an A grade.' You have to remember, he was an editor of a magazine, so he expected everything to be precise! Grades aside, he was exactly what I wanted—a non-traditional academic who was better than a lot of the academics we had and would have elevated the performance of our students. However, it seemed Northwestern didn't want him because he had a power base in the Black community and didn't need them. So, they really couldn't make him do anything; that's what the problem was."

John points out another factor leading to Lerone Bennett not assuming the Chair of African American Studies. "You had a political split in the faculty group. Jim Turner and I had a base on the left. Sterling Stuckey was and wanted a traditional Black academic to be around, like Ron Fair, Leon Forrest, and Margaret Walker. He didn't want Northwestern to be 'Black, Black' but 'integrated Black.' He was not really a Black nationalist, although he was strong on Black rights. Our hard-line nationalist thing just wasn't him. Jeff Donaldson was on campus at the time. He was one of the founders of AfriCobra. His work helped define the Black Arts Movement of the 1960's and 1970's, although he evolved from the more mainstream style that had defined him during his time painting in Hyde Park. (In 1974, Jeff Donaldson earned a PhD in art history from Northwestern University, becoming the first African American to do so in the nation.) We all were evolving.

"So, from that point after the takeover, we had to institutionalize the agreement and start to make sure the University would follow through on it." During the negotiations that followed, the students were confronted with a decision as to how efforts to implement African American Studies would be handled. The Ford Foundation had anticipated the shifts in Black student consciousness from Black integration toward Black Nationalism. "These kids didn't want to be 'First Negros.' They wanted to be representatives of Black people moving into a White institution." The move was occurring nationally, but Ford was attempting to determine how to get ahead of and manage this change. Ford decided they don't want to manage departments, but they did want to fund programs, so if this wave (of African American studies) dies down, faculty can retreat back into traditional disciplines. They were adamant about this, because the implications of Black students choosing who to hire and who would teach them had already been studied and deemed too radical. The model for Ford's approach was in place at Harvard and Yale."

"So, they come to Northwestern with that type of a proposal as a means of addressing that particular demand from the takeover of the Bursar's Office. A lot of the initial scholarship money was basically just to bring in people 'from off the street' to calm everybody down, and the enrollment numbers shot way up. If you notice, a department wasn't a part of the initial demands. We asked for people to teach African American history, not to develop a department. Only when we began to realize that they could take it away did we decide that it should be made permanent. I didn't realize how dangerous the proposition was until we went into this meeting with the Ford Foundation. They were proposing a duel program: $5 million for an Urban Studies Institute, which would have been run by Prof. Ray Mack out of Sociology, and they would study urban problems. Another $5 million was to go toward a Black Studies Institute, for which Jim Turner and I would have been the Co-Directors. We would have had scholarship money and research money. Basically, they were trying to buy us off. The Black studies piece would have pinned us down with Ford money and doing a lot that wouldn't be political, which we wouldn't have time for because now we'd be academics who would be containable.

"When the Ford official lays all out all the money that's involved, Kathy Ogletree—she was still only a sophomore at this point—kicks back from the table, and says, 'You're trying to buy us.' She puts her beret on, pushes back, and walks away, saying 'Slavery's over. You can't buy us.' Jim looks at me and says, 'Whoa. That's a lot of money.' I say, 'If Kathy goes, we've got to go.' So, we get up from the table, and we walk out. So, we don't get the five million.

"After this episode, and with the failure of Lerone Bennett and C.L.R. James to moderate, they changed how they were recruiting Black faculty. They offered all of us jobs, but only Sterling Stuckey stayed behind. He liked Evanston in a way I never did. I couldn't wait to get back to the South Side! They really were after Blacks who weren't as radical. They wanted people who were more comfortable in an integrated environment and weren't as likely to be cursing White people every five minutes. They also started shifting their recruitment patterns. They didn't focus as much on the South and West Sides of Chicago, but now efforts were being made into the suburbs and prep schools. They were after Blacks who were less scary. They wanted faculty who would fit into the Northwestern profile."

John recalls going back to Northwestern for the 40th Anniversary Commemoration of the Bursar's Office Takeover in 2008. "We were really upset at the faculty and the administrators, who were ignoring the undergraduates. They undermined our entire presentation on what we tried to make Northwestern into by claiming it was no longer necessary, as Northwestern had already moved toward that. Then, we met with the undergraduates, who were outraged. They said that the administrators were saying these things because they were getting paid, but things were really messed up for them. Then, they showed us The Black House, and we almost cried. This place was a dump! What, they can't fix the steps? You just need a carpenter and a piece of wood in some places. This was just contempt. It seems that the students were content to accept that type of abuse. That's what really bothered us a lot."

John left Northwestern in 1970, not feeling inclined to complete his doctoral work. Since 1972, he had been teaching at the W.E.B. Du Bois Department of Afro-American Studies at the University of Massachusetts at Amherst, which he calls a "movement department."

Eva Jefferson Paterson by Eva Jefferson Paterson

Eva Jefferson Paterson

Eva Jefferson Paterson was a 1971 graduate of Northwestern University's Weinberg's College of Arts and Science. This is the story of her experience at NU.

It's August 1967. My father is home from a year tour of duty in Vietnam. I have been accepted to Northwestern and am so excited. That summer, I read an article in *Seventeen* magazine that says many sororities at Northwestern do not admit Blacks or Jews. This is very disturbing.

That fall, my parents drive me to Evanston. I remember putting many of my clothes in one of my Dad's old military footlockers. When I arrive at my room, I am greeted by a long, frizzy-haired girl from California—a sign of things to come. Later that afternoon, a very, very blond girl from Ohio joins us in our triplex. She takes one look at me, leaves, and spends the night in a hotel. She is later assigned a single room down the hall.

Later that year, I was in a reading group with eleven other Black women. At one of our gatherings, the topic of college roommates came up, and everyone had a story that took one of two paths—Black girls were either roomed with each other or there were uneasy encounters between White and Black girls— another reminder of how segregated our society was.

If memory serves me well, I went through rush week but only lasted for three houses. In the third house, I was put into what I was later told was the "goon room," the place for those the sorority had no intention of rushing. After that indignity, I retreated to Willard Hall and ultimately met the three women who have been my friends for 50 years—Susan Baronoff, Lyda Phillips, and Virginia Dzurinko. I have often joked that the four of us were like one of the groups in WWII movies—or one of those jokes people tell—the Black, the Southerner, the Jew, and the Italian.

That first year at NU was mind-boggling and changed me in profound ways. Black students—although I entered calling myself a Negro—met off campus because the powers did not allow us on campus facilities because we were not an officially sanctioned group. I remember being thrilled, walking to various venues off campus.

Over the course of that year—1967—and into the new and momentous year of 1968, activist discussions turned to political action. Led by a graduate student, James Turner '68 MA, and fellow freshman, Kathryn Ogletree '71, '76 PhD, aka Twig, there were calls for militant action.

I often felt out of place because I had grown up in a desegregated Air Force milieu, but the arguments I heard made sense to me. I was at a Student Senate meeting on April 3, 1968, when word came of Dr. Martin Luther King's assassination. Chicago and most of the rest of the country burned with literal and figurative rage at the murder of the non-violent dreamer.

A month later, we took over the Bursar's Office.

We gathered in Allison Hall in the wee hours of the morning and, then, ran over to the Bursar's office. Recently, I heard that we had friends inside the office who allowed us entry. I am sure that the statute of limitations has run out, so I am comfortable telling that tale. Once inside, I cheerfully called my parents and said, "Guess where I am?" They were not amused and told me that if I did not leave, they would cut off financial support.

I talked with James Turner about this, and he suggested that I go out and collect blankets, which I did. That felt very unsatisfactory, so I decided to become an independent person and went back inside the Bursar's Office.

Turner and Twig successfully negotiated with the Dean of Students on our behalf and, thirty-eight hours later, we emerged triumphantly. The administration had agreed to a number of our demands, including the creation of what is now the Department of African American Studies and reserved housing for African American students.

The takeover impacted me in a number of ways. The following fall, as a result of our militant stance, the university hired Lerone Bennett Jr. of *Ebony* magazine to teach a course based on his book, *Before the Mayflower: A History of Black America, 1619–1962* (1962). I get emotional by just thinking about what I learned in his class. I had no idea of the magnificent cultures that had existed in Africa. I had never heard of Benin and Kush. The thought of my people thriving in vibrant cultures still fills me with deep pride. (I finally got to go to Africa in 2017 and felt so at home in Kenya.)

This course completely changed my self-image. We also learned—and this may have not been a good thing—that we could effectuate change really quickly. I think we thought that the revolution would happen that quickly.

Finally, I became my own woman. I stayed in Evanston during the summer of 1968 and shared an apartment with two other Northwestern students at 2115 Maple Avenue.

While I was living there, we decided to have a big party, so I went into Chicago to buy a dress and got off at the wrong L stop. Suddenly, I saw a large crowd of people and walked toward them. The Democratic National Convention was taking place in Chicago that August and I had just joined the protesters. I listened to speeches and accepted Dick Gregory's invitation to walk to his home on the South Side and have a Coke.

Mayor Daley had forbidden protesters to march anywhere near the convention. Well, we marched a few blocks and, then, got tear-gassed. I was infuriated by the personal affront as well as by the knowledge that the noxious fumes would be in the curtains of the people who lived along the route and would cause them much physical distress.

Over the years at Northwestern, I became increasingly radical or progressive. One of the hallmarks of those years was the teach-in, which involved speeches and presentations outside the classroom on various topics. I opposed the war in Indochina and became a feminist because of that facts I learned in these settings and what I listened to on the news. I remember watching Richard Nixon when I lived in Chapin Hall and yelling at him whenever he told one of his many lies.

In April 1970, I was elected student body president, in fact, I was Northwestern's first African American elected as such. Three weeks later, on a Sunday, I took part in a 30-mile march against hunger in a suburb north of Evanston, if memory serves me well, and walked in wooden clogs. I soaked my blistered feet in the bathtub in Chapin Hall. Little did I know that I would spend the next ten days on my feet, but I was young.

That following Monday, four students were murdered at Kent State University. I flew to Washington, D.C. for emergency meetings with other students. When I returned to Evanston, protest demonstrations against both U.S. military action in Cambodia and the murder of the Kent State students were taking place on Deering Meadow.

When I returned to Northwestern later that week, students were gathering on Deering Meadow. As student body president, I became the focal point of the rallies. Many people spoke about the Vietnam War. A pro-war student spoke and was booed. I said, "Let him speak." Later, the infamous Mayor Richard Daley quoted me when someone else was being silenced. Yikes!

There were thousands of people on the meadow. We were appalled and frightened by what had happened. Students were killed at Jackson State in Mississippi later that week. There were iron fences lining Sheridan Road that we took down. We tried to hand out leaflets to the commuters going home, but we were prevented from doing so by the police, so we blockaded Sheridan Road. It seems strange to think of what we did back then and write them in words.

Reflecting on that intense week has made me come to the following conclusion. Many people praised me for helping to maintain calm. I even persuaded students to douse their torches and not burn down Lunt Hall, home of ROTC—the Reserved Officer Training program. Years after my days at Northwestern, I was asked to give a speech in place of someone who had cancelled at the last minute. I was dog-tired, but once I started speaking, a certain energy was created. At the end of that speech, I realized that I was drawing on the energy of the audience and feeding it back to them. I then went back in my mind to those days on Deering Meadow and realized that I am a Californian, and I was channeling the desires of those assembled. We were against the war. We loved our university. We wanted to take a stand against the lawlessness of the Nixon administration. We were appalled and frightened because students much like us were shot and killed at Kent State and Jackson State. We did not want to create more violence. This may sound ethereal, but I truly believe that that is why I was able to be an effective leader. I reflected the student body for that week.

The strike ended peacefully, and things went back to normal. That fall, I applied to law school. Well, I only applied to Yale. The school was not impressed with my nineteen incomplete units and declined to admit me.

I finished my course work that summer at Northwestern and got admitted to the law school at the University of California-Berkeley, the beacon for radical students. Well, I found that campus to be rather conservative. Black students had to sit in at the

Dean's office as a medium to admit more Black and Latino students. I graduated in 1975 and passed the bar.

Since then, I've worked in East Oakland as a legal services attorney, and I have been involved in much impact litigation, challenging racism and gender bias. My years at Northwestern and what I learned about my people and my race gave me strength to fight the good fight.

On a personal level, that old maxim that the friends you make at college will be your friends for life has been true for me. I derive great pleasure from having gone to Northwestern (which we jokingly called the Harvard of the Midwest back in the day). I drove down to Pasadena when we were in the 1996 Rose Bowl. I introduced myself to fellow Wildcat Stephen Colbert when we were both on Amtrak's Acela train on the East Coast; he was on *The Daily Show* then. I cheered for our basketball team when we were in the NCAA finals last year, and I would like to brag that the future wife of England's Prince Harry, Meghan Markle, is a Wildcat.

Returning to Evanston in May to celebrate the takeover of the Bursar's office will be great, and the attendant planning by NUBAA (Northwestern University Black Alumni Association) has been wonderful. While there, I learned that I was not the only Black student who had come from integrated schools. I wish I had known that then.

I am so grateful to have gone to Northwestern.

It opened doors for me and completely transformed my life. Being at Northwestern was a part of a transformation that many in my generation experienced. We had come from our small towns or big cities to Evanston. We were exposed to new ideas and fellow students with different life experiences. The Black student movement, the anti-war movement, and the feminist movement were all coming into their own at Northwestern. Being away from home and being able think for myself changed me profoundly.

For the past 50 plus years, I have had the honor and privilege to make my avocation my vocation as President and Co-Founder of the Equal Justice Society. Much in the way that Claude Monet who loved to paint and was fortunate enough to make a living doing that, I can wake up in the morning and read the paper or watch the news, and I can engage with the struggles of our day. How fortunate am I!

My years at Northwestern laid the foundation for my life's work. For that, I am eternally grateful.

Go Cats!

Participants in the 1968 Bursar's Office Takeover

The participants in the 1968 takeover believe that everyone within the African American student body participated in that event—some contributed from the outside, but all were supportive enough to not reveal the nature of the event. The participants are also careful to acknowledge the support of many other members of the Northwestern, Evanston, and Chicago communities who provided support in a variety of ways.

The following is an image of a plaque that was hung at The Black House on May 3, 2018 by the Northwestern University Black Alumni Association (NUBAA) in honor of the participants of the Bursar's Office Takeover. The names were selected through group consensus and their best recollections. The plaque has been reproduced with permission from Northwestern University.

Northwestern | ALUMNI
NUBAA

With gratitude to the participants in the Bursar's Office Takeover on May 3 and 4, 1968.

Your courage, commitment, and vision led to the creation of this Black House and the improvement of the existence of Blacks at Northwestern.

Barbara Atkinson Perkins Melendez	Milton Gardner	Maxine Mitchell	Sandra Small Hill
Debra Avant Hill	Rene Gay	Robert "Bob" Miller	Charles Hannibal Smith
Lee Banks	Victor Goode	Janice Morris	Freddye Hill
Andre Bell	Gregory Harper	Laura Murray	LeRoy Smith
Ermetra Black Thomas	Dorothy Harrell	Harvette Nelson	Michael Smith
John Bracey	Jacquita Harris	Barbara North	Detra Smith
Elaine Brazil	Jocklyn Harris Smith	Kathryn Ogletree	Eleanor Steele Stewart-Kay
Clinton Bristow	Leslie Harris	Carol Oliver	Ibrahim Sundiata
Josephine Bronaugh	John Higginson	Dorothy Perkins	Lawrence "Lonnie" Terry
Steve Broussard	James Hill	William Eric Perkins	Adrianne Thomas Hayward
Millicent Brown Fauntleroy	Stanley Hill	Roland Person	John Trimble
Janice Bumphus Griffin	Audrey Vicurtis Hinton	James Pitts	James Turner
Nona Burney	Adrienne Hoard	Anthony Porter (Olusoji Adebayo)	Mae Tyler
Barbara Burton	Michael Joseph Hudson	Thomas Preston	Tom Vance
Widmon Butler	Gail Hush	Christine Price	Joyce Wade
Herman Cage	Marianne Jackson	Travis Pumphrey	Roger Ward
Dorothy Carter Higginson	Eva Jefferson Paterson	Lonnie Radcliffe	Wayne Watson
Paula Christopher Kelley	Nelson Johnson	Le Easther L. Redmond	Bill West
Leon Coleman	Lillian Jordan	Cora Regulus Crider	Joanne Williams
Adegoke Steve Colson	Jinx Kenan	Sue Rhoden	Judith Willoughby
Floyd Crider	Loester Lewis	Regina Rice-Luster	Dolores "Dee" Wilson
Dan Davis	Kimya Moyo	Ronald Riley	Arnold Wright
Lawrence Dillard	Daphne Maxwell Reid	Robert "Bob" Scott	Cherilyn Wright
Amassa Fauntleroy	Charles McBride	Clovis Semmes	
Vernon Ford	Mario McHarris	Charles Shepherd	
Earl "Chico" Freeman	Herbert Melton	Janice Sims	

Presented by the Northwestern University Black Alumni Association, May 2018

B100 Plaque

The Black House / Caring for the Community

- **Milton Wiggins:** Dean of the Department of African American Student Affairs

- **Alice Palmer:** Dean of the Department of African American Student Affairs

- **Karla Spurlock-Evans:** Associate Dean of Students and Director of African American Student Affairs

- **Duke Jenkins:** Assistant Dean of African American Student Affairs

- **Jerre Michelin:** Black House Administrative Assistant

- **Penny Warren:** Director, Student Life, The Graduate School

- **Debra Blade:** Interim Director, African American Student Affairs

- **Kathleen Bethel:** African American Studies Librarian & Liaison for Caribbean Students and Gender & Sexuality Studies

- **Ce Cole Dillon:** President, Northwestern University Black Alumni Association

- **Tamara Johnson:** Executive Director, Multicultural Student Affairs

- **Lesley-Ann Brown-Henderson:** Executive Director, Campus Inclusion and Community

Milton Wiggins

Milton Wiggins

Milton Wiggins served as Northwestern University's second Dean of African African Student Affairs, succeeding Paul Black in 1974. Milton first arrived at Northwestern as Assistant Dean of Students in February of 1972, having been recruited by Dick Adams, NU's Affirmative Action Officer. During his initial interview at Northwestern, Milton was impressed by the notion that there were both university and student interviewing committees—a nod to the agreement made in 1968 after the Bursar's Office Takeover. In his capacity as Assistant Dean, Milton focused on counseling Black students, and he reported directly to the Dean of Students.

Milton worked in this capacity for approximately two years, then he left Northwestern to accept a position at Indiana University as Director of the Black

Cultural Center. Little did he know at the time that his experiences at Indiana would shape the trajectory of the Black student experience back at Northwestern for years to come. It was late in 1974 that Milton was contacted by Black students at Northwestern to come back and apply for the position of Associate Dean of Students and Dean of African American Student Affairs upon Paul Black's decision to leave Northwestern. "During my absence and as a result of the efforts of the students, the Department of African American Student Affairs was created. It had a budget and became more a part of the university, instead of simply being The Black House. It became a department inside of the university. This occurred primarily through the leadership of the first Black House Director, Paul Black."

Once hired, Milton really had three areas of focus. He wanted to build upon the structure of his predecessor, work very closely with For Members Only, the Black Student Alliance of Northwestern University (FMO), and to ensure the establishment of the Department of African American Student Affairs as an integral part of the university. "I wanted to work very closely with FMO. In fact, we had an agreement. They were strategically positioned up front and, for political reasons, it kept me out of the middle of a lot of things. We had very strong and insightful student leadership back then.

"Many of the things I implemented or attempted to implement were based on my experience at Indiana University (IU). IU was a little ahead of us in that they had evolved from the 'Black House' concept to the 'Black Cultural Center' concept, which embraced many of the academic components of the university and was further integrated into the university. It wasn't something set apart from the university. I liked to use the example that The Black House could be viewed as the sixth finger on a hand. It could be cut off at any time. So, I pushed to have it further integrated into the university structure to make it more viable. We couldn't be as effective as long as we were viewed as separate from the rest of the university.

"I really tried to create an atmosphere for students to be successful academically. At that time, every quarter, there seemed to be a big list of students put on academic probation or dismissed. Our focus at that time was to look at each individual, case-by-case, to see what we could do to get dismissals reversed or to get what was primarily the colleges of Arts and Sciences and Tech (Technological Institute) to provide more support for the students."

Having come to Northwestern in 1972, Milton came to a campus still reeling from and including students who had participated in various campus actions, including the Bursar's Office Takeover and the Vietnam War protests. The revolutionary mindset on campus "… was very much still alive. Just about on a weekly basis, we had meetings and strategy sessions. Almost every day, I'd receive calls from *The Daily Northwestern*, trying to get information about what was going on or what was the position of the Department regarding a certain issue … At times, it got really hot." Even speaker events, such as the appearances of Angela Davis or the Ambassador from South Africa, threw the university into a tailspin of energy in multiple directions for several days at a time. "Now that I look back on it, I was very proud of the students and the student leadership. They took a lot of strong positions and held their ground in terms of expressing their concerns to the university. It made it easy for me to step in and submit recommendations and proposals for certain things."

Milton notes that even during his time, not all Black students were comfortable coming to The Black House, but the Department of African American Student Affairs was able to extend its reach. In one notable example, he was able to place a staff member in the offices of the College of Arts and Sciences approximately three days a week, which worked well because most of the Blacks on campus were enrolled there and, thus, most of the academic challenges were occurring there. This type of outreach was consistent with Milton's plan to integrate services within the university structure in addition to the home base of The Black House.

The staff of African American Student Affairs was put together to meet the challenges of the day, despite a total budget of just $28,000. In addition to Dean Wiggins, he had Glen Edwards positioned in the College of Arts and Sciences. A graduate student, Alice Palmer, headed the tutorial program, and Judy Goth and Everne Saxton worked through logistical challenges for students. Milton credits his past education at an HBCU (Historically Black College and University) with cultivating the necessary environment in The Black House. "You can only do what you know! I attended an HBCU, and what that offers is an opportunity to create a nurturing environment. That's what it really got down to—creating an atmosphere. Because it's through nurturing that we grow. It's how we stay motivated. I may not have all the answers to everyone's concerns, but if I can keep you focused and motivated, maybe together we can overcome these things."

Milton draws on another critical lesson he learned from having been at an HBCU that he brought to Northwestern. "At an HBCU as well as at The Black House, your color was a positive and not a negative. So, the atmosphere was natural for me to create because that was my experience. Also, I know that Northwestern was and probably still is a very alienating environment. For many students, if they get discouraged, their grades go down. What I tried to do was to keep them focused and motivated and to encourage them to not give up."

Milton didn't feel as if there was a single definable event that marked his time. "Every day was a new issue. I'd come to work sometimes, and I remember students who had tried to commit suicide." Milton recalls an example of having to take students home to protect them from issues affecting them on campus. "There were always issues involving race. Roommate conflicts ... the disciplinary board... there were always issues." Still, Milton and his team worked hard to create success for Black students, and efforts such as creation of a Black Expo led to students obtaining careers that lasted lifetimes.

Milton left Northwestern for the second time in October of 1977 to work with the federal government. However, his Northwestern experience wasn't yet complete. He returned to NU for a third time in 1982. This time, the Vice President of Student Affairs, Jim Carleton, recruited him to serve as the Director of Student Activities and Residence Halls for the Chicago campus, where he was responsible for the needs of all students in the graduate and professional schools. "These were graduate students, law students, med students, dental students, physical therapy students, and those in the MBA program ... I was in that capacity for five years."

Milton reports that the experience of the Black students in the graduate and professional schools was qualitatively much different than that experienced on the undergraduate campus, and it was not defined by racial conflict. "It was a different ballgame altogether. I was dealing with running a housing operation and all of the other concerns of middle and upper-class students..."

Milton remains entirely committed to the notion that the ongoing sustainability of The Black House is tied to the same considerations he had expressed over forty years ago. "There has been a resistance on the part of Northwestern, stronger than I've experienced at other institutions, to embrace the concepts of The Black House and African American Student Affairs, even by some Black administrators. So, I'm not surprised that there have been attempts to eliminate African American Student Affairs and roll back what The Black House does. I used to say that whatever the resistance is based upon is so deeply ingrained in the culture of that institution that they will keep doing what they have done historically, and they will continue to try to diminish the most visible sign of the presence of Black students. What The Black House does is to provide a visible sign that there are Black students attending, and I think it's very important to keep that there. Now, the tradeoff is to have a Black cultural center, in which you have recognition of Blacks and the accomplishments of Blacks. You can still integrate the academic programs and schools under the concept of a Black cultural center. This Black cultural center can provide the same services as the Department of African American Student Affairs provided, but then you run the risk of providing not only for those students but also for all students. If you stress the cultural aspects of the Blacks and the contributions we've made, to me, that is the richness of the NU experience and the richness of the Black culture, and it's something I think a lot of people could understand."

Along these same lines, Milton is quite encouraged by the current commitments to modernize The Black House and improve the Black student experience. "It seems like that sixth finger is getting stronger!" He notes that the long arc of the history of The Black House continues to move toward a Black cultural center in function, if not yet in name.

Milton's message to the current and future students is clear. "Every now and then, I hear from the graduates of NU who were at Northwestern when I was there. They're doctors, attorneys, private businessmen, presidents, and VPs. They all have achieved, and they've distinguished themselves in a multitude of ways. What comes to mind is that there is a tradition of Black success at Northwestern University. So, embrace that tradition, feel good about it. Feel good about yourselves. Go ahead and attempt to live your dreams and hopes with regard to your academic endeavors. You can succeed, as history has proven."

Milton is grateful to Northwestern for giving him the skills to understand how to impact institutions, and he appreciates both what he was able to accomplish and the seeds he was able to plant for future success. "That experience presented such a growth opportunity for me, and I am grateful for that experience. What I've attempted to do is simply what was done for me! I have been mentored by a lot of strong Black people. I still believe that my responsibility is to help, and I've always lived my life with that in the forefront of my thinking."

Alice Palmer

Alice Palmer is a 1979 graduate of Northwestern University's Graduate School, obtaining her doctorate in the School of Education and Social Policy. Unfortunately, she described experiencing some of the same elements of angst that too often marred the undergraduate experience. "I remember when I went to one professor after I had co-authored a book, and he dismissed it as irrelevant. Fortunately, I was a grown-up, and I chuckled at him. The book went on to be quite successful!"

Little did she know that the adage about time, space, and opportunity would change the lives of thousands at Northwestern. "I started here as a graduate student, and you know graduate students always need to have extra work. I asked my school if there was any place where I might work. They said, 'Oh yeah, over at that Black House!' So, I came over and met with Milton (Wiggins, the first Associate Dean of Students and Director of African American Student Affairs), and he wanted a tutor. I said fine, as earlier in life, I had been an English teacher and had written a book. So, I ensconced myself on the third floor, and students would come in. We'd have wonderful conversations about the papers they were writing and the things they were doing. Milton would be next door listening! So, when he got ready to leave Northwestern, unbeknownst to me, he recommended that I follow him and take his place." Fortunately, Alice's rise to becoming the position Dean wasn't made just on a few conversations. She had already served as an administrator, and she felt prepared for the opportunity.

"Coming to The Black House was all one could ask for as a Black person. It's a perfect example of the forward thinking of those students (who took over the Bursar's Office in 1968) that made them insist on a building. They insisted on positions that were integral to the university as it was, so I became Associate Dean of Students, as was Milton before me, under the Dean of Students, Jim Carleton. That meant we sat at the table when decisions were made, and discussions were held when it was sometimes necessary to defend the viability of having a Black House and an African American Student Affairs."

Alice speaks pointedly to a partnership with the university that has always been needed, and it is critical for the success of the Black experience. "I deeply appreciate the enlightened leadership of Vice President Carleton, Dean Jenny Landwehr, and Chaplin Jim Avery because they never got in our way, and I mean that in the best sense. They knew that we would act with integrity and wisdom, and so I appreciate that. Those were some turbulent, raucous times on campus, and I was Dean when many of those events took place."

Alice expresses a deep love for Northwestern, born out of her experiences at The Black House. "Yes! The Black House! The interactions! Being able to be here and work with them and learn from them was amazing." She notes how much she learned about South Africa, apartheid, and the divestment movement as a result of assisting students with papers and the conversations accompanying those efforts. Of course, Alice was involved in the divestment movement on campus and, later in her career, she went on to become a part of the Chicago Free South Africa movement.

Dean Palmer presided over a Black House that the students felt was a home, and the students would interact with it in ways that really displayed the fulfillment of its vision. "In my estimation, The Black House was for comfort, organizing, and enlightenment. We were a team, and everyone in The Black House was excellent at what they did. Essie Williams was the den mother of the House. If a young person had a hard time, she'd take them home with her over the weekend. Jerre Michelin always knew what to say to get them past any struggles. Everne Saxton knew every in and out of this university, so you *were* going to graduate! And Duke (Ulysses Jenkins) was a strong male presence. That back door of his … Folks would be coming into his office through a back door without having to let us women in the front know at all! So, it was a powerful team. My role was to ensure the strong presence of African American Student Affairs was on the campus."

Alice recalls an episode during which the Black student-athletes, under the banner of BAUL (Black Athletes United for the Light), were ready to protest what they felt was improper treatment by their coach. "I remember one occasion in which the Black athletes were meeting in the conference room. I was in the next room and overheard them talking. They were debating about marching over to the administration building. I told them I didn't want to interfere but asked if they'd like for me to march with them." After expressing surprise, the student-athletes happily took Alice up on her offer.

"(Former Associate Dean Milton Wiggins) had given me some excellent advice, which was 'No matter what's happening, call ahead and let them know what's going on.' So, I told the athletes that I was telling the administration we were coming over, and it would be fine. I called Irene, who was (Vice President) Jim Carleton's secretary and the only Black secretary in the entire administration building, and I told her that we were marching on them—that we were coming to see Vice President Carleton. We marched over there. We went straight up to Jim Carleton's office.

"Ben Butler was a superb spokesperson for the issues of racism that they were facing in the Athletics Department. I also had Vernon Jarrett, who was at the time a columnist at the *Chicago Sun-Times*, interview them, and an article had already been published, so there was a bit of outside pressure going on as well. So, the next day, the Athletic Director had to step down and other changes occurred (including the firing of the head football coach, Rick Venturi). That's when Dennis Green became our first Black coach."

Another hallmark of The Black House and its leadership while Alice was Dean involved the ability to directly advocate on behalf of the Blacks and the Black experience. "When revered professor Leon Forrest initially came up for tenure, he was denied by the university under the premise that Leon didn't have the academic credentials NU thought were essential to its reputation. This opinion flew in the face of the reality that Professor Forrest's first book, *There is a Tree More Ancient Than Eden*, had been lauded by Toni Morrison who, in fact, wrote the foreword to the book. For Members Only (FMO, the Black Student Alliance) was furious and was debating storming the barricades and marching on the Provost's Office.

"A team of Professor Jan Carew, Dean Palmer, and Patricia Exum (the wife of William Exum, Chair of African American Studies) came up with a plan that the students agreed with enough to hold off on their planned protest. At that time, there were only five tenured faculty members on Northwestern's campus. The thought was to organize them, go to the Provost, and make the case for Professor Forrest. Four of the five agreed initially and, after some vigorous compelling, Professor Marcus Alexis also came around. After the meeting with the Provost, three days later, Professor Leon Forrest was granted tenure.

"The Black House was every bit as good at providing day-to-day comforts as it was in facilitating student concerns. It maintained multiple programs and supported student-led programs that reinforced its purpose and served the unique needs of the Black students in a culturally specific way. These events included working with Alpha Phi Alpha fraternity to launch the Martin Luther King symposium (which has since become a week-long series of activities) and again to create the Annual Homecoming Gala. The Black House staff hosted a Christmas Bazaar that took up two floors of The Black House. *An Evening with Our Elders* brought jazz and blues legends such as Alberta Hunter and Willie Pickens to campus and highlighted Black traditions for students to learn about and uphold. The special tradition of Sunday Suppers took hold.

"I was talking to a young woman, and she was saying to me that she'd never been to Chicago. At orientation, the students had been told to never go south of the Evanston/Chicago divide, as if it would prove deadly. So, I called a team meeting and said, 'We have to deal with this!' That's how the Sunday Suppers came about. If the students were going to be squeamish about going to Chicago, home of the great migration, the Chicago Defender, and other things, then we'll bring Chicago to them.

"In the course of that, we had Harold Washington (then, U.S. Congressman and, later, Chicago Mayor) come into this living room with those awful short-sleeved shirts! We had Louis Martin, Special Advisor to three different Presidents (Kennedy, Johnson, Carter), owner of the Michigan Chronicle and part owner of the Chicago Defender come and express to students that Black newspapers were necessary to record our history because who else is going to record your living in this world!

"On another occasion, we had Charles Peters, who was far ahead of his time in understanding alternative energy. One young Brother challenged Charles, saying one of his professors had said solar energy is only 30% effective, so why bother! Charles responded to the student by pointing out that somebody had to get it up to being 30% effective, and maybe he could be the one to take it the other 70% of the way. You should have seen the look on that young man's face. You could see the look of enlightenment overtake him. That was the power of these Sunday Suppers, plus Essie and I would cook, and Everne would bring her famous lemon teacakes, and we would feed their bodies and minds."

As to why The Black House succeeded, Alice is quite clear about the structure and organization of the Department of African American Student Affairs. "It goes back to the demands of the students from fifty years ago (at the Bursar's Office Takeover) that understood that what you had to put and maintain in place were recognizable departments and positions. Without that, we would have been marginalized. Being able to be the Associate Dean and, therefore, the Dean of African American Student Affairs allowed me to operate—and Milton Wiggins and Paul Black before me—within the context of the university in ways and with positions that they understood. That was very important to the success we had."

Alice noted how The Black House maintained its relevance both by its offerings to students and partnering with students in areas of interest. "As you recall, we partnered with the Alphas (Alpha Phi Alpha Fraternity) to start the first Martin Luther King lecture, which is still going on. We partnered with Women's Studies to bring to campus and The Black House women such as the First Lady of Jamaica, Beverly Manley. We brought Gwendolyn Brooks, who was the Poet Laureate of

Illinois, and Marian Wright Edelman. So, we were very busy in making sure that the Black students' interests were hosted at The Black House in this living room.

"Then we started the Christmas Bazaar. Essie and Jerre would go into Evanston and ask merchants to help us, and they'd crochet beautiful items that would adorn The Black House. These were the kind of things that were going on in The Black House that made it what we wanted it to be."

Alice, being an activist at heart, was challenged and compelled to leave Northwestern to assist in a Chicago initiative to head voter education and registration efforts, and she was largely responsible for "Motor-Voter" efforts, which we take for granted today. She then became the founding director of Chicago Metro's YMCA Youth and Government Program, serving as the Executive Director of the Chicago Cities in Schools Program, and becoming an Illinois State Senator, notably holding the seat which, upon her leaving, immediately became future President Barack Obama's.

As Dean Palmer sits in and reflects on The Black House, she looks around and comments on the differences in what she sees and what she knew. "Right now, it's sterile. I'm sitting in the living room, and the only two remnants are the two African pieces in the window. The mural is gone. It looks like anybody's corporate conference room. This was a comfort zone along with the rest of it, so I'm hoping that type of spirit and the way it welcomed—it always held its arms out and welcomed—will get back in here somehow.

"This is not the first time I've come back to The Black House. Strange things were going on. I remember looking at the office and seeing all types of new people in here. I asked what was going on in here, and people told me this was the 'home of the multicultural,' to which I responded, 'Oh c'mon, spare me, surely not!' You see, there's been a big push in this country to be post-racial and to embrace non-identity politics, but my term is mutuality. Each of us is prone to be who we are, and it should be a matter of pride and should be the basis and foundation of how we deal with other people—with integrity and wisdom—as we were asked to do. I don't reject that. I don't reject being Black, but I do reject being invited to be multicultural in an effort to do away with all of our differences. Those differences are profound, and if they're put to righteous use, they create a wonderful world.

"All of you were my children, and I was honored to be here and to be a part of this, to know who I am and not be confused—all of us in this House knew who we —and so we did not get confused by efforts to demean us when that came up, or to marginalize us or any of the rest of that. We said to the university, 'we know who we are, and we know who these young people are, so you come over here and talk to us. It'll be all right because we'll join forces and battle off anything that doesn't make sense.'

"The Black House makes Northwestern better because it's all-encompassing. It's culturally significant and personally comforting. It is a place that if you have questions or need help getting through a course or a tangled situation, it's here." Alice relays many episodes involving students who previously didn't think they needed The Black House, who, for one reason or another, would find themselves "coming home." Regardless of the reason, there was always someone sitting on The Black House steps when Dean Palmer arrived, ready to head up to the third floor for a conversation and/or some counseling.

Alice has a pointed message for today's students and administrators who would seek to diminish Blackness in pursuit of multiculturalism or an assimilated university experience. "African Americans don't have to be 'either/or.' We can be 'both/and.' You don't have to choose. You can be both, and you can be it all for the rest of your lives. Others will know who you are and respect that you are the best of the best and not either/or. As Duke Jenkins used to say, 'Know who you are. Know where you came from. Be proud of that. Step up.' Nothing precludes a Black student from taking full advantage of all the exceptional opportunities this campus offers. At the same time, nothing should preclude a student from being very comfortable in the place where his culture and his being are most celebrated. You are to be both/and, not either/or!"

Karla Spurlock-Evans

Karla Spurlock-Evans

Karla Spurlock-Evans was the Associate Dean of Students and Director of African American Student Affairs at Northwestern University between 1985 and 1999.

"In other words, I was Dean at The Black House. That's who I was. The formal title was a little different." It is noteworthy that Karla's position marked a significant change in the title of her position. From inception, the position had held the title of

Dean of African American Student Affairs. It is also noteworthy that she was the last to hold a title overseeing African American Student Affairs.

"I had been working at Lake Forest College, and I was referred to Vice President Carleton. He found me, and I found Northwestern! As you can imagine, my experience at Northwestern was not the same as a student's, and my experience was quite good. In those initial years, I thought I had died and gone to heaven! There were multiple Black faculty, and both White and Black faculty were quite welcoming in various departments. For example, Charles Payne came to campus shortly after I arrived; Diana Slaughter was in the Department of Psychology, and Leon Forrest was an institution in and of himself as head of African American Studies. Henry Binford in the History Department was especially welcoming. I was invited to social gatherings. I got appointed to the Athletics and Recreation Committee, which put me in a circle with the Provost and others I needed to know. I felt that I pretty quickly had access to the people who influenced policy. I was very happy. I did not come from an HBCU (Historically Black College and University), so I had never been at an institution where there were more than two or three Black faculty, so this was great.

"I really liked the Vice President of Student Affairs Carleton. Jim Carleton was basically hands-off, but he kept an eye on what was going on from a distance. I didn't feel micromanaged or smothered. At one point, he essentially said to me, 'I don't know what you all are doing over there but, as long as you keep the lid on, I'm ok with it! Just do what you do!' Plus, I had Deputy General Counsel, James Perry, whispering in my ear, letting me know when things were and weren't ok. At one point, when the students were ready to protest based on the decision to reduce African American Studies to a program, Jim Carleton called The Black House and asked if I knew anything about the protest and if I was involved. When I told him I did, he responded, 'Good. I told them not to try to reduce that department! I told them they'd have trouble!' He was very pleased that the students were not going to allow this to happen. The university was trying to do this over the summer, and students came back and hit the streets! Dean Carleton just asked that they not block the streets or sidewalks to ensure no one would get arrested. That was the end of the conversation. So that's the type of relationship I had with Jim Carleton."

Karla had a specific approach to her work at Northwestern. "The challenge of a job like this is to maintain credibility and listen to students' concerns while furthering policy objectives of the university. It was probably easier for me coming of age during a period in which I knew very keenly student protests, demands, and the articulation of student needs, and the very nature of the existence of my position. I was under no delusion that this position was created because it was a part of the tradition of the university or that the university actually understood the need for this position. It was very clear to me why I was there and for whom I was responsible. At the same time, it may have been my own upbringing, but I loved being at school! In my own heart, I felt like I needed to be guided by my allegiance to the best interest of the students, understanding that if I articulated their needs and pushed for what was necessary for them to survive, the institution would be a better place. Everything we were doing was in the interest of making the institution inclusive. We wanted to have an institution that could support a wide range of students and, at that time, we particularly wanted Black people to feel as if there was room for them to be whole and as if they were in an environment in which they could fully realize their potential. We were guided by the sense that if what we're doing is in the interest of students, the institution may not realize it, but this is going to make the university a stronger place."

Karla's success wasn't just in understanding why she was there but also in understanding how to navigate the demands of the university. Her experience with her superiors made that effort more or less achievable. "The other part of it, however, is being able to have dialogue with one's supervisor and trusting that if you bring an issue clearly with integrity, that person will understand the importance of what you're doing. I can't assure that that always works, but I did have the fortune of having a boss like Jim Carleton, who was very knowledgeable about what The Black House was there to do and what the university was obligated to be for all students. After Jim Carleton left, Margaret J. Barr became the Vice President of Student Affairs. We had a much more difficult relationship. We had many of the same goals, but she expected a much different level of fidelity to her concept of what she felt people working for her ought to be doing. She wanted to have a tighter rein and actually expected me to tell her everything, especially whenever the students were about to do something in the way of protest. I remember saying to her at one point, 'Don't you have some students on your payroll who can tell you about what's going on?' If I was thought to be a conduit for information, students wouldn't trust me, and I wouldn't be of any use to the university. I couldn't be that person. It was a difficult path to walk, and that path required me having trust and credibility from both students and my colleagues. The fidelity required was to the mission of helping students thrive in what could be an alien land, not just to my boss."

Karla was pleased to have been able to retain many of the staff members who had been present through the tenures of African American Student Affairs' Deans Milton Wiggins and Alicia Palmer. "That made my job so much easier. I really characterized the staff as a family. Only those on the inside would know the degree to which we were sometimes a dysfunctional family! We were such different personalities, but there was someone for everyone, and we all worked together because we held the students' welfare as our primary focus. I really saw my job as being the intermediary between the university and these folks, who were really working as hard as much an administrator.

"It was a wonderful place to do my work. There were so many institutions that were created and named by Black students without the need for adult intervention. I was touched and educated by these various programs and institutional mechanisms. I remember *The Ritual*. I'd never seen anything like this before, and I've told administrators at many schools about how it serves as a way for new students to come to understand the history of the Black community at their school. It brings people into the community circle and family, but it's also a teaching mechanism, incorporating oral history, so that students who graduated and left Northwestern would always feel as a part of a community. Every generation of students since the Bursar's Office Takeover has been a part of *The Ritual*. They know the dance, the joining of hands that occurred with coming into the circle, and expanding back out, and they got the chain link. It was very poignant and symbolic. It helps every generation of Black students who come to Northwestern understand that they stand on the shoulders of those who came before them and to be there as the next set of shoulders upon which the next generation can stand. It's truly a way of building community.

"Here are other examples of community. I just loved going through the editions of *the Blackboard* magazine and rummaging through student history. I was inspired and in awe of the continuous production of arts and culture that was passed down from one generation to the next. The same type of cultural expression occurred in the African American Theatre Ensemble. I appreciated the double entendre in the naming of For Members Only (FMO). We had a premedical organization called One Step Before, and we had a group pulling together the Black Greek Letter Organizations. You had NSBE (National Society of Black Engineers). It was never stagnant!

"The Black House and these organizations allowed students of every ideological and cultural persuasion to find a home of like-minded people. Even though these FMO satellite organizations were separate, if there was a controversy, everyone would drop any petty animosities and come together and let the university know that the community wasn't going to put up with whatever indignity was being put upon us. They would take whatever social insult had occurred and convert it into a demand for structural change. It wasn't just 'treat our people better' but was something tangible, such as a demand for more Black faculty or graduate students. That's what helped move the University forward."

Karla notes these changes very often occurred as a result of protests. "There may have been an inclination by some administrators to do minor things, but the speed and urgency with which progress was made was turned up in these instances. I recall an episode in the '90's during a protest when about 200 students were protesting, looking like they were about 600, and you could see a wave of red, Black, and green garb as they headed to Rebecca Crown Center. As administrators looked out, were they afraid? Some. However, there were others who had actions they wanted to advance—who were responding 'Yes!' That's what I saw happening because I was in touch with both sides, including students and administration. Some administrators would tell me, 'We know you protest every two or three years! We were waiting with our ideas this time!'"

Karla continues to emphasize the nature of community advancing the Black experience during her time at Northwestern. "The beautiful thing is it wasn't just student action. Students called upon faculty and administrators. We'd often meet privately and decide who would carry which aspects of the concerns in various manners. Sometimes, it needed to be the tenured faculty members like Aldon

Morris, or people on the administrative side, like me or Joe Webb, but it was invariably the students who would open the administration up to the need to negotiate. I have to say, compared to other schools, the level of trust between Black students, faculty, and staff was greater at Northwestern than elsewhere with regard to coming together to move things forward. There was a respect for where people sat and any limitations each had with respect to the ability to further the agenda. It's a glorious thing that the Black community could work together so well in that way to accomplish collective goals."

Karla is very clear about the role of African American Student Affairs within the greater Northwestern community. "The Black House was our little piece of the pie. I've been to smaller institutions and, as was the case here, there might be concerns about when a White or certain Black person walks into a lecture hall or the cafeteria's 'Black table' and sees what they think is self-segregation. That makes me smile. Because, as with The Black House, it's at those places that our students of color can relax, be centered, and refuel to go back out onto campus and deal with everything else. The Black House is one of those places. As one student characterized our center, it's like a country store in the center of a town—you come get what you need if you need it. Events like *A Tribute to Black Men* and *A Tribute to Black Women* are student-run events. To the extent that students needed our assistance, we were there, but it was understood that it was not for us to do for them. *An Evening with Our Elders* was a little different in that it was Duke's (Ulysses Jenkins) program, and it was uniquely sponsored by African American Student

Affairs. This program was a great learning experience and an opportunity for students to be put in touch with traditions they might not have been aware of in their homes, including gospel, jazz, and other musical traditions."

Despite the multiple levels of success had at The Black House, Karla was aware that the seeds for eliminating African American Student Affairs were being planted prior to her departure from Northwestern. "I was told what was coming, but I was also told that it wouldn't happen while I was still here. A faculty member told me in confidence that, when I left, there were plans to broaden the scope of African American Students Affairs to Multicultural Student Affairs. I told them that while it may have made sense to them, politically here at Northwestern and in the greater Chicago area, that idea didn't make any kind of sense! I was glad I wasn't going to be around for that because I knew they were going to have a hard time implementing that transformation, but the decision wasn't even a discussion. It was clear that the train was coming down the tracks."

Ironically, in Karla's current position, she serves as the Dean of Multicultural Student Affairs, but she emphasizes the unique culture of different universities and speaks about how Multicultural Student Affairs can enhance the student experience. She notes that at her current institution, in addition to the Multicultural Student Affairs office, separate houses exist for Black students, Asian American students, Latino students, LGBTQ+ students, and international students. "It's not impossible to have both Multicultural Student Affairs and African American Student Affairs together. It would seem to me that anyone at Northwestern who had a frame of reference for tradition would understand why it's uniquely necessary for The Black House to remain The Black House. You just don't do this 'urban removal' and expect support from the alumni in the face of their attachment to it. Yes, you have to find a way of accommodating new generations, too, but we want to remain who we are. It's really just a matter of increasing resources."

Karla acknowledges the role increasing Asian and Latino student populations at Northwestern, in addition to the Black student population, may have had on the move to establishing Multicultural Student Affairs, noting the decision was made to shift resources away from the Department of African American Student Affairs instead of adding resources to the new entity. In fact, she notes that the resources for African American Student Affairs never increased during her nearly fifteen years at Northwestern. "One thing to which I can testify is that the resources provided in 1985 did not increase through 1999. We just had to make do with that tiny budget. It was always a struggle, but the beautiful thing was that the Black community was always ready to deal with the struggle. It was basically what we knew. Those that didn't come ready were made ready because there always was an issue to address, and there were students who wouldn't let you forget that you were a part of a community that was not only being made to struggle but also one possessing a glorious cultural tradition. So, we adjusted as well."

Karla is adamant that the loss of African American Student Affairs as a department has to change the nature of The Black House, even in the face of a change in the university's philosophy. "I think The Black House serves a purpose in helping students become more socially and politically aware and expanding their sense of identity around race. When I look back at it, we were pitiful around gender issues, but people are much more enlightened today regarding the entire spectrum of sexuality and gender identity. We just weren't about that because we were rooted in a nationalist orientation, which was popular at that time in the country and especially alive in the South Side of Chicago. However, in terms of instilling pride and teaching to do for self, I think The Black House served an invaluable service, and it was not in contradiction with the goals of the university."

Karla speaks about how her current role as the Dean of Multicultural Student Affairs seeks to avoid the dangers of further marginalizing students and works to enhance their education. "You cannot have a multicultural focus in which one size fits all. If you're going to have Multicultural Student Affairs as the overarching structure, you have to have enough staffing and support for students whose experiences are very different. To those that say such an effort fractionates students, I'd respond that it then becomes the job of Multicultural Affairs to bring those students back together. In my current job, we have a Multicultural Student Affairs council of student government, where all of those different student entities come together and work together to ensure that events don't overlap and that they can support each other socially and politically."

In addition to the trend toward Multicultural Student Affairs, Karla had also noticed an additional trend in the services provided to minority studies, which was related to those provided services. "When I travel nationally now to professional meetings, a common topic is the nature of current university administrative leadership among Blacks. A lot of these new leaders are 'careerists.' I don't know where they're getting these people. They're often more narrowly focused on their careers than the true needs of the students. Despite higher titles and loftier degrees, they're the ones truly out of touch. They're just professionals. They're not connected. Some of their actions just aren't coming from the heart. You can get a crackerjack administrator who can win a battle but, I'm telling you, they'll lose the war.

"People in these kind of positions cannot lose sight of the fact that they are there to serve the students and a wider community of people who have traditionally been marginalized. I knew I never would have even had a job if it weren't for the students, and the people who brought me in knew that too. Back then, they figured they'd either talk to me or deal with the students. These younger professionals should know there's a student community that has some power. I can't do what I do without student support because I don't have tenure. I could be fired tomorrow. It's easier to be supported by the students than opposed by them. The students aren't going to be kicked out unless they assault someone, so they have a voice. That voice gives those of us who just work here an opening to go in and advocate for their concerns and be a bridge. So, the persons in these positions, in some ways, could be the university's best friends. It takes a wise Vice President of Student Affairs to realize that if they don't empower these staff members to gain the trust of the students, there will be a whole lot of trouble later, and the university will probably end up in the pages of the *New York Times* after a protest."

Karla left Northwestern in large part to address family matters but says a part of her never left. "I am gratified seeing so many generations of students at Northwestern doing well and making important contributions to society. For me, when I go on social media, I marvel at what everyone is doing. It just makes me cry. I'm thrilled to see so many former students rise and exceed even their own wildest dreams. I'm always claiming the students as my offspring. It's a totally emotional, non-professional response. I don't know what specific difference I may have made in any one person's life, but to see everyone thriving and so distinctive just lifts my heart.

"The struggle at Northwestern was all-encompassing, but it was so filled with love and attachment that I was happy to be unhappy! The struggle was deep, and the people with whom I struggled were wonderful. It is that same love and sense of connection that has strengthened the Black alumni association so much, and I salute them for that. The efforts continue to be needed to call a new generation of Northwestern administrators to task and hold them accountable for lifting the students and the university and not just be efficient or financially prudent. I loved Northwestern, and you're all forever in my heart."

Ulysses Duke Jenkins by Emmanuel Jackson

Ulysses "Duke" Jenkins

Dr. Ulysses "Duke" Jenkins was the Associate Dean of African American Student Affairs for nineteen years. His legacy is solidified in the memories and lives of Northwestern alumni across the world. Students during Duke's time had reason to believe they knew a lot about Duke because he shared his home, his contacts, his family, and his life with everyone, as a part of his services at The Black House.

Emmanuel Jackson is the founder and CEO of Evanston Technology Partners. He is a native of Chicago and spent his early childhood years in the Cabrini Green and Bronzeville communities. Emmanuel spent his high school years at Evanston Township High School (ETHS) where, in 1982, he had a chance encounter with Dr. Jenkins on Sheridan Road.

Emmanuel felt it a blessing to find himself in Evanston and, somehow, in The Black House as a junior in high school. "I had a speech impediment, and ETHS had speech pathology five days a week. ETHS worked with a program administered through Northwestern's Communications Department weekly and while lost on campus, I run into Dr. Jenkins." Duke was wearing his usual African garb, and he invited Emmanuel into The Black House. "We begin talking and discover that we are both from Bronzeville, love Black people, and love Jazz." Emmanuel was a student activist at ETHS and, when he would see things as unfair, he would speak up. Dr. Jenkins found him interesting. "I would spend the weekends on campus for attending programs and hanging out with the Black students.

"Dr. Jenkins' stories on views of the world, about being Black, about being at William Penn College in Iowa in the 1940's were fascinating. I learned about the world through Duke. These stories shaped my thoughts." He would end up spending three evenings a week at The Black House. "Duke helped me frame how I would live the rest of my life." Emmanuel suggests that some people don't like this story but, "after a year or two of Duke studying me, we were looking out of the window at The Black

House, and he says 'a lot of these kids won't get out of here, but a lot will. They will work really hard, looking for somebody else to make an opportunity for them. It's called a job. The world's wealthiest industrialists have one thing in common, they don't have college degrees. Most of the early industrialists never made it past high school.' It was surprising to hear Duke say that, given his education and his career mentoring students. Duke went on to say that 'college isn't made for everybody. You can decide for yourself.'" So, Emmanuel decided not to attend college.

"Duke gave me an intellectual outlet. We would talk about my stories living on 47th Street, about working since the age of nine. These conversations would shape my life as an entrepreneur and my thoughts about what my community meant to me. I couldn't have those conversations with other sixteen- and seventeen-year-olds." Duke told Emmanuel about how the world works, what we needed to do as a people, and how he could make an impact. "Mostly, I learned Black self-determination. Although difficult, I still follow those principles today!"

Duke and Emmanuel's most powerful interactions were around his stories on their trips to Bronzeville on the train. Duke told a story about being in school in Iowa and having a White kid want to see his grades. Duke said, "this White guy quit school after seeing his grades. He was cursing mad and suggesting everything his parents told him was a lie, that 'niggers were inferior,' and, 'now you have better grades than I do.'" Duke was in the Navy, and he told Emmanuel that being in the military was the closest thing to being in jail for a Black man at the time.

Duke had constant words of encouragement and endless new experiences to share with Emmanuel. Duke made sure that he and the other students knew that there were plenty of great things within Black history worth celebrating. "Duke didn't demand respect, he commanded an elevated level of respect. Never asked for it". Duke told the truth, and students were blessed to be at his feet. "Because of his influence, I have and will continue to try to make that impact." Emmanuel's new tech company offices will be located in Duke's beloved Bronzeville community.

Jerre Michelin

Jerre Michelin was raised in Evanston, Illinois and worked at Northwestern from 1972 to 2012. Specifically, she worked in The Black House for thirty-five years. Jerre witnessed generations of changes in The Black House, both good and bad.

In 1972, Jerre and her husband, Donald, had two small kids, and Jerre was looking for work. Jerre's mother-in-law worked in Northwestern's mailroom, so she went to the personnel to apply for a job. Jerre was hired in the personnel department and started the next day. Jerre was promoted to recruitment and, in August 1978, she saw the job posting at The Black House and grabbed the opportunity. "I was hired by Alice Palmer, who was the Director; Essie Williams was her secretary. Glen Edwards was the Associate Dean and Everne Saxton was also an Associate Dean." When she arrived at The Black House, she remembers that Alice was new and was just finishing her PhD, Glen was on his way out, and Everne was extremely knowledgeable but very private. She especially remembers FMO (For Members Only, The Black Student Alliance) members Paula Edwards and Spain Lashley. "I wasn't too much older than the students at that time, and they thought I was mean. Northwestern students taught me a lot. I wasn't touchy feely, but they taught me to hug and be more interactive." She thought Everne and Essie had all the resources. "They knew everything."

The Black House was a very busy place. Jerre assisted the students with newsletters and facilitated Career Day. "During the month of February, one of the Deans would be in contact with different companies that were interested in hiring students. We would collect resumes from students and set up interviews. I thought it was a great program. We only did it a couple of years before we had a problem with placement." Jerre continued to print a newsletter with career opportunities and compiled the information for students "until the Directors asked me to stop." Jerre planned a Summer Academic Workshop (SAW, a new student preparatory and orientation program), Kwanzaa programs, and a Christmas Bazaar. For the Bazaar, she and Essie "would invite vendors to come in, charge them a fee, and they would sell their items. The money we collected was put in an account for student travel to conferences and other activities."

The Black House also contained information about every Black student and those students on probation. "We had a file card system for every student. The green dot meant the student was in good standing, the yellow dot meant caution, and the red dot meant you were in trouble. We sent letters to the students to set appointments to meet with the Deans." They had a directory with all the Black students' names, addresses, home addresses, and phone numbers, and they were also in charge of giving students their grades. "Someone must have misused the information, so that was discontinued."

Students sometimes misused the resources of The Black House as well. Jerre remembers a football player bursting into The Black House, requesting someone in there to type his paper, "so we did it." From that point on, she and Essie would be typing papers. It took some time, but The Black House paper typing came to an end. "Students would wait till noon to tell us they needed a twenty-page paper by 4 pm, so we had to stop that, but the students really appreciated it."

While at The Black House, Jerre worked for Alice Palmer, Karla Spurlock Evans, Glen Edwards, Duke Jenkins, Everne Saxton, Debra Blade, Coretta Cook (who became the first Director of Multicultural Student Affairs), Charles Osiris, Derrick Wilson, James Britt, Shana Cooper Gibson, Shadra Smith, and Charles Kellom. "I couldn't keep up with the title changes from Dean to Associate Dean to Director to whatever exits now. I'm not sure."

Jerre attempted to encourage hundreds of students in her capacity. Many made impressions on her. "We had one work-study student who was quiet and a good student, but something changed in her. She started looking ill, then there was a clear decline. She said she could hear the frat boys talking about her through the walls. I took her to Searle (health service) for some counseling. I got a couple of students to stay with her at The Black House because she wouldn't go home." For some time, she didn't know what had happened to the student for some but, later, found out she had graduated from another university and is now doing well. These types of students stay in Jerre's heart.

Jerre saw a multitude of concerns, but she says that what she saw most was relationship issues. "Sometimes, it got to the point where relationships would take over everything, including the schoolwork." Jerre recalls another student who was a devastated by her boyfriend of three years. "The boyfriend, after being an SAW counselor, found a new interest and 'did a number on her.' At the time, I understood how she felt because it was her first boyfriend, but I couldn't get her to understand that this would pass. I had to take her to Searle to talk to a psychiatrist."

Jerre realized early that she had to be a counselor. "The Black House was a place where students could come to us to talk and vent. We would give them money if they needed it or food if they needed it. They don't want you to tell them what to do but just to listen." Jerre had actual work to do, but the students never realized it. She learned how to listen and do her work at the same time. "Dr. Tamara Johnson saw the students sprawled on my floor and decided I needed a table in my office, so students could come in and talk to me." She recollects that many male students would mention issues involving the campus police. "The guys would come in and say that they were picked up by the campus police and taken to the Evanston Police Department for no reason. They didn't really complain about it. They mentioned it but didn't complain." She says that even her grandson would end up having issues with the Evanston Police, which he never discussed with her until he was an adult.

Essie Williams had the biggest positive impact on Jerre's time at Northwestern. "Essie had a fantastic relationship with the students. The students called her Mama Essie. She schooled me on how to manage the office and who to talk to in order to get things done. Essie retired and, then, passed away in 2002."

Jerre was already working in The Black House when Dr. Ulysses "Duke" Jenkins arrived. She found out they shared May birthdays (Jerre's was May 21st and Duke's was May 9th), and the team knew there was going to be a powerful change for the better upon his arrival. Every morning Duke would come to her office for a pow wow. "For about thirty minutes, we would discuss what was happening during that day, what happened the day before, and what was going to happen in the future." Jerre notes that Duke was "super-intelligent" and a forward thinker. "Mr. Jenkins was a wealth of knowledge. He knew about Africa and other countries, and students gravitated to him. He always had a room full of people. In the summer, even the football coaches would bring him gifts and trinkets." Duke was different, and he made The Black House different when he arrived. "Duke would eat raw garlic, he was friendly, and he could diffuse any situation."

Dr. Jenkins knew people from all over the world, and, of course, he knew the Chicago elites. "He knew musicians, politicians, and other leaders, and he brought them to campus to talk to students." Duke was a faculty associate at Jones Residential College, where he had lunch privileges, and he would always take students along with him for lunch. At lunch, with programming and while counseling, Duke kept students aware of what was happening to Black people in the real world. "I was so upset when he got sick and wasn't there anymore He impacted a lot of people; Duke was one of a kind."

Jerre doesn't remember a lot of faculty frequenting The Black House, but Professor Leon Forrest was one of the first faculty members she met. "He and his wife were full of knowledge, warm and fuzzy, and very easy to talk to." He was a grandfatherly-like figure to her, other staff, and many of the students. "He didn't seem like a professor. He had jokes! He wasn't stiff or rigid."

There were so many responsibilities to Jerre's job, but she enjoyed every single one. She loved working Kwanzaa events and Harambee. "I learned so much about Kwanzaa from the students, and I loved how Harambee brought everybody together." She remembers the university terminating a lot of services The Black House created, even when so many employers and influential people came to The Black house to recruit Black students. "It got testy when African American Student Affairs turned into Multicultural Student Affairs. The Black House had been for Black students for so long, and now here comes other groups." She remembers White kids coming in and getting candy from her desk. Jerre would say to herself, "This is not your candy!"

Jerre notes that the buildup to the transition to Multicultural Student Affairs was an especially negative experience. She liked Coretta Cook personally but knew by 2009 or 2010 that "Coretta Cook was trying to take The Black House into a different direction. What was most discouraging was when she took the mural down!" It was the symbolism of the first Director of Multicultural Student Affairs (MSA), who happened to be Black, taking down the historic mural of Black icons from the wall of The Black House conference room that planted seeds of discontent in many within the Black community with Multicultural Student Affairs and validated fears that MSA was meant to eradicate African American Student Affairs as much as support students.

Jerre recalls returning from summer vacation, walking into The Black House, and seeing a purple wall instead of the mural. Coretta said the mural was damaged, although she had never mentioned it to Jerre before. "The mural had been damaged some time before, and Karla Spurlock Evans had it repaired so I knew it wasn't damaged." Jerre thought to herself "now, what?" She knew the students would be upset because they always thought that if something were to happen to The Black House, it would happen during the summer; that has always seemed to be the pattern. She remembers telling her husband, "We've got problems now!" Then, Coretta stopped talking to the students. "She got upset with me about making an appointment for her to talk to a student. I knew that was the beginning of the end."

Jerre's impact on Northwestern and NU students is huge. Jerre has sent a treasure trove of papers and artifacts to the Northwestern Archives. She knew she wanted to preserve what happened and what was happening in The Black House. "Some things were buried, but you could find information on The Black House in the archives, including the mural." She sent essays from Duke Jenkins, materials from students, and unique pictures. Jerre knew that helping and listening to the students and staff was the most important part of her career at Northwestern. "People tell me that I had an impact on them, but I don't see it. I was doing what I normally do." Students, faculty, and staff are still in touch with her. "Former student Patty Mosley still attends church with me, many students visit me during homecoming, and I keep in touch with Duke's son, Dr. Chuka Jenkins."

Jerre hasn't been to The Black House since she retired. She knows things are changing rapidly. She heard about the Vice President of Student Affairs Patricia Telles-Irvin's attempt to further re-appropriate The Black House in 2015. She knows The Black House is a shell of what is was. "Change is not always bad, but I drove down Sheridan Road and saw the sign outside The Black House that simply read, 'The Black House.' What happed to African American Student Affairs?" She doesn't like the direction the university is heading toward, so she has not returned." She doesn't find the result of a judgment that her life's worth is deemed no longer applicable appealing enough to see up close. However, the spirit of her work lives on in the thousands of alumni who appreciate and love her.

Penelope "Penny" Warren

Penny Warren

In the discussion of faculty and administrative legends who have served on the campus of Northwestern University during the fifty years since the 1968 takeover of the Bursar's Office, you won't go too far down the list before you tick off the name Penny Warren. Penelope ("Penny") Warren was the Director and the then Assistant Dean of Campus Life and Student Affairs of The Graduate School (TGS) at Northwestern University, and she worked at NU for thirty-four years, between 1983 and 2017. It was in 1985 that Penny started working as the assistant to the Senior Associate Dean for Student Affairs (who oversaw minority affairs) at TGS. In this capacity, Penny oversaw the challenge of growing and cultivating a normalized, yet culturally-sensitive environment for what were forty minority students in 1985 and has since grown to well over four hundred students across sixteen departments and programs of The Graduate School at Northwestern.

"When I started, we didn't have anything. There were no recruiting materials. There were no fellowships. We didn't have any literature. It was a blank slate. What happened in 1986 was that the Senior Associate Director in The Graduate School (Leila S. Edwards) asked me to put together a packet (regarding issues around minority students) and present it to President Arnold Weber. So, we gave him ten points, and we said these are things we're going to need if we're going to have a minority affairs operation out of The Graduate School."

The list of recommendations was submitted without taking action and, then, "In the fall, the graduate students just happened to protest their conditions. They were asking for more minority students, more minority faculty, and more we need, we need, and we need!" It was at that time, the President recalled that he had actually been given a proposal with many solutions to many of the issues being raised, and he moved to implement Penny's initiatives. Penny laughs as she says, "That is why I always encourage the students to keep protesting, to keep their issues in front of the administration because you never know when something will click!" Thus, The Graduate School's Minority Affairs Division was implemented out of student protest, after being conceived with thoughtful prior planning.

Penny cites this initiative as immediately making the university better. "We needed this. We needed a relationship with the minority-serving (schools and other) institutions across the south and elsewhere. We need institutions here to recruit and compete." This competition was also necessary at home, in the effort to recruit Northwestern undergraduates into The Graduate School.

Penny was also instrumental in the development and implementation of The Graduate School's Summer Research Opportunity Program, which began in 1985-86. This effort extended Penny's reach (and legend) beyond The Graduate School and across campus, as she now became known for providing opportunities and career counseling to undergraduate students as well. The undergraduates usually were well aware of the prowess of Northwestern's professional schools (such as the Kellogg Business School, the Pritzker School of Law, and the Feinberg School of Medicine), but they might not have been inclined to consider the career paths that could be accessed through graduate school. "Even though they went to class every day and interacted with their professors, for a lot of students, the thought of how they became their professors never crossed their minds." Penny cites with pride the example of Makola Abdullah, who is currently the President of Virginia State University and, at age twenty-four, he had become the youngest PhD graduate of the McCormick School of Engineering. She recalls Makola's involvement with The tutoring program at The Black House after being recruited to Northwestern's The Graduate School from Howard University. Through his interactions with the undergraduates, he helped them develop an interest in graduate school, as he earned his PhD from McCormick School of Engineering.

Speaking as a positive contributor to the Black student experience, Penny emphasizes the importance of creating awareness about The Black House and other university resources for students of The Graduate School. She says it was always a good thing for graduate students to interact with the undergraduates, as it offered the vision of additional professional opportunities for the younger students and enhanced social options for everyone. Penny gleefully recalls how undergraduates would perk up and take notice when they'd learn they would be paid to attend graduate school, compared with having to pay to attend medical or law school.

All these considerations played an important role in the development of the Black Graduate Students Association (BGSA) at Northwestern during the mid-1980's. With so many disciplines and departments in The Graduate School, the BGSA created an important vehicle of fellowship, peer mentoring, financial assistance, and career opportunities, which was largely accomplished via their annual conference. Of course, Penny was instrumental in supporting and developing the BGSA since the beginning.

As a part of their conference's closing banquet, the BGSA used to give Penny a Service Award every year. In 2002, the BGSA created a Service Award in Penny's name and awarded it to other university faculty and staff who exemplified the dedication to service honored by the award. In 2017, fifteen years later, the award was given to Penny. The cycle was now complete. Penny told the students that she hopes in future years, someone else's service stands out in a way that is worthy of receiving their recognition.

When speaking of her legacy, Penny points squarely at the thousands of students she was able to support and the success they achieved. "I think that's my legacy. The people I worked with—I felt like I made a difference in their lives." Penny's enduring message to today's and tomorrow's students is to work and fight through the criticism inherent in The Graduate School's climate. "Look. You deserve to be here. You worked to be here. You were the kids in first and second grade, then elementary and high school to who everyone's parents pointed and said, 'be more like them!' You were the achievers. No matter what's going on in your lives at the moment, or with any struggles you may be having with a specific professor or your dissertation, you want to keep that in mind."

In looking across the entirety of her time at Northwestern, Penny raises a particular, ongoing challenge regarding Black males among students, faculty, staff, and administrators. She states that even in the face of a ten-fold increase of minority students across TGS during her thirty-plus years at NU, the absolute number of Black males remained approximately the same. Among undergraduates, the female to male ratio approached 3:1. At the same time, Penny expresses hope for improvement based on the recent influx of Black male administrators throughout

Northwestern, notably including Associate Provost for Diversity and Inclusion, Jabbar Bennett (the university's Chief Diversity Officer) and the Provost (Jonathan Holloway) himself.

Penny recalls the amazing level of talent that existed at Northwestern during the first few decades after the formation of the Department of African American Studies and offers a challenge to the Associate Provost for Diversity and Inclusion (Jabbar Bennett) to further enhance the current environment, such that today's generation of Black academic giants will again flock to Northwestern. "One of the things he's in charge of is faculty recruitment and development. TGS usually approves individuals when the departments have gone out and completed a faculty search; we'll approve whom they've brought in. We're at the end of the process. We need somebody at the beginning of the process when these departments are actually doing the search, to be there to say, 'Who is it that you're searching for? How many minorities are in that pool? Have you reached out to those minorities?' We need to work with the departments to go out and do this work as we recruit new faculty."

In 2017, the restructuring of the Graduate School as well as the university's diversity initiatives to embed specific diversity officers in each of the schools led to Penny Warren's departure. "I had a good thirty-four year run at TSG, and I enjoyed coming to work every day. I know life is change, and change is constant. Regarding the restructuring, I wasn't consulted, and I wasn't a part of that. It was brought to me about a week or so before the final date of my leaving. Most of my final time was spent talking to those who would be attempting to fill in my position, so the students wouldn't suffer. If I wasn't going to be there, I wanted to be able to tell these students to whom they could turn. I don't have any regrets about the Graduate School and working there and even leaving—that was done above my pay grade. I loved my work at Northwestern."

Penny remains smiling and humble about her role on campus, including the void that has been felt in her absence, but it is true that those who are a part of the Black experience in and out of The Graduate School owe her a huge debt. Having built the infrastructure for navigating The Graduate School and having seen so many students through that same process for over three decades has earned her a well-deserved spot in the hearts and minds of the students and the university itself. Ultimately, Penny Warren became more of an institution within Northwestern than a member of the administration, and her departure created more tears than she was made to shed.

In 1995, Penny was awarded employee of the year. Her nomination packet consisted of a compilation of hundreds of appreciation letters from students she had helped over the years. Penny recalls this as being a truly humbling experience. Here are a few representative thank you and goodbye notes from her past students.

- Penny, you continue to be the kind and beautiful person I know and respect and are always putting the needs of others first. You are a living testimony of selflessness.

- You have left your magical fingerprints on so many lives that will never be the same. Oh, how I loved SROP and working with you!
- I wanted to let you know how much Angie and I appreciated your support while we were at Northwestern. It was not always easy there; we were sometimes short on funding, and our family growth and degrees were on different timetables. It all worked out well in the end, thanks to your constant support. We could not have done it without you.
- Thank you again for looking out for us. We will try to follow your example.
- Penny and so many others like her continue to demonstrate that the services offered to enhance the Black student experience, whether in The Black House or otherwise within the realm of the Office of Institutional Diversity and Inclusion, work best when offered by individuals for whom the work is more a passion and a life's calling than a job. The difference is palpable.

Debra Blade

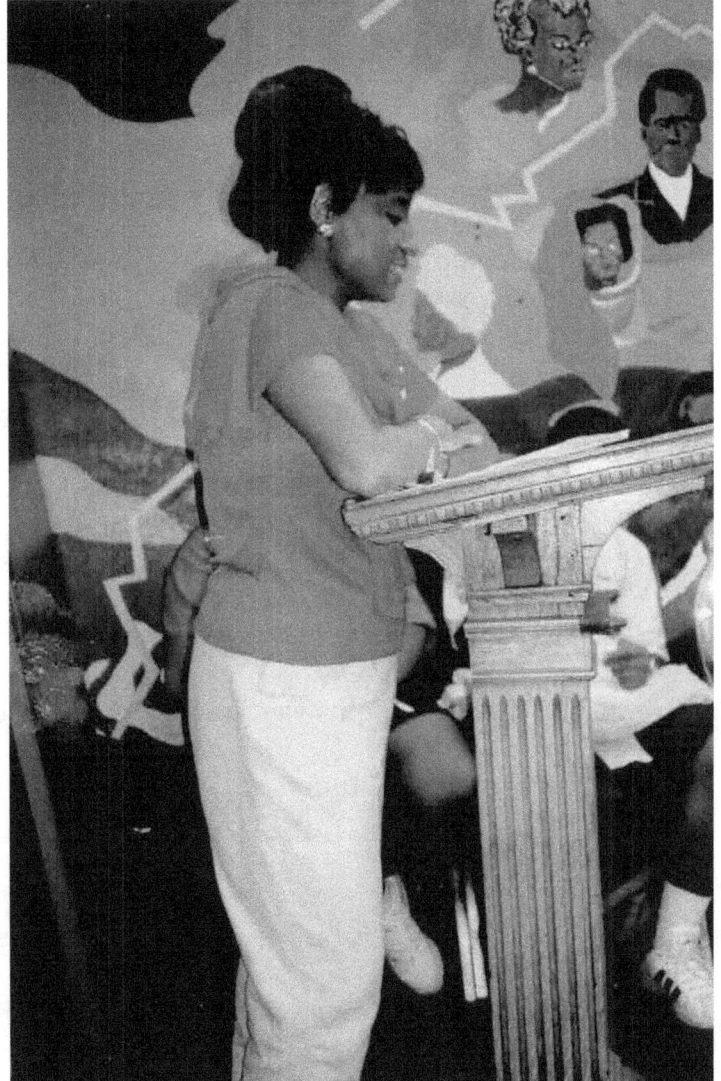

Debra Blade

Debra Blade is one of the few alums to have worked at Northwestern continuously since graduation. She graduated from the School of Speech (Communications) in 1979. Debra has been managing students and departments at Norris Center, Northwestern's Student Center for almost 40 years. She has served at Northwestern and Norris Center as Cone Zone Manager, Student Services Manager, and Assistant

Director and as Interim Director of African American Student Affairs. Debra's jobs included caring for the community that she was a member of just a couple of decades earlier. Debra has dedicated her career to Northwestern students and unpacks the administrative point of view on Black students at NU.

Debra talks about how the campus environment has evolved to produce different experiences for Black students from the 1970's to today. "Milton Wiggins was the Dean of African American Student Affairs when I arrived in 1975, and the Black Community was an exciting and nurturing environment." The 70's era fostered unification for Black people generally. "By the mid 1980's, Black students began to look outside of that cluster of The Black House, outside of culture for social life and experiences on campus, which I thought was great." Today, Debra doesn't see the same level of unification among Black Students.

Reflecting back, Debra acknowledges some fractures within the Black students in her day. "There were a few Black students who did feel isolated from the nurturing Black culture I found. Those students who might not have been heterosexual did not feel the same embrace." Black straightness was the definitive Northwestern culture that was firmly entrenched "and, in hindsight, I feel really bad about that."

Debra recalls the cliquish nature of life at Northwestern. "It was difficult for me as one of the few Black students in the Theater Department. I was in two communities—the theater community and the Black Community. I was either here or there. Northwestern becomes tribal—you join a tribe and stay in that tribe." Debra jokes that the theater tribe was abused by many other Northwestern tribes. "The engineering students would tell us that we had it easy and that we didn't have to study. Then, they'd come to the theater productions and tell us how bad it was! I would think, 'Well, you only paid $3.00 to enter, what did you expect!'" Debra declares "it was so hard for us to create productions for an ungrateful campus!" Still, in the 1970's, the theater productions would be packed. "The athlete tribe, The Black House tribe, and our other tribes would support the theater tribe! They would complain, but they would come out!"

Debra enjoyed her time at The Black House. She was appointed to The Black House in 1999 as a change agent. She knew it was going to be a lot of work, and some order was needed. "I felt that Black Students and The Black House generally deserved better. I cleaned it out, got new carpets, new furniture and generally made improvements." Debra would walk through The Black House at 7:30 am to check conditions and was critical of the students and visitors who wouldn't respect the building. She wanted students to relax but reminded them they are young adults and "to keep their shoes on because no one wants to smell their nasty feet." She moved the TV to the basement and created a lounge, so students could hang out and have fun. "I sponsored 'Brother Ed's Movie Night' that featured Blaxploitation films. That was really popular!

"I wanted to develop The Black House as a landmark. I wanted it to have landmark status at Northwestern." Debra reinstituted the African American Student Affairs Advisory Board, which included all cultures because "I wanted Northwestern to give us more money. It was a fight. I also wanted the artwork to be stellar and documented." The Black House has a great collection of African American artists' work, including Varnett Honeywood (whose work was displayed on the Cosby Show), Margaret Burroughs (artist and founder of the DuSable Museum), and many other nice portraits by other painters. "I wanted a sculptural piece to be featured on the staircase landing." Debra says Karla Spurlock-Evans did a good job of getting the artwork, "but there was no curation, maintenance, and no attention was brought to them."

Leading The Black House as an alum did have special meaning for her. "I loved it, but I was criticized by many people in Student Affairs who suggested that I wanted to take them back to the '70's." She wanted to put the energy and life back into the House with fun programs. Debra brought back the "Sunday Suppers," a program that Dean Alice Palmer had created. "'Sunday Supper' was a program that brought prominent Black alumni back to campus for dinner and discussion with students." Debra thinks she may have over programmed, but kept data on support, attendance and expenses qualifying the success. "Blacks and Whites criticized that I shouldn't forward numbers. They suggested 'that type of documentation is very westernized' and noted that the previous director never submitted hard data." As an alum who had already worked at Northwestern for twenty years, she knew what would drive the stability of The Black House—data. "NU likes data: 'show me the outcomes.' Previous annual reports had the same types of programs, the same type of pontificating; I had to justify the fight." Debra proclaims and warns that The Black House is like every other program at Northwestern. "The Black House is not operating like Hillel (Northwestern Center for Jewish Life). African American Student Affairs is just a line account. Someone could say we don't want to do this anymore, and you're down to zero."

Kathleen Bethel

Kathleen Bethel

Kathleen Bethel has been serving as Northwestern University's African American Studies Librarian since 1982. As both the field of African American Studies and Northwestern students evolved, so did the role Kathleen played in the lives of faculty, staff, and students. Kathleen is currently the African American Studies Librarian and Liaison for Caribbean Studies and Gender & Sexualities Studies. She has become one of the nation's scholars to know about the topics at hand and has served on the Board of the DuSable Museum as well as been a member of the NAACP, the Association for the Study of African American Life and History (ASALH), and the Black Caucus of the American Library Association Literary Award (BCALA) and is an official bibliographer for the Toni Morrison Society.

Kathleen always wanted to work in Black Studies, and librarianship seemed to be the way forward. She worked in a predominantly Black community at the Maywood

Public Library and then, at Johnson Publishing Company. When the Northwestern position became available, it seemed extremely enticing to her. "I had the undergraduate coursework. I had the experience. And they gave me a shot."

Kathleen never found working in Black Studies at a predominately White institution a challenge. There is a community of Black Studies Librarians in Chicago and thus, she didn't feel isolated. She enjoys the fact that at Northwestern, it's not just Black students and Black faculty researching in Black Studies. "That's not the experience here at all. It's infused throughout the curriculum and not just always the Social Sciences and Humanities." She notes that she has NSBE (National Society of Black Engineers) members frequently interested in information, statistics on their industry, and on recent scholarship.

Kathleen arrived at Northwestern in 1982 and immediately bonded with Black scholars and other Black administrators on campus. She spent a lot of time with Alice Palmer, who was the Dean of African American Student Affairs, Duke Jenkins, and Everne Saxton at The Black House. She loved Leon Forrest (the Chairman of African American studies), professor and writer, Jim Pitts, alum and professor, and Professor Sterling Stuckey. "It was a fabulous cohort of folks all over, including even Joyce Hughes down at the law library. Everybody was very welcoming, and there was a real sense of community here."

Kathleen points out that both administrative and student community outreach was strong. Black student groups were constantly programming. "From Northwestern Community Ensemble to Black Folks Theatre, there was always activity. Also, folks coming to NU from the African continent were a constant occurrence. There were some fabulous parties, and the social life was big." This trend was consistent with Northwestern having one of the oldest and most prominent programs of African Studies in the United States.

Kathleen reflects on some of the negatives of the era as well. In the 1980's and early 1990's, there were Africans who attended Northwestern that found it difficult at NU. She refers to Njoki Kamau, a twenty-five year employee of the Women's center. Njoki came to Kellogg as the only African woman student and didn't make it through. "Unfortunately, they weren't ready for her—Kellogg was essentially not ready. They weren't ready for what she was interested in. They weren't ready with her manner or her writing. They just weren't familiar." In Kathleen's estimation, changes came about in the late '90's into the 2000's. "I think some things changed for the better, even though I'm not sure that institutional racism really ever got uprooted."

Kathleen recalls that racial incidents did cause the community to respond. "In response to police harassment of a faculty member's husband on campus and the fact that many staff felt that they were training Whites, particularly White males, to come in and take jobs ahead of them, the Northwestern University Black Women in

Action to form." They set up conversations with campus police and University personnel, and they met with a number of groups and shared their concerns. Even though some concerns were addressed, many were not, and this led to the formation of a larger Association of Northwestern University Women. They hoped that this larger initiative might answer concerns quicker and with more sincerity. Kathleen is hopeful, but after working at Northwestern for over thirty years, she sees discouraging patterns. "We hear it when police still stop students on campus. We hear it when people aren't getting jobs. We hear it in the training."

Kathleen's deepest connections have always been with students, and she considers the bonds among Black students at Northwestern as having been one of the strongest she has ever seen. "It really was a community." Kathleen grew up in Washington D.C. at a time when other Blacks spoke to each other, and all Black Northwestern students were "the same" in the community, despite nuances in identity. She credits African American Student Affairs in their orientation for incoming Black students. "They told students to speak to the housekeeper, speak to the janitor, and to speak to the faculty and staff. So, walking across campus, you always spoke. Students today don't speak." It's a different era and atmosphere with the current Black student population in her assessment. "They're otherwise engaged with technology, and they may even look away." Kathleen explains the behavior to their upbringing. "It may be a holdover from segregation. the majority of students are coming out of White high schools and have White experience. They don't even have an experience of being in a Black community and perhaps are not even members of a Black church." She doesn't believe that was the case for the majority of students in the '80's and '90's. "I kind of miss when everybody spoke on campus. It was a nod, it was a 'hello,' that kind of thing." When she would see a Black student in the library, they would look up, speak, and she would ask how they were doing or discover how she could help with their studies. Now, she can't even get their attention. "Northwestern has Nigerian students, urban students, Californian students, student-athletes, LGBT students, and it's not just any kind of monolithic Black student group—which it never had been. However, the shared experiences had been more common than the different experiences that the students here have now. I miss that absence of unity."

Kathleen laments the changes to The Black House and the direction of African American Student Affairs. When Kathleen began working in the 1980's, she was barraged with students in her office daily. "I can't begin to think of the number of times students came and said, 'Duke told me to come see you' or 'Dr. Palmer told me to come see you.'" She hasn't had a referral from The Black House in a long time, not even out of Multicultural Student Affairs. "There are referrals from individuals, and certainly, the professors like Carol Lee or, before they retired, Darlene Clark Hine and Sandra Richards, but I'm not hearing it when the students are contacting me."

Kathleen reasons that the decline is due to improvements of technology. "Northwestern and the world have software that allows students to be guided remotely. They don't have to come to my office to find out about Black newspapers anymore." Northwestern students are scholars, but she knows that many are just Googling their work. Kathleen is proud that the library and archives have invested in many physical and digital resources and unique items in their collections that would enhance the studies of all students. "Students become disconnected from the research experience as well." She sees this trend as a tragedy for the Northwestern intellectual and certainly, the Black Northwestern scholar.

Kathleen has seen the rise and fall of the Black student population over the last thirty years. "I'm having a hard time understanding why the numbers aren't better. When I look around campus, I see the efforts and improvements in other minority populations. They are here and Blacks are not. I don't know what to make of it that we can hover around this low population percentage for so long."

Additionally, Kathleen is troubled when big speakers come here and the rooms are not overflowing, especially for popular Black speakers. She considers it as a missed opportunity for young people to personally meet and interact with greatness. "You name them and they've been here. The folks from our history books who come here, come here with connections." Kathleen again blames improved technologies, at least in part. "With technology and the ability to see someone's lecture at any point in time, the students become disengaged." She notices the demands and diverse interests that students have. "You almost have to be the very hot topic, the latest thing, to get any sort of attention." She recently saw that Ta-Nehisi Coates, a popular Black writer, lately drew a huge group, "but he's been here before with much smaller audiences. There is just so much available for students and not just at Northwestern, but in the Chicagoland area. Plus, there are so many activities on campus." In the 80's and 90's, Chicago had a couple of Black theater companies working. Now, Black productions are everywhere, and student productions can't compete. The kids don't have the theater spaces or access. "Students used to use the Shack (Shanley Hall) or area churches. I'm not sure if the Northwestern Community Ensemble is drawing a big crowd like they used to, but over the years, I've seen crowds."

Kathleen's name is mentioned by alumni across the globe when they reminisce about their time on campus. She was aware of the impact she was having on kids. Her first office was an open-office setting, which was a shared space in the library. She shared it with two other people; the space had no windows. She detected that it was hard for the students to have the conversations they wanted to have. "They wanted to express what was happening in class. They wanted to express what they wanted their papers or their projects to be about and needed to do it in private." She was allowed a private office that changed the dynamic immediately and enabled students to come and feel comfortable.

Kathleen's office is plastered with posters, artifacts, and books that highlight the best in Black history and scholarship. "As a librarian, I'm able to attend conferences where we get wonderful posters. The posters that are produced on campus are wonderful too." Kathleen says that she received the nicest compliment from a student recently. "He came into my office and he looked around. He's like, 'this the Blackest space I've seen on campus!' He said, 'I love it...I love it.'" Kathleen explained to the student the types of events she had posted and the logic of her poster organization. "On this wall is our campus events...he responds 'whose campus? All those people have been here?' 'Yes, yes they have and more.'"

Kathleen knows that there is a comfort in her office—that students can come and ask, and she will share. "I'm not trying to answer their questions but lead them to the resources that will help them come up with their answers." Over the years, students would come by and say, "Oh Miss Bethel, I don't really want anything. I just want to sit in your office little bit." Kathleen always responded with "well, just come on and sit down, it's all right." The students know that Kathleen has a bookmark or something to give them, something to share, and something to see. "They take a breath and get up and go. There is a need for spaces and people like that on campus. I think there is, I'm not sure if the students would agree because there are so many spaces out here but I'm still hearing from some students that lead me to think that."

Kathleen references changes in communications for Black students, changes in guidance, and changes in the faculty at NU. She used to be in The Black House all the time. The Black House held the information on Black events, news, and gossip. "I mentioned a faculty member whose husband was arrested on campus on a weekend trying to visit his wife at her office. That news spread like wildfire. How we would hear about that today. We would have to wait for The Daily to do an article, put it on

Twitter or Facebook? I don't know. I haven't listened to the radio station because there isn't a program that focuses on us. So, how that news gets shared? Once it hits the university news, it takes on a whole different channel and it's not from us, it's from them." Kathleen makes a clear comment on how we are failing each other as a Black community. The assemblage of faculty, staff, students, and the entire experience suffers when Blacks are not connected.

Kathleen has noticed trends in Black student issues among freshmen and sophomores. She looks for answers on what happens to Black students in their sophomore year when there seems to be a real dissatisfaction with the university. "We need to understand what happens to them during freshman year because they don't come back happy sophomores. That sophomore year is a challenge for them." She doesn't think it's the workload. She refers to the approaches in the classroom. "If you're the only Black student in your class talking about race, the class looks to the Black student as if they're an expert. The faculty and other students should recognize that's not really their job as a student." Kathleen has heard that complaint from countless students in her care but is unclear if the university has tackled the sensitivity training needed and thus, changes were made across the university.

Kathleen has a succinct statement of her on-going career at Northwestern. "I've had a ball!" She continues to enjoy the experience of doing the work she wanted to do and knowing that she's been helpful." She is proud when she sees young adults go out into their professions. She is equally proud of ensuring that the library and archives have the resources that are needed for the work that's being done in all fields of study. She shares her fascination with the new field of Hip Hop Studies. She laughs about tackling some of the music associated with it and unpacking the scholarship. She remembers a different day in Northwestern's music history. One of her first memories of coming to Northwestern was to see funk legion George Clinton at the Cahn Auditorium. "Parliament funked it up in 1971." She saw him again later at Patton Gym and "Somebody said you look like one of the oldest people here. I said 'yeah but I'm still younger than half of the band.'" She is one of the individuals who have played legendary roles for the Black experience and the enhancement of the university in general.

Ce Cole Dillon

Ce Cole Dillon

The Black House has been the center of the Black student existence at Northwestern for nearly fifty years. From its original location at 619 Emerson to its current space at 1914 Sheridan Road, it has been, in symbol and in reality, the icon that represents both the greatest success of African Americans at Northwestern and the entity in structure and function deemed responsible for success at NU to the vast majority of Blacks who have attended. Depending on the needs of the student, it has served to enable aspirations, insulate from campus aggressions, and enhance the Black and, as an extension, the Northwestern experience.

Ce Cole Dillon is a 1978 graduate of the Northwestern School of Education and Social Policy. As much as any other alum, the large portion of her life—over forty years at this point and counting—associated with Northwestern has been intricately tied to The Black House. As was often the case among Black students during the mid-seventies, she was the first in her family to attend college. She really had little knowledge of what to expect at college and came to NU feeling unlikely to stay the full four years. However, she soon discovered that she would become immersed in the fabric of the university's Black community.

On her very first day at Northwestern, Ce discovered that her work-study job involved an assignment at The Black House. For the first two years of her existence at NU, she spent part of nearly everyday there. This placed her squarely in the center of Black life, and that purview gave her a front row seat to all aspects of the Black experience, which, at the time, included struggles on internal matters, such as being considered a legitimate part of the greater university community, as well as external struggles, including efforts to get Northwestern to divest from its holdings with companies supporting apartheid via conducting business with South Africa. As part of her work, she often touched base with the newly emergent Black alumni community, as she was the work-study student coordinator of one of the first Black alumni social get-togethers held at the Orrington Hotel in 1977.

Ce fondly remembers the Black community coming-of-age on campus. Sometimes, this included prolonged discussions about seemingly not-so-serious (yet intensely serious at the time) subjects such as cutting one's Afro and the appropriateness of cutting or coloring one's hair. These were measures of moving from times of a campus experience of predominantly protest and radicalism to explorations of newer meanings of cultural Blackness. She recalls that her favorite class was "Black Folks' Theatre," which similarly involved both analysis of Black culture and analysis of our place in society.

Additionally, Ce learned how fervent the sentiment was that The Black House was a place of safety for students in an often-hostile environment and was a place where students could come into their own and figure out how to succeed in the university environment. This proved necessary with all too frequent tales of being on the receiving end of disparagement and racial slurs by White students while casually walking up and down campus. Ce recalls specifically being told and made to feel that she "didn't belong" at Northwestern. Partly because of these sentiments, she had a lack of interest in forging a general university experience and sought to enjoy the comforts and opportunities that were more available to her, relegating the rest of campus slights as "noise." The Black House was a safe space.

Blackness was prominent and powerful on campus. For example, the time during which Ce was a student at Northwestern included the presence of many academic giants on the faculty. There was Lerone Bennett, Leon Forrest, Mari Evans, Cyrus

Colter, Jan Carew, Joy Gleason, and Sonia Sanchez. There were professors William Sampson, Jim Pitts, and Dennis Brutus, who had been imprisoned on Robbins Island with Nelson Mandela. Not only was the faculty excellent at teaching, they were there for the students culturally, and these interactions typically occurred at The Black House.

Furthermore, there were giants in The Black House itself. Milton Wiggins was the Dean of African American Student Affairs, who was followed by Alice Palmer and Ulysses "Duke" Jenkins. These administrators and their able assistants, including Essie Williams and Annie Barnes, performed tasks ranging from keeping students focused on what they should be doing on campus to providing personal comfort and a home environment within The Black House.

The sum total of the extremely close-knit faculty, staff, and administrators served to create an environment that was protective, nurturing, and powerful. The Black House embodied a formula by which success was not only possible but became probable for the students on campus. Instead of feelings of isolation, Ce notes feeling as if she had found an additional family. You'd go to The Black House for classes and between classes. There were parties, bid-whist games, and Sunday dinners. There was music, and there were meetings. *The BlackBoard Magazine* (the Black student interest publication) was printed there, and even marriage proposals occurred there. Campus life from within The Black House effectively drowned out the slurs from other parts of campus for the duration of her time at Northwestern.

Ce notes that by the mid 1970's, not only had The Black House succeeded in providing a sense of community for students on campus but also it seemed to do so at the expense of relationships with traditional community outlets in Evanston. Although a sense of community still remained with the Second Baptist Church in Evanston, it was during this period that general feelings of "otherness" began to exist between Blacks at Northwestern and those within Evanston, which was ironic and unfortunate, based on how Northwestern Blacks felt on campus when wandering away from The Black House into the general university environment.

Regarding concerns on campus related to being a young woman, Ce was rather underwhelmed at any notion of a need for Black feminism during her time as a student at Northwestern. She notes, "I don't think that kind of sexism – the kind of sexism or the need for the kind of feminism White women talk about—is an integral part of our community. Black women have always worked. My mother worked, my grandmother worked, my great-grandmother worked. I didn't come to Northwestern with the idea that I wasn't going to work...that just wasn't part of my calculus, nor were the men that I went to school with projecting the kind of idea that they saw us as different or lesser... Gender was an issue around dating and personal relationships, not around academic relationships."

Ce's actual role in leadership arose out of necessity and out of another Black House tradition. It was a ritual of sorts that upperclassmen would be paired with incoming freshman, and these upperclassmen would accept responsibility for the development of these new students. Ce's big sister was Sidmel Estes, with whom she developed an extremely tight relationship for over 30 years, until Sidmel's death. After graduation, Sidmel served as the President of the Northwestern University Black Alumni Association (NUBAA) and subsequently "assigned" Ce to serve in the same capacity. The timing was such that it appeared NUBAA was about to collapse, and Sidmel knew that Ce would be the right person to bring it back to health. Even though Ce lived in California at that time, Sidmel didn't give Ce the option to decline. Of course, as Ce reflected on the dictate she'd been given, she came to realize that it wasn't without logic or merit, given the unique exposure Ce had to students, faculty, and staff, including those from the 1960's through the late 1980's.

Ce served her first term as the NUBAA President in 2004 and served again to fill the void through 2010. These years were a time of transition on campus from the presence of a more inner-city based student and alumni group who were likely the first in their families to attend college, toward a mix that would include significantly more middle class Blacks. However, the continuum of pride existed such that NUBAA membership presented opportunities for a better understanding of the variety of Black alumni based on the shared experiences across many considerations, and a hunger existed within the group for appreciation of the expansion of the Black experience in total.

In addition to creating unity among the new coalition of Blacks at Northwestern, and in a manner true to her strongest ties to NU, Ce notes that she was also made to face a direct university effort to pull back the purpose and function of The Black House. "This came in the context of undergraduate students who were really becoming stressed about university changes. The rise of Multicultural Student Affairs (MSA) meant the diminishment of the Department of African American Student Affairs. There was an idea that it wasn't as important to have Black identity on campus, but instead, a multicultural identity could be used to color us all. It was really clear that this was not helpful to Black students, and they were in anguish over what was happening, and that the Black population was at one of its lowest points on campus in number and morale. When I began my presidency, the Black student population was approximately 3–4% of the overall student population…"

"Furthermore, Black students found this Multicultural Student Affairs structure as being really oppressive because it was all about multiculturalism and no longer about being Black. The way I like to describe it is Multicultural Student Affairs was attempting to make a smoothie out of a salad. So, in a salad, you can look and see the green lettuce, red tomatoes, the eggs, radishes, broccoli, and whatever you put in it. In a smoothie, things just turn green. It has all the ingredients in it, but you can't see them. That's what the students were fighting against; MSA was trying to turn them into a smoothie, while we were ok being a salad. We wanted to be who we were."

During this time, Ce was approached by members of For Members Only, who were concerned about the proposed changes that would bring other multicultural groups into The Black House. The new Director of Multicultural Student Affairs, Coretta Cook, who happened to be a Black woman, was spearheading these changes. That set of circumstances was especially difficult for the students because they were conflicted and not used to having to rally or conceptually ready to rally directly against another Black person. As NUBAA President, Ce sat in on many calls with Coretta, who apparently was oblivious to her presence and addressed the students in "completely disrespectful and otherwise inappropriate ways."

After enlisting Black Board of Trustee members Wayne Watson and Don Jackson, Ce proceeded to engage Northwestern President Henry Bienan. A meeting occurred with the entire university student affairs division. The issues discussed included recruitment, academic support, safe places, and the university environment. It was a successful meeting. The results included promises from President Bienan that "The Black House would always be The Black House," a commitment from NU to fund the university's second academic chair named after an African American (Chicago Mayor and Northwestern alum Harold Washington), and assurances that substantial efforts would be made to increase Black student enrollment. It was especially notable to Ce how hard Mike Mills, the Director of Admissions, worked after this episode to implement any feasible idea and, in fact, this lead to several years of consecutive increase in Black student enrollment.

Ce notes an especially dour occurrence on campus during nearly the exact same time. The university uncharacteristically bowed to outside pressure and rescinded an offer to extend an honorary Doctorate of Sacred Theology to Rev. Jeremiah Wright, who gained fame as senior minister of Trinity United Church of Christ in Chicago and was a leader of the Black Liberation Theology movement. He was notably the long time pastor of Barack Obama, who was running for President at that time. Rev. Wright had run into quite a bit of controversy related to inflammatory comments. President Bienan's letter to Rev. Wright included the following communication: "In light of the controversy surrounding statements made by you that have recently been publicized, the celebratory character of Northwestern's commencement would be affected by our conferring of this honorary degree. Thus, I am withdrawing the offer of an honorary degree previously extended to you."

There was quite a bit of division in the Black community on this issue, but a primary point of contention for those not in favor of the revocation was that only twice before had Northwestern made such as action: with Jefferson Davis, President of the Confederate States of America, and regarding Robert Mugabe, President of Zimbabwe. It was felt by many in the Black community that creating an equivalence of any kind among the three was intellectually dishonest.

Still, this setback wasn't the biggest disappointment experienced by Ce during this time. That would be reserved to the failure of not to codify the agreement of not revisiting functional changes to The Black House. Indeed, it wasn't even five years later that yet another effort was made by the Department of Student Affairs to add university staff members into The Black House, which seemed detrimental to the space of the students.

Ce's Presidency of NUBAA had ended by then, but she was again called to action on behalf of The Black House. After efforts by the alumni, students, and faculty led to a pause on the implementation of the plans of the Department of Student Affairs, a university committee entitled The Black House Listening Group was formed to obtain input from the community and develop recommendations back to the university. Upon the recommendation of NUBAA, past President Ce Cole Dillon was the last person appointed to the committee.

The committee's report was meant to create a framework for enhancing and modernizing The Black House. It was meant to ensure The Black House's primary identity as a safe and honored space, not just for students but the entire Black community. The work of this committee led to numerous recommendations that were in sync with additional recommendations from students, alumni, and faculty. After the initial promises to adopt the committee's recommendations in total, whatever they were, the Vice President of Student Affairs, who retains administrative control over The Black House, let it be known that the recommendations would be taken "under advisement."

Ce believes that much of what's missing in today's Black House is the exposure and experiences with "the adults," quantitatively and qualitatively. From the absence of classes in The Black House to the absence of dedicated elder staff whose entire focus was the successful shepherding of students through the university experience, The Black House seems to be treated more as a building than a commitment to guiding the students it was built to serve. She lays the responsibility for this disconnect squarely at the feet of leadership of the Department of Student Affairs, which controls The Black House, made the change in university policy away from a Department of African American Student Affairs to a Division of Multicultural Student Affairs, and has repeatedly proposed changes to the function and purpose of The Black House.

"I don't think the leadership of Student Affairs is actually supportive of the kind of historical identity that The Black House has, and as long as that leadership is there, the struggle will be there. So, the vision of Student Affairs isn't there. The leadership is rooted in the idea of multiculturalism. I don't mean to be coy about it. I am talking about Patricia Telles-Irvin, a person of color (POC) who plays the POC card in basically saying that because she is a person of color, she has credibility in making these types of statements, and the university should take her status as a woman of color to believe that she actually knows what she's talking about. I think it is a great disserve to the Black students to become a pawn in that kind of game."

Ce further laments what she perceives to be an easily identifiable source of the current and ongoing rift between the university and the Black community. "It's not for me to say for any other person of color how they represent themselves and how they interact with other people, but it is up to me to say, as a longstanding member of this community and a leader in this community, that this type of thinking doesn't build the kind of community that Black students need at NU. No matter what your motive is, even if it is aspirational, these are real Black kids living in real Black moments where these are not the kind of resources and support that would help get them through Northwestern and be bonded to the university. I think that's the thing the university fails to understand.

"As an alum, the strong support I have for the university comes as a result of the support I got as an undergraduate in The Black House. If the university acts indifferent to you, why would you be committed to it? So, the people who aspire to make us fungible with other people of color have it wrong. We don't want to be a smoothie; everyone wants to be parts of the salad. It isn't just Black students who want to be seen. The Asian students want to be seen, the Latino students want to be seen, the gay students want to be seen. We want to be who we are and be accepted into the NU community, not homogenized into a smoothie."

Furthermore, Ce rejects the notion that the changing makeup of the Black university to now include approximately equal parts African Americans, Caribbeans, and Africans demands a move away from the traditional views of the Black student experience. "It's kind of interesting. You know, Malcolm X's family was from Barbados, but he saw himself strongly and proudly as part of the African American community. So, if you want to identify as an international student, there's an international house, and there should be nothing about that house that says that you can't participate if you're a person of color.

"If you want to honor the experience of being a Black American, where the majority of us are the descendants of slaves, then you could be that too, and I believe it is condescending and naïve for the university not to recognize that we have a strong history and a strong legacy of being a community that has accepted and integrated our African, Caribbean, and Black people from around the world. You know, Professor Dennis Brutus was South African. He was not a descendant of a slave. Professor Jan Carew was Afro-Caribbean. He was not a descendent of a slave. Yet, these individuals were integral leaders in our community. They accepted their role, and we honored them as elders.

"So, this is just nonsense. This failure to understand who we are as a people and how we come together within this Black American experience is nonsense. In our communities and in our hearts, we allow you to bring and allow you to take whatever you need. We don't all say that you've got to be this or that. However, when it comes to us—the descendants of slaves – everyone wants to be 'all up in our chili' and take from us. We have been here from the beginning. You can either work with us, or you can work against us, but those who have worked against us have labored into obscurity because we don't go away.

"We know who we are, an we are proud of who we are. We are part of this American existence, and all of these rights and freedoms that all of these groups claim today were built on the backs of us standing up, saying we hold these truths to be self-evident... So, for those who have managed to come along and stand on our backs, then look down to tell us who we are or who we should be or what we should be, or how we should integrate within our own community should be ashamed of themselves because everything they have, they got because we stood up and said no more. So, we require no more than for them to listen to what it is we have to say. We have been welcoming the diasporic community all of our lives. For example, when we said there should be an African American Studies Department, we didn't say just study slavery. We said study the entire diaspora. Study Afro-Caribbean communities. Study Africa. We said this is all part of us because this is the way we live our lives. Don't tell us we are a divided community because we are not. We can celebrate all that have a history that can be celebrated, that isn't connected to a history of having been a slave, but it doesn't diminish those of us who are."

Ce notes the new wave of prominent African Americans in administrative leadership positions related to the Black experience and offers the following to them. "You have to know your role and play your position. There should not be anyone in any of those roles who doesn't understand that their number one job is to be an advocate for Black students who are there. If you take the time to reach down to where the students are, you will find what we've been discussing: they come from all over the place and they're forging an identity of community and friendship. And if you don't want to do that job of being an advocate, you need to go somewhere else. Something magical happens as a result of the connections formed by the community experience. There's a continuity of experience that is up to the university administrators to keep intact. It's not about them. It's not about their idea of how things should be. We know what the experience is. We know there is something unique in the experience that's passed from generation to generation. It's not their job to change it or even to determine what it should be. They get confused about what their role is."

On account of the time Ce has spent in protecting the building at 1914 Sheridan Road, she has a poignant reminder for current and future members of the Black community at Northwestern. "The things that I talk about and the feelings that The Black House inspires in me didn't occur because of the building. It happened because of the people. The people who were in the building had no better job to do than to see that I would become the best person that I could be. So, as the university seems to want to make this about a building, we should be very clear that it's not about that. It's about failing to put leadership and resources within the grasp of young people that will catapult them to the greatness they can achieve.

"The thing I remember most about my time in The Black House was there were people all around me who were invested in developing my greatness, and if they saw something that was weak, they saw that as something that could have attention brought to it to make it better. As to today's kids, if they have weaknesses, they go unattended. There is no fire to help forge them to the greatness they can represent. The Black House is the means. If you don't put the resources in and then say to the students, 'well this is something you're not using,' well, the students aren't stupid! These are some of the brightest students in America, and they can tell there's nothing in there and feel like 'why are you trying to force me into that empty space?' We didn't' have an empty space. We had a space filled with people who cared, who are concerned, who tried to raise us up beyond what we could see for ourselves. If Northwestern wants The Black House to be what it was, then it will focus on those things. If they only want to treat it like a space, then that's what it will be. If you are so craven to use the words of children, saying it's an empty space when you've put nothing in there for them, then yes, you will get that type of outcome...and a self-fulfilling prophesy. When I think of The Black House, I think of Essie (Williams) laughing with students. I hear Annie Barnes asking me if I went to class that day. They reminded me every day what my purpose was."

Ce notes that throughout it all, and throughout the years, there seems to remain a feeling by many externals of the Black experience that somehow The Black House detracts from Northwestern and somehow lessens the general university experience. It is considered an oddity that The Black House and the surrounding history aren't considered a more integral part of the university. The Black House is not part of campus tours. Every five or so years since its creation, The Black House has been under assault in one manner or another. The university's blind eye to The Black House as a primary vehicle of the success and pride of its Black community and an integral part of the overall success found within the university – as evidenced by its ongoing desire to functionally do away with its intended purpose - remains a basic reason why the ongoing divide between the general university population continues.

Ce's message to the university is straightforward. "It's the people, not just the building. That's the communication breakdown. Today's administrators want to talk about the building. If you're an administrator, you should know better. If you want these students to be proud members of the Wildcat family, you should do better. We exhort you to do better." Ce Cole Dillon's final message is a note that is more than a connection to anything in her life other than family – more than a house or a job – the connection to Northwestern has been long lasting at over 40 years. The connection to her and The Black House represents the same entity and the clearest embodiment of the successful Black experience.

Tamara Johnson

Tamara Johnson worked at Northwestern for eight years in different capacities with students, faculty, staff, and alumni and saw changes in the student population and administration that still resonate today. Tamara served as the Executive Director of Multicultural Student Affairs at Northwestern University from 2009 to 2014.

Tamara Johnson is from Chicago's South suburbs and was living in Ohio working in consulting when she decided to return to higher education. She saw a Career Services job at Northwestern and it fit her doctoral dissertation that emphasized Black students, racial identity, and career development. It was a perfect fit! "It's kind of interesting because people often come to Northwestern because of Northwestern's reputation, but I went to the University of Illinois in Champaign. At Illinois, you think Illinois is everything. It wasn't until I started researching for my interview that I found out how highly ranked Northwestern is." It was the actual position that attracted her.

Tamara started in Career Services in March of 2006. She realized early on that the position didn't have significant enough connection with Black students and students of color. She met Penny Warren, who was the ultimate historian and knew all of the students and seemingly all of the information Tamara wanted. Penny Warren allowed Tamara to co-advise the Black Graduate Student Association. "That helped out tremendously because I was primarily focused on graduate students in my

Career Services position. So, I really needed to figure out how to incorporate some of the interest that I had with Black students into my work. The Black Graduate Student Association was a natural fit. That really provided me the access and exposure to help students in a different way. Getting Black students, Latinx students, and other students of color into a Career Services office is not as easy as one would think."

Tamara wanted to do something bigger. In 2009, when Coretta Cook stepped down from her position, William Banis, the Vice President of Student Affairs at that time, asked her to accept the interim role as Executive Director for Multicultural Affairs. At that time, I reported directly to him. She remembers the climate being really challenging because she was coming after Coretta, against whom students had been protesting. "I can't say that I knew Coretta very well, but I will say that I came to understand a lot better how things happened. The job was demanding, and the expectations were very high." The students wanted someone highly visible and it took her a while to establish her own identity. People would say "she's the new Coretta Cook."

Tamara reported directly to Vice President Banis. At that time, Vice President Banis reported to the Provost, who reported to the President. President Morty Shapiro had just started when she began as Executive Director for Multicultural Affairs. The job entailed African American Student Affairs, Asian-American Student Affairs, Hispanic-Latino Student Affairs and then, later, the LGBT Resource Center. There were four very different populations and three facilities. "You're juggling programs, trainings, individual student appointments, advising over sixty student organizations and colleagues who are trying to do collaborations with you. It's a tough undertaking."

The African American Student Affairs Director in 2009 was Shadra Smith. Shadra was there only a year and a half. "It was a lot of pressure for Shadra, but she had great ideas. She developed a Black homecoming reception, a Black male forum, and Kwanzaa activities. We ultimately launched all three. It becomes harder to manage all of the expectations and the pressure. We came at a time when students felt underserved, and so, we were overcompensating. We were at The Black House until 10 o'clock at night, most of the week. Then, we were there on the weekends. She was worn out after a year and a half."

During Tamara's first week as Executive Director, there was a big meeting with the Coalition of Colors group, which included FMO, Alianza, and many other minority groups. The Coalition of Colors, the President, The Provost, the Chief of Police and several other senior leaders were present all together in one room to hear the students' concerns. They had a list of grievances. "I'd worked at three institutions by that time, but I had never been in a meeting with all these senior administrators, where the students were actually leading the meeting. It was quite the experience." The Multicultural Student Affairs staff turned those concerns into an action plan, and she added the Coalition of Colors into her advisory board and moved forward from there. She remembers FMO leader Zachary Parker, Mark Crain, and Tyris Jones. They stood out to Tamara because they were really able to mobilize students.

In Tamara's era there was a core group of Black students that was very much unified. "Because of the activist nature of many in The Black House, there was a group that kept away from the Black community because they weren't interested in those kinds of things. I wouldn't say that I experienced the community as divided, but I would say that there were degrees of what I would consider Black consciousness and the way in which students wanted to demonstrate that Black consciousness. I think, overall during my time, the Black community was relatively cohesive, but again, I do think there were groups that were not participating very much."

Furthermore, Tamara was on the faculty at Northwestern. She met a lot of Black students who took her class because they heard that they should, but she had never seen them around. "Oftentimes, I'd talk to them. They'd come and see me outside of class. I would ask why I never saw them. They would respond 'I'm not going to get involved because I want to be able to have a happy experience.'" Tamara identified another subset of Black Students. "Some of the students clearly expressed that because they didn't do the protest, people thought they weren't 'Black enough.' There was this questioning of their identity."

Tamara engaged with NUBAA on many occasions to assist with issues concerning Black students, Black athletes, and Black Greek Letter Organizations. She noticed clear trends. "It was very easy to see that the Black athletes simply were not involved in Multicultural Student Affairs. Out of the entire football team, Tyris Jones was an exception because he was Greek (a member of Alpha Phi Alpha), an athlete, and he was a FMO coordinator. We did a lot of outreach to Athletics, including meeting with the Athletic Director, but it was still hard to get the athletes involved." She never saw groups of athletes at The Black House, which she thought unique to Northwestern.

She thought that the Black Greek Letter Organizations were engaged in their own activities for the most part. They had their meetings in The Black House and would participate in a few programs, but they were focused on their own efforts as she saw it. "Interestingly, if something happened with one of the Black Greek-Lettered Organizations, even though they were really under the umbrella of Greek Life, then it always hit my desk. I ultimately had to have a conversation with Greek Life to say these are your students too, so when things go wrong, they shouldn't just come to me. If you need some help, then we are happy to get involved."

Part of Tamara's job was to make sure that Northwestern had special initiatives for students of color. She says NU knew that Black students were less likely to graduate with plans after graduation or more likely to not have as high grade point averages, based on institutional data. She knew that she needed more time to be able to help

Black students to address unique concerns. It wasn't easy to get other offices throughout the university to understand the unique needs of this population and develop plans for their areas to address the gaps.

Knowing the concerns of Black students, Tamara made a special effort to collaborate with Police Chief Bruce Lewis. "There had been student protests against the police, so ultimately, Chief Lewis and I met regularly. Almost anything that I needed for him to do, including having the officers much more active and visible, he did. We had a barbecue once at The Black House with many of the officers present, and people were amazed." Her goal was to bridge the gap that had been widening for years. She felt good with the ongoing dialogue and the co-sponsoring of various programs.

Mary Pattillo, a faculty member, was always present, vocal, and available for the students. Other faculty members were great to The Black House and to Tamara's office, including Darlene Clark Hine and Celeste Watkins Hayes. However, she wouldn't say that there were a lot of faculty members coming to The Black House.

When she started, Tamara heard that there used to be a team of five professional staff members that were specifically assigned to African American Student Affairs. "If you have five people dedicated to African American Student Affairs, that means that you can do so much more than if you have one person that's dedicated to African American students." In terms of Black student programming, "once you go down to having one staff person for Black students, it is a lot for that person to do, and you're really focused on immediate concerns."

Tamara emphasizes that spending time with individual students was a priority, but there is a price that's paid on every level. "I spent a lot of time with individual students and appointments. One student came into the office crying because she told her professor he was a 'dream killer.' She wanted to be a physician and was discouraged by a professor. One minute you're talking to them about their professor, the next minute someone has a parent that passed away, and they're trying to get home. The next minute they're walking down the street and somebody says a racial slur at them." She could walk into the office at 8 o'clock, and a student would see her and ask, "Tamara, are you going to your office, can I come in and talk to you?" "I haven't even gotten into the office and already students needed me. It's important because they wouldn't be there if they didn't need to talk to you, but when you have that level of contact with students, then a lot of other things take the back burner. That's just the way it has to happen. You only have so many hours."

As a psychologist by training and currently an assistant chancellor, Tamara offers a few recommendations for the future. "Things probably don't change much because you have the cycle of students that come and go, and there's probably not enough pressure that's consistent and very specific on the university. There needs to be a priority list that the administrators and students continue to work on. Of course, priorities change somewhat, but it's important to regularly review student outcome data to assess if you are accomplishing your goals." Additionally, she points out that the disadvantaged tend have the underrepresented fighting for the underrepresented. "Having advocates from the majority population to be in the fight with you is critical."

Tamara also notes the reality of restructuring. "I mentioned I used to report directly to Vice President Banis, then I reported to Vice President Telles-Irvin. Then came restructuring, and I reported to Assistant Vice President Bergie Howard. Now, I understand it's the case that you don't have a Director of African American Student Affairs. You have all Assistant Directors at Northwestern now; so, there are more channels to move through for the concerns of Black students to reach the Vice President."

The current administrative structure at Northwestern has an Assistant Director who has an emphasis on Black students, who reports to a Director of Multicultural Affairs, who reports to an Executive Director of Campus Inclusion and Community, who reports to an Associate or Assistant Vice President, who reports to the Vice President of Student Affairs. This is quite the change from having a Dean of the Department of African American Student Affairs. It's difficult and an ongoing challenge to convince the Black community that the lack of status with the individual more directly responsible for the Black student experience doesn't correlate to a diminished prioritizing of Black student concerns. It certainly has correlated with a diminution of the students' ranking of their Black student experience and undergraduate education, which has been the worst of all groups on campus for several years.

As a general consideration, having really good collaborations with Admissions was important for Tamara, and she spent a lot of time with Onis Cheathams, Associate Director of Admissions. However, Tamara noted it's hard to recruit when negative issues regarding the students of color are online. "When prospective students and their parents Google search Northwestern and see the protests and forums, it can make it difficult for the recruitment side. Working in collaboration with departments who are responsible for certain kinds of student experiences, including recruitment and retention, has to remain a priority. All higher education professionals must make sure that Black students' needs aren't diluted because we're focused on 'diversity and inclusion.' There are specific challenges for Black students that are unlike other populations. It's just the reality." Tamara acknowledges the challenges that any population undergoes but asks "how do we make sure that the specific concerns of Black students remain a priority?"

Tamara remembers a conversation in which a colleague said "well, once they're accepted to Northwestern, they're all just Northwestern students." "I had to say 'yes, they are all Northwestern students, but this particular population has concerns that you will not hear from many of the other populations. I've listened to Black students all day for years. I completely revamped the entire office of Multicultural Student

Affairs, and this is what I listened to day in and day out. This is what I research. This is what I've experienced myself as a student. This is what I know.'"

Lesley-Ann Brown-Henderson

Lesley-Ann Brown-Henderson

Lesley-Ann Brown-Henderson joined Northwestern University's Division of Student Affairs in 2012 and serves as the inaugural Director of Campus Inclusion and Community.

"I've lived in a lot of places, and I think that's relevant to the work I do." Notably, Lesley-Ann's education includes a Masters in Student Affairs Administration, a Masters in Counseling Psychology, and a Doctorate in Counseling Psychology. "My dissertation specifically looked at the experiences of Black students at Predominantly White Institutions (PWIs). I was interested in a concept called minority status stress, which examines the stress Black students experience due to being Black, which is in addition to any other stress that all students endures, such as financial aid, classes, and exams. It's really stress due to being a student of color. I was interested in how Black students persisted and how leadership could explain the relationship between their minority status stress and their persistence."

Lesley-Ann has broad responsibilities related to the Black student experience at Northwestern. "In my role, I oversee three primary areas. One is Multicultural Student Affairs, the second is Student Enrichment Services, which serves the needs of our low income, first-generation and undocumented students, and the third is called Social Justice Education, which does a lot of training programs for students on issues of identity, equity, power, and privilege. In addition to that, I oversee our Posse Scholars Program, which offers college access and leadership development. I am responsible for our Bias Incident Response System and Team on campus. It's good work, it's hard work, and it's important work, but it's very busy. I'm the inaugural Director of Campus Inclusion and Community, so, in many ways, I built it (Campus Inclusion and Community) from the ground up with lots of support."

As has often been the case in matters of the Black experience, Campus Inclusion and Community was born out of controversy. "Campus Inclusion and Community (CIC) really came out of two things. The spring of 2012 on Northwestern's campus was a pretty tumultuous quarter. There were three very significant racist incidents that happened on campus. The third event involved the 'Beer Olympics' held by the ski team. The ski team held an off-campus party, and dressed up as people of other cultures and communities. One of our more activist students walked by the house, saw the activities, and made the knowledge of these activities very public. Afterwards, there were a number of forums held, and there was also demonstration and dialogue held on Deering Meadow. The students voiced that they wanted more administrative support around issues of diversity and inclusion on campus. They felt support from Multicultural Students Affairs (MSA) and other areas, but in addition to that, there really needed to be some push toward education as well as inclusion across campus. The student response to the 'Beer Olympics' occurred maybe in the April of 2012. Patricia Telles-Irvin, the Vice President of Student Affairs, posted the position in August with the financial backing of a member of the Board of Trustees, and I applied and started in September."

Lesley-Ann noted that Campus Inclusion and Community is a long-overdue effort to join units supporting our marginalized students while also placing responsibility on the majority community to develop certain sensitivities regarding diversity and inclusion. "I lean back on a theory by noted psychologist, Kurt Lewin. A person's behavior is a result of who that person is and their interaction with their environment. As we think about how we want Black students to thrive specifically on campus, we look at the person who's coming into the university. What does representation look like? In addition to that, we must also look at their environment. How do we support their identities? Do they feel like there's a place for them here? It's not one or the other; it's looking at both that need to happen in tandem.

"For so long at Northwestern, we were doing just one part of it: looking at the person. Holding folks within the university accountable for the environment hasn't happened as much. So, I think we're in a time when that's happening on multiple levels and the conversation is broadening. We're doing a lot to support students, but we've begun to think about what support from faculty, staff, and senior leadership looks like. Those conversations are gaining traction."

Lesley-Ann traces the major change in the university's current approach to its student experience back to the development of Multicultural Student Affairs (MSA). "MSA became a unit on campus in 2004, and at that time, it encompassed a few different offices, including African American Student Affairs, Hispanic/Latino Student Affairs, and Asian American Student Affairs. Campus Inclusion and

Community wasn't formed until 2012, but it wasn't until 2014 that I was asked to oversee Multicultural Student Affairs. So, the direct relationship between CIC and MSA is only a few years old.

"As far as The Black House is concerned, when MSA became a unit, The Black House as well as Multicultural Center became spaces and units under MSA, and currently, that is still the case. It's a huge part of my responsibility to be connected to The Black House, the Multicultural Center, and the Gender and Sexuality Center. I have to be mindful about how those spaces, especially with the history of The Black House, are working with and supporting the needs of students."

Regarding the university's switch from a Department of African American Student affair to Multicultural Student Affairs, Lesley-Ann doesn't necessary see a drop off in the university's focus on the Black experience. "The level of identity engagement for Blacks is still very much a priority for the university. Black students do really have a unique history here, and the way in which Black students are intended to thrive involves a few things. The identity specificity still exists within the structure in terms of programming and representation. In addition to that, what we were hearing from Black students, and really students of various marginalized identities, and our students of color across the board is their identities involve more than solely being Black. It's that 'I'm Black and I'm a woman,' or 'I identify as Black, and I'm multiracial, and I want to be able to engage and understand more about that.' Sometimes, it's 'I'm Black, and within the Black community itself, there's a lot of diversity, and we don't ever talk about that.' Other times, it's 'I'm Black, and I don't necessarily think that I want to engage or I'm allowed to engage in The Black House,' or 'I'm Black, and I love The Black House, and this is the place I feel most safe and able to be my full, authentic self on campus.' So, there are lots of things students are saying in a lot of different ways about Blackness.

"So, what we're trying to create is space to say that within Blackness there's a lot of nuance and specific experiences. Blackness is not a monolith. There's lot of diversity that exists within the Black community. We want students talking about their experiences, such as their understanding of Blackness within the diaspora and what that looks like. Is there an intersection between Blackness and the Latino community? I know a lot of people who identify as Black but have a Latino heritage. How do they make choices about where to go?

"Part of our thinking in hearing feedback from students is to say back to them their Blackness is very important, and there should be some space to experience or flow through MSA or through CIC for exploring that Blackness. There's not just one way to do it. Also, we understand that students are saying they have intersecting identities. Your Blackness is very important today, but where's the space to talk about these other things? So, creating that space to talk and explore is one of the big ways we're trying to allow for students to choose how they want to flow through NU, as well as feel supported in that journey."

Furthermore, Lesley-Ann pushes back against assertions that the university's efforts, including eliminating the Department of African American Student Affairs, presume what's best for students. "Our efforts and intentions aren't quite paternalistic. We're not deciding what's best for students; we're allowing them to decide. However, they are asking for support. I think one thing that's very clear is that our current generation of students is a different group of students than that existed in the '70's or even the '80's. From Generation X to Millennials, there are different expectations regarding who they expect to resolve their problems. There are different expectations of the university and what it should do for them. There is a difference in the mindset of 'we can figure it out ourselves' vs. 'we need you to help us figure this out' vs. 'It shouldn't be our job to figure this out. You should figure it out for us.' That is some of what we hear. They're saying 'we need you all to help us do this. Don't tell us what to do, but help us through a process that helps us figure it out.'"

It was the effort to advance those ideals that was the genesis of a significant university controversy in 2015. A plan advanced by Campus Inclusion and Community intended to move Lesley-Ann's office and services provided by Social Justice Education and Student Enrichment Services into The Black House. Widespread awareness of the plan was only obtained at the point of implementation, and the Black university community responded loudly and vehemently against the plans and the manner of implementation. The move was largely regarded as a breach of trust of the university to the Black community and a movement too far from the purposes under which The Black House was established. The feelings were exacerbated by a conference call organized by The Northwestern University Black Alumni Association (NUBAA), in which the staff member overseeing that Black House explicitly told hundreds of assembled alumni, faculty, and students that: "The decision has been made, and there's nothing you can do about it."

Lesley-Ann found herself in the center of the controversy. "The goal was to enhance access to resources, particularly across CIC to our Black students and to students overall, so what we were trying to do was to co-locate our operations, which now exist all over campus, into The Black House and the MCC. So, my office, Student Enrichment Services and Social Justice Education, would have had some staff in The Black House, and all of Multicultural Student Affairs would have been housed in the Multicultural Center. That was the primary intent. The second was to bring more students into the space of The Black House and to be able to have an opportunity to get some resources so that the walls could better speak the history of the space."

The uproar resulted in the university pausing its plan and conducting a series of "listening sessions" to obtain community input on the best route forward for The Black House. Among other things, Lesley-Ann accepted responsibility for her role in the angst generated. "I try to show up as my authentic self. I think that's important. I'm not perfect. If a mistake is made, I can own that. I can speak to my heart or what my intent was, and I did that in the first listening session."

Meanwhile, Northwestern convened a Black House Facilities Review Committee (BHFRC) to respond to the listening sessions. "The BHFRC was the committee that was established to make recommendations after the listening sessions was formed, so part of their role was to attend all of the listening sessions. Four sessions were scheduled, but after Northwestern President Morty Schapiro came to the third, the decision was made to reverse the university's plans. "There was one final listening session after President Schapiro came, and it was focused on how to move things forward."

The Black House Facilities Review Committee (BHFRC) offered multiple recommendations based on the listening sessions, including the reestablishment of an Associate Dean to oversee The Black House and to evolve The Black House to encompass services consistent with a cultural center. Lesley-Ann noted the recommendations. "The recommendations from the BHFRC did not come to me; they went way above me. I have not been a part of the conversation regarding that specific recommendation. I do know that they've been looked, reviewed, and there have been conversations around them. I stand by the structure we currently have in place."

As the 2015 Black House controversy ensued, Lesley-Ann moved forward with chairing a task force announced in the spring of 2015 to review the Black student experience at NU. This gave her an opportunity to approach the needs of Black students, and in this instance, she advocated for a systematic and data-driven approach of addressing the concerns of Black students, which included being overrepresented on matters of mental health, sexual assault, and having lower matriculation rates than other groups on campus. "Since I got here, there was an understanding that Black students were less satisfied with their Northwestern experience or specifically, undergraduate education, which is the question asked on the COFHE (Consortium on Financing Higher Education) survey, than students of other races and ethnicities. While that is an important data point, the data didn't tell us much. For instance, what I would always ask is 'what is one's undergraduate education? How would a student define that? Is that their classroom experience? Is that their co-curricular experience? Is that their social experience? Is it their experience in the residence halls or in the library?'

"Every year, the Vice President of Student Affairs takes the leadership team on a retreat, and we look at COFHE data. One of the benefits of being a part of the group within COFHE is we get benchmark data. We get our data from seniors who just graduated as well as newly enrolled students, and we can benchmark across any other institution. We can see how we're doing in our peer group. We always spent a lot of time talking about that same question of 'How satisfied are you with your undergraduate education?' Every year, when we break down the data by ethnicity, our Black students were the most dissatisfied amongst the groups by far.

"So, based on that and seeing that data point be pretty consistent over a few years, I was then asked to chair a task force to look at the Black Student Experience. That was near and dear to my heart, and it was really important work. The faculty, staff, and students who were a part of that task force put in a lot of work to really understand what that data point was telling us. From when I started, things migrated from 'Yeah, we know Black students as less satisfied,' to 'we understand, and what do we do about it?'"

The Black Student Experience committee is something that I've really felt honored to be a part of. What's going on right now is that people are taking different parts of several of the committee's recommendations to move them forward, but three of the recommendations were strategically worked on this year. One is around representation of Black students, Black faculty, and Black staff. That group is being led by the Associate Provost and Chief Diversity Officer. Then, there's another group meeting about how to listen to students intentionally and not just in times of crisis. The third one is about development of an academic hub so that there can be a place where there's central tutoring, so students don't have to go a million different places to find the resources that they need. That's pretty much done.

"We had a lot of tough conversations happening. There was financial aid, and there are tensions in lots of different ways about that topic. There was the recruitment effort: what does it mean to matriculate, and why aren't we matriculating more Black students at the rates that we want? So, we were getting more in depth. We asked how students are being academically successful here. What does the transfer rate look like from school to school within the university, and why is that? Why are students coming in pre-med or pre-law and not ending their academic career as such? We were looking at issues of mental health and sexual assault and what healthy relationships look like in the Black community. So, there's been a lot more focus and interest in learning about the Black experience, and that has extended beyond my area and even beyond the area of the Associate Provost and Chief Diversity Officer. This focus is a change over the last several years of my being here. I don't think that is directly a result of me, but I do think that's a marked difference than when I first got here.

"We did a Black Student Experience Survey, which asked questions that hadn't been asked before. The second thing was we did focus groups with our students. The way we composed the focus groups was based on what we had seen in the data. We knew Black women on campus were having a different experience than Black men. So, we wanted to hear from Black women specifically and Black men specifically. We also knew Black student-athletes were having an experience that was different than your general Northwestern student, and we wanted to know more about that. We also knew that first-year students and seniors had very different perspectives. So, we ended up with six focus groups. We sent out the surveys and got a thirty percent response rate, which is very good. The number of students who took the survey represented the highest number of Blacks who had taken a survey at Northwestern.

"We dove into the data, we listened to the focus groups, and we came up with recommendations based on what we were and weren't hearing after making sense of it all. The report was due in August of 2016 to the President, the Provost, the Executive Vice President, the Vice President of Student Affairs, the General Counsel, and the Associated Provost for Diversity and Inclusion. We met, made a presentation about how we felt the university should move forward."

Lesley-Ann insists that the new approach is not only data-driven but also responsive to students. "We're now taking multiple data points and looking to make sense of them for our current Black students. That might result in things being exactly the same as they have been, or it might be different. Blackness is a central and anchoring identity, but what it is to be Black has changed for some folks. Some people's socioeconomic status changes their view of their Blackness. I grew up being Black in a lower-middle class family. I'm a first generation college student as well. That is my experience. So, how I understand my Blackness is through those lenses. I had to beg for financial aid because I didn't have it. I had to try to navigate my university because no one could help me do so. All of those things are very much integrated into my Black experience. My son, when he goes to college eighteen years from now, will not be first generation. He likely, hopefully, will be from an upper-middle class family and yet, he is still Black. The way he'll have to navigate a university community will be much different. He'll be able to call me and say 'Mom, I don't know about this class; can you help me?' Yes, I'll be more in tune with his undergraduate experience because I know what that is. That doesn't mean that his

Blackness is less important, but those things are integrated into his Black experience at a university campus. I use that example to say generational differences do matter in terms of what the experience is.

"We need to be attuned to that because students are saying 'I'm this kind of student. I want you to be contemporary in terms of the language you use and how you see me and how I can identify.' So, for me, it's important to hear the alumni experience and what best practices were then and to hear what the students are saying. I have to find a way of integrating those things. However, I don't think it's appropriate for me to say 'so, this is what was done, and you're Black, so this is your experience, and we're going to move forward in this specific way.'"

"I'm really excited about the work we're doing now. I'm co-chairing The Black House Renovation Project with Julie Payne-Kirchmeier, the Associate Vice President and Chief of Staff for Student Affairs. We knew renovations needed to occur at The Black House, and we knew the university needed to take responsibility for and go through the full process for doing that. Thus, we have members from Facilities Management, and students, faculty, and staff are involved. It's a several-step process."

"The first step was to do a feasibility study. What we knew about The Black House was, to our knowledge, that there hadn't been any significant renovations done, at least for many, many years. Therefore, we needed to find out what the feasibility of construction on the building was. So, we needed an architectural firm to come in and do that work."

"What does our community—our Black students, our Black alumni, our Black faculty, and our Black staff—want this space to be and look like moving forward? So, we're really talking about conceptual design ideas. Our architectural firm started engaging the community to ask 'If you could put anything in here, what would you want?' We heard from the Black students, who offered every idea from a beauty salon to just space to study, from computers to no computers but places to plug in a laptop. They wanted a welcoming space. All of these things came from that. We started to engage our faculty, our alumni, and our students. We wanted to be very clear that we weren't talking about walls. We weren't at that point yet. After the charrettes, it was clear that the first floor was going to be a gathering and welcoming space. It was clear that the students wanted the second floor to be a bit more of a private space to study and congregate. The third floor was to become a meditation space away from the rest. We looked at how the basement could be used and the theme that arose there was around play. All of those things went into a very large report that was submitted in March of 2017. From everything I've heard, the students were very excited that something was happening that focused on their experience; the students we interviewed and those who served on the committee stated that this effort reflected their experience. Many saw where they could find themselves in the report.

"Now, we are at the next phase of the process, and that's conceptual design. We're starting to talk about walls and what things will look like. We have a budget of $4.5 million. With that done, we start putting ideas in place and brick and mortar to those ideas. As we go into schematic design, some of the engagements that students and other constituencies would like to see in the space will be reviewed."

Lesley-Ann remains sensitive to the notion that The Black House needs to be more than a building and notes the ongoing programming efforts. "We've done some work with the faculty. Mary Pattillo, one of our beloved Black faculty members, did an event specifically for Black women. There was a need to bring Black students together beyond student organizations, so there have been monthly Black House community meetings. Students get to come together, meet each other, and talk about issues. A group for Black women called For Us By Us (FUBU) was formed and is led by Black staff. So, there have been a lot of things that have come from the Black Student Experience Task Force that have become programs in The Black House as a result of what students have said."

Lesley-Ann is sensitive to the appearance of detaching from the history of past experience of Blacks at the university. "I'm passionate and care deeply. I think there is tension that exists based on what I do. The ways in which I like to use data I believe are important in helping us understand. I do think there's lots of data from the past that exists, and we did use information in the Black Student Experience Task Force that came from the 1990's that says a lot of similar things. That is understanding the history of alums, seeing where similarities are, and understanding the history of Northwestern and the Black experience at Northwestern and using all of that to contextualize the experience of what you're hearing now. So, it informs what we're hearing, where we're trying to go, and the work I'm trying to do. It's not to ignore those things. I'm sorry that the alumni feel like we're ignoring their experience because that is not my intent, but the experience of our alums does not trump the experience of current students. It's how those things are integrated and how we make sense of them and there are tensions that exist based on what folks are saying.

"I have not had the pleasure of meeting the past Deans of African American Student Affairs other than a sit-down with Alicia Palmer. In that conversation, I was made very aware of the past giants that served here but also of some of the history that exists. If I think about a timeline, I do wonder what my blip on that timeline might look like, what my role is here at Northwestern, and the ways in which I want to do my work. At the end of the day, for me, I lead and work from a place of deeply held beliefs, passion, and authenticity. I keep my own experience as a Black student on a predominantly White campus in front of me as I think about what some the things are that our students are navigating every day. That's not to say they're having my same experience, but it grounds me. Based on that, it brings me to a sense of urgency. I hope that the ways in which or how much we've been able to do during my time here reflects that urgency."

The Black experience at Northwestern touches on the professional staff as much as it does the students, and Lesley-Ann is part of that consideration. "Now, has everything been perfect? No. I'm not a perfect person, but my goals are always to better the experience for our students, particularly our Black students and other students of marginalized identities. This place is hard. Northwestern can be hard in lots of ways. It's rigorous, there's the quarter system, it feels like a pressure cooker sometimes, and there's opportunities for celebration and joy and representation, and for me, that's how I balance the role as well. There are tensions, and I'm pulled in lots of different ways, and with those tensions come deeply held gratitude for the giants that came before me, for the staff that's here working really hard on the ground for the students, for the students that engage me and trust me, and for opportunity to engage with the alumni. It's also meaningful to know in some ways, at least in my head, the work I've been committed to doing for a long time now in higher education is hopefully creating a better environment for students of color currently and in the future. So, I think about my son being a student someday.

"I feel the weight of my job every day. I recently have been feeling a little tired, which is not to say that I'm discouraged. Being at Northwestern and doing the amount of work that we've been able to do in less than five years is really astounding when I think back to where we were when I started. With the weight of the responsibility along with the pace in which we're trying to move—there is urgency to this, and that's important—and, then, we couple that with our national climate, I think all of that creates a pressure cooker. Not a little, but a lot! So, between our Black men being killed all the time to our current President saying racist and discriminatory things, it's a lot. It feels very heavy.

"I hold the truth of our Black students and other Black folks on this campus and many campuses have been ignored or pacified for a long time, and I feel a responsibility toward that. With that, I hold there's a lot of joy. There have been a lot of successes. There have been missteps that we've worked through and continue to work through, but Northwestern is getting better! I think the climate is improving. There's more Black staff, Black faculty, more Black students, and our numbers are beginning to get better. The number of Black students on campus is rising. This year's class has a 10.2% enrollment rate of Blacks. There is a push toward admitting and matriculating more Blacks on campus. Certainly, in this year's freshman class, I've seen more Black students on campus, more of them congregating together and building more community amongst each other from different pockets. For me, it's their experience when they get here and wanting that to be better too. I think it's important that I'm here. I think the work that I'm doing is important."

Growth of the Black Experience

- **Andre Bell:** Vice President of Admissions and Financial Aid, Bursar's Office Takeover Participant
- **Henry Binford:** Professor of History
- **Robert Moore:** Founder, Northwestern University Black Alumni Association
- **L. Stanley Davis:** Co-Founder, Northwestern Community Ensemble
- **Aldon Morris:** Interim Dean of Weinberg College of Arts and Sciences, Chair, Department of Sociology
- **Jabari Asim:** Coordinator, For Members Only, The Black Student Alliance
- **Harris Lennix:** Coordinator, For Members Only, The Black Student Alliance
- **Asadah Kirkland:** Coordinator, Form Members Only, The Black Student Alliance
- **Black Greek Letter Organizations**

Andre Bell

Andre Bell

Andre Bell was a graduate of Northwestern University's Weinberg College of Arts and Sciences in 1970 and the School of Education and Social Policy in 1974. His early Northwestern experience was defined by physical isolation. He studied engineering and lived on North Campus, only randomly coming across other Black students. Eventually, he came to enjoy the weekend excursions to the Evanston home of Charles "Doc" Glass to have some semblance of a Black experience and to discover others like him.

By his sophomore year on campus, he was part of a growing group that seems to be at the end of their rope. Andre was enlisted as part of the organizing group that planned the 1968 takeover of the Bursar's Office. "We were all kind of pissed off at how we felt we weren't being attended to very well… We had discussions about how to bring some attention to ourselves, and simply put, the decision to occupy the Bursar's Office was made because that's where the money was. If you want them to pay attention, you go where the money is." The decision to take over the Bursar's Office was not a decision made in isolation. Black students at Northwestern were emboldened by both the anger resulting from the death of Martin Luther King, Jr. just a month earlier and empowered by the success other students were having on other campuses across the country.

Andre notes the failure of earlier efforts to negotiate improvements for Black students with the administration. "We wanted to make things better… In the beginning, we were a small group, but that group was like a gnat on somebody's ass. It still wasn't good enough. There were a limited number of Black students, so we all had to come together."

Andre notes his particular role in the planning was related to his field of study. "As part of the process of planning the takeover of the Bursar's Office, I got involved in reconnaissance because I was studying architecture and interior design." He had happened across the existence of tunnels connecting Rebecca Crown Center (the administration building) and the Bursar's Office. He explored the possibility of travel between the two buildings, either as a means of entry for the students or as a means of ambush from the police. He notes there were a few Black students with work-study jobs in the Bursar's Office, so that also helped with the planning. The discovery of these tunnels and additional access points to the Bursar's office proved critical to the takeover's success by blocking sneak attacks once the building had been secured.

During the thirty-eight hours of being holed up in the Bursar's Office, Andre recalls constantly wondering if the police were coming. Still, there were no regrets. "Did I have any remorse? None. It was orderly and I felt really good about what we all did." After the takeover, Andre recalls feeling elated. "There was no pushback from the university. There was elation and feeling as if we'd done it, and we finally have their attention. The real question was 'Where do we go from here.' In a couple of years, we would have The Black House and African American Studies, although it has always tickled me that The Black House is painted white."

After his graduation in 1970, Andre had an occasion to return to Northwestern between 1972 and 1987, becoming Director of Admissions and Financial Aid. In this capacity, Andre was able to directly advance the legacy he contributed to as part of the group taking over the Bursar's Office in 1968. He was at the helm of the most precipitous period of growth of the number of African American students attending Northwestern. "We definitely worked on growing our community. We did get to the point where we had some power and the university was handling us properly.

Becoming full citizens of the university grew out of that experience. Finding qualified Blacks to attend Northwestern was a challenge but it's definitely possible if you're committed."

In October 1968, Andre took the lead in re-chartering the Northwestern chapter (Alpha Mu) of Alpha Phi Alpha fraternity, which was originally founded in 1922. Furthermore, he served as chapter advisor from his graduation until 1987.

Andre looks at the evolution of the Black experience with the viewpoint of one who directly fought to implement change. "If you have a great university with great resources, things should be better. Over time, things certainly have been." He views ongoing challenges as being as much internal as they may be coming from the institution. "The key thing is the community needs to be clear with itself. At times, we have these things that come and threaten to distract or divide us, and the challenge is still keeping everyone knowing that they're still part of this community in addition to everything else."

Tears of joy well up in Andre's eyes as he reflects on the totality of the ways Northwestern has been a part of his life and how he's contributed to his alma mater as a student, alumni, and administrator. "That's a big pot. It hits me when I'm on campus to do something or to speak to the fraternity guys. On one occasion, when we were at home watching a football game, and as they kept panning the stadium, we couldn't help but literally count the hundreds of Black kids in the crowd wearing purple. There were three Black cheerleaders regularly in front of the camera. You can throw a stick or a bomb and not hit five Blacks when we were in school. We have looked at the participation of the Blacks in those moments. I'm a part of that. I also remember for the fraternity's seventy-fifth anniversary, I was invited back to speak, and it was just amazing to have fraternity brothers from multiple generations just come up and say thank you.

"I think the first part of coming to Northwestern for Black students is 'I got in.' If you're fortunate, you'll have a great experience, and you know you'll get a great education. Now, what's critical in my view, and maybe I say this because we were in that first wave, is what's your worth to our community? How do you raise our people up by our work? I mean that in every part of the walk. It could be through your church, it could be on your job, and it could be just talking to people in your workplace so you can make it all stronger. We should all be conscious of trying to move things forward."

Henry Binford

Henry Binford came to Northwestern in the fall of 1973, joining the Department of History in what he calls his "first real job" after completing his doctoral work at Harvard University. Upon his arrival to Northwestern, it was immediately impressed upon him how much turbulence had been occurring on campus. "I was not here for the big events of 1968 or the events of 1970. However, when I arrived in 1973, there were plenty of people around who had been. Immediately, I began hearing things about what had occurred, such as the events blockading Sheridan Road as protests against the four students killed at Kent State and the two students killed at Jackson State. Then, there were stories about the enormous mass meetings that occurred that were presided over by Eva Jefferson (Paterson) regarding the Vietnam and ROTC controversies. All of that was recent memory.

"It was an exciting time. The campus was still recovering from all the protests, and there was still plenty of activism going on. However, one of the things that had happened by the time I got here was Nixon had become President. The wind had gone out of the sails of a lot of people who were advocating for help from the federal government in various ways."

Even through the numbers of African American faculty were small, Henry was able to overcome any sense of racial isolation by becoming involved in the general Black university community. "I got to very quickly know other members of the African

American faculty because there weren't very many of us at that point. There were only three African Americans in the history department: Sterling Stuckey, Ibrahim Sundiata, and myself, and there were a few others in other departments. One of the things that's changed over the years is there's a much larger community of African American faculty and staff, and it's difficult to know everybody now."

The small Black Northwestern community made it easy for Henry to carve out his area of expertise. "Leon Forrest engaged me within the African American Studies Department very soon after I arrived, and he made me a departmental affiliate, giving me a joint appointment between the Departments of History and African American Studies. So, I began taking on different roles within the departments. This allowed me to become mentor to a number of African American students, as there weren't very many of them, and they didn't have many places to go. In addition to being involved with African American Studies, and because I specialize in urban history, meaning I study cities, I was also very quickly involved with what was then called The Center for Urban Affairs, which was an institution based at Northwestern designed in part to bring Northwestern faculty and student abilities into connection with Chicago.

Henry describes an environment at Northwestern that was full of contradictions and opportunities. "I became very aware there was a sense of discouragement about governmental activities to roll progress back under the Nixon presidency, but there was also a sense of excitement on campus that there were more African American faculty and students than there had been, and things like the African American Studies program was getting going, The Black House was available, and the wonderful people of African American Student Affairs were available for students. I actually once taught an upper level undergraduate seminar in The Black House. I did hold meetings there occasionally on issues that were related to the Black experience. We wanted to make the most of the opportunities we had, and we wanted to continue to push the university in directions it seemed to be going.

"There was also a sense, especially among the undergraduate students, that they were still a tiny minority in a large sea of Whiteness at Northwestern. That hasn't gone away, but it was especially prominent then. The students too often had a sense of not belonging that was more acute than it was for the faculty. In most cases, the faculty members who hired us were delighted that we came. In the history department, people were eager to diversify what, at that time, was a small kind of gentlemen's club of White faculty members. Fortunately, they were aware of what kind of community they were, and the faculty wanted to be more diverse and inclusive."

Henry believes the students were having a tougher time than he was as a faculty member. "The students were constantly encountering extremes. There were many graduate and undergraduate students who were eager to diversify the campus and eager to welcome African Americans in greater numbers and then, there were students who really resented the Black presence. Occasionally, there were very nasty incidents on campus, just as they occur occasionally today. Students were exposed to discrimination, not from the university itself, but from organizations such as fraternities, sororities, and other clubs. My sense was the use of racial slurs and other events weren't just isolated episodes. However, the students were aware that these events weren't one extreme end of a spectrum of behavior. The African American students were just more aware of the simple fact that there weren't very many of them by comparison with lots of other groups on campus, and they were a very, very small community. I don't think things happening here were any worse than were occurring on other campuses, but it was just the way of the world at that time."

In those instances in which students, faculty, and staff were having difficulties on campus, the Black Evanston community was still available for support. "Back then, there was a significant level of interaction with the Evanston community, largely due to the ongoing efforts of African American Student Affairs. They were anxious to be a sort of bridge between the Black students and faculty on campus and the Black community in Evanston. I became involved with the Evanston branch of the NAACP, and I also was involved with the National Urban League in Chicago. I know that many of the Evanston NAACPers were eager to reach out to the students on campus."

Throughout those early days on campus, Henry and other members of the faculty and professional staff set about the work of improving the university environment over the long term in a way consistent with the aims expressed by those involved with the 1968 takeover of the Bursar's Office. "Looking back on it, it is a little different than it felt then. We were aware that we were pioneers, but we just thought of ourselves as the people laying the foundation for future greatness, rather than being the 'greatness' ourselves.

"One of the things I strongly remember about the African American Studies program was that it was struggling. It was very small. They did not have very many permanent faculty members, and it was a struggle to get more. I think there's been a sea of change in the way African American Studies fits into the rest of the university and the way the university offers support to African American Studies, from then to now. It's hard to get a sense of that because the African American Studies program now is nationally prominent, it's robust, and it has extremely distinguished people on the faculty. In those days, it was a handful, maybe a half-dozen people who were trying to get this program started and to give it permanence, and to persuade the university to expand the department. We had a sense that we had to work hard to sustain the offerings of African American Studies, but we also had to work hard to convince the university and some of the traditional departments that we needed more support, and we were a valuable part of the campus. That was a slow job."

Over the years, that "slow job" has shown dividends. "There are many more African American students, graduates and undergraduates, than there were then. There are many more African American faculty and staff than there were then. I think there's also a much greater level of diversity among the African American students. In the 1970's, they tended to be a much more tighter-knit group because they were much more aware that they were a part of a distinct, very small minority. Now, there's the thing you would want, which is a wide range of personalities and interests and talents among the Black student body. Now, there are not only people—as there were then—who'd raise the fist as activists, but there are people who just want to go off and play their violin. There's an enormous range of African Americans, which is terrific and is a big change from what it was.

"In a way, it's also the case that the presence and the enormous strength of the African American Studies department now is far beyond what we had in the beginning. This is in terms of the numbers of faculty, course offerings, the attraction of graduate students – there weren't any graduate students back then—and the ability to hold conferences and bring in distinguished scholars from elsewhere. Back in 1973–74, within the first year, I knew every African American faculty member. I couldn't do that now. It's too big of a community."

Of course, the progress is tempered by ongoing struggles, especially among the Black student experience. "Alas, some of the things that troubled us, especially for African American students, are still here. There are still difficulties of feeling invisible in some cases, and there are still occasional ugly incidents that happen to some African American students. There's an awareness of that amongst both the student and the faculty community."

To be clear, Henry doesn't view that Black experience of Northwestern to be defined by negativity. "I was delighted to get a job at a distinguished university like Northwestern in a wonderful city, but I'm even more happy to be at Northwestern now than I was then because there has been this tremendous expansion of an African American presence on the campus. We have reached the stage now, in some cases, where Blackness is not the first thing people think about when they encounter an African American faculty member on campus. We were a highly visible, tiny few in the beginning. Even people like me, being very light skinned, were distinctly noticeable. Everybody knew! Nowadays, there's too many of us for that."

Henry is especially pleased at the incremental growth of Black leadership among the administrative ranks over the years. "I think it's tremendous that the Provost of the university happens to be an African American male, but I think it's built upon certain other milestones. Aldon Morris, for a time, was Dean of the College of Arts and Sciences, and that was a big first. Dwight McBride became Dean of The Graduate School, and that was a big first. In both cases, those were extraordinarily talented and qualified individuals, and they got the campus used to the fact that there were going to be African Americans in higher-level administrative positions. So, Jonathan Holloway, in some ways, is a capstone on that kind of progression and that kind of development. I think it is tremendously valuable to the entire Northwestern community that you have someone who people will react to as Provost first –

because he is Provost. This is authority we're dealing with here! It's only been a year that he's been here, but already people are used to the fact that he is who he is, and that's not a big deal. It's not a big deal, and yet, it's a huge deal."

Henry has often been called to offer his voice on behalf of the areas of interest to the university related to the Black experience on campus. For example, in 2015 and 2016, he was asked to serve on both The Black House Review Committee and the Black Student Experience Committee. "In 2015, when a controversy erupted because the university proposed using space in The Black House for other administrative activity because the university was allegedly short on office space. They thought 'Oh, we'll just use The Black House. It's a university building, and we'll put some stuff there.' I think they really did not anticipate the psychological impact of that, and they didn't consult with the Black community before they did it. They just did it. Actually, they got started doing it, and there was an enormous backlash from the existing Black students, from the alumni, and from all kinds of other people.

"So as a result, the administration created this committee, which initially started as a mechanism for ventilation of opinions. We had an entire sequence of 'listening sessions,' in which Black students, staff, faculty, alumni, and other non-Black individuals came forward to talk about The Black House and what it meant. Sort of halfway through our proceedings, President Schapiro came to one of our sessions and heard one of the issues that kept coming up, which was The Black House as a physical structure, needed renovation as a requisite of students being inclined to use it. It's an old house, and it may not have been up to code. He heard the concerns and, in essence, said 'Ok, we're not going to do anything else with The Black House. We're not going to put any other offices in there, and we're going to see about trying to make it better.' That was a green light for a lot of other positive action.

"Since then, there have been two other committees, which I've migrated through. There was The Black House Review Committee, which was a collective brainstorming committee related to what could be done with The Black House in conjunction with some architects the university hired to think about this. That was a really productive exercise. There have been a lot of committees at Northwestern, but this was one of those occasions in which I really thought the university was doing worthwhile work. It was both setting the stage for making The Black House a better place for future African American students, faculty and staff and was also reminding the university administration of what happened to necessitate the Black House, what The Black House was, and what place in history it occupied.

"The third committee is working with those same architects to develop more detailed plans. We've now seen models and renderings, and it's going to be a truly amazing place. I think the controversy about The Black House and its resolution is the biggest confrontation that the university has had with the role of African American students probably since the 1970's and will produce meaningful progress."

The 2015 controversy over The Black House takes Henry back to an earlier series of protest that share a similar theme. "I do recall a moment in the '80's, in which there were national protests on college campuses, including at Northwestern, related to apartheid in South Africa and the support that Northwestern's investments were giving to an apartheid regime. At that point, as so often happens, a discussion of race elsewhere, whether it is in South Africa or in Mississippi, inevitably turns into a discussion about race here at Northwestern. I'm a historian, so I'm very interested in those moments in which individuals recover their history. We're living in one of those right now with The Black House renovations. However, the apartheid movement was another one where I know a certain number of African American students and faculty tried to remind the campus of its own history of race and to initiate discussions about race.

"Partly because of that episode, with the removal of African American Student Affairs, and partly because of the growth of Northwestern as a university, it is now the case that African American Studies is not the only focus of intellectual energy on issues of race that exists on campus. There are a number of other institutes and programs in which race, broadly defined, has become an issue. So, there are a lot of lively conversations going on continuously about race, as well as about class, gender, and other categories of that nature in ways that just weren't happening in the 1970's."

Regarding the university's elimination of the Department of African American Student Affairs and subsequent switch toward the focus on Multicultural Student Affairs, Henry is not yet clear on its overall effects on the Black experience. "The verdict is still out in some ways. I think the emphasis on multiculturalism is more problematic for students than it has been for the Black faculty and staff on campus because students really don't want the distinctive character of the African American experience to be normalized as just one of a diverse set of cultural experiences. One of the consequences of The Black House crisis of 2015 has been a greater recognition on the part of at least some people within the administration that, within a desirable effort to recognize multiculturalism, there is a danger of a 'one size fits all' approach. There remains a need to serve and promote the interests and viewpoints of lots of different kinds of people without thinking that they are all just representatives of a multicultural spectrum.

"What I would like to see is greater recognition of some of those specific needs of African American students through administrative channels, especially because the Black student body is now itself more diverse. In fact, Northwestern has been making an effort to increase the numbers of African Americans and underrepresented groups of all kinds, including first generation college students. I know our President and Provost are both anxious to do that. One of the things that happens when you do that is now we are getting African Americans who represent some of the most difficult circumstances in the United States while growing up, who come out of neighborhoods where it's a wonder that they finished high school, let alone got to go to college. Of course, we also have some African Americans who come from the top-level urban high schools in the nation. This diversity requires additional resources.

"Just as it is important to recognize the consequences of the long history of Blackness in the United States and at Northwestern, it's also important that the university tries to remain flexible about student needs and target resources in a finer-grained way than they sometimes do now. I'm now beginning to understand that to a greater extent than I've previously gotten in forty years because there are some undergraduate students, both Black and White, who are far less prepared for the college experience—and I don't mean academically or intellectually—but far less prepared by exposure to the world than the kind of norm of Northwestern students who come from upper-middle class, suburban backgrounds. I'm teaching a first-year seminar now, and I've got a student from Nairobi, a student from Shanghai, and a Latino student from Los Angeles, and they're all finding Northwestern to be a challenge, but all in different ways. The university, as it tries to become a more accommodating place for non-traditional students, has to keep in mind that they need to keep monitoring the experiences of very diverse kinds of people and targeting resources, so that they get a good experience at Northwestern."

Henry is encouraged that one noticeable difference in the university's approach has been to not solely appear to be reacting to protests and crises. "I think we are at a historically significant moment regarding the university's understanding that they need to be proactive about certain things related to race, and I think not only the 2015 Black House crisis but also the upcoming celebration of 1968 being held in 2018 are spurs to that kind of activity and outlook. Speaking as a member of The Black House committee, I'm very hopeful that the returning alumni will see progress and will keep the prodding going on, so the university becomes ever more aware in the future."

In recent years, Professor Henry Binford has been awarded a Career Achievement Award by the Northwestern University Black Alumni Association, the Outstanding Affiliate Award by Northwestern Department of African American Studies, the Outstanding Faculty Member Award from the Northwestern University Interfraternity Council, National Pan-Hellenic Council, and Pan-Hellenic Association, the National Faculty Award from the Association of Graduate Liberal Studies Programs, the Charles Deering McCormick Professor of Teaching Excellence, and the Northwestern University Alumni Association Award for Excellence in Teaching.

Robert Moore

Robert (Bob) Moore entered Northwestern University in 1971 from Harrisburg, Pennsylvania, joining his high school debate partner in choosing Northwestern. He received his undergraduate degree from the School of Professional Studies in 1988 and a master's degree from the Northwestern Medill School of Journalism in 1989.

"Coming from a small town in Pennsylvania, the undergraduate years were a 'Blackening' experience for me. FMO (For Members Only, The Black Student Alliance of Northwestern University) helped me because I'm a social person, and I went to FMO and got on whatever activities and committees I could to learn. We knew upon arrival there was a takeover in 1968, and I was one of the first beneficiaries of the things that were won in that takeover. So, it behooved me to get involved and make good on the promises that were made."

One especially exciting activity involved the move from the original Black House at 619 Emerson to the larger building at 1914 Sheridan Road. "That was a big move because the original building was too small, as we had a growing Black population. So, we got this new building, and we had the ability to decorate it! We had red, green, and black walls all over the place and had fluorescent paint. It was a place we certainly could call home."

Bob did very well forging relationships with other students on campus, and in fact, he remains friends with his very first roommate, "...a Jewish gentleman from Los Angeles. Believe it or not, we got along very well!" However, that too often seemed to be the exception instead of the norm. "There were a lot of growing pains on campus. A lot of the situations with students were very hard; sometimes there were multiple roommates, and there were those who were surprised that their roommate was a Black person. Thus, many of the discussions we had in The Black House were ones teaching us how to listen."

Bob was an early contributor to the growth and success of the Northwestern Community Ensemble (NCE) and recalls how difficult it was to get space on campus for activities. "My biggest disappointment at Northwestern—remember, I was here in the early '70's—is that I was one of the helpers of the Black choir, and the Alice Millar Chapel was not receptive to us. They would not give us rehearsal space on campus. So, we had to retreat to the Black community, and we went to the Ebenezer A&M Zion Church." Bob notes that resistance also came regarding the desire to have worship services and the inaugural concert for the choir. "They said, 'you want to have an all-Black worship service? Who's your faculty advisor?' Of course, we didn't have one. It was less than an inviting spirit." Through the effort of a graduate student in the School of Music, NCE eventually prevailed.

However, out of these challenges came opportunity and success. "When we had that initial performance in December of 1971, there was a university chaplain who was there. He said that he had never come to a Black worship service before, but ours affected him. So, we knew we had to stand our ground and be strident in the opinions we had because what we were doing mattered. There was a learning curve."

Later as an undergraduate, Bob became a Residence Assistant and a Hall Coordinator. He notes that his interactions with his fellow students changed again, and he was pleasantly surprised by his ability to interact with others on campus. "I wasn't Bob anymore! I had some of the most Earth-shattering discussions with White students who used me as sort of a surrogate parent who was non-judgmental."

Bob notes that during this time at Northwestern, academic difficulties were occurring disproportionately among Black students. "Some of us were on academic probation—out a year, or maybe one or two terms—but we all came back and eventually graduated." Bob himself left Northwestern in 1976 without his undergraduate degree. "I was on the 'seventeen-year plan!' It wasn't until I decided I wanted to change careers and get a master's degree that I came back and finished my last thirty credits." Bob obtained his undergraduate degree in 1988.

Bob had a myriad of challenges and difficulties through his pursuit of degrees from Northwestern, but that never interfered with the love he felt for the university. "You make the best out of situations. Was Northwestern always nurturing? I wouldn't call it that. It was more like they were saying 'We're blind to what you're feeling and thinking, and if you're not aggressive enough to speak up for yourself, you're going to find yourself a day late and a dollar short.' I was never afraid to do just that."

When asked where his love and passion for Northwestern came, Bob doesn't hesitate. "My love for Northwestern came from the Northwestern Community Ensemble (NCE). I call myself the most ardent and fervent NCE booster that's there. Even after leaving NU, while I lived and worked in Chicago, I went to every NCE concert. Over the years, it's gone from being a Black choir to a multiracial choir with Caucasians and Asians in it, but every single year, they continue to have a musical ministry. I'm so proud that this institution is going to celebrate its fiftieth anniversary at this university in the May of 2021."

Bob always held a reverence for the efforts of the students who came before him, especially the participants of the 1968 Bursar's Office Takeover, and that led to his prominent role in establishing a Black alumni association. "After I left in the mid-seventies, we had several attempts to start a Black alumni association. The first attempt was in the mid-seventies. We all had gotten together after the death of an FMO Coordinator named Melvin Wilkerson (in whose honor the conference room in The Black House was named). He was from Chicago, and he had been violently killed. We all came back on campus, and I realized it was the first time a contemporary had been killed. Afterwards, we all were of the mind that we needed to get a Black alumni association started. Well, we had a couple of meetings, and things fizzled out because people were busy.

"We then made another effort in the early '80's, which was organized around the death of a professor. It really wasn't until the mid '80's that the effort took hold because, before then, we found that when you mentioned Northwestern to a lot of our contemporaries, they'd look at you with beaded eyes and say 'Aww man, I'm not interested. My experience wasn't the greatest.' And that's the truth. We have many Black alumni who don't have a warm and fuzzy feeling, but we need to relate to that as a means of overcoming it. Thank goodness, and with the help of Dean Karla Spurlock Evans, Charles Talbert, and myself, we said we were going to go through the process.

"We met with the Northwestern Alumni Association. We created NUBAA (Northwestern University Black Alumni Association) because there was a need. The big thing at that point was we had a lot of people from the '70's who had been out and were very successful. We would ask them to come back, or you'd ask them to give for this or that, and they had that bitter spirit. We wanted to change that because, for me, coming from a small town in Pennsylvania, Northwestern had changed my life.

"So, in the fall of 1986, we were recognized by the Northwestern Alumni Association, and NUBAA was born. Now, it's only been in the last five years that we've gone from being just a laissez-faire affiliate or affinity group or club to being a power broker. I often say NUBAA is here not only for the current students but also for the alumni, for the faculty, and for the staff. We are the repository for the things those students on May 3rd and 4th of 1968 fought for. It's a covenant that was signed, and it's our job as NUBAA on whatever level to not be argumentative or racist—which are some of the things we've been accused of—but to be pragmatic. We're saying there's a covenant that was figuratively signed in sweat and blood of kids who tell me they cried during the takeover, afraid more with what their parents would say than what would happen there to them. So, that is what NUBAA is about. We're not hating or separating from our university. It's taking pride in what Northwestern has created for many Black students. Many marriages came from Northwestern. Many legacy kids are coming from Northwestern. So, my love for Northwestern continues to this day because I know the difference it made in my life and dozens and dozens of my friends' lives.

"I remember back in 1986, when we talked with the then Director of Alumni Relations, Ray Willowmagne, and Ray asked us 'Why do you guys feel like you need NUBAA?' Furthermore, he gave us suggestions of names. Of course we told him we needed NUBAA because there were certain needs and commonalities that Black alumni share. When people ask us why we can't just join NAA, we tell them we do. We're proud members of NAA, but we have to stay true to our spirit. NUBAA provides a vehicle where different groups of Black alumni with different university experiences can come together to relate, talk about, and share their experiences.

"As an example, I am so proud that in the last five to ten years, we've developed something called DH (Destination Homecoming). People now come home! I can't tell you how many times in the past the 'reunion thing' would happen, and people's responses were 'Oh God, should I come?' Then, NUBAA shows up and has a slate of three or four different things, lights up social media, and response becomes 'I'm so glad I came!' That's not only because of the NUBAA programming but the NU experience. I go back in the bleachers, and I remember going to games. So, there's a duality of appreciation that's there."

Bob notes the ability of NUBAA to have diffused the "blockage and bitterness" of many Black alumni. "By having a Black community that embraced them, and said we don't care where you're from, it creates bonds that are so unique. I not only know that because of the celebrations and NUBAA being a pleasant place to come and exchange pleasantries, but we also have funerals. When people die, the community weighs in with very lengthy accounts about how they met at Northwestern, how they were nurtured, and how these friends nurtured other people."

Bob says the presence of a Black alumni association always has seemed to bother Northwestern. "I remember when Ray Willowmagne took offense to the name. He asked, 'what happened to the name we suggested? Why don't you call yourselves the Lawyer Taylor Association or Society? As I was told, Lawyer Taylor was the first Black person to go to Northwestern way back when and get a degree!' (Lawyer

Taylor had historically been thought by Northwestern to be the first African American to receive an undergraduate degree, having done so in 1903.) Well, we certainly could honor Lawyer Taylor, but we wanted to say we were Black! We don't want anything that disguised it. We needed to say who we are, and we won. We proudly say we're Northwestern first, we're a community, and we're Black." Therefore, in 1986, NUBAA become Northwestern's first affinity group and maintains its designation as the only Association within the club structure of the Northwestern Alumni Association, and Robert Moore became the founding president.

Bob is very reflective about the evolution of NUBAA since its inception. "Originally, we got kudos just because we had a Black affinity group. Ok, now we have it. As we went through the years, we had a lot of people who said 'I'll be in NUBAA as President' because it was a resume stuffer, and that retarded the group's development. Then, we had some presidents who came in and had to deal with some real crises. So, while we had the name of NUBAA, we never had what we have now, starting about in 2015, which is a posture. We're a force. I don't want to suggest that we seek out 'point-counterpoints,' but we have an opinion. We represent people of color, and that means people who might be from the United States or Jamaica or Africa. We carry that for the alumni, the current students as well as the faculty and staff. Whenever we're asked, 'Well how can you cover all of that?' I respond, 'Because there's no one else to do that.'

"When we had confrontations over the years when Black professors didn't get tenure or were released, yeah, they'd listen to you, but you got the sense by the look in your eyes that it was insincere, like 'Oh yeah, here's the Black people. Let's listen to them... Yeah... Ok...' So, in the mid 2000's, we started getting presidents in NUBAA who had MBAs, who saw their tenure in NUBAA as not honorific in a resume stuffing way but in believing that 'I can make a difference.' So, we got organized. We started trying to recruit the masses. The university won't give us the names of all the people that are tracked as Black, so it's up to us to organize our masses so we can function beyond a current NUBAA President, and display that we have people behind us. We started getting sophisticated. I love how in 2011, during the fortieth anniversary of NCE, we worked with the NUBAA administration at that time...there was a sophistication of NUBAA helping NCE become organized in a way we couldn't have before. And from 2015 to the present, we are organized. We're organized as if we're a company. NUBAA is like that. We have interests. We know what we're about and we're going to partake of the resources of the university.

"People used to say NUBAA was just a party group. Yeah, we have entertainment, but we're much more than that. We're concerned about admissions coming in. We're concerned about the yield rate once you get that admissions letter out. When you get that acceptance rate from Northwestern, and you're a person of color, you've likely also been accepted from some of the top ten universities in the nation.

"We're also concerned about faculty. Where's the strong ombudsman for the faculty of color? If NUBAA speaks on these matters right now, the university listens. In the last four or five years, we have a NUBAA that can engage the President of the University in discussions on important issues. These aren't threats. Let's talk. Let's dialogue. And we do." "That's the power of NUBAA right now. So, how has NUBAA changed? It's a power broker for good. So, we can stop talking about what we did in the '70's. It's about the current students that are here. It's about the quality of their experience and ensuring they have a safe haven where they can come and talk. So, we participate in 'One Northwestern' and multiculturalism, but you're not going to dilute our identity. We're a force that is going to be here permanently."

Over the years, Bob became a critic of what The Black House has been allowed to become. He chooses to assign responsibility at those who have led. "The Department of African American Student Affairs had a string of Deans who came here with very pragmatic goals. They had a stake in making sure that students got in and out of Northwestern University.

"There was Milton Wiggins. Had a deep voice! He'd pick up the phone and make a call on students' behalf: 'Hi, this is Dean Wiggins over hear. We're in The Black House, and I have Bob Moore here, and we need to talk about how we can come up with a solution.' He was an ombudsman. Then when he hung up the phone, he gave you tough love and said, 'you see what spot you put me in? Now, make sure you deliver!' It's that kind of realism that was there. They were speaking the same thing your parents would say to you if they were there."

"Alice Palmer was here for a time, and then she had a brilliant political career. She inspired everyone who knew her when she was here. Karla Spurlock-Evans helped me and Charles Talbert found NUBAA. She's now a Vice President at a small exclusive eastern university for multicultural student affairs, but she got her start here. This is what we had.

"So, now with our Deans and Associate Deans gone or retired or deceased, it's become a different flavor. You don't have that nurturing force here that students and staff had. I know I'm being a critic here, but some of those administrators overseeing the concerns of African American students that have been hired in the last fifteen years haven't been worth their weight in salt at all. They came from other places, and they didn't understand the NU Black experience. So, they've tried to take fancy things that come from other universities and tried to insert them here.

"Now they've imposed hours for The Black House, when it was available 24/7. They're asking students to be homogenized. I don't think that's the role of an African American student affairs administrator. Students do that automatically and naturally. So, in the last few years, we've now had a slew of bad African American student affairs administrators. In the last ten years, they've also had roles in Multicultural Student Affairs. That's not bad, but they seem not to understand that there's a covenant in that position that they need to live up to while making it real and relevant today. That's the disconnection that's here."

Despite these circumstances, Bob retains great pride in facilitating community activities that strengthens Northwestern bonds, and he enjoys remaining a resource on behalf on NU. "Now I love being behind the scenes and providing good information to those interested in Northwestern."

L. Stanley Davis

L. Stanley Davis

L. Stanley Davis is a 1974 graduate of Northwestern's Weinberg College of Arts and Sciences, and a 1997 graduate of the School of Communication, pursuing a MA and PhD in Performance Studies. Additionally, he spent just over ten years teaching in the Department of African American Studies and the Bienan School of Music.

"My incoming class had 180 Blacks, which was the largest incoming class to that point at Northwestern. We came from everywhere across the country. What made us unique was that we, as Black students, who were chosen by Northwestern, came mostly from the hearts of inner cities. You had a few from places like Shaker Heights, Ohio and from Alpharetta, Georgia, but the main core of us was from Chicago, Detroit, St. Louis, Baltimore, and Washington, from as they say now, 'The Hood.' These were some brilliant, bright, Black folks."

From the very beginning and throughout his time at Northwestern, Stanley was influenced by and imparted discipline on his NU surroundings. "I was one of the first Black undergraduates who stayed at the NU Apartments, which had been previously reserved for graduate students and married couples. I had three White roommates. Now, I was an only child, and I had never had any roommates, except for three weeks during summer camp. It was interesting having roommates. They didn't know I was Black before I arrived, and they had all gotten there before me. They'd already picked out the rooms, but I laid down the law as to rules!

"I remember going to the first FMO (For Members Only, the Black Student Alliance of Northwestern) meeting, and I thought I'd gone to a Black Panther's meeting! The power of the leadership at that time was no-nonsense. Thanks to Clovis Semmes and the late Clinton Bristow, whom I adored, everyone stood with their fist raised high, and you went through indoctrination into the Black student community at Northwestern University at the beginning of these meetings. You'd chant 'Power to the People, Hail to the Vanguard, Black Power!' And I was like 'Whoa.' Of course, everyone had an Afro. Well, almost. I did not. My hair was short, and my mom didn't allow them in my house. She said I couldn't bring that revolutionary stuff into her home!

"The FMO leadership made some rules very clear to us. They said unequivocally that you would speak to your Brothers and Sisters as you walk this campus because our numbers were few. You were held accountable if you walked by another Black and didn't acknowledge their existence. It was reported, and you'd receive a talking to! Those FMO meetings were mandatory, and the only excuse for missing them was if you had an evening class. Then there was *The Ritual*, created and led by my dear friend, Eileen Cherry, who was the FMO Coordinator of the Arts. The handing out of the red, black, and green links symbolizing our community bond was unreal. Up until a few years ago, I still had all four of my links. You also saw dance and theater and solo performances."

As was the case with many talented Blacks at Northwestern, Stanley had unknowingly been targeted and was being groomed for leadership "They found out during New Student Week I could play the piano and asked me if I would accompany some of the Sisters that would be performing at *The Ritual*. I played for these ladies, and Eileen shared her hopes with Clifton Gerring and me about having a singing group. She said attempts had been made, but the folks doing it weren't really serious. She asked me if I would take it on. Eileen had been charged in her freshman year, so when she came back as a sophomore, she was determined that she was going to have a theatrical group, a dance troupe, a jazz group. But she really wanted a choir.

"Eileen reminded me of the commitments we made at the FMO meetings, where the Brothers who ran FMO engaged us, but they also charged and challenged us to be change agents. They insisted we be present for every event that represented the changing face of the Black community. That was in my head. I think Clovis and the others really played with our heads, and they were intimidating. My issue wasn't that. See, I was not into the Black movement in Baltimore. I didn't riot when Baltimore almost burned down. My mother wasn't going to let me out of the house to march and protest, even though I wanted to. I had been doing the music scene and choir work back in Baltimore since I was nine. I had a choir of adults that were older than me. We toured. But I came to Northwestern to go to school, to get an education, and my thing was to focus."

Stanley came to appreciate his focus and realized that the value of education wasn't just limited to academic coursework. "Northwestern had given me a full ride. I came to NU instead of U of Penn, Columbia, and other places, and I was committed. Dr. Martin Luther King, Jr. died on my sixteenth birthday, and that made a difference in my life. I kept thinking to myself 'what more could I do short of giving my life at age thirty-nine?' As the Black community kept facing challenges over my four years, I kept reflecting on what Dr. King might do.

"It was a hard fought war and took almost an entire school year, but eventually Eileen got me to do it. She stayed on me. I had been in a group in Chicago and was performing there on Sundays. I played occasionally, but that was it. I did not want that responsibility because I knew how I was. For me, it was about excellence. I wasn't going to take sixty-five or eighty percent effort, much like the FMO leaders did not accept less than total commitment. It was my getting sick, being bedridden and coming back to Northwestern for the spring quarter of 1970, nine days late, for me to realize how important the community was and what my role in it could be. It was that quarter when FMO brought the University of Illinois Black Chorus to the Alice Millar Chapel in concert. I had just been out of the hospital five days. There were 175 Blacks clad in African dashikis and with afros. The director of the choir was an alum of Northwestern, Robert Ray. And they sang! I was sitting there going 'Oh, my God.' It was on that night I turned to Eileen and said, 'You know what? I'm ready.' It was as if God had brought me back from the hospital to do this."

The Northwestern Community Ensemble was officially formed in May of 1971. "We started with a group of fifteen. We did auditions at Ebenezer A.M.E Church. We walked out to Kendall College and the National College of Education. We distributed fliers to every Black student we saw on both of those campuses. That part of the story is so important because NCE is about community. The name involved the fact that we were not just Northwestern students but included the other colleges. Because of the choir, we were a bridge to the other two schools, which also had Black students. They were proud to be able to come on our campus to do things. So, the original choir had fifteen students and three musicians, one of whom was the first Black to play in the Northwestern Wildcat Marching Band, Tony Boynes. He was our first drummer. In September of 1971, we opened NCE up for auditions and grew to twenty-seven students and four musicians."

The formation of NCE was not just a desire of the group to have its own choir. Opportunities to participate within the university were not available. "Whereas Northwestern's School of Music was ranking within the top five nationally, not one note of Black music was sung. My first work-study job was in the library in circulation, and I could hear all this music throughout the building next to Rebecca Crown, but I never heard a Negro spiritual and definitely didn't hear a gospel song. There were no Black professors at the School of Music. When we even went to the School of Music looking for a place to rehearse, I thought I had a way in because I was a known entity from the library. They asked if we had a faculty sponsor. We didn't. They asked if we were recognized by ASG. We weren't. They didn't allow us to use their facilities. That's how we ended up going into Evanston and meeting Jacob S. Blake, at that time, the Reverend of Ebenezer AME Church. We told him what we were trying to do. He granted permission. While we were practicing, he'd been in the back of the rehearsal room with the biggest handkerchief I'd ever seen. He was in tears. What we didn't know was Ebenezer had been without a youth or young adult choir at the church during his time there, and he wanted that badly. We ended up performing there during a huge Memorial Day event of the church, which led to us performing every second Sunday of the month until I graduated."

Stanley states that his university experience in effect became his Northwestern experience. "This is what I discover from alums that came out of NCE. They all would say that had it not been for NCE and their participation in it, they don't know if they'd have made it through Northwestern. There really were many who were considering dropping out of NU or transferring because the pressure of this environment was so great. For many, the Ensemble was a Saturday respite and a place of solace where people could get their mind right, get inspired, and engage with Blacks from all kinds of majors. NCE was my fraternity, and everyone came together there. Whether it was the Alphas (Alpha Phi Alpha), the Kappas (Kappa Alpha Psi), or Ques (Omega Psi Phi), they were all singing together. Whether the women were Deltas (Delta Sigma Theta) or AKAs (Alpha Kappa Alpha), it didn't matter. This was NCE."

As the Northwestern Community Ensemble grew, it's purpose outpaced simply being an extracurricular activity for students. "We started going on national tours arranged by me, Eileen, and Clifton, and NCE became a recruiting tool for the university! There were students who came to Northwestern in my junior and senior years and thereafter because of the exposure provided by NCE. We went to Memphis, Pine Bluff, Arkansas, Virginia Beach, Norfolk, Virginia, Cleveland, Baltimore, and Washington, DC. Wherever we went, application numbers went up. The university was baffled!

"Within the circle of NCE membership, we encouraged each other. We didn't necessarily preach religion. We preached feeling safe and secure within one's self and persevering through the storms. It was the lyrics of the music that brought us through the struggle. It was and has been a healing organization for the university's students. Regarding the current population, the only thing that distresses me is we were not founded as a gospel choir, and that's what separated us from everyone else. We sang cappella Negro spirituals, hymns, and anthems. We sang in foreign tongues, and we sang traditional and modern gospel. It was always about blessing the folks who came to our events, such that they would be edified and the God we serve would be glorified.

"This takes me back to the Black community during my college years. We had some revolutionaries. They were serious and didn't have any problems using different means to make their point. Some of them would not support us until the choir took on momentum and gained popularity. In fact, when the choir was formed, I remember a few FMO leaders during the next years say 'that's the problem with the Negros. You're too busy praying, singing, and getting on your knees!' By my senior year, people saw the power of the choir to bring together different parts of the Black community. NCE became a force. The theater and other groups were all excellent, but there was something about that choir."

Stanley sees parallels between participation in NCE and the Northwestern education and experience. "I think the key words are commitment and dedication. You have to put the time in. We were a unique chorus among those across the state. When we'd go to Atlanta every year for the college gospel choir workshop, we were the smallest choir, but we'd walk away with the awards. We put in the time. We really didn't experience basketball and football games or going to Chicago to the Water Tower Place. It also meant balance, time management, and a commitment, not only to the choir but also to God and to oneself and your fellow Brothers and Sisters. Individual students have to make a decision. What do you take from this university experience after having brought what you have into this experience? You are as great as the total sum, and if you bring nothing to the table, you'll only get so much from it. That will always be a concern of mine."

Almost fifty years later, the Northwestern Community Ensemble continues to be Northwestern's premier gospel choir. The ensemble still performs at various churches and public venues and holds two annual concerts, featuring local and national artists. Past participants have included Byron Cage, Kirk Franklin, Deitrick Haddon, VaShawn Mitchell, Richard Smallwood, and Hezekiah Walker. NCE strives to minister God's praises through song to strengthen, uplift, encourage, and connect the members of Northwestern's community and the surrounding areas.

Stanley has never ventured far from Northwestern and in fact, he came back to teach. "The very man that we marched on Northwestern in protest to get hired—Leon Forrest—hired me twenty years later to teach in African American studies and in the School of Music. So, I served as a faculty advisor for over ten years, from 1994 to 2005. I offered tough love, because if you're serious about being in NCE or a student at Northwestern, you've got to put in the time. If not, this is not the place for you. So, coming back as a faculty member, a graduate student, and a faculty advisor, I was really able to have a presence." Stanley's lessons and presence will continue far into the future.

Aldon Morris

Aldon Morris

Aldon Morris has worked at Northwestern since 1988. Over the last 30 years, he has served as Interim Dean of the Weinberg School of Arts and Sciences and as Chair of the Sociology Department. He enjoys teaching and is proud that Northwestern has one of the few PhD programs in African American Studies nationally. As Dean of Weinberg, Aldon worked closely with NUBAA, Ce Cole Dillon, and (at that time) NU Trustee Wayne Watson, who got an endowed chair named after Harold Washington. He remembers that Northwestern was reluctant but, in the end, and collaboratively with students, made the endowed chair happen!

Aldon loves being a Chicagoan. "Having grown up in Chicago, I got my Associates of Arts Degree from Olive-Harvey College, went to Bradley University, and decided to go to graduate school in New York." He thought naively that he was going to be in or very near New York City, but "I was way out on Long Island at the University of New York Stony Brook, which is about 60 miles out on the island!" He was itching to get back to the city. "After finishing my PhD, I had a clear-cut plan, and the clear-cut plan was to get a job back in Chicago. I received an offer from UIC, I interviewed at Loyola, and they turned me down. Then I received an offer from the University of Michigan." At the time, Aldon had no understanding of the prestige hierarchy of universities. His professors asked him when he was going to Ann Arbor and he said, "I'm not going to the University of Michigan, I'm going back to Chicago. That's always been my plan!" They hit the roof! He finally gave in to the pressure and went to the University of Michigan. Ann Arbor is a very nice college town, but it only intensified his desire to be back in Chicago, particularly when Harold Washington was elected mayor. After receiving tenure at Michigan, he got a call from Northwestern, essentially saying they were extremely interested in hiring him.

Aldon tried to make significant changes in the campus environment the second he arrived. "One of the things I should say is that from undergrad through graduate school, as an assistant professor, and as an associate professor, I was deeply involved in activism. When I got to Northwestern, I immediately sought to diversify the Department of Sociology as well as other places in the university." He believes at that time, Northwestern had a very poor record in matters of diversity, inclusion and equity. His position to administration was that it makes no sense to be next to Chicago and not be able to recruit Black students and Black faculty. "We had a lot of battles around that. I, along with others who worked with me, made a lot of real changes. Our Sociology Department is now one of the most diverse in the whole country."

Northwestern professors of color have nurtured and mentored a large number of students of color who have received PhDs and who have went on to become extremely important scholars. The list goes on and on, but people like Marcus Hunter, now at UCLA, really stand out. "The thing that really startled me, or I should say very much surprised me, was that in the middle of all these fights with my colleagues in the Sociology Department, Charles Reagan and a number of other faculty were progressive. I was never completely alone. I was the spark plug and the spear head, but there were others who agreed that changes needed to happen."

Aldon has had a steady rise to the top of Northwestern academia over the years, allowing him to implement his goals of diversity. "To my surprise, I was asked to become the Chair of the Sociology Department in '92. I chaired from '92 to '97. The typical term is three, but the Dean asked me to stay on for two more years." Since he was supportive of the Asian students and their hunger strike to get an Asian-American Studies program, he was asked to be the first Director of Asian-American Studies. "Unfortunately, there were very few faculty who even could teach courses in Asian-American Studies. They knew 'Dr. Morris' and they knew of my work in the civil rights movement (Aldon' 1984 Book, The Origins of the Civil Rights Movement, won major awards from 1984 to 1986), so they asked if I would be the director. I was like, 'Are you crazy? I don't know that much about Asian-American studies,' but they convinced me that there were a lot of parallels, so I did it."

Aldon was determined to keep the Black faculty at Northwestern. He was approached by the Dean's Office and Weinberg several times to become the Associate Dean for Faculty. The first time, he turned it down, but in that role, he knew he would be able to affect more change. He worked diligently to help build and sustain African American studies. After Charles Payne left and Leon Forrest died, African American Studies was being run by Mary Pattillo and Martha Biondi. During this time, Harvard, Skip Gates, and Cornell West made big news by making African

American studies a centerpiece and putting it on the map in ways that had never been done. "Me, Mary, Martha, and several other Black faculty at Northwestern called for a meeting at the Provost's office proposing we had the wherewithal to build a great African American Studies Department. This was 2005 and was unprecedented." They asked the Dean and the Provost for six faculty allowances for African American Studies. They shared how they did it at Harvard and asked, "Are you going to tell your own faculty that we are not capable of doing it here?" "That was the beginning of our current African American Studies Department becoming a PhD-granting institution a few years ago."

In 2007, Aldon was asked to be the Interim Dean of Weinberg, and in 2008, he came back as a professor in the Sociology Department. Among the more special honors for him was being given the Leon Forrest Professor of Sociology and African American Studies Chair. "Leon Forrest and I had a great deal of respect for each other. We were friends." A group of students and faculty got together and pushed the university to create a Chair named after Leon. "To have the Chair named after somebody you worked with and you were friends with is sort of special."

Overall, Aldon has been quite successful as a scholar. When he came back to the Sociology Department after being the Interim Dean, "my colleagues thought I was just looking for a kind of golden parachute." For some, it's hard to come out of high-level administration back into a department and produce. "I laughed because I always kept a scholarly profile even when I was in the Dean's Office." When he came back to the department, within a couple years, he published a book on W.E.B. Du Bois, who was the founder of American Scientific Sociology. It has become a very impactful work. At this point, it has won at least seven awards.

From Aldon' point of view, there's never been a sufficient number of Black faculty or Black students at Northwestern. When he arrived in 1988, Black faculty members were approximately three percent of the total. "When you take three percent, and you distribute that across the university, including the Chicago Campus, that's a miniscule number. Although it is up from back in 1968, it would be inaccurate to say that there were a lot of Black faculty members. At the same time, there might have been six or seven percent Black students. It would go up, then it would fall back down.

"In many ways, it was a very White campus. In the late 1980's and in the 1990's, Black faculty and Black students still felt very isolated, very marginalized, very much like the campus didn't really belong to them. One of the things that's different in a university that's located near a big city is that the faculty of color and the students of color can also find outlets outside the university. That's a good thing, but it could also undermine efforts to really try to change the university." Outside of African American Studies, there had been very few Black professors who had served as Chairs of their department or in the Dean capacity. Deans Dwight McBride (former Dean of The Graduate School) and Toni-Marie Montgomery (current Dean of the Bienen School of Music) only recently received their appointments.

Alden was struck by the problem that Northwestern had with diversifying and having a significant increase in the number of students and faculty of color, but Aldon acknowledges that is a national problem. "We had the same fights at Michigan. We had the same fights in undergraduate and graduate school, so there was nothing completely surprising about this.

"It was too quiescent for me in 1988. There were younger faculty members of color who came in around the same time and who were also progressive. We were able to build coalitions. Black student unrest is very important because it provided the Black faculty with a leverage to go and say to the administration, 'look, you know this is not fair.' Not only is it unfair, the real argument is that this university is impoverished by not having diverse groups of people involved in the student and faculty levels. If you really want to have a great university, all points of view must be on the table. The clash of ideas generates new and innovative scholarship." As faculty, Aldon never advanced an affirmative action argument. His argument was that they needed to make Northwestern stronger as a university. "We need to be able to prepare for a really diverse workforce. I would say that we made some headway with that approach."

The university created the first Diversity Committee at the Provost level where faculty and students argued for the systematic push to change the university. "I don't know exactly what the numbers are now, but I would say the rhetoric for change outmatched the efforts to make it happen. If you really want to understand what's important to a corporation or a university, the question you ask is, 'Let's look at the budget and let's see what portion of the budget is targeted to these efforts to diversify?' Because if you're not willing to spend money, as you are in other priority areas, then nothing is going to happen. In fact, it's not a priority."

Black faculty members constantly try to make the university live up to its rhetoric about wanting to diversify. There are some steps in the right direction but given the Northwestern's location, given the prestige and the resources of the university, Aldon knows that they could be doing a much better job. "The issue here is this—in terms of diversity, in terms of having significant, important levels of Black faculty, Hispanic faculty, Asian-American faculty as well as the same for the student body, you know something is wrong if you can't be successful year after year."

Aldon notes and warns that success in diversity recruitment can reverse itself rapidly. Universities that have very visible faculty—especially Black faculty—are very mobile. Other schools compete in the recruitment process and attempt to recruit away your faculty members, so Northwestern can't simply announce that they've reached their goals. "Numeric goals are a dangerous and unrealistic way of looking at diversity because numbers can change quickly."

However, Aldon lauds the progress and success being had. "In the Sociology Department, now we have four Black tenured faculty. Even with only four, including

Celeste Watkins Hayes, Quincy Thomas Stewart, and Mary Pattillo, our department is by far one of the leaders in the nation! The Sociology staff used to reference the 'bottom era of the '90's and 2000's.' Now, the department sees itself as setting the pace for the national community of universities. When other schools say, 'Is it possible?' they will respond 'Yes. Look at Northwestern."

Jabari Asim

Jabari Asim

Jabari Asim (born Roland Smith) was the FMO Coordinator from 1984 to 1985. He was born and raised in St. Louis, Missouri and came to Northwestern with one of his high school best friends. His high school was majority White, so the Northwestern environment was familiar to him.

Jabari had many great times at Northwestern, but attending NU became a financial drain. "I guess I could never really afford to be there." He would have constant battles at the Bursar's Office. "I had to go and beg when I couldn't get registered because there were holds on my registration. That was a regular thing for me." The people in the Bursar's office saw a lot of Jabari. "There was a woman named Judith Veitch, she was like the woman from hell! She was an ex-nun, and she was brutal! She had no compassion, and she didn't even pretend to. I would go to the Bursar's Office and say, 'I really want to register, I can't afford it, I don't have any money, my parents don't have any money, I have a job that's not enough,' and she would say, 'well transfer, why are you here?'"

Jabari actually dropped out a couple of semesters and worked. "I put in many hours at the Jewel supermarket on Chicago Avenue as a dairy clerk. When I got enough money, I would register for classes." Sometimes, he would go to classes all quarter and explain to the professor that "I'm going to be registered, eventually, just let me do the work! Most of them would go along with that."

Jabari cultivated the relationships that were important to his career. "Professor Forrest was a huge influence on me as a writer, and I would go to see him in his office whether I was registered or not." Professor Forrest was a devoted teacher who would read his work and provide honest feedback. "I learned more about how to write sitting in his office than I did in any of my formal classes." Jabari recalls Professor Forrest "had a big heart, and he always had room."

Jabari spent a lot of his time in The Black House. To his disappointment, "the Black faculty at Northwestern had nothing to do with The Black House. They never set foot in it. They avoided it." Professor Forrest was different! "He would show up! He would come to things. He was wonderful in that way." He remembers one summer working in Evanston and hanging out in The Black House with others who were around that summer, when Professor Forrest came in. He schooled them in the work of sculptor Richard Hunt and invited them to visit Mr. Hunt with him. "Professor Forrest put a signup sheet on the bulletin board, met folks back at The Black House on the particular day, and they caught the L to visit him. I can't remember who went. I know Kathleen Bethel, my friend Sidney Anderson, and maybe a handful of other students went along." They spent the afternoon at Richard Hunt's studio. "It was a turning point in my life, seeing these two African American artists, who were making a living as artists. They were simply doing their thing. It really became clear to me on that day that I could do it too."

Even with the rigors of financial worries and academics, Jabari found himself in FMO leadership. He remembers a meeting at Harris Hall and someone mentioning there was a vacancy for recording secretary on the council. Before he knew it, he had the job. "I wasn't elected. I was appointed by the coordinator!" The rest is history. The Black House became a social hub for him. "Some of my longest standing friendships stem from those days." Any negative experiences he had with FMO and/or The Black House, he turned them into a positive one.

Jabari speaks about an especially memorable episode and its resolution. "I remember once a sister was surrounded in a tunnel on campus by these guys from a White fraternity and they exposed themselves to her! She was very upset." Jabari remembers she went to the campus police and got a really bad response. "They said, you're a senior, you should know better. They totally blamed her." Jabari and JJ (John Marshall Jones) called an emergency meeting of all the Black students on campus. "We went to all of the dining halls tapping people on the shoulder." They gathered in The Black House and initially planned to interrupt the Homecoming Parade. Instead, they decided to walk beside the Homecoming Parade, chanting.

Later that semester, JJ, Valerie Boyd, and couple of other people charged into the President's office. His secretary told them he couldn't see anyone. "We just walked in. We just walked past her, busted the door open, and went off on him. At the end, JJ and I knew, they'll probably never ask us back." The positive outcome of this event was the creation of The Black House Escort service. "I got about eight brothers to sign up and we made ourselves available every night at The Black House when a Black woman on campus needed to be walked anywhere." They did that the whole year and "to be honest, we're almost hoping there would be some trouble that someone would say something to the young woman that we were escorting. They knew better."

Jabari recalls organizing to prepare for a White fraternity who would annually vandalize The Black House sign or would tear it down. During *The Ritual*, Alice Palmer came into the circle, and announced that "it's almost the end of hell week, and they will come in for the sign." Jabari recalls stepping up. "I said I will be there, I will not be defenseless, I will have a weapon of some sort, and if anybody comes for the sign, I'm coming for them." It was a fiery period! He shot an invitation to all the Brothers to join him, and only one brother showed up, Mark Arnett. "That's when Mark and I became good friends. We guarded the sign all night and no one tried to take it, because we were there, we were present."

Jabari's account of the hardships of his time at NU shows true examples of leadership. He led the students, but he also had the responsibilities of the organization. FMO, Jazz Alliance (another organization Jabari led), and A & O (activities and organizations) board planned a Gil Scott-Heron concert that two previous administrations had tried and failed. Jabari, Joan Richards (now Effie Richards), and Mark Scott worked with a very contentious A & O Board. "There was an agreement with them at the time that we would co-produce one or two concerts a year. FMO chose the artists and we got Gil." Jabari remembers that it was difficult because it wasn't a great time in Gil Scott-Heron's life. "We got him there, he gave a good concert, and we were very proud." It was one of the most positive events Jabari organized. Jabari was a jazz guy. "I really didn't want to be one of the guys who listened to what everybody else was listening to. I came from a family that respected jazz and had a deep knowledge of it. I produced a Count Basie concert while I was at Northwestern and was instrumental in bringing the Art Ensemble of Chicago to campus with the Jazz Alliance." Dr. Duke Jenkins was deep into jazz. Jabari, Ken Pierce and Duke would sit in his office and talk about jazz for hours.

The most life-changing event Jabari had at Northwestern is meeting his wife. He met her at a football game. "She called my name, I turned around, and I didn't know her. I was like, 'who is this cute girl calling my name.' She said, 'would you mind sitting down, I can't see through you.' I thought 'it's too bad she has a foul attitude, but she's fine!'" They worked it out! Jabari and his accomplished wife, Liana, have five children and two grandchildren, proving Northwestern was certainly good for something for Jabari!

Leaders care for others, but it is what sustained Jabari. He recounts the relationships that nurtured and rejuvenated him at The Black House. Essie Williams was their mother figure. She had many students over for dinner at her house with her husband Josh. "She was a straight shooter with no bias." Jabari knew having that type of unique support is rare in a campus environment. "You needed that kind of maternal contact when you're away from your home! We could go and sit with her, cry with her, and complain, and she would give you a shoulder to cry on. Then she would give you some tough love and tell you what you needed to do! She was invaluable."

Additionally, Jabari has fond memories of Jerré (Michelin). "Jerré was like a big sister to me. She was helpful in terms of navigating the network that Northwestern presented. She was very loving but real sarcastic!" Jerre and Jabari were great friends. "I remember Jerre and I used to tease each other. We had a custodian named Mr. Palmer. Mr. Palmer came through The Black House once a day to clean and we were very respectful to him, but he was a free speaker. I'll never forget, I was 'jonesin' with Jerré, she was the best "jonser." I was going back and forth with her about something, and she called Mr. Palmer into the room. She said, 'can you bring your vacuum cleaner, I want you to get this Black spot off the room.' Everybody fell out laughing, everybody thought, and I said, 'you got me.'"

There nearly always seems to be a really sad but telling story that defines the Northwestern experience as a person of African descent, and Jabari's story of his high school friend embodies the tales of those who decide that the negatives at Northwestern outweigh the positives. Jabari's high school best friend was a guy named Jamel Richardson. He and Jamel went to the St. Louis together. He was the editor of the yearbook, and Jabari was the editor of the newspaper, and they were thick as thieves. They agreed they would both go to Northwestern. Jamel was Jabari's roommate in freshman year. "Jamel transferred after two years. He graduated from Hampton. His dad was a very active Hampton alum and he wasn't happy with Northwestern. I remember when he came to get Jamel, it was a sad day for me. His dad came in a station wagon, they loaded it up, and he told me that he didn't think that Jamel's teachers were invested in him succeeding." Jamel's father was very clear on the position his son's instructors and administrators at Northwestern had: "'Northwestern doesn't think you belong here.' So, he took him away." After talking to his best friend years after, Jamel told him that at Hampton, no one wanted him to fail. If he had any trouble, everybody would drop everything to help him. He had a great experience at Hampton, met his wife there and is extremely successful.

Jabari forged relationships with the Black community in Evanston and the Evanston Police Department because he described his early interactions with the campus police as "nightmarish." Both campus and Evanston Police were constantly stopping Black male students and asking for IDs. He remembers he and Ayton Taylor were moving their furniture from The Black House to their apartment. "The campus cops rolled up on us like we were stealing furniture." There were other confrontations. "A group of us studied in The Black House every night, and we would walk to the White Hen Pantry. As we were walking, Evanston cops would roll very slowly beside us with their spotlights turned on."

The story became more serious when, one night, the surveillance became a threat to one of the group members' lives. "Harry Lennix, Phil Neely, Mark Arnett, Mark Scott, Ayton Taylor, and I were studying in The Black House, and Mark Arnett wanted to take that walk to the White Hen. For various reasons, we all backed off. None of us would go with him. We waited and waited for him to return, but he never returned because the Evanston Police had picked him up and taken him to a White man's house. The man identified him through the screen door as the man who robbed him. Mark was arrested, incarcerated, and we couldn't find him. It was a nightmare. Unfortunately, that was the typical kind of experience with police. It was combative, and it was uncomfortable." Jabari parallels the White and Black experiences with the police at Northwestern. "The police were so willing to forgive these White boys who terrorized this Black female student in a tunnel, but they don't give us the room to breathe. It was never a pleasant relationship. They didn't like us, we didn't like them, and we didn't pretend otherwise."

Jabari is a college professor and comments that there's been almost no change in what the students are up against. "There's a consistent attempt to delegitimize them to suggest that they don't really belong. There is a reluctance to acknowledge their pain, their difficulties and to take them seriously." In Jabari's assessment, "the problems haven't changed, so complacency is our enemy. Haki Madhubuti spoke in The Black House several times and told the students that 'there are people working day and night to stop your future' and I've never forgotten this."

Harris (Harry) Lennix

Harry Lennix

Harry Joseph Lennix III attended Northwestern University from 1982 to 1986 and graduated with a degree from the School of Speech (Communications). He is from the South Side of Chicago, and Northwestern was his first choice of school. He led For Members Only in the '85–'86 school year with some time off to complete a production. He took the job extremely seriously and enjoyed the experience.

Harry's South Shore neighborhood was vibrant, middle class and everchanging, with Muslims, Protestants, and Catholics, but it was mainly African American. He was thinking of going to the seminary but wanted to be an actor. He saw a special that featured prominent theatre alums who attended NU. He knew the training needed would be offered at Northwestern. He was overwhelmed after arriving. "Evanston and the North Shore were so pretty, so pristine, it was like a postcard, a Hallmark card." He eased into this new world as a part of the Summer Academic Workshop (SAW). He encountered students more well off with cars and others with less resources than he had. He was amazed at the world of new ideas and shocked about the number of diverse fields of study his classmates were attacking. "It was the perfect example of a place where the entire universe was up for discussion." Harry knew he would be able to explore and flourish at NU.

Harry was deeply immediately ensconced in the Black culture at Northwestern. He was in The Black House from day one. His counselors and mentors were deeply involved in FMO. "They knew the ropes. They said go to The Black House and study, and I did, so all of my social engagements were with Black people." He remembers the Black tables at the SAGA cafeterias. All the Black students would sit together, then endure the complaints from the White students asking why. "All the White people are sitting by themselves; what are we supposed to do? No one invited us over to eat with them." The theater department was mostly White, but his refuge was The Black House.

Harry was in Black Folks Theatre, which changed its name to African American Theatre Ensemble (Harry confirms that John Marshall Jones was the leader at the time, and he changed the name), FMO, and intramural sports, participating in football and basketball. He remembers Jeff Sterling and Glen Burress always picking him for their teams and winning. He had a work-study job but by sophomore year, he was working in his profession throughout Chicago. He became the coordinator of FMO in 1985 "because I've always had a sense of service and duty instilled in me from seminary. The idea of giving back, becoming a leader, and having other people listening to me was my obligation." Harry acknowledges that Medill student Jean Brown was a great help. "When I became the coordinator, I got a job at the Goodman, so having Jean there allowed me to become the public face, and Jean took care of the real work tackling apartheid and disinvestment issues. She was a much better organizer and administrator." She knew the important people and the best strategies by which to accomplish their goals. Harry admits, "I couldn't juggle all those things. Nicky Gilley was my spy in ASG. Angela Davis also did a ton of work for FMO." Harry remembers Black women being very active.

Harry regrets spending so much of his time on the apartheid movement. He was swept up in a concern that the society at large had, but "if I had to do it again, I would concern myself with the housing situation on the South and West sides of Chicago or the marginalization of Black people here in the United States." He remembers Dennis Brutus, who was a Professor of poetry at Northwestern, saying that "'FMO hasn't done much with regard to South Africa.' I wanted to tell him to go the hell!" Harry believes that other students thought he was engaged and concerned but maybe a little weird. He took his responsibility very seriously being the FMO leader. He knew he represented all Black people. "I wanted to defend the causes we championed, like Black women not being harassed on campus or being called out of their names in classrooms." He wanted to go up against professors and administrators but knew it was going to tough.

Dr. Ulysses "Duke" Jenkins was Harry's dear friend and mentor, and he liked Arnie Weber (Northwestern University President from 1984–1994). He thought President Weber "was always engaged even if we were not always on the same side. He made us feel that whatever we were talking about was important." Professors Sterling Stuckey, Leon Forrest, and Carlene Edie made him respect good writing and scholarly thought. These professors "exposed me to great literature and African diasporic studies." Harry considers James Coakley and David Down, his theatre instructors, as geniuses. *The Ritual, Out Da Box, Tribute to Black Men,* and *Tribute to Black Women* brought him a lot of joy. "This was Black people coming together en-mass and being there for each other. The sentiment inside all of those events 'was if you have a problem, we've got you. That was deep!'" Theatre was Harry's world! He remembers lots of productions, but one stands out. "John Marshall Jones lobbied the university to produce *A Raisin in the Sun*. It was done remarkably well for a group of college students."

There were some negative experiences. Harry remembers the White fraternity FIJI dressing up in grass skirts and bones in their noses attempting to deface The Black House—the same as they had been doing since before the takeover of the Bursar's Office in 1968. "We took the face painting and dress as mocking African culture. During FIJI's pledge week, Black women were accosted, so Jabari Asim, Mark Arnett, and others organized. We were looking to fight! We were intimidating, and we intended to be." He recounts the story of an old tenured White professor saying that "all the Black students were late." They addressed that with the Provosts office immediately. "We took it seriously and we held it down pretty well!"

Harry believes Northwestern is a reflection of what you're going to find in the real world. "There is no perfect refuge to escape the vagaries of race in this country which are so deeply entrenched." Northwestern was a laboratory, and Harry was determined to test every space along Sheridan Road. "However difficult the circumstances may seem, Northwestern has a rich legacy of people getting through in far more hostile times and eras." He acknowledges full-fledged, not imagined, hostilities were real, but we all coped. "I learned how to fight at Northwestern, academically, intellectually, personally, and culturally. I'm not sure I would have gotten that in any other place." He values his four years at Northwestern, "I grew, I stumbled, and I'm grateful for FMO and my time there!"

Asadah Kirkland

Asadah Kirkland came from New York City to Northwestern University in 1989 and was fortunate to lead For Members Only from 1992 to 1993 in her senior year, the year of the 25th anniversary of the Bursar's Office takeover. She was a Radio/TV/Film major and memorialized the occasion with a powerful short documentary on the impact of the movement.

Asadah decided on Television/Film because it allowed her to be an artist. "I minored in African Studies because I was very African-centered. I had read a bevy of books by Black people and would have sessions in my dorm called Rachael's Black Power hour! It was full of Black students who would debate for hours on history and culture." Her classmates were from Kansas, Iowa, Chicago, New York, and all over, so they had a plethora of viewpoints about being Black. Those discussions shaped a lot of them into who they became as adults and how they perceived themselves as young people.

Northwestern was a culture shock at first. She was from Harlem, New York and thus, considered herself to be extremely strong and self-confident. She arrived to Northwestern alone with no fanfare, but she was not intimidated. She remembers the Black population on campus was only eight percent, but 500 Black folks were enough for her. "I stayed in The Black House. I simply needed to be there, and I was drawn by Duke Jenkins, who helped ground me."

She met Duke in her freshman year at an orientation that Karla Spurlock Evans, Dean of African American Student Affairs, and Ulysses Duke Jenkins, Assistant Dean, hosted. After the event, probably thinking 'who is this little African-centered girl,' Duke questioned her, 'what are you about?' "As an African-centered person, I respected my elders and shared with him the books I read and my mindset, and from then on, I tried to spend as much time with Duke as I could." She would go to his office in between classes and have what she considered real Black power hours. Occasionally, they would find rides to Indian restaurants on Devon Street where they would eat and talk. Her most cherished memories are when she and Duke coordinated *"A Musical Evening with our Elders."* "This was an event where jazz greats would collaborate with the current students. The whole campus would come, but we also sent vans to senior homes in Evanston and Chicago to connect with the community and with our elders. It was an awesome intergenerational event."

Asadah had a few personal issues while at Northwestern. "The Head of the Communication Studies Department was telling staff and fellow classmates that she knew I hated her because she was White." This was an adult, someone she had to go to for transcripts and to graduate. "I had to take those types of concerns to Duke to feel recharged."

"If I didn't have a relationship with Duke Jenkins, Northwestern would have been a rougher ride. No one was rougher than me, but having a terminal to take frustrations to or get guidance from was critical. Duke was a mentor and not just a mentor for academics. I didn't need a mentor for grades. I needed a mentor for cultural stability, mental stability."

Asadah created her own environment on campus, but as she saw it, Northwestern was uncomfortable with her as a confident and smart Black woman. "Black and White students were uncomfortable with me. I was so unapologetically Black and so on top of the game." She was on the Dean's list twice and in her senior year, she received all A's. She recalls possibly having only one C her entire career at NU. She remembers one allegedly racist professor's attempt to give her a D. "I went to him with the blue (test) book and had him detail every question. He had a problem because the class was Ancient World, but he didn't relate history to its ancient African roots. He talked about Greece but never Africa, never Cush." In her view, Northwestern was more comfortable with Black students assimilating.

Asadah contributed to Black student life at Northwestern instantaneously. "I was a part of FMO from the beginning. I ran for office my freshman year as a part of a ticket. We were the SOUL ticket, the Soldiers Of Unity and Liberation. It created so much dissention amongst Blacks on campus, we decided to pull out." The next year, she ran on the FOCUS ticket, and has no idea what that stands for now, but she eventually led FMO as coordinator in the 1992–93 School year. "FMO kept me really busy. This was not running a little club! This was a big task." Because of the student movement in 1968, FMO had its own budget that Asadah considered an honored responsibility to guard. "We received $30,000, so we brought up groups like Tribe Called Quest, poet Haki Madhabuti, and there was lots of jazz and hip hop."

Asadah was extremely self-aware and knew her presence was highly felt. There were the Rodney King riots, XClan, and other issues happening in the United States in the early nineties. She knew these events, about which it was important for Black students to stay aware. She wanted Black students to attack those issues even in their own small way. "I brought all of my head wraps and 'urban flavor' to Northwestern and The Black House before Erykah Badu." *The Daily Northwestern* published an article while she was the FMO Coordinator, which was entitled *"Separatist or Not."* She was interviewed about Black student life, then thought they positioned the story in an extremely negative way. She countered that article immediately! "I had a lot of things I had to handle for FMO."

Asadah found Black women to cultivate her strength and her art at Northwestern including Kathleen Bethel. "I would sit in her office and immerse myself in everything African. She would allow me to study and provide resources. She would help with decisions made." Kathleen really made an impression on her. She proudly wore African clothing and was the kindest person anywhere on campus. "She was an African-centered woman and there were very few at NU."

Asadah took a *Black Women in Filmmaking* class. "It was awesome. The professor was Michelle Thompson. I would leave that class feeling amazing. I got to spend so many hours looking through the lens of Black women in all forms. Professor Davis, Professor Thompson, and studying filmmakers like Julie Dash and her film *Daughters of the Dust* was an ethereal experience even as I knew that mainstream America may not ever see that work." She walked on campus feeling like she was on top of the world. "That made the experience on campus a good one for me. To be exposed to Black women doing what I wanted to do in life." Asadah (which means Lioness) enjoyed the challenges Northwestern presented to her but proclaims that "Northwestern does not get credit for my excellence." She says that Northwestern or any college will enhance what you already are. Asadah knew who she was and knew what she was capable of before she arrived. The key for her was to "have her purpose tight."

Black Greek Letter Organizations

By every measure, Black Greek Letter Organizations (BGLOs) have had a substantial impact on the Black experience at Northwestern—from providing students with social outlets and socialization skills to providing scholarships and service to the surrounding community. For over a century, these fraternities and sororities have provided leadership and a needed social outlet.

Fraternities

Alpha Phi Alpha Fraternity, Alpha Mu Chapter

Alpha Phi Alpha lays claim to having the first members of a Black Greek Letter Organization on campus, when Northwestern was part of the Chicago citywide chapter (Theta). Members are documented as having attended Northwestern as early as 1910. The Alpha Mu Chapter was chartered on October 21, 1922 by Homer P. Cooper and Brother Charles Greer of Theta Chapter with charter members, Dr. Beck, Ralph Banks, Ernest Dyett, Frederick D. Jordan, A.D. Price, Samuel B. Taylor, and Warren Williams.

Kappa Alpha Psi Fraternity, Theta Chapter

Theta Chapter of Kappa Alpha Psi lays claim to having the first dedicated chapter of a Black Greek Letter Organization at Northwestern University, having chartered its chapter on April 21, 1917. Its charter members were E. Wilbur Johnson, Ira M. Henderson, T.F. Charleston, Carlyle F. Stewart, and Roy Young.

Omega Psi Phi Fraternity, Psi Sigma Chapter

Psi Sigma Chapter of Omega Psi Phi was originally chartered in 1947, but due to a decline in membership and activity, the chapter fell dormant for an extended period of time. However, on May 20, 1972, the chapter was reborn (and re-chartered) with the induction of the members of the "Crazy Eight." These members were Stephen P. Stanley, George K. Hall, Ronald Sterling, Ernest M. Stewart, William Beatie, Stanley W. Key, Ronald Sherer, and Johnathon P. Robinson.

Phi Beta Sigma Fraternity, Iota Nu Chapter

The Iota Nu Chapter of Phi Beta Sigma was chartered at Northwestern University on March 3, 1978 with the induction of Nathaniel Curry.

Sororities

Alpha Kappa Alpha Sorority, Gamma Chi Chapter

The Gamma Chi Chapter of Alpha Kappa Alpha Sorority initiated its first line at Northwestern on March 1, 1969 with eleven charter members, including Debra Avant, Nona Burney, Dorothy Harrell, Lillian Jordan, Loester Lewis, Barbara North, Regina Rice, Janice Simms, Sandra Small, Jinx Smith, and Adrianne Thomas.

Delta Sigma Theta Sorority, Theta Alpha Chapter

The Theta Alpha Chapter of Delta Sigma Theta Sorority was chartered on January 9, 1971 by twelve undergraduate charter members, although members of Delta had been on campus for years as participants in the mixed undergraduate and graduate chapter Gamma Omicron. The Theta Alpha Charter Members were Michelle Roberts Aikens, Pamela Barnes, Beverly Henry Barton, Debra Dillon, Cynthia Ramos Griffith Gale Roberts House, Esther Jenkins, Anita Brice Kelley, Karin Robinson, Binion Mitra, Patricia Prescott, Dale Wallace Thompson, and Adrian Williams.

Sigma Gamma Rho Sorority, Eta Chapter

The Eta Chapter of Sigma Gamma Rho lays claim to being the first dedicated Black Greek Letter Sorority on campus, having been installed on December 14, 1927. Edit Ward, Ida Laws, and Robert Anderson (Maloney) are noted to be the chapter's first members.

Zeta Phi Beta Sorority, Nu Sigma

The Nu Sigma Chapter of Zeta Phi Beta was chartered at Northwestern on August 28th, 2005. Its charter members were Jessica Carrasquillo, Brie Jefferson, Sara Sutton, Mayra Vega, and Keyonda Evans.

New Challenges

Charles Whitaker: Associate Professor, Medill School of Journalism, Chair, Black House Facilities Review Committee

Tanya D. Woods: President, Northwestern University Black Alumni Association

Sarah Oberholtzer: Co-Founder, Northwestern Black Lives Matter

Macs Vinson: Vice-President, Associate Student Government

Kasey Brown: Coordinator, For Members Only

Paula Pretlow: Member, Board of Trustees and Campaign Co-Chair, WE WILL

Charles Whitaker

Charles Whitaker

Charles Whitaker came to Northwestern from South Shore High School in Chicago and obtained a degree in journalism in 1980, as Northwestern was the only school he wanted to attend. He subsequently obtained a graduate degree from Northwestern's Medill School of Journalism in 1981. He is approaching the completion of twenty-five years as a member of the faculty at Medill.

"I've had this conversation with many contemporary students, and I don't say this proudly but matter-of-factly. In many ways, I went to an HBCU (Historically Black College and University), whose spirit happened to be embedded in Northwestern University. The community was such at that time that you literally could—and I absolutely did—exist within an African American bubble."

During Charles' time at Northwestern, there was a special sensitivity amongst the faculty members for the need to acclimate students from inner city communities to campus life. Charles participated in the Summer Academic Workshop (SAW), which was designed to fulfill that very purpose. He notes that the establishment of SAW created a community, within which the Black student participants felt very comfortable. This community embraced Charles and provided him with "big brothers and sisters" to guide him throughout his Northwestern education and experience, as evidenced by his remark, "I stayed very comfortably within my bubble during my time here."

Unfortunately, Charles' forays into the greater university community reinforced the notion that he was better off in his comfort zone. "I never felt reinforced and supported in my ambition to become a journalist in Medill. As such, one of my goals as an instructor in Medill is to make sure that every student feels capable and worthy of entering this business." Although Charles performed well enough in classes to subsequently achieve his professional ambitions, he never found an instructor who he believes was vested in his success and deemed him to be a talent who would be worth nurturing.

However, that reinforcement was available aplenty in the Black community and, especially, at The Black House. Charles worked as the editor of *The Blackboard* (the cultural issues' magazine of the Black community at Northwestern) for two years. At that time, *The Blackboard* was published out of The Black House. Charles reminisces happily about the opportunities that he had to reconfigure the magazine and getting access to mentors and colleagues who collaboratively worked through the required processes of publishing. This was the level of development, support and training that he had craved to accomplish.

Charles also worked on *The New Sense*, a literary magazine that was another publication of For Members Only (FMO, The Black Student Alliance of Northwestern), and he always participated in *The Ritual*, a Black community staple that embraced and celebrated the community and its traditions on campus. Charles remarks, "There was this Black community that I was deeply embedded in that was deeply formative and transformative in my university experience." The administrative leadership of The Black House, which included Alice Palmer, Milton Wiggins, and Everne Saxton, comprised the perfect curators of the Black experience and culture of the time and the needs of NU's Black students.

During Charles' time at Northwestern, twin pillars of support were uniquely available to the Black students. Of course, there was The Black House, but there was also African American studies, a still-emerging department that was formed as a result of the 1968 Bursar's Office Takeover. During Charles' time at NU, the Department of African American Studies was populated with many renowned professors. As such, it served as a place for students to learn from stalwarts of their fields about the unique qualities that one needs to exhibit on the path to success for Black people, in general, and at Northwestern, in particular.

One such professor especially stood out to a young Charles Whitaker—"Leon Forrest was a tremendous mentor of mine. I must have taken four classes with Professor Forrest not just because he was a terrific instructor but because I got the affirmation of me as a writer that I was yearning for and not getting at Medill. I felt recognized and supported, and he promoted me as a writer and scholar."

Charles is emphatic that his "bubble" was not a separatist construct sought by the Black community but was more so a means to insulate himself from the harsh general environment of the university and provide student support services in a culturally-sensitive way that he wouldn't have otherwise received. "Maybe I should have stepped outside of that bubble more often than I did, but it was so affirming and comfortable that I chose not to." Charles pointedly notes the existence of other cultural bubbles and cliques within the university, including Hillel for the Jewish community, The Women's Center, Sheil (The Catholic Center), Fraternity Row, and even the offerings to student-athletes.

Charles continually emphasizes the nature and importance of culturally sensitive options that enhanced his education. He contrasts his experience with that of Michael Wilbon, his good friend, who also was a journalism major but worked at *The Daily Northwestern*, the campus newspaper. Charles refutes the notion that either of their paths or experiences was better or worse, and he's thankful that Northwestern offers the scope for the co-existence of a multitude of robust experiences and opportunities.

Charles recalls how students participated in protests related to apartheid, in general, and a library protest, in particular, during which the Black student body withdrew the maximum allowable number of books to direct the administration's attention to any given matters of interest to the Black community. He was insistent that his student experience was met more by indifference than by overt actions of racism on campus. "I felt more invisible than anything else. I felt neglected, and that may have been the university culture in general. However, as a kid from the south side of Chicago … I largely felt a sense that I was dismissed or not expected to do well." He, in fact, notes specific occasions in which the professors expressed profound surprise at his "ability to write."

The notion of surprise that surrounded Charles' ability to do well was heightened on one particularly disturbing occasion. The *Chicago Tribune* had a tradition of selecting interns from Northwestern's journalism students, and when Charles was selected instead of another student from *The Daily Northwestern*, he faced significant hostility from the other journalism students. "People were just ballistic. They were asking, 'Who is this guy? He doesn't write for *The Daily*! He writes for this *Blackboard* thing! How could he possibly be picked?' They were just beside themselves in that I had been picked.... There certainly seemed to be racial undertones to this."

Charles also participated in another form of protest that one would find hard to believe that it ever occurred, particularly, given the lack of evidence that either the participants or Northwestern kept of the occurrences. As the story goes, during Charles' sophomore year, when two Black cheerleaders were constantly fighting with the rest of the cheerleaders (i.e. non-Black), they were being made to feel "less than equal." Consequently, these two cheerleaders concocted a plan to "take over" the cheerleading squad. "These cheerleaders recruited every Black person they knew to try out for cheerleading in 1978. So, there were about thirty-five Black people who tried out, including many who had never done anything like this before! The Black community effectively took over the cheerleading squad for three years. So, for three years, the Northwestern cheerleading squad was almost half Black and half White."

However, Charles' graduate student experience in Medill was a better experience academically. He notes that the combination of the level of the school's professionalism and his academic reputation that was developed by his familiarity with the faculty contributed to this better experience. Additionally, his past success as an undergraduate, and the opportunity to focus on magazine writing and not just "newspaper training" (as had been the case in his undergraduate years) offered him an education that was closer to what he had hoped for when he had chosen to attend Northwestern and pursue a career in journalism.

The graduate student experience empowered Charles to be both prepared for any career in journalism and to follow a career that he deemed to be aligned with his ambitions. "I can honestly say I was never discouraged away from the journalism school notion that you are a journalist, meaning you are divorced from any community. You are supposed to be this objective observer who has no allegiance whatsoever. You are an empty vessel, recording events as objectively as possible. I have personally always rejected that notion! It's ridiculous. We all are going to view things through the lens of our experiences. Objectivity is something you can strive for, but it's nothing you can ever achieve. I was savvy enough to know this, but whenever I got a chance to write about the Black community, that's always the direction I gravitated towards … I was never discouraged from doing that nor was I ever graded down for doing so, although I have had colleagues at Medill who were told it was ill-advised of them to focus on Black issues."

After obtaining his graduate degree from Medill, Charles had an impressive career as a journalist, including working for the *Miami Herald* in Louisville and serving as Senior Editor for the *Ebony Magazine*. It was during his time at *Ebony* that Northwestern came knocking at his door, seeking to bring him back home. "I had not set foot on campus for ten years after I'd left, not because I had any bad feelings but because maybe I was returning the indifference they'd shown to me as a student."

Despite Charles' indifference toward Northwestern, he had maintained his close relationship with Leon Forrest. Little did Charles know that Professor Forest would pave the way for Charles' return to NU. In 1990, as Medill was undergoing an accreditation review in the pursuit of more African American faculty, Charles was approached to return to NU at the behest of Leon Forrest. Consequently, he met Dean Michael Janeway, and, although he had decided against returning, he did begin the process of adjunct teaching in a part-time engagement with Northwestern.

After about two years of undergoing this process, and by considering it as a means of providing stability to his ever-growing family, he eventually relented and joined the faculty. "The way I joined the faculty would never happen today. I was not part of a search. I never applied. It was total serendipity." Still, during his years of teaching at the Northwestern, Charles has proven to be quite the professor, having received multiple awards and the Hurley Gurley Brown Endowed Professorship. Interestingly, Charles left Northwestern after about a six-year initial tour of duty that coincided with the departure of Dean Janeway and the arrival of a new dean,

Ken Body, who was less than enthusiastic about Charles' presence on the faculty and provided him a less than the comfortable existence one of thing a member of the faculty would receive. "He was like 'Charles Whitaker? Who are you? I don't know you! I know more famous Black people than you! There are certainly better Black folks than you whom we can have here!'" The implication was that Charles' purpose on the faculty was to maintain some Black quota, which regenerated in him old feelings of challenges to his capability and worthiness of being in the profession. Such a challenge to a professor in search of tenor was an unsettling feeling to him.

Simultaneously, another of Charles' mentors from Northwestern, Lerone Bennett, was wooing him to return to *Ebony Magazine,* and he did so while continuing at NU on a part-time basis. It took the arrival of yet another new dean at Medill, Loren Gilioni, to convince Charles to return to NU on a full-time basis again. In his second tour of duty at Northwestern, Charles has fully embraced his professorship. "After teaching for fifteen to sixteen years, I had a mid-life crisis and decided to obtain my doctorate in journalism. I've been a faux-academic all of these years. I really consider myself a journalist masquerading as a professor." Even while teaching, Charles has completed his doctorate work at Northwestern's School of Education and Social Policy and has yet to complete and defend his dissertation.

Charles' on-again, off-again favor with Northwestern based on the existing leadership reflects the way in which The Black House has been treated over the years. Indeed, Charles' generation-long history with Northwestern and The Black

House has instilled in him an interesting and evolving perspective on The Black House and its role within the university. "I would say until the 2015 Black House incident, I had bought into a narrative that said contemporary African American students didn't need a Black House anymore. They were so different than we were …. Many of us were kids from urban schools, predominantly African American schools. The range of experiences and families (familial backgrounds) was not as diverse as they are now, so I bought into the notion that maybe things are different … maybe, they can be self-sufficient. Because they are so integrated into the general university environment, maybe, they don't see the necessity of The Black House. Maybe, The Black House is underused because students don't see the need for it in the way previous generations saw …." Charles pauses and adds, "Yes, I bought that bill of goods."

"However, as I would talk to my students, I would still see and hear a level of trauma that I actually didn't see or hear among my peers, and it dawned on me that this exists because students don't know their place in this institution. They're struggling to figure out what it is, and there is no touchstone for them. I talk about my old feeling of invisibility, and many of them have that same feeling of invisibility and no place to go. I, at least, had a place to go, and I had a community where I could unpack that and no longer feel invisible."

In time, it became apparent to Charles that the feelings of students were not anecdotal but representative in a way that has never left the Black consciousness at

Northwestern. "They don't know what they're missing. They don't know what we had. They are not able to express what they are longing for ... a community that will nurture, sustain, guide, and validate them .... To be clear, I am not promoting a separatist agenda for the African American community ... but I still see and feel there is a need for a touchstone for students to see themselves feel validated in ways the general community cannot ... a culturally significant place that affirms them."

Charles suggests that since his first experiences on campus approximately forty years ago, there has been an evolving administrative belief that "a distinct African American cultural presence has outlived its usefulness to a certain extent. The pushed narrative was 'there is no longer a need for a place within the gorgeous mosaic that the university has become, and that means we need to dismantle most traces of both support and cultural celebration of distinctly African American spaces and experiences.' I'm sure people in the administration would push back on that statement tremendously, but if you look at the way things have evolved, it's hard to come to a different conclusion."

Despite a willingness to speak definitively, Charles acknowledges that the specific existence and actions of Multicultural Student Affairs at Northwestern appear to affirm and promote that premise. "The promotion of multiculturalism seems to be defined as the flapping of everything that is distinctly ... African American." Although the withdrawal of services in favor of the promotion of services for multiculturalism appears to affect only African American students, "This also allows the university to say this is why we're not going to create an Asian-American house, and we're not going to create a Latino studies house …. In service of multiculturalism, we're going to have this one place that is going to serve any and all rather than distinct places that address these burgeoning communities …." In this context, Charles notes that it was pointed out in the report produced by the 2016 Black House Facilities Review Committee (BHFRC) that many of Northwestern's peer institutions have accommodated both multicultural and distinctly ethnic communities.

In 2015, after yet another effort was made to integrate university-wide administrative services into The Black House without input or notification, the alumni and students vehemently pushed back, and the university proposed the establishment of four public forums named The Black House Listening Sessions. Northwestern created a committee named BHFRC to monitor inputs and develop recommendations on the ongoing usefulness of The Black House. Charles Whitaker was named Chairperson of the BHFRC. "I'm going to take the most benign interpretation possible. The so-called lack of use of The Black House was a self-fulfilling prophecy. I think that The Black House was made to be underused by a lack of services and lack of programming that resulted in a lack of use. I think some individuals, looking at The Black House and its use—or what they called lack of use—saw, some administrative offices that served not Blacks exclusively, but as part of their portfolio served African American and needy students, and decided that a better use for this so-called underserved facility would be to move those administrative offices into this place that had traditionally been this cultural touchstone for African American students, and The Black House would be better used for this purpose."

"The decision was made without consultation with alumni, faculty or students for that matter. It was an administrative decision that was communicated poorly, and at a time when it appeared at least, it would generate the least amount of outcry. In fact, it did generate a lot of outcry, much to the surprise of administrators. As a result of that outcry, a listening committee was formed, comprised of faculty and alumni, which was meant to gather input and determine how The Black House should be used. At least, that was my interpretation of my charge. It was later proposed—after the recommendations were delivered—that wasn't the charge of the committee at all. There are people who don't like it when I describe it this way, but I'm going to anyway. They then claimed that the committee's actual charge was to determine how The Black House was going to be decorated.

"My pushback was it doesn't matter what you do with the drapes and carpet if you actually don't have the programs and resources and think about how it's going to be used. I'm not a decorator, and it's not my thing to figure out where the computers should go! What the computers are going to be used for and who's going to be in charge of the programming is a much more substantive conversation. That's the direction in which I took the committee, I think, to the chagrin of the Vice President of Student Affairs who appointed me to Chair the committee. I think there was a different intention for the role of that committee.

"It was a great committee... I thought we prepared what I thought was ultimately a substantive report that looked at The Black House historically and in its contemporary context and tried to make some recommendations as to how it could be put to better use in the future, in many ways, restoring it to its old purpose. One of our key recommendations was the reinstitution of the position of Dean of African American Student Affairs, which we thought was critical to making The Black House a vibrant institution on campus. We didn't want it to be some artifact. We did want it to be used.

"So, we did the report. We made a presentation on it. Yet, it sits on a dusty shelf like so many reports that I have been a part of in my twenty-five years at Northwestern." Subsequent to the work of BHFRC, the Vice President of Student Affairs commissioned a different committee, a task force to protect the Black Student Experience. "Now, it became determined that it would be the recommendations of the new committee, led by staff, that would become the guiding light for how the university would move forward regarding African American students and the African American student experience ...." Meanwhile, the work of BHFRC resulted in a response from the administration that was equivalent to "Thank you for your work. We'll take it under advisement."

Charles notes that the prior submission of a discussion paper and recommendations submitted by the Northwestern University Black Alumni Association (NUBAA) also meant to steer the future direction of The Black House toward becoming a cultural center that would serve students, faculty, alumni, and the surrounding community. The students had endorsed this report via For Members Only (The Black Student Alliance of NU) and the faculty. "Many of those recommendations were woven into The Black House Facilities Review Committee. We used that report to inform The Black House Facilities Review Committee Report." Charles was reluctant to draw a conclusion regarding the motivations for disregarding the self-determined recommendations by the African American community served by The Black House.

Charles points out that the evolution of the Black students on campus to include more than traditional African Americans "feeds into the narrative that thinking about the Black student experience strictly in terms of African American students is too narrow a definition of what a Black student at Northwestern is. The narrative now suggests 'A Black student is now as much an international student as she is a domestic student' and questions how a Black House embraces those international students as well. 'Isn't it better if we have a multicultural house than a Black House that seems only to cater to the African American experience?' That seems to be the promoted narrative."

Charles is very self-effacing with respect to the notion that he is "next in line" among faculty members who, through the lens of history, are regarded as legends among the Black faculty at Northwestern. "I want students to have a better experience than I had. I left Northwestern kind of feeling indifferent about the place ... Leon Forrest, Sterling Stuckey, Ulysses Duke Jenkins, Alice Palmer are giants in my mind, and those were institutions to me. They were foundational in molding our experience with this institution."

In thinking about the Black experience at Northwestern, Charles makes an inspired comparison between the resources available to today's students and those available to students when he studied at NU. "We did have Leon Forrest and African American Student Affairs. While we don't have nearly as many African American faculty members now as we should, there are still important faculty present. However, the alumni network is huge, it's important, and it's impressive. I don't think I realized as a student that I was just ten years away from the takeover of the Bursar's Office. That seemed like ancient history to me! There really were not that many alumni for us to call upon. Today's students have a vast network of alumni to draw upon! There are people out there who are doing amazing things and who care deeply about the students' success and the university's.

"Students have to realize the alumni represent a huge level of support, with or without The Black House. They have a support network they can call upon. Of course, we have to do the job of making ourselves available. If they can look to us and look at us as a guiding light to their future, the possibilities are endless. That's why I'm so excited about what's been happening with NUBAA over the last few years. There's a sense of excitement and a sense of possibility that hasn't quite existed before. If we keep that momentum going, it should be quite exciting, exciting for the students as well to join this alumni network."

Tanya D. Woods

Tanya and Kyra Woods

Tanya D. Woods graduated from the Weinberg School of Arts and Sciences in 1989 and transferred to Northwestern from Loyola in her sophomore year. When her daughter Kyra Woods (McCormick, 2013) decided to attend Northwestern in 2009, she knew it was important to understand better how Northwestern supports its Black undergraduates. Consequently, she found an alarming deterioration of services and a disturbing disengagement of Black alumni toward students. Tanya served as President of the Northwestern University Alumni Association (NUBAA) from 2012 to 2014, a time during which NUBAA won the Northwestern Alumni Association Club of the year for 2013.

When Tanya decided to transfer to Northwestern from Loyola University, she left behind a decade of Catholic education. "I didn't find Loyola as fulfilling as I wanted, but my mother didn't want me to go far away. Northwestern was the Ivy League of the Midwest and was close to home." She applied and began attending the university in the fall of 1986. Overall, Tanya had a fantastic undergraduate experience at Northwestern. She found the Black community to be welcoming, and although her Political Science major was rigorous, it was thrilling. She received tremendous help from Duke Jenkins and others at The Black House. "It was serendipitous to be in Chicago in the 1980's as a political science major when Harold Washington was the first Black mayor of Chicago." The energy around Black politics at Northwestern with scholars including Professor Leon Forrest, Penny Warren, Charles Brantham, and Dean Karla Spurlock-Evans as her mentors made her immersion into the culture of Northwestern seamless. "There was no shortage of Black adults on campus available to help me put it all together socially and academically."

Tanya was an extremely involved undergraduate. She spent a lot of time in The Black House, joined Alpha Kappa Alpha Sorority, Incorporated and was a resident advisor on campus. Although Tanya was involved in many activities and completed her coursework diligently, she realized how much Northwestern had to offer that was never presented to her after she graduated. "There were programs and career counselors that other students enjoyed that I missed. Kids were traveling abroad, getting extra degrees, and receiving huge fellowships. This is where I felt my Northwestern (experience) fell short."

Tanya Woods graduated from Northwestern in 1989, and she was married and started a family within a year. Subsequently, she didn't stay connected with Northwestern, as she didn't live close to the campus. However, she had a small select group of Northwestern friends while she was raising her family and building a career. She was surprised when her daughter showed interest in NU in high school. "Since I wasn't allowed to attend college out of state, I encouraged Kyra to look around the country." When Kyra took a tour of Northwestern and loved it, Tanya quietly began rooting for her alma mater. Tragically, Tanya's husband of almost 20 years, Michael, died suddenly in 2008 and navigating the college selection process and grieving at the same time was not easy for her family. Kyra shared how Northwestern became her top choice. "Mom, you went there, and Dad has a connection to Northwestern." Kyra enrolled in the university in the fall of 2009 and Tanya embarked on a journey that brought her back to Northwestern for life. Kyra pledged Alpha Kappa Alpha Sorority, she became a member of the Northwestern Community Ensemble (NCE), and she was the Homecoming Queen in her senior year. Tanya enjoyed the experience of reliving her experiences as a student at Northwestern through her daughter's accomplishments. She also determined that the alumni could contribute more to the experiences of undergraduates and joined the Northwestern University Black Alumni Association (NUBAA).

In the 1990's, Tanya remembers that NUBAA was more of a social group. She knew Don Jackson, Ce Cole Dillon, Kerry Gray, Kevin Sampson, Lauren Lowery, and Scott Montgomery were organizing events, but, as a young mother, she couldn't engage in them. She knew that NUBAA was a fairly new organization and was attempting to form its identity. "When I became more involved, I knew we had to turn the corner and create a different type of agenda." In 2011, Tanya became the Vice President of NUBAA and in 2012, she became its President.

Tanya reinstituted former NUBAA President Kevin Sampson's five-point plan, infused it with the mission of NUBAA, and began working from it. "I received little transition information, but I recognized that I had to do more than simply reconnect alumni." Raising money for scholarships was important to NAA, "but NUBAA had very little infrastructure, and we had a dormant scholarship fund that we were about to lose." There were bigger concerns for NUBAA that had to be addressed in a more strategic way. "The ongoing relationship with Northwestern was surprisingly tenuous." She knew she would have succeeded in unifying alumni with respect to the endowment of the scholarship fund. Tanya believes that the same reasons for which she had drifted away from Northwestern are the same that influence many young adults, such as familial and career engagements, and the fact that simply no one communicated the value in coming together for a common cause.

Tanya dealt with the issue of scholarships because "these schools are businesses. If you're not making an impact monetarily, your agenda has less impact in the

Northwestern Alumni Association (NAA)." In Tanya's estimation, providing the scholarship would quickly repair the relationship between the students and Northwestern. Although many alumni had negative experiences at Northwestern and were reluctant to give back, "when I appealed to them about helping young Black scholars get a Northwestern education, I could break down barriers." With Tanya's passionate demand, the alumni opened their pocketbooks and their hearts to Northwestern.

Northwestern threatened to increase the endowment levels if the requisite amount of money wasn't raised within a certain date. "I thought it was cruel and unusual, but it was the reality." It was a race against the clock. They also threatened to eliminate the restrictive language that stated that the scholarship fund should be used for African American students only. "The law department at Northwestern was determined to take that restrictive language out of the fund." Tanya became aware of a west coast donor, a Black alum, who was donating a large gift to Northwestern named the Promise Scholarship. She forged a relationship with him, created a name (the NUBAA Promise Scholarship Fund), and "fought hard to maintain the integrity and mission of the fund to benefit Black students."

Tanya strategically used NUBAA's title as Northwestern's first and oldest affinity group and leveraged it with all her communications with the Northwestern leadership. NAA could see a new energy in NUBAA and, most importantly, successful leadership. "From Ce Cole Dillon to Kerry Gray, from me to Jeff Sterling, they had to pay attention and respect to the new level of organization, like it or not." She implemented the Multi City Mixers for the alumni in major cities, created a new logo for NUBAA (designed by alumni, Joeff Trimmingham), and allowed NUBAA's Vice President Lauren Lowery to improve the relationship with faculty, staff, and athletes so that NUBAA's efforts and events could be supported university-wide.

In 2013, NAA awarded NUBAA the designation of "The Alumni Club of the Year" for the first time in its history. She suggests that it was unexpected, but she always knew the work and impact NUBAA was making nationwide was worthy of being recognized. "I knew that getting that award meant a lot to the alumni community at Northwestern." She wanted to increase NUBAA's cache and credibility, as she knew that NUBAA's future requests were going to be bigger. "I knew we were going to be taken much more seriously and it let them know that NUBAA was here to stay." The award also told NUBAA members that their work and contributions were valuable. She hoped that it would garner a new level of interest, so that NUBAA could flourish in the future.

Tanya acknowledges the sacrifices that the alumni before her made. She knows that their unpleasant experiences allowed her and her daughter to have a wonderful experience at NU. "We are reaping the benefits of a NU education and most of us still put our NU degree on our resume. We represent Northwestern to the world, with both good and bad memories of taking our degrees." Tanya believes we must all do something to give back. She hopes that the Black Northwestern alumni can give just a little back to each other and a lot back to the future generations of Black students. "Racism, sexism, and classism may take another fifty years to eradicate globally," so young scholars at NU will continue to battle. She is happy that she made the time to give back using NUBAA as the vehicle. "We worked hard, and we moved the needle. My goal was to make an impact, and we did."

Sarah Oberholtzer

Sarah Oberholtzer is a March 2018 graduate of Northwestern's School of Communication in the Department of Radio/Television/Film. She finished her studies by heading abroad to study African history at the University of Ghana, which was consistent with her interest in ethnic studies while she was at NU.

Sarah is mindful and respectful of the history of struggle at Northwestern, but, as a younger voice amongst Black students at NU, she keeps her eye on the current state of the Black experience. She describes the campus environment at Northwestern as being both pre-professional and stressful. She found herself surprised that the stress found in the pre-professional (i.e., the migration from childhood through college toward adulthood and professional work) components of functioning inside the university structure were over and above what she would attribute to the stress of just being a student at a top-tier university. Conversely, she was pleased to acknowledge that the academic offerings were also more than expected, but in a positive way.

"I struggle to say that 100% of the stress was because of the Black experience, but it was a very high, high experience. Maybe 80–90% of my stress was because I was a Black person of color and low income ... so much so that it shaped all of my interactions at Northwestern, whether it was inside or outside of the classroom." Sarah found it interesting that the hyper-focus on Blackness actually benefitted her in some ways, such as when she was pursuing courses in African American or Asian-American Studies.

"I learned how I have been positioned in society as a racialized person. Outside of the classroom, my first year began great, but then toward the end of the first year, it became very difficult, as my friends didn't acknowledge or understand what it was like for me to be one of the very few Black students at Northwestern and one of the only Black students in my friend group. Being someone who also cares about Black issues, it was also difficult adjusting to a community where people didn't necessarily value the struggles of Black people."

Sarah acknowledges that Northwestern makes many efforts to provide resources to students. She notes that The Black House remains a major resource and space where students are able to congregate and feel a sense of community. "It was a nice, safe haven environment." Multicultural Student Affairs exists to provide programming to bridge the divide between diverse students and the majority. Campus Inclusion and Community (CIC) serves to facilitate interaction on campus among all students, and it has been working with her for years as a Posse Scholar, which is a nationwide program that promotes college access and leadership development. Sarah was among the first group of Posse Scholars at Northwestern. She also notes that she has been able to access counseling from the Women's Center, and she's worked with Student Enrichment Services, which provides aid for first-generation and low-income students.

Even as Sarah points out the wide variety of services that are structured to ease one's navigation throughout campus, she believes the point is still being missed. "The stress experience is much more often due to interpersonal relationships and social interactions. So, the administration can work very hard to provide services and space, but they (the administrators) currently don't appear to be structured in a way where they're constantly informed about what's happening socially, so they just don't tap into the social interactions in the pre-professional sphere culture of NU that causes stress."

Sarah surmises that the ongoing focus on diversity and inclusion work without the matched focus on enlightening the majority culture just cannot be as effective as it needs to be. "Those resources really don't seem to tap into the social aspects of Northwestern." She also believes it to be true that the focus on Multicultural Student Affairs detracts from the individual stresses that she experiences as a Black on campus. "If you don't have a specific organizing body specifically for Black students on campus, then the Black experience on campus will be washed away much more easily. We know that, historically, Black students at Northwestern have been systematically shunned." This appears to be a common refrain among the younger generation of students and alumni in their efforts to explain how their existence could possibly be more difficult than Blacks of past generations who actually had a Department of African American Student Affairs with deans and directors. These efforts have been replaced by initiatives within Multicultural Student Affairs, which has a distinctly different (and, often, conflicting) mission.

Sarah is very reflective on why she found herself becoming an activist as a student and lists a number of efforts that she eventually led and/or supported. "It started with the Michael Brown case with the non-acquittal. I was hurt, confused, and enraged. It didn't make sense to me that a White man—a police officer—could get away with killing an innocent kid. Then, I learned about other cases, like Tamir Rice and Aiyana Stanley-Jones, and really I seemed to realize that anti-Blackness was working on a systematic level to disenfranchise and get away with killing Black people. And so, enraged by the Michael Brown non-indictment, I organized a demonstration with performances and speak-outs to really let go of anger and frustration around the case and what that meant for Black people ....

"Then, I was asked to be a part of an organizing body that was reclaiming Black history month rather than thinking that the only history relevant to Blacks is the civil rights movement. Then, the Concerned Students of Northwestern movement occurred on campus (seeking to improve the experiences of Blacks on campus; this effort followed the similar efforts nationally, and notably at the University of Missouri), and I was part of the demonstration that occurred at Northwestern.

"There were budding instances of Black students on campuses listing sets of demands for universities to address Black struggles and pains on campuses. We at

Northwestern, having a body of Blacks frustrated and unheard, came up with a list of demands and found out that the President was going to be at an event (the groundbreaking for the athletics training facility), so we decided to tell him about our demands with this event, which had ESPN coverage, which allowed even more people to hear about our demands." These thirty-four demands, which were meant to improve the student experience, were delivered as planned in November of 2015, with the students interrupting the groundbreaking activities. The university has been working on the implementation of the demands since that time.

"I was also one of the founders of the Black Lives Matter chapter on campus. The efforts were primarily meant to uplift the Black social community and divest from the prison industrial complex and to provide healing and wellness opportunities to students." Interestingly, Northwestern took a major initiative and placed a Black Lives Matter banner atop the Norris University Center for a week, but the group was not notified of the decision.

Sarah notes other efforts that called her into action. "I supported the campaign to divest from the prison industrial complex, called Unshackle NU, which students also led." This effort led to Northwestern creating an Advisory Committee on Investment Responsibility. "I was a part of the Sheridan Block Group, but I didn't do as much work as others. This was the effort to turn offices and spaces in The Black House into administrative office spaces. Black students felt as if this was an infringement on The Black House and the community it aimed to create. We felt this was the administration attempting to keep an eye on the Black students at Northwestern. As we know, Black people have had a history of (being under) surveillance and (have faced) the repercussions of being heavily surveilled and policed."

When asked why students feel like they must bear the burden to improve campus relations and why she was so often involved, she responds, "I'm not on my own doing any of the things I've mentioned. Black woman and femmes (predominantly, along with Black men) had been with me throughout all of this. It didn't make sense to do anything other than that, to be quite honest. The demonstration in support of what was happening in Ferguson was creating a space that I needed to create. Because I'm so hurt and affected by the dehumanization of Black people and the struggles we are forced to endure, anything that highlights or remedies that situation is a no-brainer."

Sarah feels conflicted about the lasting effects of efforts toward change. "I'm satisfied with the creation of the Black Student Experience Task Force, which has quantified the experience with measurable looks at what we're facing. I'm not satisfied overall, though. I need every Black student to be intentionally supported, and we need to be robustly compensated (in the form of reparations for the history our ancestors were forced to take), so, no, I'm not satisfied." When asked if she can ever foresee these actions coming, Sarah responds, "For sure. When Black people tap into their beauty and resilience publicly and aren't afraid of the repercussions, things happen."

When asked about the ongoing migration from distinct diversity and inclusion efforts toward multiculturalism, Sarah laughs and says that her reaction is "I don't want one Northwestern. I want a lot of Northwesterns representing a lot of different types of people. I don't want to be solidified into one. I want thousands of variations of people living and breathing and engaging with the world." Sarah continually emphasizes the need for groups of individuals to work together to create the change they desire and notes that in her example as well as that of any other student, promoting the idea that supermen and superwomen are needed to bring about change is counterproductive. It is illuminating that she doesn't realize and doesn't necessarily need to realize how the struggles of the students in her time are reminiscent and reflective of voices from past generations, all of whom seemingly search for the same equality of experience.

Lawrence "Macs" Vinson III

Lawrence Macs Vinson

Macs Vinson is a 2017 graduate of Northwestern's McCormick School of Engineering and Applied Science.

Macs' Northwestern experience comprised four eventful years of college, even though it was characterized by struggle and controversy. "I think a lot about the problems I had with Northwestern, and I wonder whether or not I'd have had the same experiences if I'd attended another PWI (Predominantly White Institution) or if my experience would have been different if I'd attended an HBCU (Historically Black College and University). I'm coming to appreciate my Northwestern experience a lot more being removed from it and being in the working world. I will say that college was definitely a time of struggle, personally, professionally, and, especially, academically. However, I was discovering things about myself that I'd never really thought (I knew) before.

"The safety net is gone when you go to college. I was having interactions with people on different levels. You make your own decisions. You're an adult. Also, a lot of things rose to the surface emotionally by my being Black in a space where, for the first time, I was a minority. Also, when it comes to my gender identity, I was a minority among minorities. So, it was a time to struggle, but, in that struggle, I discovered a lot about myself. This is self-indulgent, but I'm very happy with who I am, coming out of it."

Macs notes that Northwestern's campus environment was not always accommodating, even throughout the struggles. "If I had to make an overarching judgment, I'd say that people who share my identities have to create space for ourselves. We have to carve out the respect we deserve. We have to fight for our right to exist. I think that is an experience unto itself, in which you simply do not come with the privilege of being taken seriously and respected or given the space to be yourself. You really have to fight for that.

"One of the biggest struggles I had at Northwestern was, in order to be yourself, you have to do a lot of work to get ready to fight battles. When my gender identity started to ebb on the femme side, in every room I went, it was awkward just to make eye contact with people. When you're wearing lipstick or when you're wearing heels, you're different than everyone else in the room, and you are hyperaware of how everyone else perceives you. It took a lot of training for me not only to walk out of my dorm room but also to enter these spaces, knowing that people were probably talking about me. Living authentically and being whom I wanted to be and not aligning myself to other's expectations needed to be a priority, so I could live in the way I wanted to. So, there's definitely a struggle when it comes to being received in the way you want to (be treated and received)."

In the quest to live authentically, Macs discovered a particular strategy to offer the strength of imposing his will on the surrounding environment. "Being at Northwestern, being a person of color, and wanting to have your voice heard, you really have to develop the confidence of a White man. What's different about that is I demanded the right to be accepted. I demanded the right to be who I was. That was non-negotiable. That's not something I'm going to compromise on or let anyone take away from me."

"So, my strength came both from the outside and inside. From inside, it was me demanding a seat, knowing there was a place for me here, and knowing I was going to take it. On the other end, strength really came from the queer and trans community, but, especially (from) the queer and trans community of color. It was especially Black women and femmes who empowered me to be myself. When I thought of gender identity and gender expression, it never really clicked with me.

"See, the reason I started growing out my hair was because I hated going to the barbershop. I hated this ultramasculine space where I never fit in. I looked like a man, but I never really felt like a man. I was always on the beauty salon side of things, talking with the women about things. I knew I didn't fit into this categorization system that everyone else seemed to identify so strongly with, and I didn't understand why. I never understood what that meant until I came to college and met other people who felt the same way. So, it was really (about) being able to see other people living authentically and rejecting the preconceived notions that others had about them and rejecting society's expectations of them. This allowed me to do the same and believe and demand that I be allowed to live authentically. So, at Northwestern, I chose not to hide who I was but to be who I was.

"I can't point to a single day or event that made me decide. It wasn't a decision as much as there was a point at which there was no longer a decision. I was never really thinking, 'Am I going to be myself today or am I going to live up to the expectations of others today?' What ended up happening is one option was no longer an option. I couldn't do it anymore. There was no longer a point in living someone else's life."

Macs did notice nuances between the challenges faced based on strictly racial considerations versus those faced because of non-adherence to a binary gender expectation. "I noticed with my hair that people immediately labeled me as Black and assumed certain things about me, for better or worse. The same things I had to go through with gender identity, I also had to go through because I am Black. When I went through this evolution with my gender identity, being Black was inextricably part of the conversation. It never was separate. I've experienced discrimination and ridicule as a result of being Black and being non-binary, both individually and simultaneously.

"I think back to a poem my mom recited to me by Marianne Williamson called 'Our Deepest Fear.' One of the lines is, '*as we let our own light shine, we unconsciously give others permission to do the same.*' I think that really encapsulated my quest for identity. With regards to Blackness, the beautiful thing about my Northwestern experience is that I was in a space with other Black people, and you're exposed to people and able to have formative relationships with people who are in the same phase of their lives. We were all just kind of figuring things out. It really gave me the space to think critically about who I wanted to be for the next few years.

"People have always said we live this life of firsts. So, when you're different at Northwestern, you're always constantly pioneering or trailblazing in spaces. In my example, that was simply because there was no one visible who had come before me in the spaces I was in. So, creating a structure where there was none was a definitive aspect of being Black and being queer at the same time at Northwestern.

"It was every day that people would react to me based on the way I looked or how they perceived me. I had professors reacting negatively to my appearance, but at the same time, some of them would be excited about my presence. There were people recited to in my education, development, and success, because they wanted to see more people like me. They want their classrooms to be more diverse. I definitely appreciated that, but it also meant I didn't have room for failure.

"At Northwestern, I was ready to go off on anyone who gave me a certain look or said something microaggressive toward me. I think that, as I am growing up, I need to start reacting more with empathy and meeting them where they are instead of trapping them. Back then, if people had something problematic to say, I would extract that out of you, then go off. Now, I'm more willing to have the conversation and let it be a learning experience for everyone involved."

Macs notes with pride that some alumni and staff have expressed appreciation and admiration of his ability to confront his issues. "I didn't build singlehandedly a space for people like myself to exist comfortably in a welcoming environment. That happened through the cooperation, understanding, and support of so many others, which has led to Northwestern being a more inclusive space. I appreciate that I left Northwestern being a more inclusive space than when I entered."

Macs' impact on the university experience was not limited to his strife for existing in truth. Macs also navigated the university much in the way any student would, which, in effect, normalized an existence. "I started in ASG (Associate Student Government) in the winter quarter of my freshman year, later was Vice President for Student Activities, and then became Executive Vice President." However, Macs states that it was the activism that arose organically or from working outside of establishment organizations that most often seemed to have the greater impact. Macs cites the 2015 pushback against proposed changes to The Black House, efforts to get Northwestern to divest from private prisons, and corporations being deemed to be supporting human rights violations and apartheid in Israel (UnshackleNU and NU Divest, respectively) that led to the university creating a socially responsible investment committee, in which initiatives, and efforts of Black Lives Matter were key examples. "Being an ally to those movements and offering them support in a way to be heard within ASG was the way I found my place in activism and was able to bridge the gap between grassroots organizing and the establishment set up for creating change in a student-driven way."

Macs is measured and reflective of one's ability to create change. "I hope that every year there is this ongoing push toward more space. It's hard when you go to a place for only four to five years, and you want to make an impact. You have to establish your name and establish your impact, and once you get power, you maybe have a year to enact your impact. So, it's really a continuing journey. So, I hope my impact was laying the groundwork for people to continue the work we did. When I see the younger classes, it's beautiful. It's great to see people who were more 'woke' than I was entering college. I know they're inheriting a campus environment that they are going to challenge, and they are going to push beyond what they had when they entered. So, if there's someone who enters Northwestern in 2020 who is Black, queer, and non-binary, they don't have to do the same level of fighting for their existence that I did."

Furthermore, Macs is skeptical about calls to promote change by simply addressing the needs of the general student population. "Too often, the dialogue around an 'average student' only serves to further marginalize students who are already underrepresented. This is a way of saying 'Sure, Black students may have this problem or LGBTQ students may have this problem on campus, but we need to focus on the average student.'

"I spent so much time questioning my place at the university and whether or not I could do the things that I set out to do. I'd want any student to know you should never question yourself and who you are. You're there for a reason. Living your life in the way you want and not for someone else's expectations is really the key to happiness. Your own internal values, beliefs, and ideals need to lead the decisions you make. When those things are misaligned, you're doing things you aren't going to be happy with. When you get out of that, you can start doing things that are purposeful to you. At the end of the day, I had some of my hardest times at Northwestern and some of my happiest times at Northwestern. You really have to take the good with the bad. This is an experience that will challenge you in ways that you haven't been before, but in my experience, it wasn't the hardest ways in which I've been challenged, and I'm very glad to have done this at Northwestern."

Kasey Brown

Kasey Brown is a senior in the Weinberg College of Arts and Sciences who is majoring in Economics and served as the 2017–18 For Members Only (FMO) Coordinator at Northwestern. In that role, Kasey was essentially the voice of Black students at Northwestern. She is a leader and loves the pressure that the job entails. Kasey has been exposed to some of the greatest institutions that the United States has to offer while being a student at NU. She has interned at Goldman Sachs, Accenture, and Northwestern's Feinberg School of Medicine and has also spent the summer of 2017 at the Harvard Business School. However, her Northwestern experience has also involved her being subject the worst kinds of trauma. She believes that her story illuminates the failures of adults in the wake of tragedy. These failures will always be amongst the memories she will have of her soon-to-be alma mater.

Kasey graduated summa cum laude from West Bloomfield High School in Michigan, which is located just outside of Detroit. She was accepted to Harvard, Princeton, and Yale, but she decided to consider Northwestern. She knew she was "the smart kid, the chosen Black kid," but she did have her doubts about how she might compete in the Ivy League. She visited Northwestern in June on an eighty-degree, beautiful sunny day with the lake glistening and thought that it might be the school for her. "I ran into some Black students on my campus visit, and they were very open about the Black experience at NU. They would say 'the Black community is strong. There may be drama, but the Black students are like family.'"

Kasey entered Northwestern as a pre-med major, but, after freshman year, she decided to switch to Economics. "No one discouraged me. I made the decision from my heart and thought it was a God-driven decision." She came from a family that dreamed of her being a doctor, so, during her freshman year, she shadowed several alums in their offices and hospitals to fully understand her career choice. She quickly realized that medicine was not what she wanted to pursue. "Every practice I visited made me know I couldn't do this. This was not what I want to do. This is not what *Grey's Anatomy* presented itself to be." It was hard for Kasey to tell her family, but she knew they would support her.

Kasey is happy with her decision to move to Economics. She considers herself extremely business-savvy, because she ran her own small business in high school. "The coursework is very difficult, but it's been a great transition." Kasey's parents were concerned when her As and Bs that she had scored in high school turned to Cs in several instances at Northwestern. "Every time the grades are delivered, my parents are like, 'What is going on! What is happening?'" She assures them that she is going to graduate on time and experience everything there is to do at Northwestern. "I tell them, 'Mom and Dad, college is the time for me to grow, and I feel like I'm growing here.'" She says her parents don't really like the response, but they accept it. Unfortunately for Kasey, there are not many Black students in

Economics, so it's hard for her to find study partners. Still, she hasn't had any major academic troubles.

Kasey was a busy freshman. She joined One Step Before (the Black premedical organization) and FMO and participated in many STEM-related activities. "I attended a predominately white high school, so I was eager to attend the Black House Wildcat Welcome Barbeque to find my community and my people. Sarah Carthen Watson was the FMO Coordinator in my freshman year, and she was my role model!" Sarah offered her and other students a ride home and food. When Sarah treated her like this, Kasey felt she had a big sister and a lifelong friend. She served on the programming committee in her freshman year and planned the State of the Black Union event.

During Kasey's sophomore year, "FMO collapsed. There was only one event and a lot of drama." During her junior year, none of the old board ran, and Cheron Mims became the coordinator with minimal institutional knowledge. "She had to work through the drama on her own with no transition or guidance, and she reached out to me." Kasey was reluctant, but she knew that there was a lack of diligent people and wanted to help. She and Cheron met with the new assistant for Multicultural Student Affairs, Heather Browning, to attempt to instill life back into FMO again. "This is a place where I can bring my skill set and advance my community." She was treasurer during her junior year, and, during her senior year, she ran for and won the Coordinator position.

Kasey has become more spiritual while being a student at Northwestern. She grew up in a Baptist church in Detroit, attended church regularly, and went to Easter services. However, the church had been just some place that she went to. "Church wasn't something that impacted my life. I didn't feel super religious." However, the STEM program Kasey attended in her freshman year had a counselor who opened her eyes. She had never seen a young person have such strong faith. "She was super candid, super cool, and would talk to me about her faith and exploring it. We prayed every night, and she taught me how to talk to God." Kasey explored her spiritual side more and applied those talks and prayers for guidance in her life.

Later, Kasey would need that spiritual guidance. In January 2017, only a month after joining Alpha Kappa Alpha Sorority, Incorporated, Jordan Hankins, her sorority sister and Northwestern women's basketball student-athlete, committed suicide. She notes that there are no protocols for properly addressing this tragedy for Black people. Suicides are almost unprecedented, and Kasey believes that it is assumed that, probably, mistakes were made in bringing young women, athletes, and the student body gathered together to ensure healing and unity and promote mental stability. "From that day, everything has not been super rosy. I've been left with a huge void and lots of regrets. How didn't I know this was going on? How didn't I see it?" Kasey has still not gotten over this heartbreak. Kasey notes that she has not had any time to grieve and has had to be strong for so many people. Kasey loves Alpha Kappa Alpha and Northwestern, but it becomes fair to ask whether Kasey is the same mistakes are being made with respect to interpreting her strength, stillness, and resilience as complete wellness.

Unfortunately, there are no older Black women or men in The Black House to guide Kasey or the other FMO leaders, which is even more annoying to Kasey based on her understanding of how robust the support used to be in The Black House earlier. Heather Browning, the Assistant Director of Multicultural Student Affairs, was new to Northwestern and new to the job during Kasey's junior year. In Heather's role, she was responsible for guiding and supporting FMO and other Black satellite organizations, although her title and work did not specifically focus on Black students. "She held retreats for us to get to know each other, so we felt that there were good intentions." By the time Kasey became the Coordinator and wanted to "find funding to execute programs, I realized that Black students were not her priority." Kasey felt Heather was giving her the runaround, which deteriorated into no communication at all by the time Heather quit in the December of 2017. Kasey feels like she and FMO "are on our own, and it just sucks. At Northwestern, I feel like I never get hugs. No one hugs me here."

When Kasey took the job as FMO Coordinator, she didn't realize that it was the 50th year anniversary of the Bursar's Office Takeover and the anniversary of the formation of FMO. Consequently, she was thrown into meetings and conference calls that were completely unexpected. "I truly love meeting alumni and meeting with administration, but Northwestern, NUBAA, and FMO must do a better job of sharing and helping us understand the vast and important history of the organization." She knows that in 2018 the idea of FMO being the "sole voice of Black Northwestern is void." However, Kasey has enjoyed every minute of being the face of FMO in this pivotal year. Therefore, she continues to embrace the job as the liaison between the community and the university. "I'm so honored to be here after fifty remarkable years of FMO. I can see that I'm impacting change now that will continue 50 or 100 years after me. I love it!"

Paula Pretlow

Paula Pretlow

Paula Pretlow graduated from Northwestern University's Weinberg College of Arts and Sciences in 1977 with a B.S. in Political Science and again in 1978 from the Kellogg School of Management after obtaining her MBA. Paula came to NU in 1973 from Oklahoma, at a time that was removed from the Bursar's Office Takeover by five years and during which NU was especially focused on admitting a larger number of quality Black students. "I was part of that wave. Some might call it affirmative action, but I don't because I competed on every measure, and I think most of us who were admitted to Northwestern competed (more) on every level than anybody else, any White students, competed on for admission."

From the very beginning, Paula was insistent on having a "normal" campus existence. "The campus atmosphere for me at that point was one of normalcy—maybe, I was too naïve—but, I never went into the atmosphere thinking that I wouldn't be anything other than accepted. But, of course, I come from a tradition, a family, who decided to integrate the Oklahoma City Public School System voluntarily. I was used to walking into situations believing 'I belonged to be here' because I chose to be here. Call it naïve or just call it being what your expectations are, but I found the atmosphere to be welcoming.

"I lived in what used to be known as the NU Apartments. Back in the old days, it was a relatively newly made co-ed dorm, where men and women are actually on the same floor. That was a great experience. It was a great place to live, and I was consumed with dorm life, had wonderful friends, and was totally absorbed in being a freshman, going to parties, and studying!" In fact, Paula was fortunate enough not to have experienced a single negative racially or sexually charged episode during her freshman year when she lived on campus.

"I think there was an opening and an expectation that it was going to be a great experience. I didn't feel any push or pull one way or another. I had three White roommates, and we all got along as roommates do. But, my experience was different from most students, Black, White, green, yellow, red, or whatever, because I met a fellow student early in my freshman year, got married in my sophomore year, and moved off campus! My experience was as a commuter student, really, because there was no married student housing for undergraduates."

Paula is reflective about how her ability to have a normal student experience rendered the need to access resources within which others thrived as relatively unnecessary. "I went to The Black House occasionally, but it was not where I felt I had to go for refuge. I'm a person who kind of goes my own way, and I always have been. From childhood, I had to find my way everywhere. It wasn't a place that I sought out as much as some of my friends, and that's ok! These days, it seems to be too often the case that people of color, African American students, come to Northwestern and don't have a good experience. I'm concerned about that.

"I was used to being one of the only Blacks in the environment (when) I was in Oklahoma. I was very used to having to deal with, negotiate with, thinking around, and being around White people. Had I had any problems or needed to confront anyone (at Northwestern), I'd have had no problems doing so!

"I actually had people helping me along the way. I was a work-study student. I was a poor student when I came to Northwestern on full financial aid. I think I started at eighty cents an hour. I was a hall monitor—of all things—in one of the North Campus' all-male dorms. I had guys who just took me under their wing who were just like big brothers to me, and that was really cool! In my second year, my work-study job was in the Office of Financial Aid, so I had people in the administration who actually became mentor figures to me. That helped. I was able to use those folks as sounding boards when I made it known that I wanted to apply to the 3/2 program (a Northwestern undergraduate and Kellogg Business School combined degree program in place at the time), and the Director of Financial Aid ended up writing a letter of recommendation for me." Paula fondly recalls the late Professor Leon Forrest as also being a father figure to her during her time at NU.

"So, I think I learned in my previous experience in Oklahoma that having mentors—Black mentors and finding White ones, too—served me well. So, it was natural that when I got to Northwestern, I would look for helpers and people to guide me, and I did. What does that mean for a student entering Northwestern today? How might that work for a student today? We didn't have Posse or, other than The Black House, places to go for support like that. (The Posse Scholars program, introduced at Northwestern in 2012, identifies high school students for academic and leadership potential who begin working together in their senior year of high school to prepare for college and, once on campus, they meet weekly with a campus mentor.) So, unless you come to college with a mindset like that or knowledge on how to get it, it can be really difficult. So, my advice to an entering student—but advice can't and doesn't apply to everybody because we're all (unique) individuals—is I love the idea of pairing up. I think there's a lot to be said for pairing a student up with a buddy or someone who can show them the ropes. I'm not even suggesting it necessarily needs to be Black on Black or color on color, but I think having a buddy or someone who has your best interests and can show you the ropes is helpful."

For many Black students at Northwestern, memories of protests or other campus activist events might be embedded in their minds as a memory of the campus experience. For Paula, however, her memories comprise a different yet specific occurrence. "One thing that reinforced my pre-Northwestern experience was arriving at Northwestern and observing the dining halls. Because no one group claimed me or I would not be claimed, it was at times uncomfortable to say 'No, I'm not going to sit at the 'Black Table.' I'm going to sit with these friends.' But, I got over it. So, for me, that reinforced this notion that I would have to find my own way. Today, I may choose to sit with these friends, and tomorrow I may choose to sit with my all-Black friends and wave at my White friends from across the room. But ... this segregation that occurred was a continuation of what happened in high school, as voluntarily segregation gave way to mandatory desegregation, and people went off in their groups, and I wandered between them all. That has been a lasting hallmark, and that's how I live my life today."

Paula harps on the possibility that many Blacks don't segregate themselves and simply sit where they are most comfortable, "but I can assure you, some students, whether they were Black or White, didn't feel comfortable sitting outside of that clique, outside of that segregated table. I know this still happens from my son's experience. He was targeted for not sitting at the 'Black Table' with comments such as 'Are you too good to sit with us?' But no one ever said anything to me and, when I sat at the 'Black Table,' I was welcomed.

"I credit my Black mother, who in 1968 sat us down—her five Black kids—and said we were going to desegregate the Oklahoma City Public Schools. In 1968, she said 'You're smart. Your competition in life is going to be the brightest White kids and Black kids in the world. You may as well get used to hanging around White people right now. You're not going to have any problems because you're just as smart as anybody else. You're just as smart as those White kids. So, you're going to go. You're going to learn, and I'm here as your support.' So, I credit my mother for putting us in that situation, in an uncomfortable situation, and knowing she was always there to support us."

Paula is very clear on the impact that Northwestern had on her and how it gave her opportunities to engage in the university after graduation. "I realize that Northwestern made a difference in my life. I realized that Northwestern would make a difference in my life the first day I stepped foot on campus. I've always given back in gratitude. Before I could give back financially very much, I would spend my time interviewing prospective students. It's always been important to me to make sure I express gratitude and help others who—I hope—have a similar experience or at least have the possibility of a similar experience."

In fact, Paula insisted that she be given the opportunity to help. "I was working at a small firm, and when a development officer came to call on one of the principals of the firm, I thought, 'Development Officer? You're not calling on me?' I asked why and told them they were losing out by not calling on me. Word got back, and somebody was assigned to me. It forged a relationship. It's finding that person that's going to pay attention to you and saying, 'I deserve to be paid attention to, and it could be in your best interest—and I want you to.'

"I was involved in different ways, first more so through Kellogg, then more so through the undergraduate school, Weinberg. I loved giving back to Northwestern in ways that involved me being there physically and ways that involved me contributing financially, because I credit the university with opening doors for me."

Paula targeted to become a member of the Northwestern Board of Trustees and says, "It took me longer than I thought it would! I wanted to have a seat at the table." Paula joined the board in the September of 2016. "I'm in my second year on the Board, and I'm finally feeling confident enough in that room to lend my voice in ways that are collegial and without being shy and speaking up when I feel something I need to say needs to be heard."

Paula explains how issues of importance, such as issues related to the Black experience, get handled. "Most work gets done in committees. There is a student affairs committee that would take up most of these issues (related to the Black experience at Northwestern). I happen not to be on that committee, but through the work I do with Weinberg College of Arts and Sciences' Board of Visitors as another voice and having those conversations one on one with people who are on the committee, and in having conversations with people in the administration, I raise my concerns, I raise my commitment to try to make it better, and I try to listen to students, because we've got to get it right. I view it as a part of my fiduciary responsibility as a board member to address those concerns."

Paula notes the limitation of addressing concerns based on the relative paucity of Blacks on the Board. "Here, in December 2017, there are only two African American women on the Board of Trustees, and as far as African American men, there are only two. So, there are only four Black board members at Northwestern University, and there should be more."

In addition to her role on the Board of Trustees, Paula has assumed the mantle of Campaign Co-Chair for Northwestern University's $3.75 billion "WE WILL" fundraising campaign, succeeding another prominent African American member of the Board of Trustees, Adam Karr. "I think it's pretty cool that I was asked to follow Adam Karr. I'm such a huge fan of Adam, my little brother. He's absolutely fantastic and working with 'WE WILL' was one of the first things I was asked to do upon joining the Board. It never occurred to me to say no, because I viewed it as an opportunity to continue the symbolism, to continue to show the world that we are here too and representing—as a person of color—the University. I jumped at the opportunity.

"Hopefully, it means I get to be an inspiration to people who look like me. We can all participate, no matter how small or large (our participation is). The point is participation. That's what I represent here. I'm the Campaign Co-chair for participation. We have goals for that, and I'm the face and voice of that part of our campaign. I'm on the Board's Alumni Development Committee. I look forward to the day when we have more people's names come up who are African American who are on that list of 'We really need to be in touch with them!' Part of my plan is to make that more of a focus, because there are more of us. We are a giving people. The poorest among us always find a way to give, whether in time or in financial resources, even if it's that last dollar. I want to make it my agenda at the Board level, because I just want it spoken out loud. One thing I want to speak about is the giving and the increased participation among Blacks and the fact that Adam's face first and my face now makes a difference. I have gotten notes and feedback from Black people who have done so because I was the one asking (the relevant questions). That's huge."

Paula is reflective of her current and future work with Northwestern and appreciates that her efforts comprise very high-level means of impacting multiple components of the Black experience. "I currently serve on the Alumni Relations and Development Committee and the Investment Committee. I take my work on the Investment Committee very seriously, because as the university hires managers, it is important to have a diversity of managers, and I get to have a voice in that." Paula has been at the table for student-led conversations about Northwestern divesting from corporations involved with the prison industrial complex and addressing the concerns of the BDS movement. (The Boycott, Divestment, Sanctions movement's self-described mission is "... to end international support for Israel's oppression of Palestinians and pressure Israel to comply with international law.")

Paula provides an evolved view of the journey of Blacks at Northwestern today. "I don't think that there is a singular Black experience. The 'Black experience' encompasses a variety of experiences, which is a beautiful thing. I think we all can learn from one another by having conversations like this about what they are: what makes them good, what makes them great, and what makes them awful. Especially, in what makes it awful, we need to spend particular time and attention to make sure that this not normal, and I'm committed to doing that, because I believe that every African American student, every Black student who steps foot on campus deserves to have a good-to-great experience at Northwestern and to the extent to which that is not happening, then we as alum and administrators and interested parties have a job to do. I'm committed to that idea that we should have a good-to-great experience.

"The members of today's Black community are faced with realities that just weren't as prevalent when I attended. There are a whole set of circumstances that students today are faced with, and I think we have a responsibility as a university and Black people within the University to have support systems that help students adjust and thrive. We have to provide the support and the safety net for students who make it into this university. Even the most brilliant of us need support. I don't want to discount or gloss over any of that in my aspirational expectations, because we owe it to the students."

Paula appreciates that her experience was exceptional and hopes that it is aspirational in demonstrating that a path for a normal campus experience can be navigated. Her impact on Northwestern and its Black experience wasn't implemented through a protest, but by displaying a commitment to elevating and normalizing the university experience for all. She is clear that her contributions are not close to being done. "What's next for me? I will continue to serve on this Board for as long as they will have me."

Modern Evolution of the Black Experience & A New Future

- **Alexandria Bobbitt:** President, Black Campus Ministry
- **Charla Wilson:** Inaugural Archivist for the Black Experience
- **Phil Harris:** Vice-President and General Counsel, Vice-Chair, Board of Trustees
- **Sonia Waiters:** Vice President, Northwestern University Black Alumni Association
- **Michael Wilbon:** Member, Board of Trustees
- **Jabbar Bennett:** Associate Provost for Diversity and Inclusion, Chief Diversity Officer
- **Jonathan Holloway:** Provost
- **Jeffrey Sterling:** President, Northwestern University Black Alumni Association

Alexandria Bobbitt

Alexandria Bobbitt

Alexandria Bobbitt is a 2016 Northwestern graduate from the School of Education and Social Policy. Although Alex's Northwestern experience is entirely her own, her story perfectly captures the essence of the multifaceted experiences of modern-day Blacks at Northwestern. Discussing the Black experience with Alexander invokes a roller coaster of emotions in one. Although her exuberance and smile are always on display, she spontaneously bursts into tears, depending on the direction towards which the conversation is headed. Knowing Alex entails knowing the following two things about her: Northwestern is deeply embedded in her, and so is her Christian faith.

Alexandria's Northwestern legacy is not hers alone. She is only the latest of a long line of family members to attend Northwestern, the Bobbitt "family school." Her mother and father, Kecia and James, met at NU. Their cousins, aunts, and uncles had attended the university before them. Her brother studied here after her. As such, she knew from a very early age that Northwestern University was a major part of her family's life and would be a major part of her life. She was so sure of her Northwestern destiny that she applied early decision and would have applied the earlier decision, if that had been a thing. She admits to having been "brainwashed" a long time before she arrived on campus.

The Bobbitt family legacy offered Alexandria a more acute understanding of what Northwestern had to offer. After a lifetime of hearing about the beautiful campus, the Black Northwestern experience, how her parents found love at NU, and the stories about her father as a member of the football team and her mother as a member of Alpha Kappa Alpha Sorority and observing the career success of all of her relatives, she came to NU ready not only to embark upon discovering herself and enjoying a college experience but also to immerse herself in and building upon the Black experience.

True to form, upon arrival, she jumped into the Black experience. She notes, "I was definitively going to be a part of that!" There was an opportunity for active participation in For Members Only, the Black Student Alliance at Northwestern. She was also a peer advisor and a student coordinator for the Ambassadors program, which meant to assist with student enrollment. She spent three years as Chaplain of the Northwestern Community Ensemble (NCE) and was immersed in House on the Rock (a chapter of the InterVarsity Christian Fellowship and the local Black Campus Ministry for over twenty-five years), subsequently becoming its President during her senior year.

However, Alexandria's Northwestern journey wasn't defined by her activities as much as by her experiences. As she describes it, there's a seemingly inescapable part of the Black experience with which she became all too familiar that comprised the distinctive parts of injustice and beauty. "I saw blatant racism. I saw covert racism. I was witness to the microaggressions and the different experiences of my classmates based on their race or sexuality. There was a stark contrast between the beauty of how Northwestern looks and the ugliness of how it can make you feel." She allows for a reasonable degree of stress that is a part of the learning process but notes frequent occasions in which that stress becomes oppressive. She, just like many other graduates, refuses to say that "on average" one outweighs the other. From her perspective, the Black experience is defined by wild swings of emotions more than which can simply be ascribed to the process of becoming an adult. She notes that an essential part of being a Black student at NU entails learning not to allow "what's put upon us to get into us." She states that it seems to be this trait that allows the alumni to return to Northwestern and fiercely display not only a love for their college-made friends but also for the university.

However, Alexandria suggests that, in some very significant ways, the Black experience at Northwestern is actually becoming worse. Even as she allows for the possibility that the experience will look better "in the rearview mirror" and some portion of the struggles experienced are a necessary part of the learning process, she believes that this generation of Blacks faces challenges on campus that are more difficult to navigate than at other times in the past. In this instance, it's not that the challenges themselves are more (or less) onerous. She argues that the distinguishing factor is the community itself.

According to Alexandria, today's Black Northwestern community isn't inherently in solidarity as much as the communities in the past generations. Starting from the subtleties of Blacks who no longer universally acknowledge each other when coming across each other on campus to occasional larger failures to support each other in times of crisis to the failure of interacting with the Evanston community in the same ways as in the past, the current environment doesn't seem to offer the same amount of internal support as has historically (and legendarily) been the case.

An additional consideration here involved the evolving backgrounds of Blacks on campus. Over the years, there has been a clear movement away from predominantly

African Americans ("the descendants of slaves") toward a mix of the African diaspora, including approximately equal parts Africans, African Americans, and Caribbeans. Alexandria is careful to distinguish between this reality as being a consideration as opposed to an obstacle, noting that, for the most part, today's Blacks still have more in common than they have differences, and those differences don't interfere with the needs of the larger community in times of crisis. If anything appears to be lost, it's the casual levels of comfort that seem to have defined the past generations of Blacks at Northwestern. It's important to note that, in many other ways, this newer level of diversity enhances and enriches the current Black experience.

Alexandria's Northwestern experience has been special in many aspects, including because how illustrative it is of the prototypical modern Black student experience, how suggestive it is of the ability of a Northwestern education to create success and a family legacy, and the role of spirituality in the lives of many Black students. It also displays how students who come to Northwestern wanting to get an education become caught up in experiences that are beyond their control.

One example of this last consideration involved the national wave of student protests that originated at the University of Missouri in 2015–2016 after which the institution dealt with a series of race-based hate crimes. A football team boycott and a hunger strike by a student resulted in the resignations of the president of the University of Missouri System and the chancellor of the Columbia campus. These actions emboldened students across the country, and the series of protests reached Northwestern's campus as well, where smoldering feelings about the seemingly oppressive environment on campus were ready to explode.

During a groundbreaking for Northwestern's fantastic new 260-million-dollar, 500,000-square feet lakefront athletic facility, the Black students assembled at The Black House and proceeded en masse to the event. After maneuvering their way into the event to deliver a message of concerns over the Black students' feelings of struggle and oppression, Alexandria found herself in the midst of a movement that crystalized why she felt she had been brought to NU. Even though she wasn't an event organizer, she found herself in the center of a prayer circle, generating love and goodwill for the entire campus. She describes the event and the resultant improvements in services to the NU Black community as embodying the reason behind why she was meant to attend Northwestern.

On a different occasion, Alexandria similarly found herself at the center of a different campus crisis related to the treatment of Blacks. During her time at Northwestern, The Black House, the single facility on campus born of struggle and protest and meant to be the safe space for Black students on campus, was slated to have additional student services integrated into it that were designed to impact the university community, in general, instead of the Black community, in particular. Furthermore, certain administrators had begun to question the ongoing relevance of The Black House for students on campus. This train of thought seemed especially tied to the idea that the soon-to-be-constructed student center was intended to have specialty-designed spaces for various campus "constituency groups."

This type of effort to reclaim The Black House has been made several times over the, approximately, forty-five-year span of existence of The Black House as the focal point of Black life on campus and have always been successfully thwarted. In this example, the effort seemed especially cruel, as these changes were occurring at a time when the Black student experience was ranked to be the lowest on campus from among the different ethnic groups, and the Blacks were suffering from other considerations such as mental health and matriculation at a rate disproportionate to other groups on campus. Furthermore, these changes that were being imposed were decided without acceptable significant notification of or input from the various stakeholders in the Black Northwestern community.

After substantial pushback, which included drafting of petitions and making emails and phone calls, the university agreed to a series of what was to be four events entitled "The Black House Listening Sessions," in which the administrators would hear the concerns of those who were affected. Whether or not one believed in the sincerity of the process in advance, the passion generated at these sessions was unmistakable, and Alexandria's voice in the conversation was as passionate and prominent as that of any other Black student. As she described it, "if you all can't see the importance of this space for African American students and what it does for the Black experience, I don't see the need to have my children here ... this is so disrespectful, so disrespectful to those who fought and gave blood sweat and tears for this place. You're basically telling your Black students that you don't care and don't see our spaces and experiences are sacred, even if it's not universally used by Black students on campus. This is the height of arrogance and patronizing." Her comments, tears, and force of logic were a big influence on President Schapiro's decision of ending the process after the third session and commissioning a series of actions meant to upgrade, enhance, and modernize The Black House for a new generation.

Even as Alexandria cherished being Black at Northwestern, she enjoyed her Christian experience in equal parts. She reminisces about seeking out opportunities to engage Christian organizations immediately upon her arriving on campus. However, she found "home" within House on the Rock, the InterVarsity Christian ministry on campus. House on the Rock allowed Alex to "just be" both Christian and Black without having to explain the nuance of either experience to a general Christian environment that assumed that its Eurocentric orientation was compelling to all. As Alex describes it, the nuance of the worship experience is such that one's spirituality is enhanced when you don't have to question the relevance and applicability of the message to your life, culture, and environment. She notes that the beauty and achievement of the House on the Rock is that it allows for an expression of Christian faith and Blackness without necessitating those two considerations to be at odds with each other.

In fact, Alexandria notes that House on the Rock allows those two considerations to complement each other by fully exploring and activating the Black student experience and making worship relevant to life's challenges and realities, including being successful at Northwestern. One particularly resonant paradigm is the shift in Christian philosophy from "not yet" to "now"—the rejection of deferring any considerations of heavenly type treasures on earth in favor of receiving heavenly rewards in total after death. As stated, the goal is to live your life but to do so with Christianity as the foundation (the rock) upon which your life (the house) is built.

When asked to describe the lessons that she learned, which she'd like to share with others in the university community, she offers the following to current and future students: "I'm thankful that Northwestern is blessed to be graced with your presence and that NU is a place where you can go to not only be changed but to make change …. Black people are necessary. Despite efforts to demonize and criminalize our existence and experience, Black people are beautiful and even more so when we are united. It's the illustration of the African proverb Ubuntu—I am because we are. We need to remember that we belong to each other and we are because who each of us is, and we're better together…. Your experience is what you make it. So, love each other—hard—for the time that you're together." This has truly been the central tenet of the successful Black experience at Northwestern.

Charla Wilson

Charla Wilson

The effort to preserve the legacies of African Americans at Northwestern began in earnest in 2012. Initially conceptualized by Lauren Lowery and then developed and implemented with Northwestern University Black Alumni Association's (NUBAA's) President Jeffrey Sterling, the NUBAA Archives were considered as a necessary means to research, organize, disseminate, publicize, and archive the history of persons of African descent who were either students or faculty at Northwestern University, beginning from its inception to the modern day. The NUBAA Archives is meant to include the implementation of a comprehensive survey of Northwestern schools and departments, the showcasing of collections held by community organizations, and bringing together independent historians and creators to compile the history of Blacks at Northwestern.

The NUBAA Archives will present the history of the Black experience at Northwestern by digitizing and displaying information on African Americans at Northwestern. This information will be easily accessible to students, parents, the entire Northwestern community, and visitors. The NUBAA Archives will improve public awareness of collections related to the study of African American culture and history to which research communities have limited or no means of access. It will improve research access through expanded, integrated, and networked cataloging and searching programs that will build on an assessment of the preservation, processing, and other access needs of NUBAA members and that of current undergraduate and graduate school scholars. It will serve as a means of outreach to members who are the custodians of the at-risk manuscripts and archival materials. Through the NUBAA Archives, we seek to honor the pioneers who paved the way for scholars of color to matriculate through Northwestern University.

In 2017, after collaborative efforts involving the University Librarian Sarah Pritchard, University Archivist Kevin Leonard, Provost Daniel Linzer, and Associate

Provost for Diversity and Inclusion Jabbar Bennett, Northwestern University, NUBAA agreed to the framework for this important addition to the university's archives. To that end, the university hired Charla Wilson to be Northwestern's Archivist for the Black experience.

"I began working at Northwestern University Library in July 2017. I was deeply drawn to the position, Archivist for the Black Experience, because of the unique opportunity of doing work that involves full dedication to the preservation and documentation of African American history in the university's archives. As someone who is originally from San Diego where the history of African Americans is grossly underdocumented and overlooked, having the opportunity to support this endeavor is very exciting. My introduction to African American archival material was through research of the San Diego Young Women's Christian Association's (YWCA) segregated Clay Avenue facility for African American women and girls from the 1920's to 1950's. It is a fascinating story of Black women who transformed a traditionally recreational organization at the local level into a body that serviced the larger Black community. It was the first and only social services agency for African Americans that provided employment opportunities, housing, and functioned as a space to mobilize for civil rights in the city. Unfortunately, there is very little archival material that captures additional stories about African Americans in San Diego. The realization that there are hidden and forgotten histories of African Americans in San Diego was my motivation for building a career around safeguarding accounts of African American history in archives. Therefore, I recognize how special and important my responsibilities are at the Northwestern University.

"Previously, I worked at Barona Cultural Center & Museum as librarian/archivist for the (history of the) Kumeyaay Indians of San Diego and Women's Museum of California as Library, Archive, and Museum Collections Manager. My educational background is in American Studies with an emphasis on African American History from Scripps College, History from California State University San Marcos, and Education from Claremont Graduate University.

"The project I have undertaken is an extension of the mission of Northwestern University Archives to collect and house records pertaining to every aspect of Northwestern University's history, including the personal papers and manuscripts of faculty, alumni, students, staff, and organizations. My role as an archivist for the Black Experience gives me the distinct honor of having a specialized focus on documenting African American history at the Northwestern University. There is a great responsibility in uncovering histories and stories that are not yet captured in the archives. Time is of the essence for acquiring these stories and filling in the gaps in the repository.

"The position of archivist for the Black Experience is quite unique. I have yet to find another archivist at a university that is not at a Historically Black College and University (HBCUs) that has the same mission. I have, however, met a few archivists and curators from throughout the country who are in similar positions that focus broadly on the African diaspora, race, and ethnicity and, in particular, on communities and regions. The university's emphasis certainly sets Northwestern apart from other institutions. I like to think of the work I do at the Northwestern University as a study of local (history) or microhistory. Though it has a narrow focus, there is a rich history that can illuminate a broader understanding of the history of Chicago, the Midwest, and African Americans.

"While collecting priorities at Northwestern are different from other institutions, we have a shared mission of compiling (the records of significant events of)Black history. We also experience similar challenges in doing so. Something that I have to continually keep in mind is not to assume that everyone is familiar with archives, that some might be skeptical about placing their material in archives that will be publicly available for research and possibly displayed in exhibitions, and that some might not see themselves as valuable contributors to a repository. Perhaps, for some African Americans, their unfamiliarity with archives could be due to the practice of the oral tradition, where African American history is passed down through the story and not through physical records or the documents available were not created by African Americans. It could also be because, historically, museums and archives have not prioritized the acquisition of African American material as valued historical records. There is also a history of distrust from institutions, and rightly so, where there were past cases of stereotypical portrayals or misrepresentations of African American history and culture. Therefore, I see my role as remedying attempts to erase Black history from the archive while being sensitive to the concerns of potential donors, as it relates to representations of Black people. It is the joy and challenge of my job to ensure that endangered histories are preserved while assuring potential donors that their experiences matter and are historically significant.

"One of the most fascinating aspects of studying history and collecting archival material is that one gets to interact with the past in tangible ways. Therefore, in addition to collecting material, outreach is important for educating the public about the history and making them aware of collections available for research. Providing access and visibility to these collections can be achieved in a number of ways, including outreach, research and reference consultation, collaboration with neighboring institutions to extend this mission, and exhibitions.

"While I was not part of the discussions that transpired prior to my arrival, I applaud the Black Alumni Association (NUBAA) and the University for working together to establish a framework that will strengthen collecting in the area of African American history at Northwestern. There is an undeniable energy surrounding the mission. For example, I enjoy sharing what I learn from archival research with others. I find it particularly motivating to hear students express the inspiration they draw from learning about students who came before them and who have contributed to shaping the campus they are part of today. There are stories such as (that of) Eva Jefferson Paterson addressing 5000 students on the Deering

Meadow in the aftermath of the Kent State shootings, who led the campus in a week-long peaceful protest of the war. Another inspiring story is that of Daphne Maxwell Reid who shares so poignantly the discrimination she faced in response to becoming the first African American homecoming queen in 1967 at Northwestern. The energy and interest on campus for learning about Black history at Northwestern continues to motivate me to uncover hidden stories.

"It is important to note that African American history at Northwestern University IS Northwestern history. It is wonderful that the university has devised a committee comprised of interracial and interdepartmental representatives in a campus-wide effort to commemorate the 50th anniversary of the 1968 Bursar's Office Takeover. The campus has responded with great enthusiasm and interest in celebrating and calling attention to this once divisive event to now honor the participants who bravely took a stand 50 years ago. It is a history that the entire campus is taking an interest in. A benefit of the creation of this position is that resources are directed to support related projects, including exhibitions, programming, and travel to meet with donors and alumni. Projects such as these offer exposure to this history in tangible ways.

"While there is great enthusiasm on campus and among alumni, I am often surprised by how far news of the position has reached. Archivists from the across the country have expressed their excitement and support. This has allowed for greater resources to be allocated to this effort and is allowing for promising collaborative opportunities to make the mission a reality.

"I often find myself thinking about the subject of responsibility in my roles as archivist and historian. Something I am aware of is that I am a gatekeeper, where I can decide what is and not preserved. This could have negative and positive connotations. I certainly do not want to look back years from now and recognize that there are gaps in the historical record that I did not address. I recently participated in a history conference at which the theme was 'hearing silences' in archives, libraries, and museums. What I like about this theme is that it implies that one is conscious of the fact that voices, perspectives, and experiences are on mute or are overlooked. This suggests that something can be done to bring attention to those histories. However, there is a danger if one recognizes missing voices but does not take action to represent them. I heard a quote recently that visually solidifies this issue from Emory University's Professor of History, Dr. Carol Anderson, who stated, 'We, historians, know that one of the problems of history as a discipline being so archives-driven is that it means that if there is not an archive with you in it, then you cease to exist.' That is a haunting thought that there is a correlation between the absence of archival documentation and the erasure of a people's history and existence. It is words like these and experiences like those I had in San Diego that remind me of the importance of archives for capturing history and that it is a powerful tool for ensuring that the histories of underrepresented peoples are well documented. Therefore, I practice forming a habit of reflection, considering missing perspectives, biases, and misrepresentations. As I am becoming familiar with early Black students of Northwestern, where there is not an enormous amount of documentation, such as (in the cases of) Lawyer Taylor (possibly the first African American to graduate from Northwestern University) and Isabella Ellis (known for being rejected from a Northwestern dormitory in 1901 because of her race), names I am certain are unfamiliar to many, I think of how they could be better represented. There is a sense that you want to do right by them and make sure that their stories live on so that people in the future will remember they existed. These efforts extend to engaging alumni and students in asking what is important to them as they are my main subjects and have a wealth of knowledge and perspective.

"I am also aware that some history is already lost. That is a somber realization. However, that should not deter strategizing creative approaches for representing and calling attention to those silences when identifying gaps in the archives.

"Alumni have expressed that appointing someone who is fully devoted to capturing these histories at Northwestern is greatly needed. It serves as a good faith commitment to building diversity on campus, developing genuine relationships with alumni, students, staff, faculty, and external communities, and educating the community about the university's history. Additionally, there is an infrastructure in place and resources available to support African Americans affiliated with Northwestern to tell their truths and experiences (in an) unfiltered manner. The alumni have been very responsive and generous with their time and energy to share their stories and donate material to the archives. I hope we can sustain that interest and collaboration. Many have also expressed that they are delighted that the university has an interest in them and wants to document their lives. For some, this has special meaning if they did not have pleasant relationships with the university due to experiences of discrimination and exclusion. For some, that has resulted in distancing themselves from the university and (they) have since reestablished that relationship. It benefits all to ensure that all voices and experiences are represented in the archives to ensure that accurate and uncensored sources live on. It goes without saying that NUBAA leadership has been instrumental in making this new initiative a reality. It is an enormous advantage to have an alumni association that wants to be involved. They, of course, are most closely connected to alumni and do admirable work to honor and recognize this history.

"The question of how the Black Experience at Northwestern has changed over time is possibly the principal topic I will address, and one I look forward to exploring in great depth. Since my inaugural assignment is working on 1968 Bursar's Office Takeover related projects, most of my research has been concentrated on that history. This was a very particular moment in Northwestern history. With that event as an example, I see variation based on a number of factors, social climates, demographic shifts, home communities, student's relationship with Black Evanston and Chicago communities, university policies, federal laws to name a few. On the other hand, it is clear that there are also common threads. In particular, the November 2015 student demonstrations illuminated that some of the issues brought up in the 1968 demands are relevant 50 years later. It is remarkable observing the impact of the 1968 protest as it lives in For Members Only (FMO) today, keeping with the tradition of passing down the history of the Bursar's Office Takeover with *The Ritual*, State of the Black Union, and planning race-conscious events and programs. There is much to be explored from the standpoint of students, faculty, staff, organizations, movements, decades, relationships with greater Chicago.

"Again, I commend NUBAA and the University for working together to support greater diversity initiatives at Northwestern. It is a positive move, and I look forward to seeing its long-term impact. I look forward to future research projects, a growing physical collection, and outreach and collaboration opportunities that support education. I hope that other universities will be inspired to initiate similar work in their campuses. I feel very honored to have the opportunity to do this work."

Philip Harris

Phil Harris

Philip L. Harris was a political science major at Northwestern University. He describes his time at Northwestern as having been spent in being a library nerd and playing basketball at the Patton Gym. He graduated in 1980. "My social life was not well developed at Northwestern. I grew up in Cedar Rapids, Iowa, in an environment in which the Black community was very important to my family. However, in terms of my upbringing, it was very different from being in a big urban area, such as most of my fellow Black students. So, I was immediately thrown into this environment, that for me, even though I was with Brothers and Sisters, was culturally very different."

Phil's early awkwardness was advantageous in that his shyness left him with the option of focusing on studying. As his father had gone to high school in Chicago and had introduced Chicago to Phil at a young age, Phil thought his Northwestern experience would include significant parts of a Chicago and Evanston community experience. However, that proved not to be the case. "I knew academically it was going to be tough for me, and so I was just studying all the time. I was surrounded by a lot of engineers, and they were just really, really smart. I knew I was up for a difficult challenge." Still, Phil didn't allow the difficulty of the challenge to reduce the brilliance of the opportunity presented by attending Northwestern. "I felt the opportunities were greater than the obstacles."

Phil recalls the story of what might have been the only party he attended at Northwestern. "I remember one social event. I went to The Black House for a party. I saw all these people out on the dance floor dancing, and I didn't even know what was going on. I was just very shy back then! So, I went and sat down by myself, then I left.

"Northwestern was very segregated back then, much more so than now. I knew if I was going to do anything socially, it was going to be at The Black House. The Black House was the only place where I really felt comfortable going for anything like that. For my generation, that was it. That's where you went to hang out and to study and meet friends and have a good time."

Regarding any negative and racially tinged events occurring on campus, Phil's focus on why he came to Northwestern worked to his advantage. "I just said, 'To hell with it all' and studied. I think I was helped by having four siblings older than me who had gone to college and had been through similar experiences. I just felt a lot of internal pressure to make certain that it worked. I never wanted to let my parents down. I figured if I studied ten hours a day as a sacrifice to my social life, and I got through here, it's going to be ok."

Phil's Northwestern experience never got more complicated than his social woes, and he graduated in 1980 with his degree in political science. Little did he know at the time that he would return before very long—and not as a graduate student. Phil had been working at a prestigious downtown Chicago law firm when his alma mater came calling. "I was asked to join the Northwestern Alumni Association in the late '80's, and so I did that. Through that, I was nominated to be in a special category—young alumni trustee. So, I ended up being on the Board from 1990–1992." Back in the 1990's, as an alumni trustee, you necessarily had to cycle off the Board after your term, but it was through the intervention of Lester Crown (son of Rebecca Crown, the namesake of Northwestern's administrative office building, among many other accomplishments) that Phil ended up back on the Board as a full-time trustee. Phil then stayed on the NU Board of Trustees between 1994 and 2016 and was promoted to become Vice-Chairman of the Board and a member of the Executive Committee.

Although Phil is careful to point out that he was not Northwestern's first Black trustee, he was able to interact and learn from a few of them, including Darryl Grishow (from Parker House Sausage), George Johnson, and Don Jackson. "They mentored me in a way that brought out what I loved about Northwestern without expressing their frustration. Don Jackson never complained about anything—and he was from the Class of '65! I don't even know if he had been able to live on campus. They taught me how to interact with other trustees, many of whom were very wealthy individuals with whom I'd never had any social experiences." Phil worked extremely hard to belong and find a place on the Board of Trustees, and his effectiveness on the Board led to his being asked to chair its Student Affairs Committee, which he did for a decade.

Phil notes a unique challenge in being a Black male on the Board of Trustees in that the university has an agenda and work that literally spans the world. Given the nature of the job description of being a trustee, it may not be as easy as one would imagine to address seemingly fundamental issues with respect to one's interests, such as Black experiences in Phil's example. However, Phil found ways to have a substantial impact. "To be really honest, whenever there was anything affecting Black people, I wanted to be involved. There were a number of task forces I served on that were somehow related to the Black experience at Northwestern and, whether it was faculty-, student-, or staff-related, I wanted to be involved. Fortunately, I had Board Chairs who would ask me to be involved."

Phil agrees with the assessment that Northwestern has done better recently with respect to addressing concerns related to the Black experience than at any past time in its history. "I really don't think the university has understood the Black experience that well, and the reason I think we have the understanding we do now is largely because of alumni leadership. I think the history in the '60's and '70's was just not well understood. I think it's been something I've known. I've known that Black students' satisfaction has lagged behind (that of the students from) the rest of the campus, and there are a lot of reasons for that, but it's always been on our plate—and on my plate as a leader here—to do something about it. I think part of the response has been that we need to be more inclusive. We need to find a way to make Black students and the Black experience more of a part of the greater Northwestern experience. While I bought into that, I also know we have a very different history here, and we really need to understand our history, which is very different from the experience of other students of color in this campus. So, what I find now is Northwestern is trying to understand, and we're reaching out. We're reaching out to Black alums, understanding that there's a connection between the undergraduate experience and the experience of alums. We're understanding that The Black House has always been a fundamental part of Northwestern and the Northwestern experience for Black students.

"So, I would say, I don't want to sound as if, during the twenty-five years I was a trustee, we had this figured out. I think a lot of progress has been made in the last five years, and it has been driven by the Black alumni leadership, among a few others. We're piecing together a history that's going to make us a lot better as a result.

"Our journey needs to be understood in a broader context. What I've learned is our history is not recorded anywhere. You can find snippets here and there, but you can't go to a book and say, 'Here's the recorded history of the Black experience at Northwestern.' So, now we're doing that. I really believe that to advance and to have a more inclusive experience and to have a great university, we have to understand and embrace that history before we can move forward. That's what's missing."

As an example, Phil muses about the Foster-Walker Complex, a favored dorm on campus for the Black community, that features approximately 600 rooms, all of which are singles and co-ed in nature. It is an amazing exercise to trace the origins of the preference for "The Plex" back to the times prior to the takeover of Bursar's Office in 1968 when Blacks were not able to live on campus, then to recall the early attempts towards achieving integration on campus, and the refusals by a majority of students to share dorm rooms with Blacks. The Plex, with its location immediately behind The Black House and closeness to the classrooms of the courses preferred by many Black students, proved to be a perfect solution to many of the problems and challenges that were faced by Blacks, who had grown from a population of approximately one hundred and seventy five students to nearly 1000 students during Phil's years at Northwestern. This evolution of a seemingly simple dorm preference is steeped in a much more functional reality that refutes the seemingly logical notion that any student would prefer a co-ed dorm with single rooms.

In 2016, Phil became Northwestern's Vice President and General Counsel and, in the role, he has been able to directly impact every aspect of the university, including the Black experience in ways that are obvious and not. Still, he remains deferential while speaking about the impact he's able to implement. "I could not do anything as a leader here if not for Morty Schapiro. President Schapiro, who's a very good friend of mine, is very committed to inclusion. He's really the first leader here with whom I've really heard talk about inclusion and not just diversity. So, when I was discussing with him (about) coming here, he had a whole plate of issues he wanted to focus on and challenges he wanted to meet, all of which involved inclusion. He knew nothing was going to be sustainable programmatically unless he had a sustainable environment. It's not because it's good politically, it's just the way he thinks. So, I have seen that in almost everything that I take on. If it has to do with Black students or students of color, it's coming from his heart."

Phil offers two examples of this focus on inclusion in action. "From a legal perspective, when I arrived here, I learned that we were not working with any Black attorneys as lead counsels on principal engagements. I talked to him about it and noted we had a supplier diversity plan but no attorneys. President Schapiro told me to go out and hire them. I spent months doing just that …. Also, in leadership positions at the university, President Schapiro is always thinking about diversity. So,

I was hopeful that when we were in a search for a new provost, that it could end up being an African American. The President's commitment to diversity made this a possibility."

Phil makes a compelling case that changes in the Black experience on all levels at Northwestern will follow the eradication of negative feelings and the negation of intellectual inferiority among Blacks. He strongly asserts that such changes will be most effective when they are leadership-driven and supported by the top members of the institution. "You really need people like President Schapiro who believe there is no such thing as intellectual inferiority and that we are all equals, intellectually and in other ways."

As such, it is not lost on Phil that the modern-day presence of prominent African Americans in prominent administrative positions is similar to the past presence of legendary African Americans among the faculty. "If you want to hire great Blacks, whether faculty or administrators, the message has got to come from the top, and then you have to go out and do it and not wait for people to argue about qualifications or relative accomplishments."

Phil asserts that the presence of increased numbers of administrators and faculty of color could have a profound impact on the Black experience. "When I go back to my days, I think about Leon Forrest, who was absolutely brilliant, and I think about Robert Hill, who was writing on Marcus Garvey. I remember looking at this guy and reading his book, and just thinking how brilliant he was. Those were the role models I needed. Any course I could take from them, I took. Just being in their classrooms really got me where I am today."

Phil is simultaneously modest and decisive in describing his roles in an impact upon Northwestern. "I don't like to talk about myself that way, but I think I worked really hard to gain credibility as a trustee. I think because I was able to develop credibility as a trustee, I was able to develop relationships that have helped us move forward. So, whenever there was an issue on the table that involved us, I was always talking about it.

"There are subtle ways (in which) you can have an effect as a leader. There's mentoring and demonstrating a passion for issues, and part of it is bringing people together for (solving) issues." Phil still notes the need for the university to develop trust with portions of the Black community as a means of moving relations forward. "We don't have the kind of history that has created any particular reason for people to trust the university."

Phil Harris has navigated the halls of power in Northwestern University as much, if not more, as any other African American. He has indeed served the university and his community without compromising either concern. "I am always first and foremost a Black man. That's my experience. That's my life. That's how I view myself. The people in the communities we serve and are a part of us should know that's how I think. In every issue I take on, that's what I'm thinking about. I feel I owe that to myself, my family, and to Northwestern; otherwise, I'm not sure I would bring anything different to the position than anyone else."

Sonia Waiters

Sonia Waiters

Sonia Waiters is a 1989 graduate of Northwestern University's School of Education and Social Policy. Her desire to attend Northwestern was consistent with her wide view of exploring what the world had to offer. "After attending a girl's Catholic high school in the Chicago suburbs, I turned down a four-year scholarship to Spelman to attend Northwestern. I support Historically Black Colleges and Universities (HBCUs) but felt that the world was not all Black or White and wanted the same exposure to connections and academics as those I would encounter in the real world."

The experiences Sonia gathered at Northwestern gave her everything she had sought, but not always in the most affirming manner. "Frankly, I was astonished at the mindset of an institution of higher education. I recall diversity experiences: Once, in a social policy class, I almost got into fisticuffs with a football player regarding the merits of Title VII. He voiced a reverse discrimination claim that Title VII disadvantaged White job applicants. I countered, stating that I would like to see Title VII disappear too. It only exists to counter overwhelming racially prejudice in (the) hiring (process). If this prejudice did not exist, there would be no need for the law. I told him that I look forward to the day that Title VII goes away."

Sonia expressed surprise at some of her interactions with schoolmates. "One year, I drew a residential dorm in the lottery. The fastest way to my room was through the sorority quads. On one warm, sunny day, I was passing through a sorority house, and an unknown resident who was sunbathing held up a tanned arm and said, "Look, I am almost as dark as you." My response was that mine (tan) was year-round and that you (resident) could not handle what it means to be Black."

As to the question of the ongoing issues of diversity, Sonia always aspired to find the best the university had to offer, but too often she found herself addressing issues that were more fundamental than she would have hoped to need to address. "During my undergrad years, I recall participating in a diversity project comprised of dramatic vignettes performed around campus and aimed at heightening racial sensitivity and inclusion. It saddens me that some 30 years later there is still a need for these activities."

Sonia has always visualized and sought out the best of Northwestern. To that end, she re-engaged in the university in an effort to contribute. "More than two decades after graduating from Northwestern, I decided that it was time that I become active as part of a 'One Northwestern.' As a carry-over from my student years, I felt NU did not embrace me. As a student, I mostly associated with other Black students with whom I remain friends today. However, I realize that there were others who made up my NU experience and (I) wanted to connect with them. Thus, I became active with Northwestern Alumni Association (NAA). I wanted to bring the Black perspective to the NAA board.

"I served on the Leadership Symposium for a couple of years. My goal was to give back to the university and get a better understanding of its focus on Black alumni. The Symposium members oversaw the selection of topics and speakers for the annual meeting of alumni leaders. At the time, there was no attention given to cultural diversity and inclusion among speakers and board members or as a topic. The Northwestern University Black Alumni Association (NUBAA) is the oldest, largest, and most active national alumni club. NUBAA was voted the 2013–14 NAA Club of the Year, received the 2014–15 Membership award, and the 2015–16

Governance award, yet, curiously, the NUBAA members have never been selected to share their expertise at the Symposium in panel discussions or as keynote speakers."

Fortunately, an additional avenue opened up for Sonia to directly and dramatically contribute to the NAA and the cause of alumni. "While working at the Leadership Symposium, I met the then-Vice President of NUBAA, Jeffrey Sterling. Between workshops, we discussed the challenges and opportunities to align NUBAA with NAA while remaining true to NUBAA's mission. I learned that we were like-minded in our commitment to advance NUBAA. When Jeffrey subsequently became NUBAA's President, he asked me to serve as Vice President and to implement his vision of a grand event to bring together and celebrate our best alumni toward developing business and entrepreneurial objectives. Thus, the NUBAA Summit and Salute to Excellence Gala (The Summit) was born. I have served as the Chairperson of The Summit since its inception in 2015.

"The NUBAA Summit and Salute to Excellence Gala has always been two separate events. The purpose of The Summit portion is to feature personal and professional growth seminars and panel discussions from some of our most successful entrepreneurs, corporate and non-profit leaders and professionals. The first Summit was held in Florida with eighty attendees. Currently, it attracts hundreds of participants from across the country annually and has been vital for re-engaging previously unattached (and prominent) members back to NUBAA and to

Northwestern. NU's President and Professor, Morton Schapiro, attended the 2017 Summit in Los Angeles, CA, along with a dozen other NU administrators."

"The purpose of The Salute to Excellence Gala is to recognize some of our members who have distinguished themselves in their careers and community affairs. It allows us to celebrate the accomplishments of our membership and NUBAA's influence and enrichment of the world around us. This black-tie event has two award components: The Salute to Excellence Awards and the Legacy Award. The Salute to Excellence awards spotlight those who have excelled in their career and community endeavors. Honorees have included Dr. Charles Modlin, one of eight kidney specialists in the country having established a health center focused on treating issues often afflicting Black men, stars of stage and screen such as Harry Lennix and Daphne Maxwell Reid, as well as those who bring stories of the Black experience to life to such as Mara Brock Akil. There have also been honorees who advocate for the Black experience before Northwestern in the role of trustees such as Michael Wilbon and Paula Pretlow.

Each year, the goal is to highlight the accomplishments of the graduates from various NU undergraduate and graduate schools across a variety of professions. The Legacy Award recognizes those who have advanced the purpose and mission of NUBAA and is NUBAA's highest honor. Past recipients have included the first NUBAA Board, the first Black Associated Student Government (ASG) President, and the founders of the Northwestern Community Ensemble. In Commemoration of the

50th Anniversary of the Bursar's Takeover, the cosmic event that dawned NUBAA, Excellence honorees will include those who were first in their profession or within NU's history. The Legacy award will acknowledge the contributions of the student negotiators to the agreements that followed the 1968 takeover of the Bursar's Office and the founder of For Members Only (FMO), the Black Student Alliance of Northwestern University.

The Summit has become a galvanizing event for Black alumni. It serves as an annual executive networking event with Black MBAs, physicians, lawyers, sports figures, and others who are prominent in their fields. NUBAA members attend the event to explore the opportunities for partnerships and seek out supplier diversity opportunities. They return to reconnect with old friends and make new ones. It has become NUBAA's culturally sensitive leadership symposium. Financial success and growth are vital parts of The Summit. Insights on philanthropy are part of the seminar series. The Black student experience is discussed, and contributions to NU from NUBAA members have risen each year. The Summit has caused increased number of donations and awards of scholarships to Black students. Similarly, Summit participation has led to an increase in non-monetary gifts to the university. Members have begun to contribute hundreds of materials to the NUBAA Archive to chronicle the Black experience at Northwestern. In short, The Summit has served as means for Black alumni to re-engage with NU. Overall, it has expanded the bridge for re-engagement and provided a high-profile venue for support.

"Northwestern has made great strides in diversity and inclusion since my time as a student, but there is more to be done. I hope that a sustained NUBAA Summit & Salute to Excellence Gala will serve to highlight the character, commitment, and achievements that Northwestern produces in its graduates.

"Upon its establishment, the NUBAA Summit was an event unprecedented within the clubs of the Northwestern Alumni Association and was a distinctly Black approach to connecting with our membership base. It has elevated the Black alumni experience and made our community much more connected. It is of note that The NUBAA Summit and Salute to Excellence Gala's audience has increasingly attracted a more diverse audience. It's a positive step that the entire university community would choose to celebrate the accomplishments of the Black community. Diversity initiatives should flow in multiple directions.

"As the Vice President of NUBAA and a member of The Black House Steering Committee, I seek to fulfill the promises of NU administration to the NUBAA members. Out of creative tension can come great innovation."

Michael Wilbon

Michael Wilbon

Michael Wilbon is a 1980 graduate of Northwestern's Medill School of Journalism.

"My four years were as close to ideal college life as a Black student at a White college could get. I was not some fish out of the water. I grew up on the south side of Chicago like everyone else back then, but I went to a Jesuit high school (St. Ignatius College Preparatory) that was 85% White. I had never gone to a White person's house when I was growing up—ever, including any of my classmates' homes who were not Black. So, that part of my life was segregated and typical of anybody growing up in any urban environment at the time.

"However, still my world was one that was like W.E.B. DuBois talked about, with 'double consciousness.' I was certainly part of that scenario. I had the segregated Black life of anyone who was growing up in Chicago, Detroit, Washington, or in most urban places. I also had a life similar to (that of) people who look different than me whom I saw every day. So, when I got to campus, I hated when people talked about some shock value, as if it's supposed to be so different! I didn't understand that, and I didn't get it. Northwestern was no different than any of the classes I'd taken for three years in high school. It looked like the world to me. I wasn't going to Tennessee State. I wasn't reporting for duty at Howard, Tuskegee, or Fisk. I was going to Northwestern. I knew what it was. So, to me, a lot of that stuff didn't and still doesn't resonate.

"Still, when I got there, most of my friends were Black—the closest friends in my life to this day are people from Northwestern. Most of them are Black, but not all of them. The people I hung out with back then were all Black. I ate with Black people in the cafeteria every day and partied with Black people on Friday and Saturday of every week. I sat with Black people at the football games and sat with Black people at the basketball games. But that doesn't mean that, walking around campus, I expected it to look like Tennessee State. I expected it to look like Northwestern.

"I hung out in The Black House a little bit—enough for me to get what I needed and enough to know that was a different experience." Mike agrees with the commonly expressed notion that The Black House could have felt like a historically Black college and university inside a predominantly White institution. "That was ok, and that was a place for everything, if you needed that. For me, none of the processes of getting what I needed was conscious. I really wasn't sitting around making choices. I was going to avail myself of everything. I did work on *Third World Report* (*TWR*, a Black issues radio program) on WNUA, and I worked at *The Daily Northwestern*. *TWR* had an all-Black staff.

"See, I don't need some thread to connect every part of life, so it can be the same. To me, that would be preposterous. I will not let my son do that, and I wouldn't let myself do that. So much of this depends on your experiences before Northwestern. If you had traumatic experiences before attending, maybe you wouldn't be so willing to step out of a shell, but I didn't have any of those. I didn't have any unpleasant experiences. Now, if that's different than the reality of others, so be it, but I was going to take advantage of the things that the university offered that my parents paid for.

"See, I didn't have any financial aid. I didn't have any grants, loans, or anything. I just paid—from $6,000 to $10,000—each year. I remember delivering that last tuition check to the Bursar's Office in my senior year in 1980: $9,997. My parents paid full freight, so I wasn't going in there discount shopping. I was going to take advantage of everything that was available to me, which is everything by definition! That meant I was going to hang at The Black House or I might go somewhere else and do something else. Hell, I was a member of NCE (Northwestern Community Ensemble) in my freshman year! So, my experiences, by choice, were predominantly Black experiences—not exclusively, but predominantly. It was like the people I dated: predominantly, but not exclusively! I don't owe anybody exclusivity. If they got mad about that in 1976 or get mad about it in 2018, I don't care. I did what I wanted to do, and I navigated my way through that campus. Now, in reality, I didn't go to (White) frat parties, but I went to our frat parties! Whether it was Alphas, Kappas, Ques, AKAs or Deltas ..., I went to all of that, even though I ain't Greek! I didn't go to keg parties because I don't drink and didn't like to slosh around in the beer. My experiences were mostly dealing with Marvin Gaye on a Saturday night and chasing some AKA or Delta girl around at The Shack—but not exclusively! If my son went there tomorrow, I would tell him you don't owe anybody anything in this experience but yourself.

"I think my pre-professional activities were much broader at Northwestern than my personal activities. My personal experiences were a lot closer to those that we expect young Black students of that time to have. My personal experiences conformed, but my pre-professional experiences did not. Those were such that a journalist-in training would undergo. Those weren't up for vote or discussion or any of that. I did various things that I thought would get me ready for this career, and there was no apologizing or explaining. I just did it.

"Look, I didn't have to sacrifice a thing at Northwestern. The Bursar's takeover group did all of that for me. They sat in that office for thirty-eight hours for me. They made it, so I'd have a Black House to hang out in. They got enough students admitted for me to party and study with, so I wasn't isolated. They made it, so we could have Greek organizations and the subculture we had. So ... I don't have a lot of patience for people who were there between 1976 and 1980 who talk about how much they sacrificed! I worked—but I didn't sacrifice. Yet, I think if I were a student now, my experience would be vastly different (from) what it was then."

Mike left Northwestern and forged an amazing career as a journalist with an intermittent engagement with Northwestern (including being named the top sports columnist by the Society of Professional Journalists in 2001), but he found himself surprised when a huge opportunity to re-engage in NU presented itself. "I don't get involved in stuff. If asked and I respect the body asking, I'll do. I was completely oblivious to the Board (of Trustees). Then, Morty Schapiro became President, and he and others knew I had a certain level of involvement. I know he wanted to change up the makeup of the Board a little bit. So, now there was room for people like me who weren't in banking. So, Morty asked me to join the Board, and I said, 'Yes.' He literally ticked off the things he wanted the Board to address and how he wanted it to look and feel different."

"Being on the Board is eye-opening. It's actually kind of scary. It's one thing to see a university that you're prominently involved with from the outside. It's another thing to be inside of it and see how the sausage is made. It's scary, it's empowering, it's enlightening, and it's inspiring.

"I know I can make a tremendous impact in a 'boosterism' kind of way and also in a meaningful way in that I am representing not just myself but people who associate you with other things." To that end, in the face of the multitude of responsibilities Northwestern has and addresses, Mike is very pleased with the level of Northwestern's focus on the challenges faced by its Black students since he has been on the board. "There are a few key people who I know are tuned into that issue. I learned how to tell that because, to a degree, I get involved a little bit with the University of Virginia because my wife has been on a few boards. You end up listening in a different way when you're with a spouse, and you're that drag-along at a retreat. One of the things I know is the number of times through private or very bold public communications is Morty (President Schapiro) doesn't consider this a back-burner issue. I've known from the very beginning that he wanted student diversity and he wanted inclusion in the undergraduate experience to be one of his primary areas of impact.

"The topic just comes up. There are just a lot of things involved with the Black experience. You have to have honest communication in those Board sessions and behind the scenes. Look at the Provost (Jonathan Holloway) and look at Phil Harris (General Counsel). Look at the people prominently involved in dealing with the university's most intimate affairs, and Morty's not afraid for that to look whatever way that needs to look. He trusts those people, regardless of ethnicity, race, religion, or culture. It makes it easier when that's a part of what's going on. That's leadership.

It doesn't mean everything is done that you want to get done, and it doesn't mean the place is perfect, but you know it's not being ignored.

"I haven't had an experience yet where I've felt excluded, or someone didn't want my input. In fact, my input is usually sought, and that's all you can ask for. Inclusion is what you want. If you've got people at the top who say we've got to have inclusion, then I think people are going to be ok, even in the areas where we might fall short because you know people are not obstructionists. I've never felt that."

Mike has been involved with Northwestern for forty-two years and has been on the Board of Trustees during seven of the last eight years. During that time, he has seen many changes in the Black experience. "One thing that scared me was the drop in Black student enrollment. When I was a student, African Americans were about ten percent (of the student body), and that was about the same as Stanford, Harvard, and other such places. Then, when I reconnected with the University, some fifteen years later, and I'd go back to campus to speak to students, I found out at that time we were down to about six percent. What happened here?

"Well, it happened to the entire country. The Reagan years happened to the whole country for those of us who were in school during the Jimmy Carter administration, when people used to have money at their disposal to borrow or be granted or otherwise have access to. That was no longer available by the last few years of the Reagan administration and beyond. My God! How did we go from 'the talented tenth' to this number, and then it got down to five percent and four percent and three percent? It seems like it's gotten back to the point where the only Black males being admitted are scholarship Black athletes. That was a bit frightening, and I was unaware. People who went to school in my day likely took for granted that we had a certain standing in certain elite universities in America such as Northwestern. It disheartened me to see Black students experience what they did in those late nineties into the aughts. I realized I didn't know much about the Black student experience during those years, and I regret that. It clearly wasn't as triumphant as we thought our period was.

"Now, we're in such a transition as a culture, and, obviously, the cultural transition inside of universities is going to result in a bit of upheaval and uncertainty. I wonder how to best address it, but I honestly don't know because I'm not a part of it. That double consciousness was something that we all lived with on a daily basis. Now, I don't know what percentage of these students that applies to. Exactly what is it that they need? It has changed, and I don't know (how) universities (can) prepare for this era, although it is clearly the perception among some of our most elite students that other institutions deal with this in a way that is more welcoming. Going back to how things have evolved, I think it's fairly representative of hundreds of other institutions that there is a transition and a real difficulty in figuring out how they fit within. Even with all the other challenges we faced, it was easier for us to figure out how we fit in."

Mike has a clear view regarding a university's responsibility to provide specific types of environments to its students. "I think it's really more up to the individual students and the supporting community more than it's the responsibility of the university per se. I don't look to the university to provide all the answers for students. Now, I had Sterling Stuckey in history and other professors and graduate students who offered support as well as education. Still, that part of the Black community was smaller forty years ago. Of course, the institution is providing it indirectly, because it hires and selects staff, faculty, and people who will impact the university on multiple levels. I just think it's up to the students to find some of that. I have never been one to leave that to the mainstream, predominantly White institutions. Why should I do that? Look, if they do, fine. When you're lucky enough to get people like Morty Schapiro, great! That's wonderful. Do I expect that? Do I think they owe us that? Hmm. I'm not leaving that to anybody else.

"We are determinate enough, and we should be independent enough as a community. Northwestern's Black community has been intact since the 1960's. We were about sixty students in 1966, and we were about 150 students by 1968. We were up to 600 Black students by 1976. We've got enough of our own resources. I don't need to go hat in hand to somebody else. I'm not saying I wouldn't access it or not be appreciative; I just don't want it to be necessary."

All things considered, Mike's message to students and younger alumni is pretty clear, and he shares a message that he shared with his goddaughter, fellow alum,

Brittany Wilbon. "She's twenty-nine years, soon to be. She's been out seven years. I ran into one of the SESP (School of Education and Social Policy) deans, who said, 'I know Brittany's doing really well. We've got to tap into her.' So, I called her. I said, 'Hey. You're almost thirty years old. The baton needs to be passed. These students aren't trying to listen to someone (who is) fifty-nine years old when they can listen to someone (who is) twenty-nine years old!'

"I consider all of our alumni's institutional resources. To me, they are as reflective of Northwestern as anything else that's purple. I spend a lot of time telling people to take advantage of everything Northwestern has to offer. You're paying $70,000 a year? If someone tells you that you can't walk through a door, call him or her out, and if they didn't, then you get inside whatever part of the university that is. I never had anyone telling me 'no' in the '70's, so I know they're not telling anyone that now!

"As I think about it, the only unpleasant experience I had at Northwestern was having an advisor who didn't think I was going to amount to much. She asked me why I was applying to *The Washington Post*. Then, I get this job, and three or four years later, I'm a young veteran and pretty well entrenched, and she calls me asking to help her as a job reference. It was unbelievable! Still, I didn't walk around thinking this had been some racist person at Northwestern, because also I think about my advisor, Craig Klugman. I wouldn't have my current career without Craig Klugman. He sat with me, nurtured me, and did all of these things for me. So, am I supposed to believe one experience is reflective of the institution, and the other isn't? Northwestern is a big place. There are subsets and smaller communities and subcultures that you have to plug into, and we're smart enough to do all of this stuff that students do to get into all of these universities. So, they're smart enough to know how to reach out and make themselves available and make any part of the institution theirs.

"So, when kids ask me what obstacles they're going to face, I ask them, 'What obstacles have you got? You're eighteen years old! You're attending one of the top universities in the United States of America. Go to school. Make yourself available to anyone who can help you.' So, stop with the notion of obstacles. Kids are too smart and too resourceful when they want to be. Here's the proof in the pudding. Look at all the people who we know and the successes they've had in various industries to radically triumphant degrees, and I'm not supposed to think they're not representative of my school? I can't do that. Look at us in performing arts, in Hollywood, on Wall Street, in medicine and science, and technology professions and in journalism. There are too many shining examples for me to need to look at what didn't happen. So, I just don't—and students shouldn't."

Jabbar Bennett

Jabbar Bennett

Jabbar Bennett is Northwestern University's inaugural Associate Provost for Diversity and Inclusion and Chief Diversity Officer. He also holds a position as Associate Professor of Medicine at Northwestern's Feinberg School of Medicine. Immediately prior to coming to NU, he served as Director of the Office of Multicultural Faculty at Brigham and Women's Hospital and Associate Dean of

Brown University's Graduate School and its division of Biology and Medicine. He came to Northwestern in 2015.

One of the most distinguishing and defining characteristics of Jabbar's role and presence at Northwestern is that it marks a clear effort of the university to be proactive in addressing issues of diversity, equity, and inclusion across the entirety of its infrastructure in a way that was not previously done and has been long desired. "In my current role as Associate Provost and Chief Diversity Officer, I help to oversee and coordinate our broad diversity, equity, and inclusion efforts as it relates to our undergraduates, graduate, and professional students, faculty, and staff. Also, we engage and work with our alumni groups that are filled with diverse members and who have diverse interests, and we work similarly with some of our external partners and stakeholders, both locally and beyond."

Jabbar's work involves a long-term vision of having a university apparatus to monitor, engage, and interact with the community on relevant issues. "I created the Office of Institutional Diversity and Inclusion after I joined, so people wouldn't just see me as the person doing all of this work. We want people to understand there is an office and a broader set of efforts and group of people who make this work possible. We want every member of the university to understand that it is everyone's role to think about, advocate for, and execute solutions on the issues of diversity, equity, and inclusion.

"When I was brought on as the inaugural Associate Provost for Diversity and Inclusion and Chief Diversity Officer, I understood the scope of my work to span across all twelve of our schools and everything we do as an institution, because diversity, equity, and inclusion do touch all activities. So, I set out to form key partnerships and relationships with everyone who is involved in this work, whether they work on the undergraduate side with admissions and financial aid or are faculty, as is related to their recruitment, retention, and advancement. That involves staff and alumni as well. So, I had the opportunity to think about how to make this work successful, important, and impactful at Northwestern.

"In doing that, I identified four areas that I believe are the key to success in doing this work: access, equity, enrichment, and well-being. That involves thinking about points of entry, thinking about (what) happens when people are here, providing education and ongoing training to members of our community, and focusing on the well-being of individuals and across affinity groups for people who may be underrepresented or who may have been historically and/or traditionally underserved and under-supported. With that thought and with that vision, carrying it forward was and still remains well received by our President, our Provost, and our other senior leaders. I'm grateful that the institution has embraced what my philosophy is regarding how this work should be done and can be done well here at Northwestern."

Because the student experience results in visible and often vocal signs of progress and/or protest, Jabbar is keenly aware of the need to form a viable partnership with the Department of Student Affairs. "Student Affairs is the overarching umbrella for Campus Inclusion and Community and under that falls Multicultural Student Affairs. I see Student Affairs and the Vice President for Student Affairs as key partners in the work I do, because they oversee the co-curricular components of the student experience, which involves everything that happens outside of the classroom for underrepresented minority students, Black students, low-income students, first-generation students, and others. Student Affairs helps to support that work and programming in the residential spaces and otherwise. So, I work closely with the Vice President of Student Affairs, and we meet regularly, communicating and partnering on various initiatives.

"Also, within Student Affairs, I work specifically and partner a lot with Campus Inclusion and Community (CIC) and the Executive Director there. Under CIC, there are Multicultural Student Affairs, Student Enrichment Services, and Social Justice Education. I also work with the directors of those areas to ensure we are providing sufficient support to all of our students both outside of the academic space but also in the space, making sure they have what they need to be successful.

"Outside of these individual meetings, I do convene on a bi-monthly basis with the leaders of those groups in various capacities. One is via the University Diversity Council (UDC), which meets quarterly and consists of faculty, staff, and students from across the institution. In the UDC, we talk about big-picture goals and ideas that my office may be undertaking and those that impact various members of our community. It also gives those individuals opportunities to share information and updates with others and me in the room. The second group is the Diversity Leaders Group. These are staff members who sit in schools and units across the university and have explicit responsibility for diversity, equity, and inclusion work. This work occurs in a smaller setting, with about fifteen individuals from across the university, and we're able to have conversations about how to support each other's work. My office gives feedback on initiatives we're moving forward and, often, we test these initiatives out with this group before we move this to a broader audience. Also, we help to support these people who are in their department and units who do this work often alone and without support and co-workers in their spaces. They help move this work forward, and we let them know we care about them, we support them, and we want to collaborate and partner with them in any way that we can."

Jabbar is appreciative of Northwestern's willingness to approach the challenges of the Black experience innovatively. "The way that I do the work here at Northwestern is different than I believe many of my peers do, and I'll just focus on my Big Ten Academic Allies peers, because that's the group I see on a biannual basis. The way I do things and have been allowed to are different. This gets back to me being able to present a plan and process of this work, so it could be successful at Northwestern. It required an understanding this would require cross-unit collaboration for it to work. I will say that because I believe I was brought in the right way, meaning the Provost and the President really supported the work and have empowered me to move forward in the way we, the institution, sees fit and has entrusted me to do, I've been pretty well received by colleagues who oversee various units, including deans who oversee schools and others within units across the board. There have been questions and challenges, and there will continue to be, but none of them came unexpectedly, and I don't believe any of them will be insurmountable. Some of this does just comes along with the work. A lot of education comes along the way. It's human nature for people to feel threatened by things when they don't understand it, it's new, and it hasn't yet been fully explained."

Despite expected challenges, Jabbar believes the times and the need have made Northwestern very receptive to the broad changes and construction of the infrastructure that are being proposed. "There has not been, and I'm just being honest, any direct, overt resistance or things that have occurred that would cause me to raise any red flags or feel like there's an issue that I could not deal with on my own or overcome in some way. I'm grateful for that. However, because this is an institution that is predominantly White and has been since 1851, I'm not naïve enough to believe that there aren't structures in place that oppress or discourage people who are a part of the underrepresented groups or who may not be more explicitly defined as a cis-gendered, heterosexual White man. I spend a lot of time every day educating people on why this work is important for the people I advocate for and also why it's important for them, their units, and the university more broadly. You get pushback when people don't understand or have a fear that what we're doing may negatively impact them, their work, livelihood, or reputation, but the reality is that (the more) everything is enriched and enhanced, the more diverse it becomes.

"Northwestern is a place that is and is beginning to do a better job of being a place that is acknowledging its history. We acknowledge not only our history but also the history of institutions of higher education in the United States, especially those that are elite, which is a category we place ourselves in. It's those histories that we have attempted to better acknowledge, and it's the systemic barriers we are attempting to address. I've been happy with the progress we're making, and that's not only in the (context of) the conversations we're having to begin to address issues, but in the actions that we've been taking."

Even though the phrases "diversity and inclusion" seem to have become synonymous, Jabbar points out the important distinctions between them. "When I think and talk about diversity and inclusion here on campus, I mention diversity as being something that you can assess quantitatively and inclusion as something you might think about in a qualitative sense. I think it's one thing to get people here to build these various differences in things you can enumerate and count up. However, once you get them here and amass these things, how do they all go together and complement one another? In the case of individuals, how do you acknowledge the differences that others may have, understand and embrace those and again, work together, collaborate, live and operate in this reasonably harmonious state without a feeling of threat and without one trying to somehow undermine, undercut, or dismiss the other? That's inclusion. I do see those things as being very different. Diversity, often, without inclusion does not lead to success. Whether we're talking about students, faculty, or staff, as we diversify, we have to talk about equity as well. We need to ensure that everyone has what they need to be successful: thinking about fairness and thinking about justice in some cases. I think it's really important to distinguish that as well."

Jabbar's arrival at Northwestern coincided with the 2015 controversy related to proposed changes to the services provided by The Black House. "(During) My first two years here, I responded to several things occurring upon my arrival. Within about a month of my being here, there were student protests and demands on our campus, and there were these episodes happening across the country. These were often underrepresented minorities who participated in these events, so I was responding quite a bit.

"My perception of that entire Black House incident is that it stemmed from a miscommunication. What I understood and still believe to this day is Campus Inclusion and Community (CIC) wanted to move two staff members into The Black House who didn't have an explicit responsibility to support Black students. However, as CIC does, it supports Black students as well as others, such as low-income and first-generation students. For what I understand and still believe is the

CIC staff were split across several locations, and this was an attempt to bring people together and not an attempt to take away space, services, or support for Black students or the staff who support those students. What I know is, a miscommunication or not, there were people who were really upset about the entire situation. I am not in that unit, and I did not believe my role was to fix anything, but to listen, learn, engage, and be supportive. That support was not only to my colleagues in Student Affairs but also to hear what the alumni had to say and what the students had to say about that move and how they interpreted what the intention of the proposed move may have been."

Jabbar states emphatically that those first few months created immediate impressions on him and an urgency to create a strategy. "Along with colleagues here at the university, I have created initiatives to better support and acknowledge students, faculty, and staff. What we are embarking on in this year involves the launch of a university-wide diversity, equity, and inclusion strategic planning process. Out of that process, we will look at developing metrics and thinking about what our goals would be to sufficiently diversify, execute inclusion, and promote being equitable across the board. So, whether we're talking about students, faculty, and staff, engagement with alumni, Board of Trustee representation and participation, and so forth, we're engaging consultants to help us think about this more broadly and actually have a firm plan in writing that we can all refer to as a master plan. Then, the schools can also use this to develop their own diversity plans and goals."

In the 1990's, the Department of African American Student Affairs ceased to exist, and services began to be provided under the guidance of Multicultural Student Affairs. Jabbar describes the nature of how services to Black students are now provided. "Multicultural Student Affairs operates within Campus Inclusion and Community, and, as a part of Student Affairs, it specifically addresses the experience of Blacks and other underrepresented students. There are several efforts ongoing that have been birthed out of the university's colleges and other units to help support Black students and also students of color, first-generation and low-income students. There are various summer bridge programs; there are now six of them. There are mentoring programs that exist within schools. There are clubs that are supportive of students with specialty interests. For example, pre-meds have the group One Step Before. There's the National Society of Black Engineers and others. Similarly, there are several specific programs in the Weinberg College of Arts and Sciences alone that have been birthed over the past decade that also support students who are Black or otherwise underrepresented, independent of Multicultural Student Affairs.

"I can talk about three things that my office and I are involved in that benefit Black students and underrepresented students more broadly. In the first project, I am helping to lead the charge on three recommendations that came out of the Black Student Experience Taskforce. The administration prioritized these out of the fourteen recommendations made, because they needed institutional and higher level administrative support to address. As a result, we're looking at how to more quickly implement these. We're not revisiting and recasting these recommendations but trying to determine how do we take these recommendations (into account) and put them into action. One of these is to increase the number of Black students, faculty, and staff, and I oversee the group implementing this with various colleagues from across the institution. One is to create an academic hub or physical space where students can go for (gathering) support. That hub essentially exists now, and there are parts of it that are functional and physically placed within the university's libraries. The third is to commit to listen to Black students and not only in times of crisis. There's been a significant amount of work done since this past summer to look at these.

"A second project I'm working on specifically is an initiative to look at the success of Black pre-med students. This was birthed out of a multiyear gift by a Weinberg (College of Arts and Science) alum who wanted to specifically support Black pre-med students. What this gift has done is allowed us to leverage resources to think about more broad support from beginning to end for these students and more underrepresented pre-health students.

"The third project that I'll mention is (one that) we have for a while had what we call a transitions-plus workgroup that looks at pre-matriculation and summer bridge programs. We've looked at students who have participated in these, how they were identified, and the level of support they've been given essentially between their freshman and sophomore years. Now, what we're looking at is how do we support underrepresented minority students, including Black students, first-gen and low-income students across the entire student lifecycle? So, now, we're looking at support from pre-matriculation to post-graduation and thinking about outcomes. This is exciting work that's in the early phases. So, what we're attempting to do is to look at all of the little things that units and schools are and have been doing, and we're trying to coordinate efforts to ensure we are supporting and benefitting all students to ensure they are being successful."

In response to the concerns related to the current levels of dissatisfaction reported by students today under the Multicultural Student Affairs paradigm compared with the past successes that African-African students achieved under the Department of African American Student Affairs, Jabbar focuses on the affirmative strategies being put in place to address today's generation of students. "Let me admit I don't know the full history of the Department of African American Student Affairs at Northwestern, including how it was staffed, how many staff (members it had), what the roles and responsibilities of those staff members were, or what was the scope of the work. So, with that said, and I'm aware that there had been a dean and now there's an assistant director, I can't say that because there's no longer a department. That's the reason why Black students are or aren't perceiving that they're receiving the same level of support as they once did. That's not in defense of any structural changes or the evolution of how Student Affairs looks at or thinks about this work. The institution itself has changed over time as well as the entire student body. The demographics of students in various ways, what students need, what their expectations are, and what our desired outcomes are, whether it's from the institution's perspective or their own has changed. So, I would assume that a change in the structure was to help accommodate a specific need. It may have been an attempt at forecasting how the university might better position itself to address the future needs based on the evolving demographics of the students or the changing priorities of the institution. So, I don't have the best answer for that."

To that end, Jabbar and the university are moving forward in what is really the most proactive approach seen at Northwestern to address the needs and challenges of today's environment. "I have been here now (since) officially just over two years. I am pleased with the progress we are making. This progress has been possible, because it builds upon many pre-existing efforts and the goodwill, hard work, and persistence of many people. Progress is one thing, but that also inherently states we are not where we need to be. We're not at the finish line just yet. So, I, the President, and the Provost, acknowledge we're not yet at a place where we can comfortably say, nor might it ever be our goal to say, we will ensure the success of every student. I think success is different for everybody. However, what we can surely do is ensure equitable access and opportunity for every student to be successful. I am pleased with the progress we are making, with the receptivity to the ideas that my office is putting forward and moving forward, not alone. There's still a lot to do, and not just for students, faculty, and staff of color but for many, many members of other groups as well."

Of course, Jabbar's interests and work go beyond students and include the faculty, staff, alumni, and even the Board of Trustees. "My office is just now beginning to work with human resources on the staff side to identify issues and also to help think about solutions as to how we can address (students') satisfaction and advancement. We just conducted our first-ever staff engagement survey at Northwestern, and that survey contained questions about diversity. We will look at and examine the data, and we will look at how our Black and underrepresented staff are responding versus others. We did a faculty survey for the first time in 2015, and it produced a separate report on diversity and inclusion that talks about experiences based on how the faculty identify and in which schools and units they sit. The next step to that work is to take some action to address those concerns. That work is being done separately for students. We've gotten some data from existing surveys that have been given to students. In partnership with Student Affairs, The Graduate School, and others, my office is launching the first-ever student climate survey for all graduate and undergraduate students to get an idea about how students feel about belonging and perceptions and the value of diversity on campus."

Jabbar's sphere of influence facilitates and includes the opportunity to have conversations about and with the Board of Trustees. "I do have that opportunity, and I've had some preliminary conversations about diversity and inclusion at the level of the Board of Trustees. The Board itself, without my presence to directly having to pursue those conversations, has diversified somewhat during my time here. I am not shut out of those conversations, and I do have an opinion. If it is requested, I can offer it, and it will be taken into consideration."

Jabbar has a vision of how a successful Northwestern would look with respect to diversity, inclusion, and equity. "An ultimate goal for me as it relates to the Black experience would be for every Black to feel welcome, confident in knowing they were selected to be a member of this community because they truly can succeed here. Also, they would feel like they have the support to be successful in whatever way they see fit and in whatever way they imagine success to be for themselves. Success would be to be in an environment that acknowledges them as people, as students, and as Black people, but, more importantly, to be seen as members of the Northwestern community. That acknowledgment and acceptance have to occur both inside and outside of the classroom. That's what I would want for all members of our Black community regarding an equitable and supportive Black experience."

Jonathan Holloway

Jonathan Holloway

Jonathan Holloway formally became the Provost of Northwestern University in the August of 2017.

"The simplest way to understand my role is (as follows): The President sets the agenda for the university and is the chief fundraiser for the university, and my job as Provost is to take the President's vision and work really hard to make it a reality. I'm responsible for anything related to academic affairs at the university, and anything related to academics will roll up to me one way or another, whether it's related to the deans of the university, tenure decisions, or the library, you name it. That's the short version."

As Provost, Jonathan is responsible for the academic well-being of all, be it the students or members of the administration, in the university, and that necessarily serves as his focus. "The philosophy for me is pretty simple. Everybody we admit and enroll—every single person—is a Northwestern University student and deserves all the rights and privileges that come along with being a Northwestern University student. So, I want to make sure that I am there for every single student, and I don't differentiate between one student's needs and another's. Now, I know—I'm not naïve—that there are different kinds of needs that take precedence at different moments. Of course, they do. But I want to start from the premise that I actually think is kind of radical: that every Northwestern student deserves respect and access to resources. Now, if that means we have to work harder so that some of those resources get to students or to make sure that students feel properly supported, then we're talking about implementation and how we get to that place. I want to start from the high, ethical standpoint of every one of our students is our student, and President Schapiro understands that."

Jonathan places the considerations of the needs of Black students in context based on his overarching philosophy. "There are unique needs across communities that are driven by different sets of cultural experiences, racial experiences, class-based experiences, etc., but I think it's always important to articulate that fact that we are going to do the best we can so that every student can just be a student."

Northwestern University has a specific mechanism in place to ensure that such a philosophy is put into action and is enforced as it is related to Blacks and other diversity students. "Northwestern's Office of Institutional Diversity and Inclusion is a clear acknowledgment that this is a country with a long history of resistance to frankly acknowledging its own heterogeneity, and that it's been a country that's provided great access to certain demographics and limited access to others. Any great university must be paying attention to the actual heterogeneity of this country and the world, and the Office of Diversity and Inclusion is recognition that this is important work. We can't just say it's important and presume people are just going to get on board, but we actually have to have someone in place who has the authority—which comes from Provost's Office—to cut across the entire University, whether its medicine, law, Weinberg, or Medill doesn't matter, to make sure that best practices, as we understand them today, are being followed to make sure our university is pursuing in earnest diversity and inclusion at the highest level. That's the genesis of this office and certainly what I expect it to do while I am Provost. To that end, Jabbar Bennett, while holding the position of associate provost for Diversity and Inclusion, serves as the Chief Diversity Officer for Northwestern."

The Provost has an appreciation for the storied history of the Black faculty at Northwestern and speaks about the university's approach to building on that legacy. "When it comes to thinking about a university, it is composed of all different types of people in the community. There are faculty, staff, and students, minimally. When it comes to faculty, Northwestern is not unlike its peers that have quite a low percentage of African American faculty members on campus. I absolutely pledge to try to do everything I can to increase that percentage. It is hard work, and people will claim it's a pipeline. It's really because of a very complex set of reasons, with pipeline being part of it, but not exclusively. It's going to take a commitment of resources and vision to make sure that we diversify our faculty along these lines specifically.

"This is one of the places where things get complicated. We could, for instance, pursue the other great faculty out there in the country—we'll do some of that as well—but then, we're not growing the pool. In that methodology, we're just taking things from one place and putting them in another place. So, we need to do that, but we also need to actually increase the pool, which means we need to diversify the presence of Black graduate and professional students. Under Dwight McBride's leadership as Dean of The Graduate School until August 1 of 2017, and now with Theresa Woodruff in place, progress is being made, and numbers of underrepresented minorities are going up—shockingly so! That's real progress, and we have to be committed to it. That's a decade-long kind of commitment."

Northwestern is recovering dramatically from a nadir of a three-percent Black student proportion in the undergraduate population and the lowest student satisfaction rates among diversity groups. However, in the student class of 2016, the Black admission rate increased to over ten percent. "The last piece is the undergraduates. The numbers have grown impressively over the last decade, as far the number of Black undergraduates at Northwestern (is concerned). Our current application pool reflects that growth. It's still lower than what I want it to be, though. So, we've got to find ways to find the most talented undergraduates who happen to be Black and admit them—and we're doing that—but then, we have to convince them to come. This is a place where we struggle against Harvard, Yale, Princeton, and Stanford. Those are our four chief competitors in that regard. That is work that's ongoing. Part of the way we are going to make improvements there is to demonstrate is through the commitment of resources, that we are going to do everything that we can for Black students while they are here. Word of mouth will travel around, and people will understand that this place is really receptive. But, we have a couple of decades of a different type of energy that we're fighting against in this regard. So, I think with the President's leadership on this, and I'm certainly part of what I hope to be the solution, I think we're going to see some real progress on this. So, major universities are all fighting for a lot of the same students, actually, and that's a challenge right now."

As much as the Provost's Office is responsible for safeguarding the university's academic culture, it is comparatively limited with respect to the direct impact it has on the students' experience. "My job as Provost is not a student-facing job, which is actually one of the parts of the job that I don't like a whole bunch. I wish I was much more student-facing, as that's very familiar to me. My job is much more (involved with) resource management and faculty management than it is meeting with students." At Northwestern, the Department of Student Affairs reports directly to the President rather than to the Provost. "There are two different models, in which Student Affairs either reports to the Provost or not, and there's, mostly, an even split between these scenarios around the country. I prefer it to report to the Provost. When I was Dean of Yale College, Student Affairs reported to me, so I'm familiar with the Student Affairs' world. The thing is, I do collaborate often with Student Affairs, so it's not part of my reporting line, but it is part of my operation."

Jonathan appreciates that the question and challenge of solving the riddle that improving the Black experience doesn't simply involve the implementation of a set of actions but involves a global philosophy from which actions can follow. "Northwestern is one of the world's great universities, and it lays claim to that, but if you're going to be that kind of university, you have to have the world at your university. Yours must be a place that really values diversity and, literally, not because it makes you feel good but values—almost in a coldly pragmatic way—what you get from having a diverse campus. You get better ideas. You get a better product. Things get better. All the research points in this direction. So, I want us to be a world-class university, tackling all of the world's problems, and, therefore, that means having the world locally. That means having a very broad commitment to diversity and inclusion, and that's an entry and starting point for me."

Jonathan takes note of and supports Northwestern's history of being willing to confront and have conversions related to challenges, such as the Black experience. "I also want us to be historically respectful of our own history in all of its complications. That means we recognize the great things about Northwestern's past but also recognize the flaws in its past and that we find ways as a community to talk about them openly, engage them, and then learn from it, so we don't repeat things (the past mistakes). Now, that's actually a heavy lift for a lot of universities. They don't like talking about the mistakes they've made. As a historian of the African American experience, to me, what makes a place more interesting, more impressive, is that it does talk about these things. A place that says we were a different place that made decisions then that we wouldn't accept now. We acknowledge that, and we're going to make sure it doesn't happen again. To me, that (makes it) a great and ethical institution, and I want Northwestern to do that kind of work as well. That is about demographic complexity and ethical engagement with who you are in the past and in the present, and you've got to do both.

"Then, it comes down to the real grassroots: in this case, the actual lived experience of African American students or faculty or staff. I've got to be vigilant. Leadership has to be vigilant to make sure that we are always listening to what this experience is like, because the place is so complex and so big that if people are not coming forward to talk about those places where we are not performing at the highest level, then I am not going to know, because my attention is in so many places all at once. Now, if people are talking to me and I am ignoring them, as it often happens at universities or big institutions, then, that's my fault. That's my failing. That's when you get Bursar's Office Takeovers, to be honest.

"I have no problems with student protests, not at all. I'm hoping that I'll be able to manage a university in such a way that they'll know that you don't have to protest to get our attention. Know that we're going to do our best, always. Sometimes, we'll fall short, and the students or the alumni or the faculty will tell us that 'You're not doing this right.' Then, we'll have to listen and adjust. That's the kind of place I want us to be."

Jonathan is fully aware of the significance that his role has in every aspect of the Northwestern University, including in action and in symbol as a Black administrative figure and a Black Provost who was hired in the year leading up to the 50th Anniversary of the 1968 Bursar's Office Takeover. "I appreciate the support. I know, sometimes, it will come in the form of creative tension, but I know that it's coming from a place of love, and that's great. Look, I'm not naïve, I have lived in this skin for fifty years, and I have specialized on topics related to the Black experience for twenty-five years, and I get it. Even though it is 2018, the fact remains that in everything I do, almost certainly, in terms of positions that I hold, I will be the first Black person to hold that, regardless of the school I'm going to be at. That is its own commentary.

"I come from a very long line of educators. My maternal grandfather was the first Executive Director of the United Negro College Fund. Being in my skin, being involved in higher education is sort of what my family has done ... but the UNCF was founded a long time ago, and it has only been within the last ten years that we're seeing Black leaders recognized in executive positions outside of the UNCF in anything approaching faculty representation numbers. We are a small group. If we don't show up and do that work, how long is it going to be? If I weren't the Provost at Northwestern in my Black skin, how long was it going to be before there was one? I mean, who knows? That's the fact of it. That's not a critique of anybody's vision, but a fact that there are so few people who are qualified for this position at this time. The work continues.

"I know that I will have to be a symbol, and there are times when that will be welcomed, and there are times in which that will be terrible. I'd be silly to think I'm not one. However, I insist that I be much more than a symbol. I will be doing the work of not just being a Black Provost or the first Black Provost at Northwestern but simply of being the Provost, which takes us all the way back to my first statement. I'm interested in students, and I actually believe that's a pretty radical statement. Every student we welcome is our student. Period."

In fact, that's all that's ever been asked: to make the Black experience at Northwestern equivalent in opportunity and outcome to the students' experience in general while acknowledging the cultural sensitivities of the community. Jonathan would likely agree that his success is to be celebrated not for his glory but for the effects that it will have on the students, faculty, and staff of Northwestern.

Jeffrey Sterling

Jeffrey Sterling

My name is Jeffrey Sterling, and I am a 1985 graduate of the Weinberg College of Arts and Sciences with a degree in psychology. My Northwestern experience has been both representative and defensive of a wide variety of components that encompasses the Black experience. My representation of the interests of the Black community in different capacities for over thirty-five years has both enhanced and, occasionally, interfered with my ability to enjoy my deep attachment to NU. Having said that, I've been incredibly fortunate to have the majority of my life comprise experiences at Northwestern. Out of all the places I've been and all the things I've done in my life (excluding building my family), I identify with this place more than any other.

There's just something about the place. I have degrees from other prestigious universities, but Northwestern has this unique essence and, curiously, I've heard the same opinion expressed independently time and again in my casual conversations with faculty, staff, alumni, and administrators. You just feel as if you own part of the place, even long after your engagements in life have distanced you from this beautiful campus.

However, the really crazy thing is that the proverbial "best four years of your life" only become so in retrospect for so many. In real time, college was hard. I would never have thought that it actually represented the formative years of my life and that it would continue to be such an integral part of my life, decades after completing my graduation. A major reason for that view was because, for many years, I never felt that I received any love back from the university itself.

I have no recollection of ever wanting to attend any other university. Therefore, I don't believe I applied anywhere else. I was shocked when I got in, certainly not because I was a marginal candidate, but because from where I had come from and what my getting accepted represented. I was the stereotypical Black student from the south side of Chicago and the first in my family to go to college. I was raised by my mother and siblings after my father died from a gunshot wound when I was six. We were terribly impoverished and, even when I was at Northwestern, there was never a time when I was comfortable financially. Given that this was how I'd lived my entire life, it didn't seem as difficult at Northwestern as it actually was, but I do recall it being embarrassing relative to the experiences that everyone else on campus seemed to have.

When arrive at the campus, the variety of resources is so abundant that the options are actually intimidating, if not overwhelming. When you land on campus straight from the circumstance of being underprivileged and underrepresented, it's easy to believe a lot of things on campus are "not for you" and, in the case of many Blacks, someone will most likely be around to tell you that or try to make you feel that way. If you buy into that narrative, there will always be enough factors present to reinforce that self-limiting view. As has been evidenced throughout this book, the Blacks who have been the most successful while at Northwestern have been compelled or have learned to be oblivious to those self-depreciating instincts.

In my example, when I think about Northwestern, certain stories always come to mind that represent the mental roadblocks that I had to overcome. As an aspiring medical student, I attempted to learn as much as possible about how to position myself for achieving success. An especially poignant encounter with the Dean of Student Affairs (which was subsequently repeated in a near-exact mode with about fifteen other African American students) ended with the Dean telling me that I had absolutely no chance at getting into medical school. It turns out that the Dean should have been more precise in his assertion. I got accepted to every medical school to which I applied, except Northwestern (well, at least, I was wait-listed, but that didn't turn into final selection prior to my selecting a different medical school).

Similarly, when I was the Vice President of the For Members Only (Northwestern's Black student alliance), a particularly memorable debate with the President of the Associate Student Government ended with him pausing, musing, and telling me, "Now I know what my father meant when he told me he was sending me here to learn how to *deal* with *you*." I didn't realize it at the time, but a big part of my education was also centered on how "to deal with" my counterparts.

The financial roadblock was very real for me. When I was a student, my family was dirt poor, and the struggle imposed by the required parental contribution was palpable, even though I was far away from the south side of Chicago. Both my family back home and me, on campus, seemed to be making it by encashing our Social Security checks each month. "The final ignominy came during my graduation. Our ongoing struggle perpetually had us behind on tuition and when graduation came, we still weren't caught up. As such, I was allowed to participate in the ceremony, but the box used to hand out diplomas didn't have mine. I spent what was supposed to be the happiest day of my life explaining to everyone who had attended the ceremony as to why I actually didn't have a diploma to show them.

As a student, Northwestern represented such an odd confluence of positive and negative emotions and reality to me. I was so proud and honored to be at such a great institution, yet I never felt wanted when I wandered into the general campus community. It wasn't even a sense of isolation—it was more about survival and then about a drive to flourish. If was as if the notion was, "You're here, isn't that enough?" It seemed as if the term "unrequited love" was coined for this very scenario. The resources available were truly world-class, but, for the vast majority of African American students, in order to navigate and/or access student resources, you had to retreat to The Black House, a dedicated building that was won during the Bursar's Office Takeover of 1968 and was once home to the Department of African American Student Affairs. It was not only a safe space but also a culturally sensitive location where students could not only receive help but also be made to understand how best to succeed in an environment that was rife with ongoing microaggressions and outright institutional racism. It simultaneously made Northwestern special for having such a place and raised suspicions, as it needed such a place.

The sentiment of oppression on campus is very much as objective as it is subjective. For years, African Americans have been disproportionately impacted by the bad conditions that have existed on campus, including sexual assault, suicides, and other mental health challenges. Blacks have long had lower matriculation and satisfaction rates and have reported the lowest student experience ratings. The perception was a reality, largely because there was a documentable reality within what was, too often, a hostile environment. Too often, the all-too-often protests of Blacks on campus were the results of survival instincts. Despite the presence of verifiable data, I can't ever remember a time when I was a student when a proactive effort was made to address our situation. Ever step forward always seemed to be propelled by a confrontation or stimulated by some campus crisis.

As an individual, I did a pretty fair job of navigating the university. I had the briefest stint possible as a walk-on on the baseball team before realizing that I couldn't risk engaging any activity that could put my grades at risk, as I had too much to lose. I ended up taking leadership positions in multiple campus organizations. My friends and I won seven intramural basketball championships. My membership in the Alpha Phi Alpha fraternity offered me an unexpected level of support throughout the Black subsection of campus and proved to be the most accessible portal of entry into the greater university environment in an unthreatening way. You couldn't convince me there was a better time to have been had, even with all of the challenges I endured.

After graduation and with maturity comes perspective. Looking back on my college days, I realize that, whether I intended it or otherwise, it were those very experiences that prepared me for life after my education. As luck would have it, those experiences provided me with the perspective of returning to Northwestern later in life and, much to my surprise, duty kept calling.

For almost fifteen years, I had nothing (and wanted to have nothing) to do with Northwestern. Disgruntlement was a very common sentiment among the Black alumni, who, in overwhelmingly large numbers, chose to disengage from the university that, in fact, has paved the way for the success many of us enjoyed in life. By this point in life, I'd had achieved a very good amount of success professionally and was definitely in the mode of trying to give back. My fraternity, which was always in the business of service and scholarship, appeared to be a prime target for creating a scholarship for students like I had been. I spent the next ten years creating an endowment fund that accomplished just that.

It appears that the activities involved in creating the endowment fund were just setting the table for further engagement. By the time the fraternity fund had been endowed, my consulting company (Sterling Initiatives) had provided me with access to C-suites and heads of governments and corporations around the world. So, when I was approached to take on the challenge of heading the Northwestern University Black Alumni Association (NUBAA), I knew exactly what the challenges entailed and had a wealth of experience and expertise in organizational dynamics.

Fortunately, I correctly calculated that NUBAA had a trump card available that could be effectively deployed to overcome the typically slow pace of progress. At the time when I became the President of NUBAA, Northwestern was four years away from the 50th anniversary of the defining moment in the history of the African American experience at Northwestern—the takeover of the Bursar's Office in 1968. Prior to this event, there was no meaningful African American presence outside of athletics, either with respect to population or cultural considerations on campus. After the thirty-eight-hour duration of Bursar's Office Takeover, many concessions have been made, including increases in the numbers of students, enhanced provision of financial aid, the development of an African American Studies department, a Department of African American Student Affairs, and a dedicated building that serves as a safe space for students—The Black House. The specific importance of the 50th anniversary was the following: Despite any feelings of angst that were being nurtured by the alumni, we could anticipate the presence of thousands of Blacks back in the campus for the commemoration. The challenge was to turn the event into a celebration of the university's progress as opposed to yet another opportunity to protest and otherwise express anger about the ongoing disparity between the experiences of Black students and other diversity students within the NU community.

First, I began the process of re-engaging Northwestern and the alumni constituency much in the same manner as I would any other consulting job: with the end in mind. I had two main objectives that needed to be accomplished to move forward. First, I knew I needed an understanding of the university's goals and beliefs and the evolution of its culture, particularly within the African American community, as I had last engaged in it approximately twenty years ago. It was a different place than I had attended in many ways. However, in many significant ways, especially for the students, faculty, and staff on campus, it seemed to be the same as it always was.

This understanding was critical to the process of developing specific, desired, and achievable outcomes on which everyone could agree.

Second, I knew I needed to be able to bring together the African American alumni community to support the effort. In general, organizations understand robust ideas, but they respond to shows of strength. Taking into consideration the magnitude of changes that I was about to propose, a university that was otherwise occupied with the business of running a university would need to be compelled to respond to our suggestions, and that would most likely only happen in the midst of a unified community for acknowledging our organization as the vehicle for communication and addressing our concerns. In other words, I need both a competent board and a large alumni membership.

As I mentioned, for several generations, the Black alumni at Northwestern comprised disgruntled students. Many of us loved the experiences we had, the friends we made, and the successes we enjoyed. However, it was always a subject of debate as to whether or not those affinities were because of or in spite of the university. Conversations about supporting Northwestern were much more likely to include the word "hate" than "love." As such, the level of participation in alumni activities, including NUBAA, was much lower than it should have been. However, there existed a core group of mainly Chicago-based alumni who for years had not only held down the fort but also performed and that kept the process of achieving NUBAA's goals moving forward. NUBAA was already a forceful entity, having been the first of Northwestern's national alumni clubs. This made it much easier for it to succeed, as there were many shoulders to lean on in the form of a wealth of talented, successful, and willing individuals who were waiting to be convinced. As luck would have it, my predecessor as NUBAA President, Tonya Woods, provided an excellent set of shoulders on which I could stand and advance the organization's mission and goals. I did so serving as Vice President prior to starting my term as President.

As a result of my success as a consultant, I've come to believe emphatically that we slot ourselves into levels of success based on our assumptions of individual merit. NUBAA didn't need us to aspire to "move the ball forward" or to "shoot for the stars and land on the moon." We wanted the occasion of the 50th anniversary of the Bursar's Office Takeover to represent as close to a *fixing* (i.e., a normalization) of the Black experience at Northwestern as human nature would allow. As such, we needed a plan that would represent exactly what that would look like. After a few months of having hundreds of conversations with students, alumni, faculty, staff, and administrators in advance of beginning my first term as NUBAA President, I developed a "Programmatic Agenda."

The NUBAA Programmatic Agenda was either a radical agenda or a clear path forward, depending on the audience. It was meant to be a document with a direct and traceable lineage to the founding ideals of NUBAA, which was created through the best efforts of the nine NUBAA Presidents that preceded me. It meant to respect the students' right to quiet enjoyment of their university experience, but it served as a clear signal to the university as to how those of us who had successfully navigated the university believed that experience could be improved. It was a move away from a mostly well-intentioned but still paternalistic approach to direct our existence on campus toward a more self-determined path.

I was pleasantly surprised at how readily President Morton O. Schapiro granted an audience with most of his senior administrative staff to hear our ideas and plans. We presumed this "NUBAA Advisory Board" meeting must have been the largest amongst such gatherings since the Bursar's Office Takeover negotiations. I was even more amazed at how willingly he was to debate the path forward and how he subsequently deployed his staff toward the full implementation of the plan. The Programmatic Agenda became widely disseminated within the university's administration and provided an unprecedented amount of access to university officials toward implementation.

Truth be told, it was obvious which administrators were on board and which were not. The underlying sentiment in some cases was skepticism with respect to whether the Black community either agreed on the path forward or had the ability to accomplish the parts of the plan that were required to be completed by us. The funny part about this was that those concerns were fair. Our team, in fact, did have work to do. However, I still had the allure of the 50th anniversary in my back pocket and, most importantly, President Schapiro's leadership on the matter never wavered and the efforts continually remained largely self-directed efforts to improve the Black experience.

The first job for NUBAA was fixing our shop. We couldn't engage the students properly and adequately offer them resources without having achieved real internal strength within NUBAA first. We needed to build an infrastructure that is meant to perform and last. One of our very first actions was to eliminate membership dues as a means of removing that obstacle to alumni participation. Consequently, the number of our members increased eight-fold from the hundreds to the thousands. Our board changed from a core board of directors comprising six individuals to an extended board of over one hundred. Our national chapter affiliates grew from four to twenty-nine.

Another key step in building our infrastructure was being able to control our communication and membership. All too often, what we deemed as adequate support from the university was not being made available to us. We weren't given access to our membership database and couldn't use the alumni web network in ways that would guarantee our culturally effective means of communicating within our group. As a result, we created NUBAA.org (our independent website) and recreated our membership roster from scratch. Doing both of these things allowed us to have measures of control in our message and methods, all the while sharing the same goals of serving our alma mater—just in a self-directed way. Furthermore, we extended the NUBAA umbrella in ways that we hadn't fully explored before.

The act of growing membership wasn't meant to be just an exercise in obtaining donors for the university (even though it was in the midst of a wildly successful, nearly $4-billion fundraising event for the university endowment). We strove to have a membership that could be activated for the following multiple purposes: support of students via mentorship, the attraction of sponsors for our many events, and mobilization during times of need. Unfortunately (and fortunately), an early opportunity presented that allowed us to demonstrate just how mobilized we'd become.

For years, it seemed that some people in the university had their minds set on rolling back the commitment made regarding The Black House. They had largely shifted away from addressing the concerns of individual groups of students based on race and additional considerations and had moved toward the trend of Multicultural Student Affairs. It had eliminated the Department of African American Student Affairs and the status of having a Dean of African American Student Affairs. In fact, the support staff was no longer dedicated to the Black student experience and was rolled into the Multicultural Student Affairs' effort. In many instances, the staff was moved out of The Black House and into the Multicultural Student Affairs' building. The activities and artifacts in the Black House seemingly had been cored out. Pictures, plaques, and murals consistent with our history had been removed and replaced with less meaningful and more generic adornments.

Over the years, this systematic dilution of services (or "the new approach" to student services) rendered The Black House less meaningful and, as a result, less used. New students didn't see the intended benefit of action, so they didn't appreciate the benefit. In the act of the tail wagging the dog, the university attempted to fill the void by intermittently bringing other groups into the building. In fact, this had occurred several times over the years and had always been pushed back. However, on this occasion, things appeared to be different.

A few months after a conversation with the Vice President of Student Affairs in which she explicitly offered me assurances that the university was committed to The Black House and that it wasn't going to be altered in purpose, a proposal was announced to take steps to bring additional services into the building, which would involve the net effort of irrevocably removing the spirit by which The Black House was established. They might as well have torn it down. It sure appeared as if that was their intention. This would have been the proverbial straw that broke the camel's back after years of quiet reversal of components of The Black House that made it what it had been.

Against this backdrop, it was rather easy for NUBAA to mobilize alumni, students, and faculty in an effort to combat the university's initiative. In fact, after a petition by 2500 individuals as well as more than two hundred emails were forwarded to the university's president, the provost, and the vice-president of student affairs, the brakes were placed on the effort. However, we were done playing defense. Our primary goal remained to fix our relationship with the university and to improve the quality of existence of the students, faculty, and staff on campus. Prior to the university's actions, we had already prepared a proposal for revitalizing The Black House and transforming it into not only a student resource center but also a cultural center for the entire community. As these things go, the university's administration had to convince itself that it was the "right path." After several comments and internal efforts, including a robust group of listening sessions and a specially designed committee to analyze those sessions, the university agreed with our assessment and agreed to complete a renovation of the entire building keeping in mind both its original mission and the evolved needs of the Black community.

This success really wasn't just the rebuttal of a flawed university policy. It facilitated a direct link back to the alumni community. Over the years, when all else failed, The Black House always served as a galvanizing force for the Black community and a reminder of why everyone cared and how everyone succeeded. NUBAA very much had a captive audience. With that in mind, we had the numbers and had demonstrated the power needed to engage the university in further discussions on how to fix the environment and experience for Blacks on campus.

Irrespective of those individuals who felt personally rebuked over what occurred in the controversy over The Black House, NUBAA and the university truly were operating as a partnership with a defined set of objectives directed toward achieving the same ultimate goal and a defined timetable. In a relatively rapid timeframe (by the standards of large organizations), we were able to put in place some amazing initiatives that served to both improve our great university and the experience of Blacks on campus.

It is of note that despite a campus presence of over 125 years (Daniel Hale Williams, the physician noted to create the processes for blood transfusions, famously attended Northwestern in 1875), there had been no organized effort to collect, chronicle, and otherwise celebrate the history of the African American experience at Northwestern (recall that the informal displays at The Black House had all been removed). Therefore, we proposed a university initiative, The NUBAA Archives, to do just that. Working with the Office of the Provost and the University Library the framework for the proposed archive was approved and funding was generated in about a year.

An analysis of the reasons behind such a low level of satisfaction among students revealed a rather simple contributor—the ongoing feeling of isolation. The enrollment rate at Northwestern has long been lower than what would be proportionate with the percentage of Blacks in the general population. The history of the university had shone with exemplary efforts to provide opportunities to students in need, but it wasn't competing especially well with the peer institutions for other categories of African American student aspirants, even though it was admitted that the number was very impressive. A major issue appeared to be the lack of the provision of financial aid to students for merit. Out of this concern,

NUBAA convinced the university to allow us to fundraise for a trial scholarship, as a means to compile collective data to assess the impact of a new category of financial aid to better convert students who had been accepted to those ultimately choosing to attend Northwestern. Thus, the NUBAA Achievement Scholarship (NAS) was born. Immediately, NUBAA was able to obtain large amounts of pledges and gifts toward the effort, and the impact was immediately felt in the admissions rate. As a result of the NAS, the university has agreed to offer a series of financial aid options, targeting individuals based on merit, and NUBAA continues to use the NAS as a means of contributing in a way that directly increases the proportion of Black students on campus and incrementally reduces the level of isolation felt by students.

One of the unique recruiting tools that our great university is able to offer is the visual of the fully formed alumni. NUBAA has gone to great lengths to familiarize the alumni with students and applicants and to demonstrate how our university's degree offers lifelong value. To that end, we now directly contact each accepted applicant and have hundreds of alumni in an active mentoring program named the NUBAA Student Based Initiatives (SBI), which offers support, jobs, and professional development. The NUBAA SBIs now hold alumni–mentor workshops annually in six different disciplines (The Arts, Athletics, Business & Entrepreneurship, Engineering, The Health/Medical Careers and Legal Careers).

Our efforts at career development are no longer limited to students. NUBAA has embraced the notion that service to alumni is equally important to our effort for students and the university. To that end, in 2014, I created what is now our signature event, The NUBAA Summit and Salute to Excellence Gala, as a means of providing ongoing opportunities for alumni to network, access procurement opportunities, and celebrate success. This event has not only provided a forum for "hall-of-fame" worthy recognition of more than twenty alumni during the first three years of the event, but it has featured financial opportunities in the hundreds of millions of dollars. The event is especially notable for bringing together the more successful components of the Black alumni community to support the ever-higher levels of achievement and support of our alma mater.

Even beyond The NUBAA Summit, NUBAA has now prioritized advancing opportunities for alumni to exchange commerce and support each other's entrepreneurial aspirations. We have worked notably with well-positioned alumni, such as Oliver Kupe, formerly at Merrill Lynch Wealth Advisors, to strategically leverage corporate sponsors not just to advertise but also to become partners in the success of students and alumni. This particular initiative has resulted in jobs, support of programming, and massive networking.

In addition to university support for all the aforementioned activities, the university has taken additional significant steps to improve the entirety of the university experience directly. A Chief Diversity Officer (Associate Provost for Diversity and Inclusion) position has been established and filled with an African American. The newly appointed Provost also happens to be an African American, just as the new

Director of the Women's Center. Northwestern's General Counsel is an African American and former alum. It is truly an example of the impossible coming to reality to think that such things would not have been possible based on where we were five years ago, much less fifty years ago.

This sampling of our activities and events, all of which have built within my terms as President can each be predicted to improve the university experience dramatically and to diffuse the tensions that have always been a part of the Black student experience. Even though I'd like to believe I've been able to make a meaningful contribution back to my alma mater, I still wonder. I have a teen son whose academic performance will warrant admission to a school with the caliber of Northwestern. Although I don't know if he will choose to attend my alma mater, and I certainly don't pretend to know whether he would be accepted, I do know that Northwestern's willingness to face and address its issues related to Black students has been phenomenal, even as it has been needed. I can now say that with first-hand knowledge of its inner workings and direction. I can also say that the 50th Anniversary Commemoration of the Bursar's Office Takeover will largely be a well-deserved celebration.

It took a long time, but now my primary memories of my times at Northwestern have evolved. I recall going back and speaking at the 30th annual event of the Medical School Day that I inaugurated. I think of the look on my mother's face when I became the first member of my family to graduate from college successfully. Most recently, I remember the look on my son's face when I first brought him to campus to watch me officiate a NUBAA Annual Meeting and that he later told me (in the way only a teen can) that it was "actually interesting!" Despite a rough history and a mixed, still-evolving Black experience, I am certain the university has been more proactive in the last five years than at any prior time in its history in its efforts to "get things right."

I once had a conversation with the president of a university that is known for popularizing the notion of affirmative action in education. His rationale defied my expectations. Their rationale had much less to do with morality or the nobility of equal opportunity than I would have thought. The fundamental concept involved preparation. In a nation with changing demographics, if one aspires to retain this nation's greatness, all who participate in the democracy (and the capitalist economy) necessarily need to be competent and excellent. In this context, affirmative action and equal opportunity are the means to an end.

This has fundamentally been my approach in my volunteer work with Northwestern University on all levels, but especially in addressing components of the Black experience of the student, faculty, staff, and alumni. If NU is to reach its fullest measure of greatness, its diverse communities must be positioned to make the same level of contributions to it via enrollment, teaching, administration, and charitable donations as is done by the majority community. This can only happen if and when certain levels of success have been achieved by these same communities. It stands to reason that the best means to that end is a largely self-determined implementation of best practices, which should create success. Too often, we have been subject to the paternalistic inclinations of those with good intentions but without a sufficient appreciation for the culturally sensitive nuances of diverse communities, especially the Black community.

My final set of major accomplishments have involved serving as Chairperson of the activities involved in the 50th Anniversary Commemoration of the Bursar's Office Takeover. NUBAA began planning these events more than two years ago in advance of the May 2018 activities. We have coordinated efforts that will include a full-length documentary, a major symposium featuring the university president, the participants of the takeover, and myself, the presentation of a commemorative in honor of the takeover participants, the groundbreaking of the renovations slated to occur in The Black House, the completion of this book, musical and theatrical performances, and the return of the participants of the Bursar's Office Takeover back to Northwestern, as many have not returned to the university since they left Northwestern. The commemoration has compelled various schools and departments to compile previously uncollected inventories of their own students' Black experiences in an effort to further the work of the NUBAA Archives. It is a sign of progress that Northwestern assembled its committee to coordinate activities for the commemoration in the fall of 2017.

In total, this period of reviewing the Black experience has not only propelled things forward in ways not previously achieved but has actually extended the line on which the Black experience has always continued to move forward. It is with optimism that the entire university community should review the efforts and successes that have been accomplished. However, the final measures of success must be objective and also long, as metrics showing a suboptimal Black student experience exist, and there will be work that would need to be done. NUBAA will continue to be on standby in a capacity of oversight to ensure our best traditions are honored and advanced and is proud to celebrate Northwestern's reconfigured infrastructure that is meant to address concerns for every student who is admitted. Because at the end of the day, we know that Northwestern's internal requirements and further aspirations of greatness necessitate not only moving beyond but also successfully addressing the needs of a community with the legacy held by its Blacks.

About the Authors

Jeffrey Sterling

Jeffrey Emery Sterling, MD, MPH, FACEP

Dr. Jeffrey Sterling is an innovator in community-based medicine and health care.

- He serves as President and CEO of SterlingMedicalAdvice.com, an international public health initiative that provides personal and immediate healthcare information, advice, and telemedicine to consumers, businesses, corporations, and governments.

- Dr. Sterling is also President and CEO of Sterling Initiatives (SI), a healthcare consulting and implementation firm that assists entities with clinical, operational, and financial best practices. SI has assisted health systems, health plans, state governments, and medical practices in three-dozen states and countries. SI has gained particular notoriety for its work in creating "centers of excellence" among hospitals and other healthcare entities. Dr. Sterling is also the author of the healthcare blog "Straight, No Chaser" at www.jeffreysterlingmd.com.

- Dr. Sterling is also President and CEO of SI-STEMS, an emergency medicine contract medical group that provides staffing and management services to hospitals across the United States.

Additionally, Dr. Sterling is also involved in the following:

- Dr. Sterling serves as President of the Northwestern University Black Alumni Association, representing approximately 5,000 alumni who are nationally organized in twenty-six local chapters.

- Dr. Sterling has served as CEO, senior VP, corporate medical officer, national physician practice director, and regional medical director for various healthcare contract management groups, and as medical director for seventeen emergency medical system units and home health companies.

- o Dr. Sterling has served as chairman and/or medical director of the departments of emergency medicine at Level I trauma emergency departments in Fort Worth, TX, Metro DC, and Milwaukee, WI.
- Dr. Sterling founded DFW Urgent Care, a series of award-winning urgent care centers in Texas, New York, and California, to provide quality-equivalent and cost-effective care alternatives to hospital emergency rooms.
- Dr. Sterling founded the Minority Association of Pre-Health Students (MAPS), a national organization for premedical and other health career aspirants with chapters in over 300 colleges nationally.
- Dr. Sterling served as the founding medical director for JPS Health Network's Sexual Assault Nurse Examiner (SANE) program and created the first SANE program in the state of Connecticut at Connecticut Children's Medical Center.
- Dr. Sterling founded US Asthma Care, a series of outcome-based, best-practice disease management treatment facilities in Texas and Illinois while working with health plans to reduce hospitalization and improve clinical outcomes among asthmatics.
- Dr. Sterling founded and served as Medical Director of the Covenant Healthcare Asthma Clinics in Milwaukee, which was then the largest asthma education clinic in Wisconsin.
- Dr. Sterling has served on the board of the Asthma & Allergy Foundation of America, Texas Chapter and the American Lung Association in the Central States Region.

- Dr. Sterling served as Chairman of the DFW Minority Business Council's Health Industry Group, a consortium of over seventy healthcare business enterprises across the Dallas–Fort Worth Metroplex.
- Dr. Sterling is the author of *Behind the Curtain, A Peek at Life from within the Emergency Room*, *There are 72 Hours in a Day: Using Efficiency to Improve Every Part of Your Life*, and *The 72 Hours in a Day Workbook: 72 Days to the 72 Hours Life*.

Dr. Sterling has degrees from Northwestern University, Harvard University School of Public Health (Health Policy and Management), and the University of Illinois College of Medicine. Additionally, he completed his emergency medicine residency at Cook County Hospital in Chicago. He has obtained executive education from the Tuck School of Business of Dartmouth College.

Dr. Sterling is a speaker in high demand on topics of asthma, pneumonia, acute coronary syndromes, healthcare economics, and healthcare disparities, having delivered over one thousand lectures nationally. He is also a Life Member of Alpha Phi Alpha Fraternity, Inc.

About the Authors

Lauren Lowery

Lauren G. Lowery

Lauren@BlackIntellectual.org

Archivist/Independent Scholar/ Inner City Specialist

Lauren G. Lowery is Principal and Managing Broker at Finders Plus Real Estate and FP Commercial Advisors based in Chicago, Illinois. During her extensive twenty-five-year career, Ms. Lowery has been involved in the development and representation of retail and residential properties throughout the greater Chicagoland Area with an emphasis on Chicago's urban, downtown, and South Side communities. She has successfully managed and negotiated retail transactions with KinderCare Learning Centers, Dunkin Donuts/Baskin Robbins, State Farm Insurance, Uber, Inc., Motorola Inc., Quaker Products, the city of Markham, Illinois, Bronzeville Retail Initiative, Edgewater Development Corporation, Neighborhood Housing Services of Illinois, and West Humboldt Park Development Corporation. Previously, Ms. Lowery managed a portfolio of more than 1.5 million square feet of retail space and has facilitated successful negotiations in over 500 sale and lease transactions. Ms. Lowery was named Top Producer by the Chicago Association of Realtors.

Ms. Lowery is Co-Founder and Chief Archivist at the Modern Dance Music Research and Archiving Foundation based in Chicago, IL. The MDM Foundation documents and preserves house and dance music artifacts, scholarship, and memories to reveal the genre's significance and impact on music and Black music globally. She is the co-curator and co-host of Vintage House radio show and podcast on WNUR.org (89.3FM) in the Street beat format. She has curated and moderated events at Columbia College Chicago, Northwestern University, Chicago State University, The Old Town School of Folk Music, and CIMM Fest.

Ms. Lowery received her Bachelor's Degree from Northwestern University in Evanston, IL and a Master of Arts in Inner City Studies from Northeastern Illinois University, Carruthers School. Ms. Lowery is a member of the International Council of Shopping Centers and an Illinois state-licensed managing real estate broker. Lowery is a former member and award winner of the Chicago Urban League, Metroboard, a Silver Star Member of Alpha Kappa Alpha Sorority, Incorporated, and a member of the Society of American Archivists. Ms. Lowery held a professional certificate from the Modern Archives Institute at the National Archives and Records Administration in Washington DC and has also served as Vice President of the Northwestern University Black Alumni Association.

www.ingramcontent.com/pod-product-compliance
Lightning Source LLC
Chambersburg PA
CBHW081351290426
44110CB00018B/2347